Emerging Themes in Cognitive Development

Volume I

Mark L. Howe Robert Pasnak
Editors

Emerging Themes in Cognitive Development

Volume I: Foundations

With 36 Illustrations

Springer-Verlag
New York Berlin Heidelberg London Paris
Tokyo Hong Kong Barcelona Budapest

Mark L. Howe, Ph.D.
Department of Psychology
Memorial University
St. John's, Newfoundland A1B 3X9
Canada

Robert Pasnak, Ph.D.
Department of Psychology
George Mason University
Fairfax, Virginia 22030
USA

Library of Congress Cataloging-in-Publication Data
Emerging themes in cognitive development/edited by Mark L. Howe and Robert Pasnak.
p. cm.
Includes bibliographical references and indexes.
Contents: v. 1. Foundations—v. 2. Competencies.
ISBN-13: 978-1-4613-9222-4 e-ISBN-13: 978-1-4613-9220-0
DOI: 10.1007/978-1-4613-9220-0
1. Cognition in children. 2. Human information processing in children. I. Howe, Mark L. II. Pasnak, Robert.
BF723.C5E48 1992
155.4'13—dc20 92-297

Printed on acid-free paper.

Softcover reprint of the hardcover 1st edition 1993

Production managed by Natalie Johnson; manufacturing supervised by Jacqui Ashri.
Typeset by Best-set Typesetter Ltd., Hong Kong.

9 8 7 6 5 4 3 2 1

Preface

Emerging Themes in Cognitive Development presents two volumes of the newest research and theory in cognitive development available at the outset of the 1990s. These ideas are firmly rooted in research from the 1980s and, in some sense, these volumes represent a culmination of that research and of even earlier work. Nevertheless, these volumes are offered as catalysts more than summaries, because each presents the freshest and most recently gathered data of many scientists whose insights have had an important impact on the field.

The latest ideas of these researchers will, in some cases, immediately prove to be dominant themes of research and theory. In other cases, of course, it will take longer for the concepts presented to capture the imagination of students and colleagues who are still invested in meritorious research on other themes. In either case, the syntheses and innovations proposed are not likely to escape the careful study of the serious scholar, and it is to such scholars that these volumes are dedicated.

The first volume provides a foundation by describing some fundamental aspects of cognitive development. In part, this proceeds through the development of theories and explanations that make sense out of extant and new data. Dempster describes how the common process of resistance to interference underlies many cognitive performances. This theoretical approach is advanced with sufficient precision and detail to reveal relations among phenomena previously thought unrelated, and thus it provides a welcome step toward a unitary theoretical explanation of diverse expressions of cognitive development. Harnishfeger and Bjorklund present an equally welcome analysis of the development of efficiency in inhibition, leading to a carefully constructed theory that inefficient inhibition is a major cause of poor cognitive performances by young children. Finally, fuzzy-trace theory, an outgrowth of recent trends in cognitive development, is presented in its most complete and up-to-date form. Brainerd and Reyna offer theoretical explanations of the development of a broad range of memory and reasoning phenomena. An excellent summary of this theory, exemplified by illustrations of age changes on a variety of reasoning tasks, is presented, and implications for developmental trends in memory are discussed.

This first volume also contains several demonstrations of formal modeling. The gains in prediction and precision that can be won by such mathematical analyses is the hallmark of cognitive developmental psychology as a maturing science. First, the reader is asked to consider the basic issue of speed of processing from a developmental perspective. Kail presents evidence that there is a common mechanism in cognitive processing that permits mathematical prediction of age differences. This model is designed to permit at least a first approximation to prediction of differences in processing rates at all ages from childhood to old age. It is followed by Thomas' analysis of individual differences on a variety of cognitive tasks. This advance in methodology is potentially quite important, particularly as it may lead to more accurate prediction of individual performance instead of merely accounting for group tendencies. This section ends with Cooney and Constas' superb analysis of the complex determinants of learning even simple cognitive skills. The nonlinear dynamic modeling approach they use is proving to be extremely productive and it is significant that at this time cognitive developmental psychology is joining other sciences in profiting from it.

This volume proceeds to the development of memory, a foundation for cognitive competence. Leichtman and Ceci describe the development of early memory capabilities and show how fuzzy-trace theory can be applied to the problem of infantile amnesia. Lehman and Bovasso explore another area of research that is just blossoming, namely, the intentional control of forgetting. They are able to show that improved methods uncover developmental trends that were previously hidden and identify the mechanisms by which children intentionally forget. Finally, Ausley and Guttentag present some of the first studies using indirect assessments of memory to identify developmental changes in associative learning. They are able to demonstrate indirect memory for associations during childhood and suggest that this paradigm may be an important tool for studying developmental changes in memory.

The first volume thus provides a foundation for understanding cognitive development. The most recent theories and models of cognitive development are described and key discoveries in new areas of research are presented. The second volume builds on this foundation by revealing new insights into the continued development of cognitive skills. We have labeled the improvements in cognitive performance that occur throughout the child's development cognitive "competence," a term that signifies simply a change or increment in cognitive proficiency, understanding, or mastery. The chapters in this volume provide descriptions of how cognitive abilities increase or may be increased on either narrow or broad fronts as children mature; these disparate gains in capacities and prowess may collectively be considered to represent competence.

The second volume begins with three chapters that present new analyses of children's cognitive competence and proceeds to five chapters that suggest how that competence may be changed. Gelman and Kalish's chapter introduces the volume by offering new insight into the ways in which children organize knowledge intelligently and efficiently. The chapter focuses on the link between children's understanding of causality and the categories by which they classify aspects of their environment. Their use of noncausal, statistical information to draw inferences based on categorizations is also described with a presentation of recent data.

The next chapter, by Siegel, deals with a significant cognitive deficit from which many children suffer. The cognitive basis of dyslexia is discussed, and evidence for and against alternative explanations is described. A model of this cognitive handicap as a modular processing deficit independent of general cognitive functioning is ultimately developed. This chapter leads into a consideration of differences in cognitive ability and how they should be assessed. A novel, modern theory of intelligence underlies Project Spectrum, which has developed new techniques for assessing a wide range of cognitive abilities. In their chapter, Adams and Feldman discuss the distinctive theoretical underpinnings and describe the assessment techniques of this innovative project. Implications for classroom observation and program planning are outlined, and the latest theoretical and research developments are described.

The next five chapters present new research and theory on children's increasing cognitive competence. These chapters offer cogent descriptions of the educational responsibilities and challenges now facing experts in cognitive development. Bjorklund, Gaultney, and Green lead off with a discussion of children's inferences about their own performances. Innovative and previously unpublished studies of children's predictions and interpretations of their own ability to duplicate another person's actions are analyzed in this research on meta-imitation. Surprising developmental trends are noted and interpreted in terms of the adaptive nature of cognitive immaturity.

A model of parental guidance of children's performance of cognitive tasks is presented by Rosengren, Behrend, and Perlmutter in the next chapter. Interactions of parental style, the cognitive ability and age of the child, and the cognitive performance desired are described, predicted, and tested empirically. This pioneering research is followed by Pressley and Van Meter's masterful description and analysis of the circumstances that favor discovery of cognitive strategies. This chapter describes the nature of this aspect of cognitive development and competence and explains the conditions that favor either unassisted acquisition of new strategies or that make explicit instruction necessary.

O'Sullivan's chapter develops the theme that principles of cognitive development can be used to enrich educational theory and practice. Examples of such applications in reading and memory are offered, and a recently developed program for young school children is used to emphasize this point. The view that developmental psychologists have the responsibility to ensure that the latest theory and research in cognitive development is incorporated into education, and the variety of challenges such efforts face, are elaborated.

Finally, Weikart and Hohmann describe two classic efforts to use principles of cognitive developmental psychology to assist disadvantaged children. The renowned Perry Preschool Project and Preschool Curriculum studies are described in depth, and follow-up data spanning nearly two decades are presented. This research, based on a Piagetian framework but fully anticipating Vygotskian perspectives, has valuable implications for efforts to apply cognitive developmental psychology to assist needy children today.

The second volume thus traces the development of cognitive competence and examines conditions that support or assist cognitive development. The primary challenge issued by many of these authors is to ensure the incorporation of our knowledge of cognitive development into educational practices.

Each volume also contains an afterword in which we, the editors, have done our best to draw together the major points contained in the different contributions to each volume. We have also tried to identify the emerging themes in cognitive development today, the final decade of the 20th century. How well we have succeeded only you can judge. Meanwhile, we thank the contributors for being responsive to both of us throughout the editorial process and for presenting their latest views and research in these volumes. It is our hope, as it must be theirs, that you the readers will reap the benefits.

Acknowledgment. Preparation of these volumes was facilitated by a research grant from the Natural Sciences and Engineering Research Council of Canada (OGP0003334) to Mark L. Howe.

Robert Pasnak and Mark L. Howe

Contents

Contents of Volume II

Contributors

JAYNE ANN AUSLEY Department of Psychology, University of North Carolina at Greensboro, Greensboro, NC 27412, USA

DAVID F. BJORKLUND Department of Psychology, Florida Atlantic University, Boca Raton, FL 33431-0991, USA

MARGARET BOVASSO Department of Psychology, George Mason University, Fairfax, VA 22030, USA

C.J. BRAINERD Department of Educational Psychology, University of Arizona, Tucson, AZ 85721, USA

STEPHEN J. CECI Human Development and Family Studies, Cornell University, Ithaca, NY 14853, USA

MARK A. CONSTAS Department of Educational Psychology, University of Northern Colorado, Greeley, CO 80639, USA

JOHN B. COONEY Department of Educational Psychology, University of Northern Colorado, Greeley, CO 80639, USA

FRANK N. DEMPSTER Department of Educational Psychology, College of Education, University of Nevada, Las Vegas, NV 89154-3003, USA

ROBERT E. GUTTENTAG Department of Psychology, University of North Carolina at Greensboro, Greensboro, NC 27412, USA

KATHERINE KIPP HARNISHFEGER Department of Psychology, University of Georgia, Athens, GA, 30602, USA

MARK L. HOWE Department of Psychology, Memorial University, St. John's, Newfoundland, A1B 3X9, Canada

ROBERT KAIL Department of Psychological Sciences, Purdue University, West Lafayette, IN 47907, USA

ELYSE BRAUCH LEHMAN Department of Psychology, George Mason University, Fairfax, VA 22030, USA

MICHELLE D. LEICHTMAN Human Development and Family Studies, Cornell University, Ithaca, NY 14853, USA

ROBERT PASNAK Department of Psychology, George Mason University, Fairfax, VA 22030, USA

V.F. REYNA Department of Educational Psychology, University of Arizona, Tucson, AZ 85721, USA

HOBEN THOMAS Department of Psychology, Pennsylvania State University, 513 Moore Building, University Park, PA 16802, USA

Contributors to Volume II

MARGARET L. ADAMS Eliot-Pearson Department of Child Study, Tufts University, Medford, MA 02155, USA

DOUGLAS A. BEHREND Department of Psychology, University of Arkansas, Fayetteville, AK 72701, USA

DAVID F. BJORKLUND Department of Psychology, Florida Atlantic University, Boca Raton, FL 33431, USA

DAVID HENRY FELDMAN Eliot-Pearson Department of Child Study, Tufts University, Medford, MA 02155, USA

JANE F. GAULTNEY Department of Psychology, University of North Carolina at Charlotte, Charlotte, NC 28223, USA

SUSAN A. GELMAN Department of Psychology, University of Michigan, Ann Arbor, MI 48109, USA

BRANDI L. GREEN Department of Psychology, Florida Atlantic University, Boca Raton, FL 33431, USA

MARY N. HOHMANN High/Scope Educational Research Foundation, Ypsilanti, MI 48198, USA

MARK L. HOWE Department of Psychology, Memorial University of Newfoundland, St. John's, Newfoundland, A1B 3X9, Canada

CHARLES W. KALISH Department of Psychology, University of Michigan, Ann Arbor, MI 48109, USA

JULIA T. O'SULLIVAN Faculty of Education, Memorial University of Newfoundland, St. John's, Newfoundland, A1B 3X8, Canada

ROBERT PASNAK Department of Psychology, George Mason University, Fairfax, VA 22030, USA

MARION PERLMUTTER Institute of Gerontology, University of Michigan, Ann Arbor, MI 48109, USA

MICHAEL PRESSLEY Department of Human Development, University of Maryland, College Park, MD 20742, USA

KARL S. ROSENGREN Department of Psychology, University of Illinois, Champaign, IL 61820, USA

LINDA S. SIEGEL Ontario Institute for Studies in Education, Toronto, Ontario, M5S 1V6, Canada

PEGGY VAN METER Department of Human Development, University of Maryland, College Park, MD 20742, USA

DAVID P. WEIKART High/Scope Educational Research Foundation, Ypsilanti, MI 48198, USA

Part I
New Theoretical Directions

1
Resistance to Interference: Developmental Changes in a Basic Processing Mechanism

FRANK N. DEMPSTER

Historically, theories of cognitive development have focused on two general processes: knowledge accumulation and information activation. Central to Piaget's grand design, for example, is the notion that cognition is rule-governed (Reyna & Brainerd, 1991). He frequently stressed the importance of rule-based "operations" that, as they are acquired, progressively enlarge the child's intellectual repertoire. Likewise, many more recent developments inspired by the rise of information-processing theories have explained age-related improvements in performance on the grounds that individuals acquire and implement more powerful rules, skills, or strategies (such as rehearsal, elaboration, and imagery) as they grow older (e.g., Fischer, 1980; Moely, 1977; Siegler, 1984). Although there are many points of divergence between Piagetian-type rules and information-processing rules, both traditions have nurtured the view that intellectual development is, in considerable part, a product of the accumulation of certain forms of knowledge.

Another view fostered by the rise of information-processing theories is that age-related changes in intellectual performance depend critically on the maturation of an activation resource. Two examples that come immediately to mind are working-memory capacity and information-processing speed. Changes in capacity are assumed to enable the child to activate an increasing number of stored units simultaneously (Case, 1974; Halford, 1982; Pascual-Leone, 1970), whereas changes in processing speed allow the developing child to activate information more quickly (Bjorklund, 1985, 1987).

For the most part, then, theories of cognitive development have stressed the importance of knowledge structures and their activation or excitation. By contrast, the role of inhibitory processes, such as resistance to interference, in cognitive development has received relatively little attention. At first glance, this disparity seems curious because it is self-evident that intelligent behavior relies both on the ability to resist or suppress task-irrelevant information as well as on the ability to activate task-relevant information. Upon reflection, however, this neglect is understandable. There appear to be at least three reasons why little attention has been given to the role of inhibitory processes and interference in cognitive development.

First, interference theory was originally a theory of forgetting (McGeoch, 1943) and until recently (e.g., Howe & Brainerd, 1989) there has been little interest in the development of forgetting. To some extent, this neglect is rooted in the mistaken belief that there are no significant age trends in retention. But, it may also reflect the fact that interference theory has failed to provide an adequate account of memory disruption, despite numerous attempts to do so (e.g., response-set suppression). Theoretically, interference theory has been beset by internal inconsistencies and complications (Crowder, 1976). From the present perspective, the failure to link interference phenomena to mechanisms that appear to have developmental implications has been particularly disappointing.

Second, during the past several decades the study of cognitive development has been predicated largely on the computer metaphor. Although this metaphor easily invokes terms such as storage and retrieval, it is only recently as computers have been used to model psychological function in physiological terms that the computer metaphor has prompted interest in inhibitory mechanisms. In particular, inhibitory processes are frequently implemented in terms of activation/suppression weights in parallel distributed processing models (Sejnowski & Rosenberg, 1988). In these models, as in connectionist models in general, simple processing units at varying levels of complexity are in continual interaction, each unit being able to send excitatory and inhibitory signals to other units via the connections among them. So far, however, these models have contributed little to developmental issues.

A third reason for overlooking interference processes in the study of intellectual development may be that inhibitory processes seem empirically intractable. As Titchener noted in 1911, inhibitory processes appear to operate at the lower levels of consciousness. If excitatory processes and inhibitory processes are considered analogous to "on cells" and "off cells," respectively, then this intuition seems well founded. Inhibitory processes are in some sense more obscure, and thus more difficult to observe, than excitatory processes.

Nevertheless, recent developments suggest that inhibitory processes, including interference, are beginning to be taken more seriously by behavioral scientists. Three associated developments are noteworthy. First, Bjork (1989) has suggested that inhibitory processes play a critical role in the retrieval of list information, and Reyna and Brainerd (1991) have suggested that young children's recall is more susceptible than older children's to output interference. Thus, memory research appears to be becoming increasingly sensitive to the potential usefulness of inhibitory processes in explaining various memory phenomena. Second, Dempster (1985a, 1989, 1991) and Dempster and Cooney (1982) have argued that susceptibility to interference is an important source of individual differences in cognition, and Dempster (1991) has suggested that these individual differences reflect differences in the efficiency of the frontal lobes. Third, inhibitory processes have recently been invoked to account for a variety of phenomena in cognitive development (Bjorklund & Harnishfeger, 1990; Dempster, 1985b; 1990; Harnishfeger & Bjorklund, this volume) and cognitive aging (Dempster, 1990; Hasher & Zacks, 1988). For example, Bjorklund and Harnishfeger (1990) have argued that neurologically based changes in the efficiency of inhibitory processing contributes to increased working-memory efficiency, whereas Hasher and Zacks (1988) have proposed an interference-based view of text processing in the elderly. Although the larger implications of inhibitory processes have been largely ignored in the past, there are at least some signs that inhibition, particularly in the form of resistance to interference, is an emerging theme in the study of cognition. The present chapter is intended to be a further step in that direction.

Specifically, the present chapter has two goals. The first is to develop the thesis that developmental changes in resistance to interference are important factors in cognitive development. To this end, a review of evidence is presented that depicts developmental differences on a diverse variety of interference-sensitive tasks—namely, search tasks, the Wisconsin Card Sorting Test, measures of field dependence, conservation tasks, selective attention tasks, and the Brown-Peterson task. The second goal is to develop the view that changes in resistance to interference reflect changes in the efficiency of the frontal lobes. To that end, the second major section is focused on the frontal cortex, and includes a discussion of its phylogeny and its ontogeny, as well as a discussion of its structure and function. In the third major section the larger theoretical and developmental issues raised by the preceding sections are discussed. The chapter closes with a brief summary.

Developmental Changes in Interference-Sensitive Tasks

Search Tasks

Piaget (1954) observed that 8- to 10-month-old human infants can find a hidden object at an initial location (A). However, after several successful searches at A, many infants continue to search there when an object is hidden at a different location (B), even though the displacement is visible and the infant watches as the object is hidden. This phenomenon is known as the *A-not-B* or Stage IV error (Gratch, 1976). Although there are alternative interpretations of this phenomenon, several findings favor the hypothesis that infants younger than 10 to 12 months of age are extremely susceptible to the effects of proactive interference generated by the initial search(es) at location A (Diamond, 1988; Harris, 1973; Schacter & Moscovitch, 1984). First, infants of this age display nearly perfect recall on trials not preceded by similar, potentially interfering, activities (Schacter, Moscovitch, Tulving, McLachlan, & Freedman, 1986). Second, the spatial similarity or closeness of the alternative location to the currently correct location of the object appears to be a primary determiner of whether that location will be the locus of any incorrect search attempt (Bjork & Cummings, 1984). Third, the results of a study using a nonsearch variant of this task call into serious question attempts at explaining infants' search errors in terms of faulty memory mechanisms per se (Baillargeon, DeVos, & Graber, 1989). The search errors are, however, readily explained by the hypothesis that infants are unable to suppress a previously correct solution.

Although older children make fewer errors on search tasks than infants, the errors they do make often involve searching in the location where the object was found on the preceding trial (Sophian, Larkin, & Kadane, 1985). Errors of this sort continue to occur as late as $4\frac{1}{2}$ years of age (Sophian & Wellman, 1983). Thus, there is a developmental shift from relatively error-prone search performance during infancy to predominantly correct search patterns during early childhood; however, the types of errors made are remarkably similar. One way of interpreting this trend is to view it in terms of increasing resistance to interference.

Wisconsin Card Sorting Test

In the Wisconsin Card Sorting Test (WCST) the subject must sort cards according to the color, shape, and number of stimuli that are depicted (Berg, 1948). The examiner initially reinforces one category, but then begins reinforcing the next category (without explicitly alerting the subject) after the subject makes 10 consecutive correct responses, and so forth until all the cards have been sorted. For example, if the required sorting principle is color, the correct placement of a red card is under one red triangle, regardless of the symbol or number (see Fig. 1.1). Thus, the WCST requires participation in many trials, and assesses the subject's ability to shift response sets in the presence of irrelevant dimensions.

Although adult norms have been available for some time (Heaton, 1981), developmental norms are a relatively recent addition to the literature (Chelune & Baer, 1986). In their study, Chelune and Baer (1986)

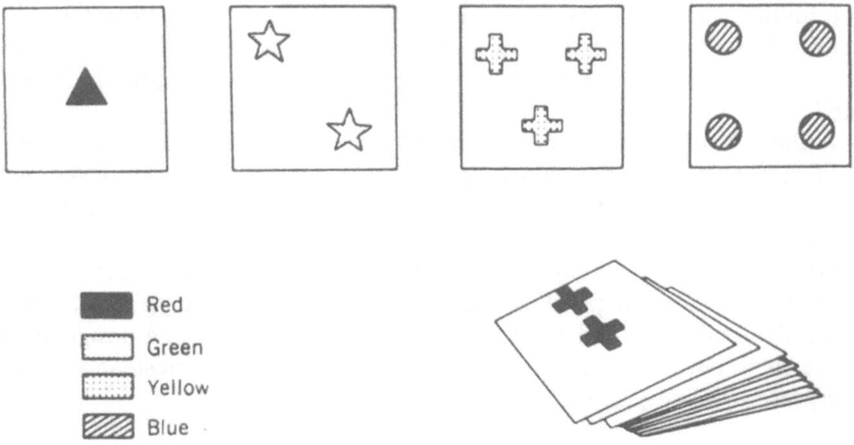

FIGURE 1.1. The Wisconsin Card Sorting Test (Milner, 1964).

tested 105 children in grades 1 through 6, and found that with advancing age children made substantial gains in the number of categories achieved and significantly reduced their tendency to make perseverative errors (the same dimension is chosen even after it has been called "wrong"). Examination of performance changes by age indicates that improvements were most rapid between ages 6 and 7, whereas somewhat lesser growth spurts occurred between the ages of 8 and 9 and 9 and 10. By the time children were 10 years old, their performance on categories achieved was indistinguishable from that of normal adults. Perseverative errors, however, did not decline to adult levels until age 12.

Measures of Field Dependence

Field dependence-independence has received a great deal of attention in the literature on individual and developmental differences. Originally, the criterion task was the Body Adjustment Test (BAT) (Witkin, Dyk, Faterson, Goodenough, & Karp, 1962), but the use of the cumbersome BAT has declined in favor of two mutually correlated measures that require the disembedding of a specific form from a distracting field—namely, the Embedded Figures Test (EFT) and the Rod and Frame Test (RFT). In both the EFT and the RFT, the subject encounters conflicting visual cues and must "interrupt" the tendency to activate the irrelevant information in order to achieve a correct solution (e.g., Pascual-Leone, Ammon, Goodman, & Subleman, 1978).

Perhaps the best known finding associated with these measures is that children normally become increasingly field independent with age until the middle teenage years when performance tends to asymptote (Witkin et al., 1962). As a consequence, children become progressively able to resist the perceptual "pull" of irrelevant visual cues found in the EFT and RFT.

Although field dependence-independence is often considered a dimension that reflects an individual "preference" for processing information, evidence suggests that this should not be interpreted to mean that the individual has any real choice in the matter. Although children tend to become progressively field independent with age, individual differences in field dependence-independence tend to remain stable. In general, field-dependent subjects tend to obtain little benefit from training designed to make them more resistant to misleading visual cues when misleading cues are present (Case, 1974; Linn, 1978; Zelniker, 1989).

Conservation Tasks

Conservation refers to the ability to understand that certain properties of objects may remain unchanged despite changes in the appearance of the objects. Thus, Piaget's conservation tasks are, in some sense, interference paradigms.

Historically, conservation tasks have served as an index of logical thinking, and age-related increases in the ability to conserve using standard conservation tasks are well known. Early research, however, called attention to the misleading structure of many of Piaget's tasks (Bruner, 1966; Gelman, 1969; Wallach, Wall, & Anderson, 1967; Zimilies, 1963) and showed that preconservers could "conserve" if the misleading cues were absent (Bruner, 1966), or if they were taught to ignore the irrelevant features of the task, such as changes in size, shape, and color (Gelman, 1969). Conversely, more recent research has demonstrated that "conservers" can be made to provide nonconservation responses to misleading questions, such as "when do you weigh more, when you are standing up or sitting?" (Winer, Hemphill, & Craig, 1988). Thus, the difficulty level of conservation tasks may have more to do with the presence or absence of irrelevant stimuli than it does with the subject's ability to grasp their underlying "logic."

Selective Attention Tasks

Measures of selective attention include speeded classification and visual search tasks, selective listening tasks, priming tasks, and the Stroop Test. In general, performance on these tasks has been regarded as an index of the ability to focus, divide, or maintain attention in the face of irrelevant stimuli (see Davies, Jones, & Taylor, 1984; Lane & Pearson, 1982).

It is now well established that children are less efficient selectors than young adults. For example, Strutt, Anderson, and Well (1975), using a speeded classification task, asked subjects age 6, 9, 12, and 20 years to sort cards varying in one relevant and either zero, one, or two irrelevant dimensions as rapidly as possible without making any errors. They found that sorting times for 6-year-old children were significantly increased by the presence of an irrelevant dimension, and that two irrelevant dimensions produced significantly more interference than did one. The same patterns of results was obtained, although less clearly, for older children, but it was absent in adults, who showed no interference effects.

In general, these results typify the results of studies with children on interference-sensitive visual search and speeded classification tasks (Enns & Akhtar, 1989; Enns & Cameron, 1987; Plude & Hoyer, 1985). The ability to listen selectively, that is, to repeat words spoken by one voice in the presence of an irrelevant and potentially distracting voice, also improves during childhood (see Davies et al., 1984, and Lane & Pearson, 1982, for reviews). For example, in a now classic study, Doyle (1973) found that children's (aged 8, 11, and 14 years) intrusions from the distracting message during the selection tasks decreased greatly between 8 and 14 years of age and the retention of distracting material declined progressively with age. Moreover, there was a positive correlation between the number of intrusions from the unattended message and the number of items from the unattended message subsequently retained by the 8-year-olds, but not among the 14-year-olds. On the basis of these and other data, Doyle concluded that the superior listening performance of the older children was due in large part to an improved "ability to inhibit intrusions from the distracting material during the selection task" (p. 100), a conclusion subsequently endorsed by Anooshian and McCulloch (1979).

In the priming paradigm, normally two objects, one of which is irrelevant and one of which is a probe, are briefly presented, followed by the probe that is to be named. If on subsequent trials the irrelevant object is the probe, naming latencies are ordinarily impaired. This effect, known as *negative priming*, has been interpreted to mean that the irrelevant item was inhibited (cf. Tipper, 1985). Although negative priming tends to be a consistent finding among normal adults, it is not always evident in children, particularly in children below the age of 8 years (Tipper, Bourque, Anderson, & Brehaut, 1989).

The Stroop Test has its origins in the work of Wilhelm Wundt in 1883 (Jensen & Rohwer, 1966). However, application of the interference portion of the test did not gain a foothold until the introduction of the Stroop Color-Word Interference Test (Stroop, 1935). The conflict or interference situation requires the subject to name the color of the ink in which an incongruent word is written (e.g., the word red printed in green ink) as quickly as possible. The amount of time to do so is compared with some other timed measure (e.g., naming colors on a color chart) to provide an estimate of interference. Thus, Stroop interference is an index of the individual's ability to focus attention on a relevant stimulus dimension (ink color) and to ignore an irrelevant one (word meaning).

The most comprehensive study of age differences in Stroop performance was conducted by Comalli, Wapner, and Werner (1962), who tested more than 200 individuals ranging in age from 7 to 80 years. They found that interference declined with age from 7 years to adulthood, remained relatively stable over the young and middle adult years, and increased for the oldest group tested (65–80 years). Other, less comprehensive studies have generally confirmed Comalli et al.'s findings with respect to age-related improvements in Stroop interference performance (e.g., Wise, Sutton, & Gibbons, 1975). In addition, there is some evidence that the type of errors most likely to decline with age, aside from errors of omission, are what might be called *intrusion* errors (Rand, Wapner, Werner, & McFarland, 1963). These include naming the word instead of the color and "contaminated" responses such as "gred," "brue," and "reen."

Brown-Peterson Task

In the Brown-Peterson task (Peterson & Peterson, 1959), the subject participates in a series of trials, three or four of which ordinarily occur in rapid succession. Furthermore, the stimuli used on each trial are usually similar to each other in terms of some salient dimension, and each trial includes a distractor-filled delay interval interposed between presentation and recall. Thus, the task has at least three characteristics that should make it a sensitive measure of susceptibility to interference. The sensitivity of this task to proactive interference is, in fact, well documented (e.g., Crowder, 1989; Murdock, 1974).

Only one study appears to have focused specifically on the question of age-related changes in Brown-Peterson interference during childhood. In that study (Leslie, 1979), second-graders and fifth-graders received 12 trials in which a different combination of the same set of pictures were used on each trial, followed by a shift trial with a different set of pictures. The subject's task on each trial was to reconstruct the order in which the pictures were presented. As expected, the performance of both groups reflected a build-up of proactive interference and a release from proactive interference on the final trial. However, the decline in performance from trial 1 to trial 12 (which is assumed to reflect proactive interference) amounted to about 42% for second graders and only about 27% for fifth-graders. Moreover, large age differences were found on nearly every trial except the first and the shift trial, in which age differences were absent.

In other developmental studies of Brown-Peterson task performance, differences in susceptibility to proactive interference are difficult to assess. Typically the results of many trials are averaged together and often no measures are taken to dissipate the effects of proactive interference across blocks of trials. Since proactive interference tends to develop rapidly, this practice may obscure differential susceptibility to proactive interference (see Dempster, 1981, for further discussion). In order to estimate such differences effectively, subjects should either participate in just a few trials or a 2-min rest interval should be interpolated between blocks of trials to prevent the spread of proactive interference across blocks (Loess & Waugh, 1967). In a study in which this first condition was met, the results were generally consistent with those of Leslie (1979); the decline across trials were considerably greater for 7-year-olds than for 11-year-olds (Kail & Levine, 1976). Together, these studies at least raise the possibility that young children are more susceptible to interference, as defined by the Brown-Peterson task, than older children.

In sum, developmental changes in a variety of interference-sensitive tasks—namely, search tasks, the Wisconsin Card Sorting Test, measures of field dependence, conservation tasks, selective attention tasks, and the Brown-Peterson task, suggest that resistance to interference is a basic cognitive process with considerable explanatory power. This in turn suggests that resistance to interference is an important and neglected dimension of cognitive development.

The Frontal Lobes

One possible way of understanding developmental changes in resistance to interference is in terms of the operation of the frontal lobes of the brain. This view is based on at least three considerations. First, the frontal lobes are the logical locus of control from both an ontogenetic perspective and a structural perspective. Second, the brain clearly contains inhibitory mechanisms as well as excitatory mechanisms, and the frontal lobes are heavily involved in inhibitory control. Third, frontally lesioned adults display deficits on interference-sensitive tasks that are remarkably similar to those of young children. Each of these considerations is discussed below.

Phylogeny and Ontogeny

The frontal lobes—or to be more precise, the prefrontal divisions of the brain (i.e., frontal cortex)—are the most recent structures to appear in the phylogenetic development of the brain. This can be inferred from the study of the brains of existing animals as well as from paleoneurological data (Fuster, 1989). Although the frontal lobes represent only a small fraction of the total cortex in lower mammals, they are well developed in nonhuman primates, and greatly enlarged in humans, where they comprise roughly 30% of the total mass of the cerebral hemispheres (see Fig. 1.2).

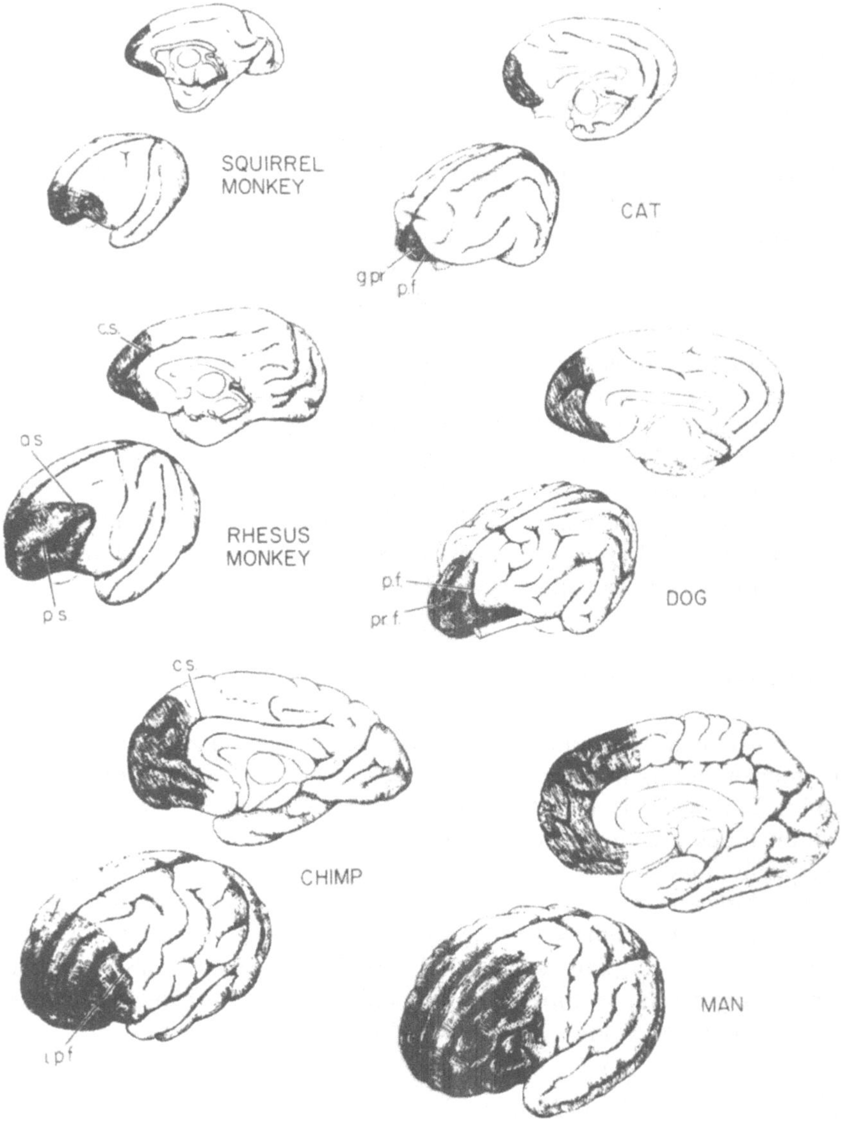

FIGURE 1.2. The prefrontal cortex (*shading*) in six different species. Abbreviations: a.s., arcuate sulcus; c.s., cingulate sulcus; g.pr., gyrus proreus; i.p.f., inferior precentral fissure; p.f., presvivian fissure; p.s., principal sulcus; pr. f., proreal fissure.

In size and weight the frontal lobes are the most distinctive structures of the human brain, a fact that has fueled speculation that their development in man has ushered in a new way of thinking. Perhaps so, but it should be noted that the vaunted increase in the size of the frontal lobes is not particular to hominids, and does not by itself explain human supremacy. For example, the frontal lobes of the horse also gained in size more than other parts of its cerebrum (Sarnat & Netsky, 1981).

In humans, the frontal lobes are also the last brain system to develop on the ontogenetic time scale. Presumably, postpubertal maturation proceeds from the posterior to the frontal areas of the brain (Hudspeth & Pribram, 1990). The area comprised by the frontal lobes increases sharply from birth to the second year of life, followed by a less pronounced growth spurt from about 4 years of age to about 7 years of age. Thereafter, there is a slow and much less dramatic increase in the size of the frontal lobes until young adulthood (Luria, 1973).

Much of this growth is due to an increase in the size and complexity of nerve cells (Reinis & Goldman, 1980), but there are other significant changes as well. For example, myelination of the sensory and motor areas of the brain is almost complete by age 2 years; in the frontal lobes, however, myelination is generally not complete until the early teenage years (Reinis & Goldman, 1980; Yakovlev & LeCours, 1967).

Two other significant changes that take place in the development of the frontal lobes are in cortical fissuration, which is associated with more refined control of behavior (Rourke, Bakker, Fisk, & Strang, 1983), and in synaptic density. Synaptic density increases during infancy and reaches a maximum at 1 to 2 years of age, at which time it is about 50% above the adult mean (Huttenlocher, 1979). Following this period of synapse accumulation, excess synapses are progressively eliminated, a process that continues throughout childhood and adolescence (Goldman-Rakic, 1987; Huttenlocher, 1979). Although it is too early to tell precisely what role synapse accretion and synapse elimination play in human behavior, it may be that a critical mass of synapses is a necessary condition for the emergence of some abilities, but not a sufficient condition for adult competence (Goldman-Rakic, 1987). Since synapse elimination is consistent with the general principle of competitive elimination in the mammalian central nervous system, and is associated with the removal of unproductive axons (La Mantia & Rakic, 1984), a high level of adult competence may depend on an optimal level of synapse pruning. It may not be coincidental, therefore, that in some instances of mental retardation, low synaptic densities have been reported in the frontal cortex (Goldman-Rakic, 1987), whereas in others, relatively high synaptic densities have been reported (Cragg, 1975).

Structure and Function

For more than a century, scientists have attempted to solve "the riddle of the frontal lobes"—that is, to unravel the "hidden secrets" relating the frontal lobes to intellectual functioning. Early descriptions of the functional significance of the frontal cortex were based largely on naturalistic observations and were much affected by the relative prominence of the frontal lobes in the brain of humans. As a consequence, these descriptions were "riddled with preconceptions of frontal lobe supremacy and anthropomorphic interpretations" (Fuster, 1989, p. 51). Some early students of brain function went so far, in fact, to conclude that the prefrontal cortex is the substrate of human intelligence (Wechsler, 1958). Gall, for example, believed the frontal lobes were the seat of the intellect because of his observation that the brightest students had protruding eyes (Hynd & Willis, 1985).

Other pioneers in the study of the brain, however, were more circumspect in their accounts of frontal lobe function. For example, Ferrier (cited in Fuster, 1989) believed that attention was the primary function of the prefrontal cortex. Pavlov (1949), on the other hand, emphasized the importance of the prefrontal cortex for the integration of goal-directed movements and behavior. Although in light of present evidence none of these functions seem to be localized entirely in the prefrontal cortex, there is a grain of truth to each of these claims.

Perhaps the most accurate early assessment of frontal lobe function can be attributed to Bianchi (1895), who hypothesized "that the frontal lobes are the seat of co-ordination [sic] and fusion of the incoming and outgoing products of the several sensory and motor areas of the cortex" (p. 34). Indeed, a distinguishing feature of the prefrontal region is that it has a very rich system of connections and feedback loops both with lower levels of the brain and with virtually all other parts of the cortex (Luria, 1973). Pathways carrying information about the external environment from the posterior cortex and information about internal states from the limbic system also converge in the frontal lobes (Lezak, 1983). Significantly, practically all prefrontal connections are reciprocal in character: Structures projecting fibers to the prefrontal cortex are the recipients of fibers from it (Fuster, 1989). The frontal lobes also figure prominently in the selective control of the access of sensory inputs to higher cerebral structures, including the prefrontal cortex itself (Fuster, 1989), confirming Ferrier's earlier speculation that the prefrontal cortex plays a major role in attention. In short, the frontal lobes are where correlated information from all sources is integrated and enters into ongoing activity (Lezak, 1983).

Despite these rather impressive anatomical and neurophysiological characteristics and their recent expansion in evolution, there is no evidence that the frontal lobes play a superior role in human intelligence. The most telling evidence in this regard is that significant frontal lobe damage usually has little effect on global measures of intelligence (Hebb, 1939), including the Wechsler Adult Intelligence Scale (WAIS) (Stuss, Benson, Kaplan, Weir, Naeser, Lieberman, & Ferril, 1983; Wechsler, 1958). Intellectual impairment associated with loss or disconnection of frontal lobe tissue usually does not appear as a loss of specific well established skills or old learning (Teuber, 1964), and there may be little evidence of a deficit in abstract thinking, such as the ability to understand and explain linguistic metaphors (Stuss, Kaplan, Benson, Weir, Chivilli, & Sarazin, 1982). In fact, patients with frontal lobe lesions typically perform within normal limits on almost any formal intelligence test in which another person directs the examination and makes all the discretionary decisions (Lezak, 1983). Closed-ended questions concerning common facts or familiar situations, as well as structured puzzles presented in the absence of distracting stimuli, are not likely to present special problems for most patients with frontal lobe injuries.

Although it may seem paradoxical, frontal lobe lesions tend not to disrupt specific cognitive functions as obviously as do lesions in other areas of the brain. The most obvious changes occur to the personality, where unrestrained, childishly egocentric behavior is often observed (Stuss & Benson, 1984). Nevertheless, it is now clear that certain aspects of intellectual functioning are typically compromised by prefrontal damage. Moreover, since the frontal lobes appear to be heavily involved in the planning and execution of goal-directed activities (e.g., Lezak, 1983; Stuss & Benson, 1984), frontal lobe disturbances tend to have repercussions throughout the behavioral repertoire. Frontal lobe patients tend to become distracted or stalled in carrying out almost any intentional activity that is sensitive to either external or internal sources of interference (Lezak, 1983).

One of the clearest and best documented phenomena in studies of frontal lobe function is the deficit on the delayed response task that results from frontal lobe impairments. In this task, the subject watches as an object or food is hidden in one of two or more locations. After a delay period in which the subject is effectively prevented from responding (vision may be obscured as well), the subject is allowed to select one of the alternatives, a procedure that is continued for any number of trials. In tasks of this sort, both human and nonhuman subjects with frontal lobe impairments perform much more poorly than suitably matched controls (Diamond & Goldman-Rakic, 1986; Freedman & Oscar-Berman, 1986; Hacean & Albert, 1978; Milner, 1964). Since the position of the hidden object is varied from trial to trial, the subject must keep the different trials separate and concentrate on the predelay stimulus during the delay. Thus, the delayed response task is similar in all formal respects to the A-not-B task (Goldman-Rakic, 1987), provided the latter includes a delay interpolated between the placement of the object and the response.

Although there is some disagreement about the exact nature of this deficit, evidence suggests that frontal lobe lesions impair the subject's ability to suppress the memory of earlier trials and thus to inhibit irrelevant stimuli (e.g., Diamond, 1988a; Hacean & Albert, 1978; Luria, 1973). For example, normal delayed responses have been restored by minimizing distractions that might reactivate memory of previous trials during the delay (see Fuster, 1989, p. 62). In addition, both prefrontally operated monkeys (Diamond & Goldman-Rakic, 1986; Stamm, 1987) and amnesiacs with pronounced frontal lobe damage (Schacter & Moscovitch, 1984, Schacter et al., 1986) tend to select the location that was correct on the previous trials, just as they do on the A-not-B task. Thus, it appears that sensitivity to proactive interference generated on previous trials is the principal source of errors on delayed response tasks and A-not-B tasks (Diamond, 1988a). As Diamond (1988b) noted, "any interpretation of A-not-B must take into account that the delay aspect of the task is critical" (p. 524).

Several other tasks in which adults with frontal lobe lesions perform poorly are also tasks in which young children perform more poorly than older children. Like the delayed response task, the WCST has a lengthy empirical history of discriminating patients with frontal lobe lesions from controls. Patients with frontal lobe lesions make significantly more errors and achieve significantly fewer shifts than do controls (e.g., patients with lesions in other parts of the brain). In addition, a high percentage of errors are perseverative (Milner, 1964), just as they are in young children. In fact, a comparison of the means of adult patients with focal frontal and focal nonfrontal lesions (Heaton, 1981) and children's means (Chelune & Baer, 1986) indicates that patients with focal frontal lesions perform in a manner similar to normal 6-year-old children on categories achieved and perseverative errors.

From the present perspective, the most important finding linking field dependence-independence to a basic processing dimension that reflects the operation of the frontal cortex stems from research with frontal lobe patients. Relative to controls, patients with frontal lobe lesions perform much more poorly on a task that is remarkably similar to the BAT (Teuber, 1964), and on the Gottshalt Hidden Figures Test, from which the EFT was derived (Teuber, 1972). In addition, frontal lobe patients perform poorly on the Block Design—the most sensitive of the Wechsler subtests to frontal lobe damage (Lezak, 1983), and a task that has itself gained acceptance as an indicator of field dependence (Waber, 1989).

Adequate selective attention is thought to require an intact frontal system (Albert & Kaplan, 1980) and patients with frontal lobe dysfunction do indeed tend to perform poorly on selective attention tasks (e.g., Stuss & Benson, 1984). For example, patients with frontal lobe syndromes are more susceptible than controls to Stroop interference (Perret, 1974). In addition, schizophrenic patients who exhibit varying degrees of atrophy and reduced metabolism in the prefrontal cortex, and who perform poorly on the WCST (Weinberger, 1987), have been found to exhibit a weakened negative priming effect relative to controls (Beech, Powell, McWilliams, & Claridge, 1989).

Although the Brown-Peterson task does not have a lengthy history of discriminating between frontal lobe patients and controls, there is growing evidence that Korsakoff patients, who have been found to have frontal lobe damage (e.g., Janowsky, Shimamura, Kritchevsky, & Squire, 1989), are especially sensitive to Brown-Peterson interference. In fact, estimates of the extent of frontal lobe damage in Korsakoff patients, as measured by the WCST, are negatively correlated with performance on the Brown-Peterson task (Parkin & Leng, 1987). Significantly, Korsakoff patients make many more prior-trial item specific intrusion errors than controls, suggesting an increased vulnerability to proactive interference, and the recall advantage of control subjects increases as the length of the distractor-filled delay interval increases (Longmore & Knight, 1988).

Unfortunately, the effects of frontal lobe damage on conservation task performance does not appear to have been investigated. Frontal lobe patients, however, are known to be poor problem-solvers when the problem contains misleading cues, conflicting messages, or when previous responses are no longer correct (Luria, 1966; Oscar-Berman, 1980). These findings at least raise the possibility that frontal lobe patients would perform relatively poorly on conservation tasks.

In sum, the functional organization of the human frontal cortex is still one of the most complex problems in modern science. However, it is now reasonably clear that frontal lobe damage leads to various disturbances in the selection, regulation, and verification of human behavior, including the ability to resist distracting, potentially interfering, stimuli. In short, the frontal lobes appear to play a decisive role in the inhibition of irrelevant stimuli and in the preservation of goal-directed behavior.

Conclusions and Unresolved Issues

Taken together, the findings reviewed in the previous sections indicate an impressive degree of similarity between the behavior of young children and frontally lesioned adults in a wide variety of interference-sensitive tasks. This in turn suggests that the maturation of the frontal cortex plays an important role in the development of behaviors that require inhibitory control for effective performance. From a theoretical perspective, the significance of this synthesis is that it represents a step toward a unitary theoretical explanation of diverse expressions of cognitive development.

Perhaps the basic developmental issue raised by this synthesis is whether resistance to interference is best thought of as a singular process or as a multifaceted process. Among the arguments for viewing age-related changes in resistance to interference as a singular process is that interference-sensitive tasks all share a core similarity: One or more task-irrelevant stimuli must be inhibited for effective performance. This implies that the basic unit of analysis common to any interference-sensitive task is competition between two or more cognitive entities. Such a view implies a greater amount of continuity between infancy and late childhood than does a multiprocess view.

Competition implies selection, and indeed, one of the most noticeable aspects of cognitive development is that children become more selective and more exhaustive of relevant information as they grow older (cf. Siegler, 1989). The behavior of infants (and to a greater extent the behavior of most lower animals) appears to be controlled by the presence of salient stimuli in the here-and-now. As the frontal cortex matures, the child, although still impressed by salient stimuli, becomes increasingly able to shift attention away from stimuli and associations that have not proven satisfactory in a given context and to attend selectively to ever more subtle features of the environment. Those processing units (and presumably the underlying synaptic connections) that have proven useful under the particular circumstances encountered by the child will tend to be preserved whereas those that have not will tend to be deleted (cf. Siegler, 1989). A reasonable corollary is that in the absence of the maturation of the frontal cortex, the child would continue to be dominated by either preprogrammed behaviors or behaviors that are guided by prepotent stimuli or recently reinforced contingencies.

The main argument for viewing changes in resistance to interference as a multifaceted process, on the other hand, is that interference has a variety of operating characteristics. As can be seen in Table 1.1, these operating characteristics vary along several dimensions, including temporal (proactive, retroactive, coactive or concurrent) and formal (motoric, perceptual, linguistic). In addition, interference can originate in either external stimuli, as shown by measures of field dependence, or internal events (e.g., distractor task activity or associations occurring during a delay interval).

A related, more speculative, argument is presented in Figure 1.3, which depicts the hypothetical relation between age and the formal

TABLE 1.1. Dimensions of interference corresponding to six interference-sensitive tasks[a].

Task	Temporal	Formal
Search tasks	Proactive Coactive	Motoric Perceptual
WCST	Proactive Coactive	Motoric Perceptual
Measures of field dependence	Coactive	Perceptual
Conservation tasks	Coactive	Perceptual
Selective-attention tasks	Coactive	Perceptual Linguistic
Brown-Peterson task	Proactive Retroactive	Linguistic

[a] Based on simple task analysis.
WCST, Wisconsin Card Sorting Test.

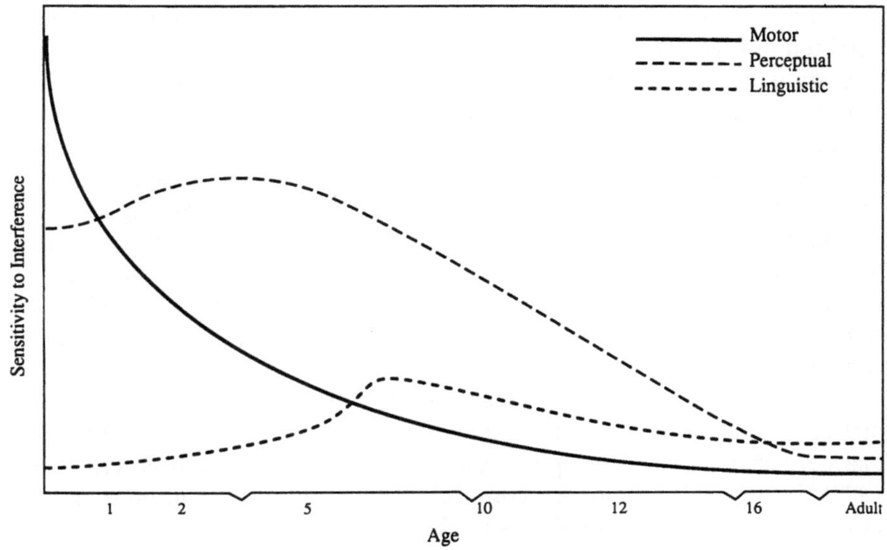

FIGURE 1.3. Hypothesized relation between age and sensitivity to interference.

categories of interference. As can be seen, age-related changes in resistance to interference do not follow an even course. Instead, decreases in sensitivity to one form of interference are accompanied by increases in sensitivity to one or more other forms of interference during the first decade of life. In other words, there is a stage-like quality to the developing child's sensitivity to interference. Initially, the child is particularly sensitive to motoric forms of interference. This, in turn, is followed by an increased sensitivity to perceptual forms of interference, accompanied by a decline in sensitivity to motoric forms of interference. Finally, these shifts are followed by an increased sensitivity to linguistic forms of interference, followed by a decrease in susceptibility to perceptual forms of interference.

The basis for this claim is threefold. First, many of the errors made on search tasks during infancy are perseverative (eye movements suggest that infants "know" the correct location, but cannot suppress their reaching behavior), which implies that the infant has difficulty resisting the repetition of a motor action that is no longer appropriate. By age 2 years, however, tasks with salient irrelevant visual or auditory stimuli, such as measures of field dependence, conservation tasks, and selective attention tasks, prove especially difficult. Finally, interference from tasks with an obvious linguistic component, such as the Stroop test (which is not normally interference-sensitive before the age of 6 years or so) and the Brown-Peterson task, begin to disrupt performance just as the child becomes increasingly resistant to perceptual sources of interference.

Second, there are obvious parallels between the stage-like progression depicted in Figure 1.3 and the sensorimotor → preoperational → concrete operational progression described by Piaget. Although the validity of Piaget's notion of stages is in doubt, there is little question that infancy is dominated by sensorimotor behavior and that the ability to overcome conflicts between perception and logic is the hallmark of the concrete operational period. Although there are other interpretations (e.g., Howe & Rabinowitz, 1991), the present perspective suggests that the changes that normally take place between the ages of 4 and 7 years on Piaget's visual illusion problems, such as conservation and class inclusion (Reyna & Brainerd, 1991), are largely due to improved ability to resist perceptual sources of interference.

A final argument for viewing resistance to interference as a multifaceted process is that cerebral maturation appears to proceed in a discontinuous manner, characterized by spurts and plateaus (cf. Hudspeth & Pribram, 1990). In particular, there is a considerable amount of discontinuity in the development of the frontal lobes. As indicated earlier, both the area comprised by the frontal lobes and synaptic density exhibit an irregular pattern of change over the course of development. Similarly, fissuration of the frontal lobes exhibits growth spurts at ages 2 and 6 years. Thus, changes in overall frontal lobe growth and synaptic density may be in part responsible for the transition from sensorimotor to perceptual forms of interference, whereas changes in overall frontal lobe growth and changes in fissuration may contribute to the transition from perceptual forms of interference to linguistic forms of interference.

Although the issue of singularity versus distinctive processes cannot be resolved on the basis of existing evidence, there is probably some truth to each side of the argument. In a general sense, changes in resistance to interference, whatever their source, are likely to reflect a common underlying mechanism—namely, the frontal cortex. At a more detailed level, however, there is probably a family of inhibitory processes, each of which is specialized to deal with somewhat different processing demands.

Another, more general, issue raised by the present synthesis centers on the mechanisms by which interference is resisted and inhibitory control is exerted. Presumably, one function of the prefrontal cortex is to protect the behavior structure from intrusions from a variety of internal and external influences that would divert it from serving in an adaptive manner. Theoretically, this function fills the need for suppressive neural influences that weaken or eliminate elements of behavior or cognition that are not germane to the task at hand. In this sense, the present synthesis provides a framework for investigating the adaptive nature of human intelligence. However, the process that preserves and strengthens some processing units and prunes away others is far from clear.

Although little is known about the details of inhibitory function in the frontal lobes, it may be helpful to invoke some analogies from sensory mechanisms: lateral, forward, and feedback inhibition. In the visual system, lateral or "sideways" inhibition—because it operates between adjacent cells—acts to sharpen contours. Activity in one neuron is modified (inhibited) by the activation of an adjacent neuron. Similarly, the activation of irrelevant dimensions in the EFT and conservation tasks, for example, may be weakened by the activation of "adjacent" relevant dimensions, so that the developing child comes to see these visual configurations differently.

Forward and feedback inhibition are thought to act to sharpen neural responses to temporal changes in illumination, by means of differential rates of excitatory and inhibitory build-up (cf. Lindsay & Norman, 1972). The basic strategy seems to be to enhance changing aspects of external signals and to suppress older, more familiar aspects. The development of such a mechanism might be responsible for the child's growing resistance to proactive interference.

More generally, the present perspective suggests that inhibitory mechanisms regulate the process of activation, promote resistance to interference, and gradually tranform the child intellectually in two basic ways. First, an activated irrelevant processing unit may be weakened or deactivated. Second, the activation of an irrelevant processing unit may be made more difficult or prevented altogether.

Summary

The thesis of this chapter is that resistance to interference is a major factor in cognitive development and that it is a basic processing mechanism linked to the efficiency of the frontal lobes. This perspective is the product of two converging areas of research: developmental research and recent advances in the neurosciences. Developmental research suggests that the common process of resistance to interference contributes to diverse expressions of cognitive development, whereas research on the brain is consistent with the view that the frontal lobes are slow to mature and that they play a major role in interference-sensitive tasks. From the present perspective, an especially revealing point of cross-disciplinary convergence is the striking degree of correspondence between the performance of young children and the performance of frontally lesioned adults on interference-sensitive tasks.

The present theoretical framework is, in effect, a new synthesis that seeks to reveal relationships among phenomena that previously seemed unrelated and that seeks to clarify the issues it raises. One such issue is whether resistance to interference is a singular process or a multifaceted process. Examination of this issue suggests that resistance to interference reflects a common underlying mechanism and that developmental change in resistance to interference is discontinuous in nature, and that there is a family of inhibitory processes, each of which has evolved to deal with different sources of interference.

Acknowledgments. Preparation of this chapter was supported in part by a grant from the University Research Council, University of Nevada, Las Vegas. I thank Chuck Brainerd and Laurie Hahn for their assistance and encouragement.

References

Albert, M.S., & Kaplan, E. (1980). Organic implications of neuropsychological deficits in the elderly. In L.W. Poon, J.L. Fozard, L.S. Cermak, D. Arenberg, & L.W. Thompson (Eds.), *New directions in memory and aging* (pp. 403–432). Hillsdale, NJ: Erlbaum.

Anooshian, L.J., & McCulloch, R.A. (1979). Developmental changes in dichotic listening with categorized word lists. *Developmental Psychology*, *15*, 280–287.

Baillargeon, R., DeVos, T., & Graber, M. (1989). Location memory in 8-month-old infants in a non-search AB task: Further evidence. *Cognitive Development*, *4*, 345–367.

Beech, A., Powell, T., McWilliams, J., & Claridge, G. (1989). Evidence of reduced "cognitive inhibition" in schizophrenia. *British Journal of Clinical Psychology*, *28*, 110–116.

Berg, E.A. (1948). A simple objective test for measuring flexibility in thinking. *Journal of General Psychology*, *39*, 378–379.

Bianchi, L. (1895). The function of the frontal lobes. *Brain*, *18*, 497–530.

Bjork E.L., & Cummings, E.M. (1984). Infant search errors: Stage of concept development or stage of memory development. *Memory & Cognition*, *12*, 1–19.

Bjork, R.A. (1989). Retrieval inhibition as an adaptive mechanism in human memory. In H.L. Roediger, III & F.I.M. Craik (Eds.), *Varieties of memory and consciousness* (pp. 309–330). Hillsdale, NJ: Erlbaum.

Bjorklund, D.F. (1985). The role of conceptual knowledge in the development of organization in children's memory. In C.J. Brained & M. Pressley (Eds.), *Basic processes in memory development: Progress in cognitive development research* (pp. 103–142). New York: Springer–Verlag.

Bjorklund, D.F. (1987). How age changes in knowledge base contribute to the development of children's memory: An interpretive review. *Developmental Review*, *7*, 93–130.

Bjorklund, D.F., & Harnishfeger, K.K. (1990). The resources construct in cognitive development: Diverse sources of evidence and a theory of inefficient inhibition. *Developmental Review*, *10*, 48–71.

Bruner, J.S. (1966). On the conservation of liquids. In J.S. Bruner, R.R. Olver, & P.M. Greenfield, et al., (Eds.), *Studies in cognitive growth* (pp. 183–207). New York: John Wiley.

Case, R. (1974). Structures and strictures: Some functional limitations on the course of cognitive growth. *Cognitive Psychology*, *6*, 544–573.

Chelune, G.J., & Baer, R.A. (1986). Developmental norms for the Wisconsin Card Sorting Test. *Journal of Clinical and Experimental Neurospychology*, *8*, 219–228.

Comalli, P.E., Wapner, S., & Werner, H. (1962). Interference effects of Stroop Color-Word test in children, adulthood and aging. *Journal of Genetic Psychology*, *100*, 47–53.

Cragg, B.C. (1975). The density of synapses and neurons in normal, mentally defective and aging human brains. *Brain*, *98*, 81–90.

Crowder, R.G. (1976). *Principles of learning and memory*. Hillsdale, NJ: Erlbaum.

Crowder, R.G. (1989). Modularity and dissociations in memory systems. In H.L. Roediger, III. & F.I.M. Craik (Eds.), *Varieties of memory and consciousness* (pp. 271–294). Hillsdale, NJ: Erlbaum.

Davies, D.R., Jones, D.M., & Taylor, A. (1984). Selective and sustained-attention tasks: Individual and group differences. In R. Parasuraman, D.R. Davies, & J. Beatty (Eds.), *Varieties of attention* (pp. 395–447). New York: Academic Press.

Dempster, F.N. (1981). Memory span: Sources of individual and developmental differences. *Psychological Bulletin*, *89*, 63–100.

Dempster, F.N. (1985a). Proactive interference in sentence recall: Topic similarity effects and individual differences. *Memory & Cognition*, *13*, 81–89.

Dempster, F.N. (1985b). Short-term memory development in childhood and adolescence. In C.J. Brainerd & M. Pressley (Eds.), *Basic processes in memory development* (pp. 208–248). New York: Springer–Verlag.

Dempster, F.N. (1989). Reflections on the nature and sources of individual differences in learning. *Learning and Individual Differences*, *1*, 1–6.

Dempster, F.N. (in press). The rise and fall of the inhibitory mechanism: Toward a unified theory of cognitive development and aging. *Developmental Review*.

Dempster, F.N. (1991). Inhibitory processes: A neglected dimension of intelligence. *Intelligence*, *15*, 157–173.

Dempster F.N., & Cooney, J.B. (1982). Individual differences in digit span, susceptibility to proactive interference, and aptitude/achievement test scores. *Intelligence*, *6*, 399–416.

Diamond, A. (1988a). Abilities and neural mechanisms underlying A$\bar{B}$ performance. *Child Development*, *59*, 523–527.

Diamond, A. (1988b). Differences between adult and infant cognition: Is the crucial variable presence or absence of language. In L. Weiskrantz (Ed.), *Thought without language* (pp. 337–370). Oxford, England: Clarendon.

Diamond, A., & Goldman-Rakic, P.S. (1986). Comparative development of human infants and infant rhesus monkeys of cognitive functions that depend on prefronal cortex. *Neurosciences Abstracts*, *12*, 274.

Doyle, A.B. (1973). Listening to distraction: A development study of selective attention. *Journal of Experimental Child Psychology*, *15*, 100–115.

Enns, J.T., & Akhtar, N. (1989). A developmental study of filtering in visual attention. *Child Development*, *60*, 1188–1199.

Enns, J.T., & Cameron, S. (1987). Selective attention in young children: The relations between visual search, filtering, and priming. *Journal of Experimental Child Psychology*, *44*, 38–63.

Fischer, K.W. (1980). A theory of cognitive development: The control and construction of hierarchies of skills. *Psychological Review*, *87*, 477–531.

Freedman, M., & Oscar-Berman, M. (1986). Bilateral frontal lobe disease and selective delayed response deficits in humans. *Behavioral Neuroscience*, *100*, 337–342.

Fuster, J.M. (1989). *The prefrontal cortex* (2nd ed.). New York: Raven Press.

Gelman, R. (1969). Conservation acquisition: A problem of learning to attend to relevant attributes. *Journal of Experimental Child Psychology*, *7*, 167–187.

Goldman-Rakic, P.S. (1987). Development of cortical circuitry and cognitive function. *Child Development*, *58*, 601–622.

Gratch, G. (1976). On levels of awareness of objects in infants and students thereof. *Merrill-Palmer Quarterly*, *22*, 157–176.

Halford, G.S. (1982). *The development of thought*. Hillsdale, NJ: Erlbaum.

Harris, P.L. (1973). Perseverative errors in search by young infants. *Child Development*, *44*, 28–33.

Hasher, L., & Zacks, R.T. (1988). Working memory, comprehension, and aging: A review and a new view. In G.H. Bower (Ed.), *The psychology of learning and motivation* (Vol. 22, pp. 193–224). New York: Academic Press.

Heaton, R.K. (1981). *Wisconsin card sorting test manual*. Odessa, FL: Psychological Assessment Resources.

Hebb, D.O. (1939). Intelligence in man after large removals of cerebral tissue: Report of four left frontal lobe cases. *Journal of General Psychology*, *21*, 73–87.

Hecaen, H., & Albert, M.L. (1978). *Human neuropsychology*. New York: Wiley.

Howe, M.L., & Brainerd, C.J. (1989). Development of children's long-term retention. *Developmental Review*, *9*, 301–340.

Howe, M.L., & Rabinowitz, F.M. (1991). Gist another panacea? Or just the illusion of inclusion. *Developmental Review*, *11*, 305–316.

Hudspeth, W.J., & Pribram, K.H. (1990). Stages of brain and cognitive maturation. *Journal of Educational Psychology*, *82*, 881–884.

Huttenlocher, P.R. (1979). Synaptic density in human frontal cortex—developmental changes and effects of aging. *Brain Research*, *163*, 195–205.

Hynd, G.W., & Willis, G. (1985). Neurological foundations of intelligence. In B.B. Wolman (Ed.), *Handbook of intelligence: Theories, measurements, and applications* (pp. 119–157). New York: Wiley.

Janowsky, J.S., Shimamura, A.P., Kritchevsky, M., & Squire, L.R. (1989). Cognitive impairment following frontal lobe damage and its relevance to human amnesia. *Behavioral Neuroscience*, *103*, 548–560.

Jensen, A.R., & Rohwer, W.D., Jr. (1966). The Stroop Color-Word test: A review. *Acta Psychologica*, *25*, 36–93.

Kail, R.V., Jr., & Levine, L.A. (1976). Encoding processes and sex-role preferences. *Journal of Experimental Child Psychology*, *21*, 256–263.

LaMantia, A., & Rakic, P. (1984). The number, size, myelination and regional variations in the corpus callosum and anterior commissure of the developing rhesus monkey. *Society of Neuroscience Abstracts*, *10*, 1373.

Lane, D.M., & Pearson, D.A. (1982). The development of selective attention. *Merrill-Palmer Quarterly*, *28*, 317–337.

Leslie, L. (1979, April). *Mediation or production deficiency in disabled readers?* Paper presented at the annual meeting of the American Educational Research Association, San Francisco, CA.

Lezak, M. (1983). *Neuropsychological assessment* (2nd ed.). New York: Oxford University Press.

Lindsay, P.H., & Norman, D.A. (1972). *Human information processing*. New York: Academic Press.

Linn, M.C. (1978). Influence of cognitive style and training on tasks requiring the separation of variables schema. *Child Development*, *49*, 874–877.

Loess, H., & Waugh, N.C. (1967). Short-term memory and inter-trial interval. *Journal of Verbal Learning and Verbal Behavior*, *6*, 455–460.

Longmore, B.E., & Knight, R.G. (1988). The effect of intellectual deterioration on retention deficits in amnesic alcoholics. *Journal of Abnormal Psychology*, *97*, 448–454.

Luria, A.R. (1966). *Higher cortical functions in man*. New York: Basic Books.

Luria, A.R. (1973). *The working brain: An introduction for neuropsychology*. New York: Basic Books.

McGeoch, J.A. (1943). *The psychology of human learning*. New York: Longmans Green.

Milner, B. (1964). Some effects of frontal lobectomy in man. In J.M. Warren & K. Akert (Eds.), *The frontal granular cortex and behavior* (pp. 313–334). New York: McGraw-Hill.

Moely, B.E. (1977). Organizational factors in the development of memory. In R.V. Kail, Jr., & J.W. Hagen (Eds.), *Perspectives on the development of memory and cognition* (pp. 203–236). Hillsdale, NJ: Erlbaum.

Murdock, B.B. (1974). *Human memory: Theory and data*. New York: John Wiley.

Oscar-Berman, M. (1980). Neuropsychological consequences of long-term chronic alcoholism. *American Scientist*, *68*, 410–419.

Parkin, A.J., & Leng, N.R.C. (1987). Aetiological variation in the amnesic syndrome. In M.M. Gruneberg, P.E. Morris, & R.N. Sykes (Eds.), *Practical aspects of memory: Current research and issues* (Vol. 2, pp. 16–21). Chichester, England: Wiley.

Pascual-Leone, J. (1970). A mathematical model for the transition rule in Piaget's developmental stages. *Acta Psychologia*, *63*, 301–345.

Pascual-Leone, J. (1989). An organismic process model of Witkins's field-dependence-independence. In T. Globerson & T. Zelniker (Eds.), *Cognitive style and cognitive development* (pp. 36–70). Norwood, NJ: Ablex.

Pascual-Leone, J., Ammon, P., Goodman, D., & Subleman, I. (1978). Piagetian theory and Neo-Piagetion analysis as psychological guides in education. In J.M. Gallagher & J. Easley (Eds.), *Knowledge and development: Piaget and education* (Vol. 2). New York: Plenum Press.

Pavlov, I.P. (1949). *Complete Collected Works* (Vols. 1–6). Moscow: Nauk SSSR.

Peterson, L.R., & Peterson, M.J. (1959). Short-term retention of individual verbal items. *Journal of Experimental Psychology*, *58*, 193–198.

Perret, E. (1974). The left frontal lobe of man and the suppression of habitual responses in verbal categorical behavior. *Neuropsychologia*, *12*, 323–330.

Piaget, J. (1954). *The construction of reality in the child*. New York: Basic Books.

Plude, D.J., & Hoyer, W.J. (1985). Attention and performance: Identifying and localizing age deficits. In N. Charness (Ed.), *Aging and human performance* (pp. 47–99). New York: Academic Press.

Rand, G., Wapner, S., Werner, H., & McFarland, J.H. (1963). Age differences in performance on the Stroop Color-Word test. *Journal of Personality, 31*, 534–558.

Reinis, S., & Goldman, J.M. (1980). *The development of the brain.* Sprinfield, II: Charles C. Thomas.

Reyna, V.F., & Brainerd, C.J. (1991). Fuzzy-trace theory and children's acquisition of mathematical and scientific concepts. *Learning and Individual Differences, 3*, 27–59.

Rourke, B.P., Bakker, D.J., Fisk, J.L., & Stang, J.D. (1983). *Child neuropsychology: An introduction to theory, research and clinical practice.* New York: Guilford.

Sarnat, H.B., & Netsky, M.G. (1981). *Evolution of the nervous system* (2nd ed.). New York: Oxford University Press.

Schacter, L.L., & Moscovitch, M. (1984). Infants, amnesiacs, and dissociable memory systems. In M. Moscovitch (Ed.), *Infant memory* (pp. 173–216). New York: Plenum.

Schacter, D.L., Moscovitch, M., Tulving, E., McLachlan, D.R., & Frendman, M. (1986). Mnemonic precedence in amnesiac patients: An analogue of the A$\bar{B}$ error in infants. *Child Development, 57*, 816–823.

Sejnowski, T.J., & Rosenberg, C.R. (1988). Learning and representation in connectionist models. In M.S. Gazzaniga (Ed.), *Perspectives in memory research* (pp. 135–178). Cambridge, MA: The MIT Press.

Siegler, R.S. (1984). Mechanisms of cognitive growth: Variation and selection. In R.J. Sternberg (Ed.), *Mechanisms of cognitive development* (pp. 141–162). New York: Freeman.

Siegler, R.S. (1989). Mechanisms of cognitive development. In M.R. Rosenzweig & L.W. Porter (Eds.), *Annual Review of Psychology* (Vol. 40, pp. 353–379). Palo Alto, CA. Annual Reviews.

Sophian, C., Larking, J.H., & Kadane, J.B. (1985). A developmental model of search: Stochastic estimation of children's rule use. In H.M. Wellman (Ed.), *Children's searching* (pp. 185–214). Hillsdale, NJ: Erlbaum.

Sophian, C., & Wellman, H.M. (1983). Selective information use and perseveration in the search behavior of infants and young children. *Journal of Experimental Child Psychology, 35*, 369–390.

Stamm, J.S. (1987). The riddle of the monkey's delayed response deficit has been solved. In E. Perceman (Ed.), *The frontal lobes revisited* (pp. 73–89). New York: The IRBN Press.

Stroop, J.R. (1935). Studies of interference in serial verbal reactions. *Journal of Experimental Psychology, 18*, 643–662.

Strutt, G.F., Anderson, D.R., & Well, A.D. (1975). A developmental study of the effects of irrelevant information on speeded classification. *Journal of Experimental Child Psychology, 20*, 127–135.

Stuss, D.T., & Benson, D.F. (1984). Neuropsychological Studies of the frontal lobes. *Psychological Bulletin, 95*, 3–28.

Stuss, D.T., Benson, D.F., Kaplan, E.F., Weir, W.S., Naeser, M.A., Lieberman, I., & Ferrill, D. (1983). The involvement of orbitofrontal cerebrum in cognitive tasks. *Neuropsychologia, 21*, 235–248.

Stuss, D.T., Kaplan, E.F., Benson, D.F., Weir, W.S., Chivilli, S., & Sarazin, F.F. (1982). Evidence for the involvement of orbitofrontal cortex in memory functions: An interference effect. *Journal of Comparative and Physiological Psychology*, *96*, 913–925.

Teuber, H.L. (1964). The riddle of frontal lobe function in man. In J.M. Warren & K. Akert (Eds.), *The frontal granular cortex and behavior* (pp. 410–444). New York: McGraw-Hill.

Teuber, H.L. (1972). Unity and diversity of frontal lobe functions. *Acta Neurobiologica Experimenta*, *32*, 615–656.

Tipper, S.P. (1985). The negative priming effect: Inhibitory priming by ignored objects. *The Quarterly Journal of Experimental Psychology*, *37A*, 571–590.

Tipper, S.P., Bourque, T.A., Anderson, S.H., & Brehaut, J.C. (1989). Mechanisms of attention: A developmental study. *Journal of Experimental Child Psychology*, *48*, 353–378.

Waber, D. (1989). The biological boundaries of cognitive styles: A neuropsychological analysis. In T. Golberson & T. Zelniker (Eds.), *Cognitive style and cognitive development* (pp. 11–35). Norwood, NJ: Ablex.

Wallach, L., Wall, A.J., & Anderson, L. (1967). Number conservation: The roles of reversibility, addition-subtraction, and misleading perceptual cues. *Child Development*, *38*, 425–442.

Wechsler, D. (1958). *The measurement and appraisal of adult intelligence*. Baltimore: Williams & Wilkins.

Weinberger, D.R. (1987). Implications of normal brain development for the pathogenesis of schizophrenia. *Archives of General Psychiatry*, *44*, 660–669.

Winer, G.A., Hemphill, J., & Craig, R.K. (1988). The effect of misleading questions in promoting nonconservation responses in children and adults. *Developmental Psychology*, *24*, 197–202.

Wise, L.A., Sutton, J.A., & Gibbons, P.O. (1975). Decrement in Stroop interference time with age. *Perceptual and Motor Skills*, *41*, 149–150.

Witkin, H.A., Dyk, R.B., Faterson, G.E., Goodenough, D.R., & Karp, S.A. (1962). *Psychological differentiation*. New York: John Wiley.

Yakovlev, P.I., & LeCours, A.R. (1967). The myelogenetic cycles of regional maturation of the brain. In A. Minkowski (Ed.), *Regional development of the brain in early life* (pp. 3–70). Oxford: Blackwell.

Zelniker, T. (1989). Cognitive style and dimensions of information processing. In T. Globerson & T. Zelniker (Eds.), *Cognitive style and cognitive development* (pp. 172–191). Norwood, NJ: Ablex.

Zimilies, H. (1963). A note on Piaget's concept of conservation. *Child Development*, *34*, 691–695.

2 The Ontogeny of Inhibition Mechanisms: A Renewed Approach to Cognitive Development

KATHERINE KIPP HARNISHFEGER AND DAVID F. BJORKLUND

A major focus of developmental researchers has concerned the isolation of the mechanisms behind age-related improvements in cognition. Working memory capacity, metacognitive abilities, strategies, and knowledge base have all been touted as important causative agents in children's thinking (e.g., Bjorklund, 1990; Schneider & Pressley, 1989). Meanwhile, although inhibition processes enjoyed a role in early theories of cognition and development (Luria, 1961; Underwood, 1957), inhibition has been neglected, in part, because it has not appeared to be compatible with the computer metaphor of cognition (Bjork, 1989; Dempster, this volume). Currently, the developmental significance of inhibitory processing is garnering renewed support from such diverse areas as memory development (Bjorklund & Harnishfeger, 1990), object permanence in infancy (Diamond, 1988), and discourse processing in the aged (Hasher & Zacks, 1989). It is time to reexamine inhibition as a central mechanism in accounts of cognitive development.

In an earlier paper (Bjorklund & Harnishfeger, 1990), we outlined a developmental theory of *inefficient inhibition*. We proposed that, with age, children are increasingly able to keep task-irrelevant information out of working memory. Younger children's poor inhibitory mechanisms result in less efficient cognitive processing because working memory space is consumed with irrelevant information, leaving less mental space available for other aspects of processing. We proposed this theory in response to recent attacks on the resources hypothesis of cognitive development (Brainerd & Reyna, 1989, 1990; Howe & Rabinowitz, 1990; Stanovich, 1990). Basically, the resources hypothesis holds that developmental differences in cognitive functioning are due to differences in children's efficiency in allocating their limited mental resources; this efficiency improves with experience, knowledge, and maturation (Bjorklund & Harnishfeger, 1990; Case, 1985). A model of inefficient inhibition maintains many of the explanatory powers of the resources hypothesis and provides a broader context in which a new framework of cognitive development can be formulated (Bjorklund & Harnishfeger, 1990).

In this chapter, we expand our earlier hypothesis, demonstrating developmental changes in inhibitory processes for a wide range of phenomena. We begin with a look at older literature examining age changes in abilities to inhibit motor responses, followed by an examination of developmental differences in children's abilities to inhibit their attention to external distractors. The primary emphasis of the chapter concerns more recent evidence of age-related changes in children's abilities to inhibit *internal*, or *mental* distractors, and we present new data showing developmental differences in inhibitory processes in a memory task. We conclude by proposing that developmental changes in inhibitory processes can serve as the basis of a theory of cognitive development and are consistent with our current knowledge of brain development, making a theory based on inhibitory mechanisms an attractive one as a broad account of cognitive development.

Inhibition of Motor Behavior

Inhibition of Motor Behavior in Infancy

The importance of inhibitory function can be seen very early in development. In Piaget's Stage IV object permanence task, an infant watches as the experimenter hides an attractive toy in one of two wells, a brief delay is then imposed during which time the infant is distracted. On the initial trials, infants are able to reach (correctly) into the well in which the toy was hidden to retrieve it. On a subsequent trial, in which the hiding place is changed (from well "A" to well "B") infants typically err by reaching back to the same well from which they had successfully retrieved the toy on the previous trials. This has been called the *A not B* (A$\bar{\text{B}}$) error.

There are strict boundaries for production of this phenomenon (Diamond, 1988). There must be a delay between the hiding of the toy and the infant's reach. If the infant is allowed to stare at or maintain a bodily orientation to the correct well, the error is typically not seen. Furthermore, the error is not seen on all trials, but only on reversal trials (i.e., it is seen when the hiding place is changed from a previously successful location).

One interpretation of the A$\bar{\text{B}}$ error is that it is due to a memory failure, such as proactive interference (Harris, 1973) or poor information processing (Cummings & Bjork, 1983). Clearly, short-term memory is a necessary condition for correct performance, as infants do not err when there is no delay between hiding and retrieval (Gratch, Appel, Evans, LeCompte, & Wright, 1974; Harris, 1973). However, proactive interference alone is not sufficient to account for the phenomenon, for infants make the error even when the toy remains visible during the B hiding trials and transparent covers are used for the wells (Butterworth, 1977; Harris, 1974). In addition, the infants' erroneous reaches are not random. When there are multiple wells in the task, infants' errors are clustered between the A and B wells, but there are virtually no responses to the side of the B well farthest from A (Cummings & Bjork, 1983).

Diamond (1985, 1988) has argued that failures on the A$\bar{B}$ task are due to a combination of forgetting and an inability to resist the tendency to reach to the conditioned well. Diamond discusses instances in which infants appear to remember the correct location but are unable to inhibit their prepotent response: "infants often uncover the wrong well, do not look in to see if the toy is there, reach immediately to the correct well, and retrieve the toy. . . . Infants occasionally look squarely at the correct well as their hand reaches back to uncover the well where the toy used to be" (Diamond, 1985, p. 881).

Inhibition and Verbal Self-Regulation

Inefficient inhibition of motor behavior has also been investigated in older children. Luria (1961) examined the development of the verbal regulation of behavior in experiments in which young children were told to squeeze a rubber ball in response to various kinds of visual and auditory signals. The complexity of the directions was varied, and in some experiments the children were instructed to verbalize as well as perform the action. Interpreting Luria's work, American researchers have conceptualized the development of verbal self-regulation as occurring in stages (Fuson, 1979; Wozniak, 1972). Between about 1.5 and 5.5 years, children gradually become able to direct their own behavior through self-verbalizations. Children are first able to control their behavior in accordance with adult instructions; only later is verbal self-control possible. The developmental progression also reveals that speech has both initiative and inhibitory self-regulation functions. The initiative functions are the first to come under control, and at early stages speech can initiate, but not inhibit, behavior.

For example, toddlers can respond to direct, immediate instructions ("Squeeze the ball") from an adult. However, instructions that are in conflict with an ongoing activity ("Don't squeeze the ball") will neither inhibit nor alter that activity and often actually intensify the child's actions. The only way to inhibit an ongoing motor response at this stage is to provide a new action instruction, such as "Touch your knee" (Luria, 1961). With slightly older children, Tikhomirov (in Luria, 1961) demonstrated the impulsive effect of speech and the poor inhibitory function of verbal control. Children instructed to squeeze to a red light and not squeeze to a green light were able to comply, with fairly good inhibition to the green light. When they were also required to say "Press" when pressing to the red light and "Don't press" to the green light, their inhibition performance deteriorated greatly. In this condition, the children squeezed the bulb both when saying "Press" and when saying "Don't press." Luria's work suggests that verbal self-regulation reaches mature function sometime after 4.5 to 5.5 years.

Response Inhibition

The process of inhibiting motor responses continues to be of interest in older children. Constantini and Hoving (1973a) defined response inhibition as "the ability to slow down, delay, or withhold a previously learned or preferred response" (p. 484). Various tasks have been used to assess behavioral response inhibition in children, such as the Draw-a-Line Slowly Test and the Reel-up-Slowly Test, both of which require motoric control. Response inhibition has been found to increase with age (Constantini & Hoving, 1973a), to correlate with IQ (Maccoby, Dowley, Hagen, & Degerman, 1965), to be influenced by overt and covert self-instructions (Meichenbaum & Goodman, 1969), and to improve with training (Constantini & Hoving, 1973b).

The ability to inhibit motor impulsivity may be a composite of an immediate response inhibition function and a more sustained inhibition or attention function that occurs over protracted delay periods. For example, Masters and Binger (1978) distinguished between interruption of an ongoing activity and maintenance of action suppression (such as in a delay of gratification paradigm), and found developmental improvements in both processes. Similarly, Olson (1989) has proposed that "by the onset of the early school-age period, two different subtypes of impulsivity may exist: a 'cognitive' dimension indexing ability to inhibit overt behaviors in highly structured task situations and a 'delay' dimension indexing compliance with social expectations for 'correct' behavior" (p. 182).

Logan and his colleagues have looked more closely at the immediate inhibition of motor behaviors (Logan & Cowan, 1984; Schachar & Logan, 1990). They proposed that young children's poor inhibitory control may be caused by inefficient response inhibition, which is demonstrated by "impulsive behaviors such as responding before the task is understood, answering before sufficient information is available, allowing attention to be captured by irrelevant stimuli (i.e., distractibility), or failing to correct obviously inappropriate responses" (Schachar & Logan, 1990, p. 710). To assess inhibitory control, Logan developed the stop-signal test, performance on which is independent of IQ, metacognition, and motivation (Logan, Cowan, & Davis, 1984; Logan & Cowan, 1984). The stop-signal paradigm consists of a primary task that engages the subject's attention, such as a forced-choice letter discrimination task. On one-quarter of the primary-task trials, an auditory signal is presented and the subject is to inhibit his or her response to the primary task when this signal is heard.

Logan and his colleagues have been primarily interested in the inhibition of action (Logan & Cowan, 1984; Logan et al., 1984). In one study, Schachar and Logan (1990) looked for developmental and individual differences in inhibition functions among normal and disabled children. Differences in inhibition between second grade children and adults were not significant, although they did find poorer inhibitory performance in hyperactive than normal children. This suggests that the mechanism of inhibitory control of a motor response may be developed by the second grade.

In this section we have briefly reviewed research demonstrating the progressive development of the inhibitory control of motor behavior. Inhibition of action begins to come under control in infancy and becomes more and more refined through the early childhood years. Although the inhibitory function of simple actions may be mature by age 7 years, variations in task and response requirements continue to tax inhibitory processes throughout childhood.

Inhibition of External Distractors

One of the most important cognitive functions of inhibition is its role in selective attention. At any given moment, we are capable of receiving an almost infinite array of stimuli. In order to function effectively, we need to be able to select from that array the critical stimulus and ignore the other irrelevant, distracting stimuli. Our ability to do this is a central cognitive skill and, as such, has been the focus of a large body of research (see reviews by Davies, Jones, & Taylor, 1984, and Lane & Pearson, 1982).

Several investigators have demonstrated that inhibitory processes operate in selective attention performance (e.g., Neill, 1977; Tipper, 1985; Tipper & Cranston, 1985). For example, Tipper has demonstrated a "negative priming" effect in a Stroop task. The Stroop task is a selective attention test in which the subject's task is to name the color of the ink of a series of words, which are themselves color names. The test has long been used as a measure of selective attention and interference. In Tipper's paradigm, performance in the standard Stroop condition is compared with a negative-priming condition, in which the color to be named on trial n is identical to the color word on trial n-1. The color *word* on trial n-1 was an irrelevant stimulus and thus should have been ignored. Tipper found that adults' performance was impaired in these conditions, compared to the standard Stroop conditions. This supports the idea that ignored stimuli (the color word on trial n-1) are actively inhibited, and so when those words subsequently become target stimuli, processing is impaired (Tipper, 1985; Tipper & Cranston, 1985).

There has been a great deal of research examining the development of selective attention abilities. Generally, a developmental trend of increasing ability has been demonstrated for selective attention tasks such as speeded classification (Strutt, Anderson, & Well, 1975), incidental learning (Hagen & Hale, 1973; Hagen & Stanovich, 1977), selective listening (Doyle, 1973), and Stroop tests (Comalli, Wapner, & Werner, 1962).

Lane and Pearson (1982), in their review of the literature, argue that developmental improvements in selective attention are not a function of older children's ability to filter out irrelevant information before it reaches meaning. Rather, in concordance with Tipper's work, it appears that multiple stimuli are processed for meaning in parallel, and then the target stimuli are selected into a limited-capacity system as the distractor stimuli are actively inhibited (see also Duncan, 1980). Others have argued that developmental improvements are the result of improved ability to maintain inhibition of irrelevant information (Hale & Alderman, 1978) and the ability to inhibit intrusions of irrelevant information in primary-task processing (Doyle, 1973).

Another hypothesis suggests that facilitation of selective attention performance after repeated exposure to the same distracting stimuli occurs as a result of habituation to the repeated stimulus, and that older children may be more efficient in this process (Lorch, Anderson, & Well, 1984; Lorch & Horn, 1986). In a speeded classification task in which some children were given prior exposure to irrelevant, distracting stimuli, Lorch and Horn found that children given preexposure and practice showed less interference than those who did not receive preexposure. Furthermore, younger children (kindergartners through second-graders) benefitted more from the preexposure than older children (fourth- through sixth-graders). Lorch and Horn suggested that such short-term facilitation afforded by efficient habituation (i.e., through preexposure and practice) may contribute significantly to the developmental improvements in selective attention (see Jeffrey, 1968, and Wright & Vlietstra, 1975, for similar views).

Tipper, Bourque, Anderson, and Brehaut (1989) examined the contributions of habituation and inhibition processes to developmental changes in selective attention in a Stroop paradigm. They were specifically interested in determining whether habituation and inhibition processes each contributed independently to selective attention. They found that (a) children (second-graders) were more distracted in the Stroop condition than adults; (b) negative priming, a demonstration of inhibition, was significant for the adults, but not the children; and (c) habituation was significant for both groups, but larger for the children (cf. Hale & Flaugher, 1977; Hale & Stevenson, 1974). These results demonstrated that habituation and inhibition are dissociated and show different developmental patterns: the automatic processing of stimuli and habituation to repeated stimuli develop rapidly and are functional by second grade, whereas the inhibitory mechanism is not firmly established until sometime later. Tipper et al. concluded that "the greater distractability of children in certain situations may be due in part to the underutilization of this inhibitory mechanism" (p. 353).

In summary, children become increasingly efficient at establishing and maintaining selective attention with age. Although processes of inhibition and habituation both contribute to efficient selective attention, developmental improvements in inhibition most likely are responsible for the developmental trends seen in selective attention performance.

Inhibition of Internal Distractors

In addition to the inhibition of inappropriate motor behaviors and of distracting stimuli in the environment, efficient inhibition requires the inhibition of internal distractors. This is a central concept in current theories of attention. For example, Posner and Friedrich (1986) discuss the activation and inhibition processes of a limited capacity, semantic network system. In semantic network models, knowledge is represented by an expanded body of nodes, corresponding to units of knowledge such as words or concepts. The nodes are connected by links, representing the various relationships among the concepts. Executing a cognitive task via this network occurs through the spreading activation of nodes and links. Processing within such a network requires both the excitation and inhibition of links. For the system to operate effectively, task-relevant links and nodes must be activated, while task-irrelevant links and nodes must remain unactivated. In many cases, NON-activation translates into an active process of inhibition. Some theories of attention propose that spreading activation is an automatic process that occurs upon presentation of a stimulus, whereas inhibition of activation occurs later, and may be a slower, more conscious process (Neely, 1977; Posner & Friedrich, 1986).

Lexical Ambiguity

One avenue to investigating inhibitory processes that work on internal distractors is the study of lexical ambiguity. When we encounter a polysemous word such as *scale*, we must have some process to select the correct meaning of the word for the particular context. Current research has converged in support of an exhaustive-access model of lexical ambiguity (Onifer & Swinney, 1981; Seidenberg, Tanenhaus, Leiman, & Bienkowski, 1982; Swinney, Zurif, & Nicol, 1989). The model proposes that immediately after the presentation of a polysemous word, all meanings of the word are automatically accessed. The initial access is followed by a decision stage, when the contextually appropriate meaning is selected. Finally, the alternative, inappropriate meanings are suppressed. Research investigating developmental differences in lexical access has generally supported the idea that there are different developmental courses for the automatic and conscious components of lexical access (Simpson & Lorsbach, 1983; West & Stanovich, 1978). The initial phase, an automatic spreading activation process, is thought to reach maturity early and operate efficiently in very young children (as early as age 4 years). A subsequent, conscious allocation phase of attentional processing is thought to emerge later in development (by fifth or sixth grade, depending on the task).

Swinney and Prather (1989) investigated developmental differences in lexical ambiguity processing. They used a cross-modal priming task to examine which meanings of polysemous words are activated within a biasing sentence context (e.g., which meanings of *bat* are activated when the child hears the sentence: The baseball player picked up the bat lying in the park). Swinney and Prather found that 5-year-old children accessed all meanings of the ambiguous words, whereas 4-year-old children only accessed the dominant meanings of the words. There was no facilitation for the subordinate meanings of polysemous words (e.g., *bat* the mammal) for the 4-year-old children, even when the sentence context was biased to prime for that meaning (e.g., The birdwatcher picked up the *bat* lying in the park).

Swinney and Prather suggested that these findings may be a result of the younger children having a *protracted rise time* for exhaustive access of the various meanings of the ambiguous words (cf. Swinney, Zurif, & Nicol, 1989). According to the protracted rise time hypothesis, the failure of the younger children to activate all meanings of the polysemous words is due to a slower word-access process. Swinney and Prather suggested that if processing had been tapped downstream, perhaps after a few syllables, the younger children may have demonstrated exhaustive access of all meanings. An investigation of lexical ambiguity processing in second-, fourth-, and sixth-graders supports this hypothesis (Simpson & Foster, 1986). Simpson and Foster varied the time interval between prime offset and target onset in a task similar to Swinney and Prather's. Children saw the targets 150, 300, or 750 msec after the primes. Results from this experiment suggested that all the children initially accessed both meanings of the homographs. However, by 750 msec the older children were actively attending to the dominant meanings of the words, as evidenced by facilitation for dominant associates and by interference for subordinate associates, whereas the second- and fourth-graders continued to show facilitation for both dominant and subordinate associates. That is, by 750 msec after prime offset the older children had exhaustively accessed all meanings and had restricted activation to the dominant meaning; the younger children had only reached the phase of exhaustive activation of all meanings by that time. This experiment was interpreted as supporting the two-process theory of ambiguity processing in which initial activation is followed by inhibition of irrelevant, or subordinate, meanings. Further, the data suggested that the inhibitory aspect of this process reaches maturity at a later age than the activation aspect.

Age-related dfferences in lexical processing can be accounted for by the poorer inhibitory processing of young children. The studies reviewed in this section have demonstrated that younger children are competent and efficient in an initial automatic activation stage of processing. Young children are inefficient, however, in the subsequent suppression of context-irrelevant meanings. Although it is possible that the inhibition stage of processing would occur further downstream than these investigations monitored, this possibility is unlikely, as Simpson and Lorsbach (1983) failed to find inhibition of irrelevant information in young children even after 2,000 msec.

Discourse Processing

Hasher and Zacks (1989) have examined adult developmental trends in discourse processing and have proposed that inefficient inhibition may account for deficits in performance among the aged. In a study examining inferences made during the reading of a discourse passage, young and old adults read passages that either maintained the meaning of the passage inferred in the early sentences (expected versions) or that altered the meaning of the passage so that the initial inferences were invalidated by the end of the passage (unexpected versions) (V. Hamm, cited in Hasher & Zacks, 1989). As the adults were reading the passages, they were periodically presented with a single word that they were to judge as either consistent or inconsistent with their *current* understanding of the passage. Hamm found that, although older adults did maintain the correct inference at the end of both the expected and unexpected versions (as demonstrated by their consistency ratings), they were also likely to maintain the incorrect inference at the end of the unexpected versions. That is, the older adults maintained erroneous and irrelevant information in working memory, along with the correct information, for longer periods than young adults. Hasher and Zacks interpreted these results as evidence for the reduced efficiency of inhibitory processes in the aged. Their model of discourse processing posits that when inhibition is not effective, irrelevant information will be entered into and maintained in working memory. This will result in cross-talk among competing messages and difficulties in the retrieval of relevant information, which will seriously impair the processing of discourse.

Several others lines of research have suggested that adults may suffer from increasingly less efficient inhibitory processes with age. For example, interference on the Stoop task has been found to increase with age (Cohn, Dustman, & Bradford, 1984; Comalli et al., 1962). The elderly have also been found to make more false-recognition errors and more intrusions in free recall (Rankin & Kausler, 1979; Stine & Wingfield, 1987).

Memory

Recent models of memory have emphasized the roles of knowledge base, limited mental resources, and strategies in accounting for developmental improvements in memory performance (e.g., Bjorklund, Muir-Broaddus, & Schneider, 1990). In an extension of this model, we proposed that developmental improvements in inhibition are central to the operation and development of memory (Bjorklund & Harnishfeger, 1990). This inefficient inhibition model posits that young children are not able to block the activation of task-irrelevant information and associations efficiently during cognitive processing. Consequently, task-irrelevant information becomes activated and maintained in working memory. This poses a problem because of the limited-capacity nature of working memory. With space being consumed by off-task activations, less capacity remains for the storage and retrieval of task-relevant information. Therefore, task performance will suffer whenever inhibition processes are inefficient.

There is some evidence in the developmental literature pointing to the deleterious influence of inefficient inhibition on memory. Early investigations demonstrated that one source of problem for memory performance was proactive interference, the interruption of a current memory task by previously remembered materials (Underwood, 1957). Developmental improvements in resistance to proactive interference have been documented and may contribute generally to developmental improvements in memory (cf., Dempster, 1985, 1989).

Another consistent line of evidence concerns children's false recognition errors and intrusions in memory tasks. The theory proposes that young children will have more activations of information that is not directly tied to the memory task. This information may be demonstrated by false recognitions and intrusions. In support of this, Brown, Smiley, Day, Townsend, and Lawton (1977) examined developmental improvements in memory for prose passages and found that younger children made many more intrusions of irrelevant information during memory performance than older children. Similarly, Shepard, Cohen, Gold and Orbino (1976) investigated the hypothesis that false recognition errors are promoted by implicit associations and found that children made more false recognition errors to their own word associations than to those of their peers.

A Study of Inefficient Inhibition in Memory

We found evidence for inefficient inhibition during a memory task in a reanalysis of data from a cued recall experiment with nursery school, kindergarten, third-, and sixth-grade children (Bjorklund & Harnishfeger,

TABLE 2.1. Cue and target words for cued recall experiment.

Cue type	Cue word	Target word
Category	Furniture	Bed
	Weapons	Knife
Function	Listen	Ear
	Throw	Ball
Acoustic	Teach	Peach
	Like	Bike

1990). The task involved the presentation of words to be remembered, along with a cue that was given at presentation and at recall. The targets and cues were related in one of three ways: categorically, functionally, or acoustically (see Table 2.1). At recall, children were given cues and asked to give one response to each cue. To examine children's failures to keep off-task information from interfering with the task, we measured the proportion of intrusions (i.e., words recalled that were not on the list) in the child's recall. The rate of instrusions decreased with age, with the nursery school and kindergarten children making a significantly higher percentage of intrusions than the third- and sixth-graders (see Fig. 2.1).

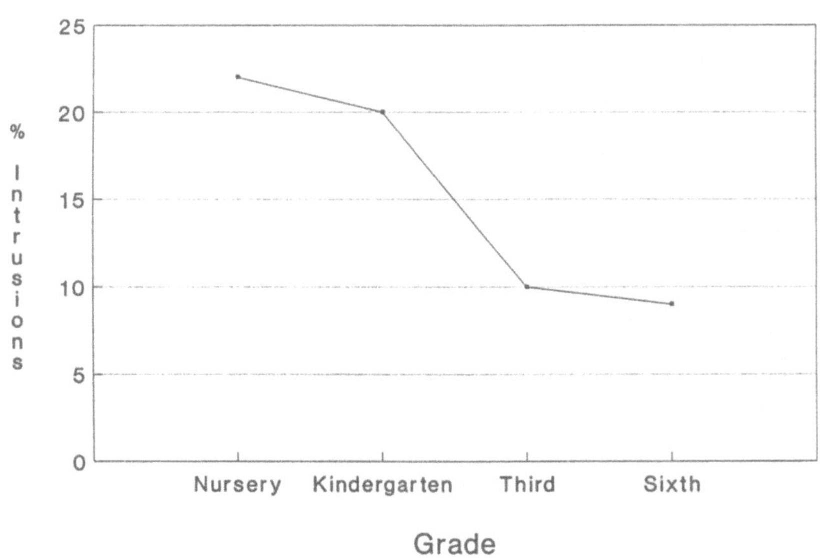

FIGURE 2.1. Percentage of intrusions in cued recall for nursery school, kindergarten, third-, and sixth-grade children.

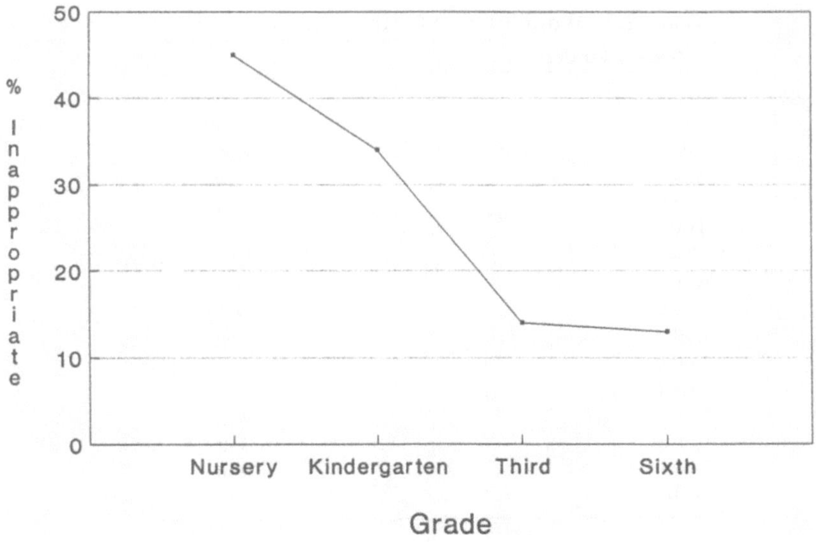

FIGURE 2.2. Percentage of inappropriate intrusions in cued recall for nursery school, kindergarten, third-, and sixth-grade children.

The inefficient inhibition hypothesis predicts not only that young children will have more intrusions in recall, but more specifically, that their intrusions will be task-irrelevant. To examine this, we classified each intrusion as task-appropriate or task-inappropriate. Task-appropriate intrusions were defined as words recalled that were not on the list but that were related to the cue in one of the three relationships used in the experiment (i.e., categorical, functional, or acoustic). For example, if the child received the cue word *throw*, to which the correct target word is *ball*, *blow* would be an appropriate intrusion, whereas *needle* or *zow* (or any other nonword) would be inappropriate. The proportion of inappropriate intrusions to total number of intrusions (appropriate + inappropriate) was computed and entered into a one-way analysis of variance. The analysis was significant, $F(3, 60) = 5.74$, $p < 0.01$. Subsequent Bonferroni t tests indicated that the younger children produced more inappropriate intrusions, relative to appropriate intrusions, than the older children (see Fig. 2.2). These findings were consistent with the inefficient inhibition hypothesis, suggesting that, with age, children are better able to keep irrelevant information from working memory, thus reducing the number of inappropriate responses made to a specific probe.

As a further test of the inefficient inhibition hypothesis, we investigated intrusion effects in a free-recall paradigm. Thirty-two kindergarten, 32 second-, and 32 fourth-grade children attempted immediate free-recall of lists of 16 words that were categorically and acoustically related. That is, each word was *categorically* related to one word in the list and was

TABLE 2.2. Word list used for free recall experiment.

Categorical order	Acoustic order
Eagle	Eagle
Parrot	Beagle
Red	Red
Blue	Head
Four	Four
Two	Door
Head	Knees
Knees	Peas
Dolly	Dolly
Ball	Collie
Collie	Parrot
Beagle	Carrot
Peas	Wall
Carrot	Ball
Door	Blue
Wall	Two

acoustically related to another list item. We manipulated the salience of the relation dimension for the children by emphasizing either the categorical or acoustic relations through word order (see Table 2.2).

An analysis of the proportion of intrusions in recall indicated that intrusions decreased with age ($F(2, 85) = 7.72$, $p < 0.001$) between the kindergarten and second-grade children, with no difference in intrusion rates between second- and fourth-graders (see Fig. 2.3). The absolute levels of intrusions were lower in this experiment than in the cued-recall experiment, which is most likely due to the differences in the tasks. In this experiment, the children spontaneously produced the free-recall stream, whereas in the cued-recall experiment, the children were exposed to a probe prior to each recall attempt. This presentation of the cue may cause to reactivate the cue word and so intrusions in recall may reflect either inhibition failures during presentation (which are stored and remembered at recall), or failure to inhibit the spreading activation to the cue during recall. If inefficient inhibition affects processing at all stages, then the exposure to cues during recall would likely add this additional burden to the young children's poor inhibitory functioning.

To investigate the appropriateness of the intrusions made by the children, we again classified the intrusions as appropriate or inappropriate. Because there were so few intrusions in the second and fourth grades, we performed the appropriateness analysis collapsing across the upper two grades, yielding an older and a younger group. This analysis again revealed a higher percentage of inappropriate intrusions in the younger children's recall (61%) than the older children's recall (26%): $F(1, 31) = 4.99$, $p < 0.05$.

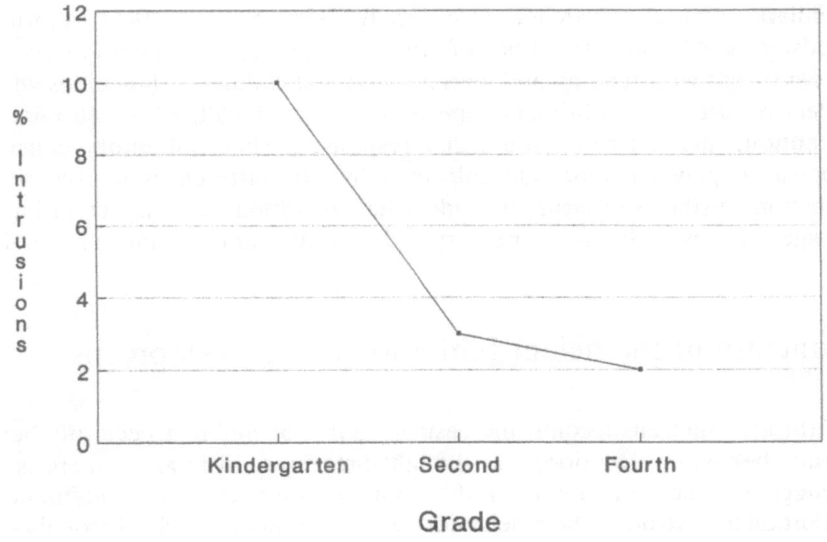

FIGURE 2.3. Percentage of intrusions in free recall for kindergarten, second-, and fourth-grade children.

In summary, the inefficient inhibition model proposes that young children's failure to inhibit the activation of task-irrelevant information detrimentally impacts their cognitive task performance. In support of this, we found that children make fewer intrusions in their recall with age, and that the intrusions older children do make are more task-appropriate than those made by younger children.

Individual Differences in Inhibitory Functioning

Although this chapter specifically addresses developmental function, a short note on individual differences is warranted. Research investigating a number of different areas of individual differences has implicated the role of inhibition in accounting for those differences. For example, Frith and his colleagues (1979; Joseph, Frith, & Waddington, 1979) have proposed that an inhibitory failure to limit and control the contents of consciousness may be responsible for the hallucinations, delusions, and thought disorders suffered by schizophrenics. This model has received some empirical support (e.g., Bullen & Hemsley, 1987).

Inefficient inhibition appears to be a central deficit in disorders of hyperactivity (deHaas, 1986; Gorenstein, Mammato, & Sandy, 1989; Lufi, Cohen, & Parish-Plass, 1990). For example, deHaas (1986; deHaas & Young, 1984) has found that hyperative children suffer primarily from deficits of sustained attention and inhibition of impulsive behaviors.

Similarly, several researchers (e.g., Kelly, Best, & Kirk, 1989; Lazarus, Ludwig, & Aberson, 1984) have found that the idea of inhibitory deficits is consistent with reading and learning disabled children's difficulties with selective attention to primary aspects of tasks, difficulties with sustained attention, and inhibiting routinized responses. Thus, inhibitory deficits appear to play an important role in individual differences in cognitive function, further supporting the idea that inhibition may also contribute to age changes in children's memory and cognitive processesing in general.

Conclusion: Inefficient Inhibition and Development

With age children become increasingly able to inhibit aspects of their motor behavior, attention, and thought processes. In infancy, there is a struggle between the inhibition of prepotent motor responses and infants' intentional control of their behavior (e.g., Diamond, 1988). Throughout childhood, children continue to have difficulties with the inhibition of impulsive or perseverative motor actions. Development occurs in an outward-in direction, with commands from adults directing inhibition first, followed by the child's own, overt, self-directions, and finally with the child being able to control both the inhibition and initiation of behavior covertly (e.g., Luria, 1961).

Inhibition is a basic function in cognition as well. Children must be able to control their attention within a realm of unending distractions from without and within. Numerous studies have documented children's increasing abilities to ignore external distractors and maintain attention to the task at hand (e.g., Lane & Pearson, 1982). These studies have demonstrated that, with age, children become more efficient in the inhibition of impulsive attentional shifts as well as the maintenance of inhibitory control over longer periods of time. Furthermore, the central role of inhibition, rather than habituation or some other process, in the development of attentional maintenance has been empirically demonstrated (e.g., Tipper et al., 1989). Finally, recent evidence is accumulating that suggests that inhibition of internal associations or activations is a process that becomes more efficient with age and that contributes significantly to cognitive function.

With respect to cognition, we propose that changes in children's ability to keep inappropriate information out of working memory is a major factor influencing cognitive development (e.g., Bjorklund & Harnishfeger, 1990). Evidence from research on lexical decisions (e.g., Simpson & Foster, 1986; Swinney & Prather, 1989), discourse processing (e.g., Hasher & Zacks, 1989), and memory (reported herein) illustrates developmental differences in the suppression of task-irrelevant information—with age, children are increasingly able to keep inappropriate information out of working memory. Task-irrelevant information clogs working memory and uses some of the limited mental space (or resources) that could better be used for other aspects of task processing. Thus, with age, children do not necessarily have more mental resources to allocate to various aspects of a task, but have less competing (and inappropriate) information in working memory, permitting them to devote more of their limited resources to the task-relevant operations and information.

There are a number of factors that influence changes in inhibitory processes. As children become more experienced with a specific task or with a particular domain of knowledge, they process task- or domain-relevant information more quickly (e.g., Bjorklund, 1987; Case, 1985; Harnishfeger & Bjorklund, 1990). Accompanying the processing advantage is an increased ability to inhibit irrelevant task information. For example, Siegler (1988) has proposed a model of children's arithmetic problem-solving and word-identification strategies. In this model, the most efficient strategy is that of direct fact retrieval (e.g., just "knowing" that $3 + 5 = 8$, or the meaning of the word *dog*). For any particular problem, several alternative answers may be activated in long-term memory (e.g., for the $3 + 5 = ?$ problem, potential alternatives may be 7, 8, and 9). When one alternative reaches a critical level of activation, that answer is directly retrieved. If none of the alternatives reach that level, children use a fall-back strategy to solve the problem (e.g., counting for arithmetic problems, phonological analysis for word identification). With repeated experience retrieving the correct answer, activation of that alternative becomes higher and the activation of the incorrect alternatives becomes lower. We further propose, following Case (1985), that experience with retrieving correct alternatives not only increases the activation of that answer, but also strengthens the inhibition of alternative responses.

There is also clear evidence of a biological basis to developmental changes in inhibitory mechanisms. Numerous sources point to the frontal lobes as the location of important inhibitory processing. For example, Diamond (1985, 1988) has proposed that immaturity of the frontal lobes underlies the $A\bar{B}$ error seen in infants. Evidence in support of this has been found in monkeys, who typically solve the $A\bar{B}$ object permanence task between 2 and 4 months of age. Damage to the frontal cortex of adult monkeys, however, causes them to make the $A\bar{B}$ error, performing much like 7- to 9-month-old human infants do; on delays during the B trials, they fail to search where the object was recently hidden but rather search where it had been hidden on the immediately previous trial (see Goldman-Rakic, 1987). In monkeys, the period associated with improved performance on the $A\bar{B}$ task corresponds to the time when there is excess synaptic density in the frontal area of the brain (many of these cells subsequently die) (Goldman-Rakic, 1987). The corresponding period of frontal lobe synaptic excess in humans is between 8 months and 2 years of age, a period when major cognitive changes occur (Huttenlocher, 1979).

Other evidence of a link between frontal lobe development and inhibitory processes can be found in the timing of myelinization of the brain. The frontal cortex is the last brain area to be fully myelinized, with degree of myelinization being related to cognitive accomplishments from infancy through adolescence (Lecours, 1975; Yakovlev & Lecours, 1967). Moreover, a host of cognitive deficits have been associated with brain damage to the frontal area, with patients showing impairments in a wide range of tasks that require suppression of prepotent responses (see Dempster, this volume; Goldman-Rakic, 1987). Finally, frontal lobe dysfunction has been proposed to underlie the inhibitory deficits of hyperactive (Gorenstein et al., 1989; Chelune, Ferguson, Koon, & Dickey, 1986) and reading disabled children (Kelly et al., 1989).

We propose a general theory of development with inhibition playing a central role. With age, children become more efficient inhibitors, and this affects many aspects of their behavior and cognition. Efficient inhibition allows children to guide their motor behavior, to direct and sustain their attention in the face of distraction, and to monitor and control their own cognitive processes. Furthermore, we propose that inhibition mechanisms affect cognitive development through their interaction with limited mental resources. With age, task-irrelevant information is increasingly screened out from working memory, affording children greater functional mental resources, which translates into enhanced performance. The ontogeny of inhibition is influenced both by experience and maturationally paced factors. We believe that inhibition will be increasingly found to be a powerful explanatory mechanism for cognitive development.

Acknowledgements. We thank the students and staff of Coral Sunset Elementary School and Henderson University School for their cooperation in the execution of the memory experiment, and Thomas R. Coyle and Cherie Everett for help in conducting the memory experiment. We also thank Elizabeth Ashley, William S. Cassel and Wolfgang Schneider for comments on earlier drafts of this chapter. Correspondence should be sent to Katherine Kipp Harnishfeger at the Department of Psychology, University of Georgia, Athens, GA, 30602, or David F. Bjorklund at the Department of Psychology, Florida Atlantic University, Boca Raton, FL, 33431.

References

Bjork, R.A. (1989). Retrieval inhibition as an adaptive mechanism in human memory. In H.L. Roediger, III, & F.I.M. Craik (Eds.), *Varieties of memory and consciousness*. Hillsdale, NJ: Erlbaum.

Bjorklund, D.F. (1987). How age changes in knowledge base contribute to the development of children's memory: An interpretive review. *Developmental Review*, *7*, 93–103.

Bjorklund, D.F. (1990). *Children's strategies: Contemporary views of cognitive development*. Hillsdale, NJ: Erlbaum.

Bjorklund, D.F., & Harnishfeger, K.K. (1990). The resources construct in cognitive development: Diverse sources of evidence and a theory of inefficient inhibition. *Developmental Review*, *10*, 48–71.

Bjorklund, D.F., Muir-Broaddus, J.E., & Schneider, W. (1990). The role of knowledge in the development of strategies. In D.F. Bjorklund (Ed.), *Children's strategies: Contemporary views of cognitive development*. Hillsdale, NJ: Erlbaum.

Brainerd, C.J., & Reyna, V.F. (1989). Output interference theory of dual-task deficits in memory development. *Journal of Experimental Child Psychology*, *47*, 1–18.

Brainerd, C.J., & Reyna, V.F. (1990). Gist is the grist: Fuzzy-trace theory and the new intuitionism. *Developmental Review*, *10*, 3–47.

Brown, A.L., Smiley, S.S., Day, J.D., Townsend, M.A.R., & Lawton, S.C. (1977). Intrusion of a thematic idea in children's comprehension and retention of stories. *Child Development*, *48*, 1454–1466.

Bullen, J.G., & Hemsley, D.R. (1987). Schizophrenia: A failure to control the contents of consciousness? *British Journal of Clinical Psychology*, *26*, 25–33.

Butterworth, G. (1977). Object identity in infants: The interaction of spatial location codes in determining search errors. *Child Development*, *46*, 866–870.

Case, R. (1985). *Intellectual development: Birth to adulthood*. New York: Academic Press.

Chelune, G.J., Ferguson, W., Koon, R., & Dickey, T.O. (1986). Frontal lobe disinhibition in attention deficit disorder. *Child Psychiatry and Human Development*, *16*, 221–234.

Cohn, N.B., Dustman, R.E., & Bradford, D.C. (1984). Age-related decrements in Stroop color test performance. *Journal of Clinical Psychology*, *40*, 1244–1250.

Comalli, P.E., Wapner, S., & Werner, H. (1962). Interference effects of Stroop Color-Word test in children, adulthood and aging. *Journal of Genetic Psychology*, *100*, 47–53.

Constantini, A.F., & Hoving, K.L. (1973a). The relationship of cognitive and motor response inhibition to age and IQ. *Journal of Genetic Psychology*, *123*, 309–320.

Constantini, A.F., & Hoving, K.L. (1973b). The effectiveness of reward and punishment contingencies on response inhibition. *Journal of Experimental Child Psychology*, *16*, 484–494.

Cummings, E.M., & Bjork, E.L. (1983). Search behavior on multi-choice hiding tasks: Evidence for an objective conception of space in infancy. *International Journal of Behavioral Development*, *1*, 71–88.

Davies, D.R., Jones, D.M., & Taylor, A. (1984). Selective and sustained-attention tasks: Individual and group differences. In R. Parasuraman, R. Davies, & J. Beatty (Eds.), *Varieties of attention*. New York: Academic Press.

deHaas, P.A. (1986). Attention styles and peer relationships of hyperactive and normal boys and girls. *Journal of Abnormal Child Psychology*, *14*, 457–467.

deHaas, P.A., & Young, R.D. (1984). Attention styles of hyperactive and normal girls. *Journal of Abnormal Child Psychology*, *12*, 531–545.

Dempster, F.N. (1985). Proactive interference in sentence recall: Topic similarity effects and individual differences. *Memory & Cognition*, *13*, 81–89.

Dempster, F.N. (1989). Reflections on the nature and sources of individual differences in learning. *Learning and Individual Differences*, *1*, 1–6.
Diamond, A. (1985). Development of the ability to use recall to guide action, as indicated by infants' performance on A not B. *Child Development*, *56*, 868–883.
Diamond, A. (1988). Abilities and neural mechanisms underlying A not B performance. *Child Development*, *59*, 523–527.
Doyle, A.B. (1973). Listening to distraction: A developmental study of selective attention. *Journal of Experimental Child Psychology*, *15*, 100–115.
Duncan, I. (1980). The locus of interference in the perception of simultaneous stimuli. *Psychological Review*, *87*, 272–300.
Frith, C.D. (1979). Consciousness, information processing and schizophrenia. *British Journal of Psychiatry*, *134*, 225–235.
Fuson, K.C. (1979). The development of self-regulating aspects of speech: A review. In G. Zivin (Ed.), *The development of self-regulation through private speech*. New York: John Wiley.
Goldman-Rakic, P.S. (1987). Development of cortical circuitry and cognitive function. *Child Development*, *58*, 601–622.
Gorenstein, E.E., Mammato, C.A., & Sandy, J.M. (1989). Performance of inattentive-overactive children on selected measures of prefrontal-type function. *Journal of Clinical Psychology*, *45*, 619–632.
Gratch, G., Appel, K.J., Evans, W.F., LeCompte, G.K., & Wright, N.A. (1974). Piaget's stage IV object concept error: Evidence of forgetting or object conception? *Child Development*, *45*, 71–77.
Hagen, J.W., & Hale, G.A. (1973). The development of attention in children. In A.D. Pick (Ed.), *Minnesota symposium on child psychology* (Vol. 7). Minneapolis: University of Minnesota Press.
Hagen, J.W., & Stanovich, K.G. (1977). Memory: Strategies of acquisition. In R.V. Kail & J.W. Hagen (Eds.), *Perspectives on the development of memory and cognition*. Hillsdale, NJ: Erlbaum.
Hale, G.A., & Alderman, L.B. (1978). Children's selective attention with variation in amount of stimulus exposure. *Journal of Experimental Child Psychology*, *26*, 320–327.
Hale, G.A., & Flaugher, J. (1977). Distraction effects in tasks of varying difficulty: Methodological issues in measuring development of distractibility. *Journal of Experimental Child Psychology*, *24*, 212–218.
Hale, G.A., & Stevenson, E.E., Jr. (1974). The effects of auditory and visual distractors on children's performance in a short-term memory task. *Journal of Experimental Child Psychology*, *18*, 280–292.
Harnishfeger, K.K., & Bjorklund, D.F. (1990). Strategic and nonstrategic factors in gifted children's free recall. *Contemporary Educational Psychology*, *15*, 346–363.
Harris, D.L. (1973). Perseveration errors in search by young children. *Child Development*, *44*, 28–33.
Harris, D.L. (1974). Perseverative search at a visibly empty place by young infants. *Journal of Experimental Child Psychology*, *18*, 535–542.
Hasher, L., & Zacks, R.T. (1989). Working memory, comprehension, and aging: A review and a new view. In G.H. Bower (Ed.), *The psychology of learning and motivation: Advances in research and theory* (Vol. 22). San Diego, CA: Academic Press.

Howe, M.L., & Rabinowitz, F.M. (1990). Resource panacea? Or just another day in the developmental forest. *Developmental Review*, *10*, 125–154.

Huttenlocher, P.R. (1979). Synaptic density in human frontal cortex—Developmental changes and effects of aging. *Brain Research*, *163*, 195–205.

Jeffrey, W.E. (1968). The orienting reflex and attention in cognitive development. *Psychological Review*, *75*, 323–334.

Joseph, M.H., Frith, C.D., & Waddington, J.L. (1979). Dopaminergic mechanisms and cognitive deficit in schizophrenia. *Psychopharmacology*, *63*, 273–280.

Kelly, M.S., Best, C.T., & Kirk, U. (1989). Cognitive processing deficits in reading disabilities: A prefrontal cortical hypothesis. *Brain & Cognition*, *11*, 275–293.

Lecours, A.R. (1975). Myelogenetic correlates of the development of speech and language. In E.H. Lenneberg & E. Lenneberg (Eds.), *Foundations of language development: A multidisciplinary approach* (Vol. 1). New York: Academic Press.

Lane, D.M., & Pearson, D.A. (1982). The development of selective attention. *Merrill-Palmer Quarterly*, *28*, 317–337.

Lazarus, P.J., Ludwig, R.P., & Aberson, B. (1984). Stroop color-word test: A screening measure of selective attention to differentiate LD from non LD children. *Psychology in the Schools*, *21*, 53–60.

Logan, D.G., & Cowan, W.B. (1984). On the ability to inhibit thought and action: A theory of an act of control. *Psychological Review*, *91*, 295–327.

Logan, G.D., Cowan, W.B., & Davis, K.A. (1984). On the ability to inhibit simple and choice reaction time responses: A model and a method. *Journal of Experimental Psychology: Human Perception and Performance*, *10*, 276–291.

Lorch, E.P., Anderson, D.R., & Well, A.D. (1984). Effects of irrelevant information on speeded classification tasks: Interference is reduced by habituation. *Journal of Experimental Psychology: Human Perception and Performance*, *10*, 850–864.

Lorch, E.P., & Horn, D.G. (1986). Habituation of attention to irrelevant stimuli in elementary school children. *Journal of Experimental Child Psychology*, *41*, 184–197.

Lufi, D., Cohen, A., & Parish-Plass, J. (1990). Identifying attention deficit hyperactive disorder with the WISC-R and the Stroop Color and Word Test. *Psychology in the Schools*, *27*, 28–34.

Luria, A.R. (1961). *The role of speech in the regulation of normal and abnormal behavior*. New York: Pergamon Press.

Maccoby, E.E., Dowley, E.E., Hagen, J.W., & Degerman, R. (1965). Activity level and intellectual functioning in normal preschool children. *Child Development*, *36*, 761–770.

Masters, J.C., & Binger, C.G. (1978). Interrupting the flow of behavior: The stability and development of children's initiation and maintenance of compliant response inhibition. *Merrill-Palmer Quarterly*, *24*, 229–242.

Meichenbaum, D., & Goodman, J. (1969). The developmental control of operant motor responding by verbal operants. *Journal of Experimental Child Psychology*, *7*, 553–565.

Neill, W.T. (1977). Inhibition and facilitation processes in selective attention. Journal of Experimental Psychology: Human perception and performance, *3*, 444–450.

Neely, J.H. (1977). Semantic priming and retrieval from lexical memory: Roles of inhibitionless spreading activation and limited-capacity attention. *Journal of Experimental Psychology: General, 106*, 226–254.

Olson, S.L. (1989). Assessment of impulsivity in preschoolers: Cross-measure convergences, longitudinal stability, and relevance to social competence. *Journal of Clinical Child Psychology, 18*, 176–183.

Onifer, W., & Swinney, D.A. (1981). Accessing lexical ambiguities during sentence comprehension: Effects of frequency of meaning and contextual bias. *Memory & Cognition, 9*, 225–236.

Posner, M.I., & Friedrich, F.J. (1986). Attention and the control of cognition. In S.L. Friedman, K.A. Klivington, & R.W. Peterson (Eds.), *The brain, cognition, and education.* Orlando, FL: Academic Press.

Rankin, J.L. & Kausler, D.H. (1979). Adult age differences in false recognitions. *Journal of Gerontology, 34*, 58–65.

Schachar, R., & Logan, G.D. (1990). Impulsivity and inhibitory control in normal development and childhood psychopathology. *Developmental Psychology, 26*, 710–720.

Schneider, W., & Pressley, M. (1989). *Memory development between 2 and 20.* New York: Springer.

Seidenberg, M.S., Tanenhaus, M.K., Leiman, J.M., & Bienkowski, M. (1982). Automatic access of the meanings of ambiguous words in context: Some limitations of knowledge-based processing. *Cognitive Psychology, 14*, 489–537.

Shepard, W.O., Cohen, D., Gold, L., & Orbino, P. (1976). Personal and peer's word associations in relation to children's false recognition errors. *Developmental Psychology, 12*, 477–478.

Siegler, R.S. (1988). Individual differences in strategy choices: Good students, not-so-good students, and perfectionists. *Child Development, 59*, 833–851.

Simpson, G.B., & Foster, M.R. (1986). Lexical ambiguity and children's word recognition. *Developmental Psychology, 22*, 147–154.

Simpson, G.B., & Lorsbach, T.C. (1983). The development of automatic and conscious components of contextual facilitation. *Child Development, 54*, 760–772.

Stanovich, K.E. (1990). Concepts in developmental theories of reading skill: Cognitive resources, automaticity, and modularity. *Developmental Review, 10*, 72–100.

Stine, E.L., & Wingfield, A. (1987). Process and strategy in memory for speech among younger and older adults. *Psychology and Aging, 2*, 272–279.

Strutt, G.F., Anderson, D.R., & Well, A.D. (1975). A developmental study of the effects of irrelevant information on speeded classification. *Journal of Experimental Child Psychology, 20*, 127–135.

Swinney, D.A., & Prather, P. (1989). On the comprehension of lexical ambiguity by young children: Investigations into the development of mental modularity. In D.S. Gorfein (Ed.), *Resolving Semantic Ambiguity.* New York: Springer-Verlag.

Swinney, D.A., Zurif, E., & Nicol, J. (1989). The effects of focal brain damage on sentence processing: An examination of the neurological organization of a mental module. *Journal of Cognitive Neuropsychology, 1*, 25–37.

Tipper, S.P. (1985). The negative priming effect: Inhibitory priming by ignored objects. *Quarterly Journal of Experimental Psychology, 37A*, 571–590.

Tipper, S.P., Bourque, T.A., Anderson, S.H., & Brehaut, J. (1989). Mechanisms of attention: A developmental study. *Joural of Experimental Child Psychology*, *48*, 353–378.

Tipper, S.P., & Cranston, M. (1985). Selective attention and priming: Inhibitory and facilitatory effects of ignored primes. *Quarterly Journal of Experimental Psychology*, *37A*, 591–611.

Underwood, B.J. (1957). Interference and forgetting. *Psychological Review*, *64*, 49–60.

West, R.F., & Stanovich, K.E. (1978). Automatic contextual facilitation in readers of three ages. *Child Development*, *49*, 717–727.

Wozniak, R.H. (1972). Verbal regulation of motor behavior—Soviet research and non-Soviet replications. *Human Development*, *15*, 13–57.

Wright, J.C., & Vlietstra, A.G. (1975). The development of selective attention: From perceptual exploration to logical search. In H.W. Reese (Ed.), *Advances in child development and behavior* (Vol. 10). New York: Academic Press.

Yakovlev, P.I., & Lecours, A.R. (1967). The myelenogenetic cycles of regoinal maturation of the brain. In A. Minkowski (Ed.), *Regional development of the brain in early life*. Oxford: Blackwell.

3
Domains of Fuzzy-Trace Theory

C.J. Brainerd and V.F. Reyna

The chronicle of cognitive-developmental theory is a tale of waxing and waning commitments to competing metaphors of the mind. Following Thorndike (1911), the stimulus-response connection was psychology's preeminent mental metaphor for half a century. Over the years, it had profound influences on cognitive development (cf. Berlyne, 1970), with theories of children's discrimination transfer (e.g., Kendler & Kendler, 1962) being the quintessential artifacts of those days. In the 1960s, interest shifted toward another metaphor, Piaget's (e.g., 1953) logician in the mind, with much of the momentum coming from Flavell's (1963) virtuoso exposition of Piaget's work. By the end of the decade, cognitive development had become synonymous with logical development. Within adult psychology, however, Piagetian logicism never gained the foothold that it did in child development. There, S-R connectionism was first challenged by information theory (e.g., Broadbent, 1957) and then supplanted by its descendent, information-processing theory (e.g., Newell & Simon, 1972). Eventually, the formalist metaphor of information processing, which saw the mind as an abstract symbol-manipulating machine, seeped into cognitive development (e.g., Siegler, 1981). By the time of Piaget's death, it had become the modal metaphor, although pockets of allegiance to logicism remain to this day (e.g., Chapman & Lindenberger, 1992).

Fuzzy-trace theory (FTT) is a new iteration in this historical cycle (Brainerd & Reyna, 1990b, 1990c, in press-a; Reyna & Brainerd, 1990; 1991a, 1991b). It adopts intuition as its basal mental metaphor, where intuition is defined, as it is in the foundations of mathematics, as fuzzy representations (senses, patterns, gists) in combination with construction rules that operate on those representations. FTT grew out of the Piagetian and information-processing traditions inasmuch as its impetus was supplied by certain findings that both the logician in the mind and the computer in the mind have difficulty handling (Brainerd & Kingma, 1984, 1985). The ties run far deeper, however. It would be impossible to imagine tackling the complex phenomenon of intuition without the rich data base on cognitive development that has been generated by the Piagetian and information-processing traditions.

Our general approach has been to apply the intuition metaphor systematically to different research domains, expanding and refining it as we go, with the twin objectives of reinterpreting established findings and generating new ones. The purpose of this chapter is to sketch the progress that has been made so far. We organize the conspectus around five domains where activity has been concentrated: encoding, storage, processing, output, and forgetting.

Encoding: Gist Extraction, Parallelism, and the Verbatim → Gist Shift

For concreteness, we introduce the material in this and subsequent sections with reference to some reasoning paradigms that will be familiar to most readers; e.g., class inclusion, framing, probability judgment, and transitive inference. Structurally, their common feature is that they involve three phases: a *background phase* in which subjects receive some facts (e.g., cardinal numbers in probability judgment or relative magnitudes in transitive inference) that are critical to reasoning, a *problem phase* in which certain questions are posed to subjects, and a *response phase* in which subjects offer their solutions.

Gist Extraction

In traditional psycholinguistics, gist is like the Cheshire cat's smile; it is the residue of linguistic input that remains as time passes. FTT broadens this concept to encompass nonlinguistic, as well as linguistic, patterns or senses that are present in incoming information, especially the crucial background data that accompany thinking, reasoning, and learning tasks. In FTT, gist is not simply the ghost of degraded verbatim information. Instead, it consists of memory representations that are extracted in parallel with the encoding of such information, and it is thought to function independently of verbatim information once it has been stored (for reviews of relevant evidence, see Brainerd & Reyna, in press-a; Reyna & Brainerd, 1991b).

FTT assumes that encoding is governed by a gist-extraction imperative, called the *reduction to essence rule* (Brainerd & Reyna, 1990b). As verbatim information is encoded, so are patterns and other skeletal information. Traditional cognitive science regards verbatim information, not gist, as the foundation of reasoning and memory. Although there is little disagreement as to the universality of gist extraction, and although the existence of gist-based intuitive reasoning has been acknowledged by many theorists, the normal tendency is to regard such processes as primitive and as sources of noise when it comes to the study of higher cognitive abilities. For example, this position is the cornerstone of the long-standing belief of Piagetian investigators (e.g., Smedslund, 1963, 1969) that childhood reasoning tasks should be so purified and complexified that solutions must be based on logical deductions from verbatim information (Brainerd & Reyna, 1992; Reyna & Brainerd, 1990).

It would be difficult to countenance any position that did not assume universal gist extraction because instances of it are so common, even in animal memory. Latent learning (e.g., Tolman & Honzik, 1930) and learning sets (e.g., Harlow, 1949) are textbook examples that have been studied for decades. In the former case, rats store generic spatial maps of mazes as they learn to run them. These templates are independent of reinforcement contingencies because they are stored during preconditioning familiarization periods, when such contingencies are not operative. The maps are also generic because rats transfer them from one maze layout to another. But perhaps most important of all, the acquisition of such maps exerts strong forward control over the course of maze conditioning. Learning sets, another example of animal gist extraction, refer to higher vertebrates' tendency to store generic representations of discrimination-learning situations as they solve individual problems. After a learning set is established, discriminations that once required long trial-and-error sequences to acquire are now acquired suddenly, as though by insight. The change is dramatic: Harlow (1949) reported that monkeys who initially committed 20 or more errors in learning color, shape, and size discriminations committed only a single error in new tasks after forming a learning set.

In humans, probability judgment is an often-studied paradigm in which preschoolers, elementary schoolers, adolescents, and adults are known to extract prototypical forms of relational and nominal gist. In the standard problem, the cardinal numbers of a small collection of sets are presented as background facts (e.g., $A_1 = 5$, $A_2 = 4$, $B_1 = 7$, $B_2 = 1$). Subjects then forecast the results of sequences of random draws from sampling spaces that contain these numbers of elements. If gist probes are administered after the numbers are encoded, it is found (Brainerd, 1981) that even 3- and 4-year-olds will have stored both relational gist (e.g., A_1 has more than A_2, B_1 has more than B_2) and nominal gist (e.g., A_1 has the most, B_2 has the least). Further, these gist representations are more enduring than traces of the verbatim numbers, and, more often than not, they are the basis for prediction (Reyna, 1992).

In psycholinguistics, data on memory for gist have led investigators to postulate that linguistic inputs necessarily lead to the encoding of certain types of gist. For instance, Kintsch, Welsch, Schmalhofer, and Zimny (1990) proposed that theories of text memory are constrained to assume, at a minimum, that text produces three distinct levels of memory representation: "At one level, a text is characterized by the exact words and phrases used . . . At another level, not the exact wording but the semantic content of the text must be represented. Both the local (microstructure) and global (macrostructure) characteristics of the text play a role here . . . The situation model is the third level . . . What is represented is not the text structure proper, but the situation described in the text, detached from the text structure proper, and embedded in pre-established fields of knowledge" (p. 135). Situation-level traces could also be generated for familiar childhood reasoning paradigms such as transitivity or class inclusion. With repeated exposure to the patterns that are present in these paradigms, reasoners will begin to recognize recurrences, and, perhaps, organize them into situation models, such as "this is a linear magnitude series" (transitive inference) or "this is an inclusion hierarchy" (class inclusion).

Parallelism: Time Course of Gistification

Since gist memories are fundamental in FTT, considerable interest attaches to the question of *when* they are deposited. In tasks where the background information is numerical (e.g., class inclusion, probability judgment), for instance, at what point during the background phase is relational information ("more As than Bs") and nominal information ("the As are most") stored? There are two basic positions (Brainerd & Reyna, 1990b; Reyna & Brainerd, 1991a). At one extreme, subjects might postpone extraction until the background phase is complete, storing only gist that is consistent with all the facts. This serial gistification of verbatim information has the advantages of economy and accuracy, and it is also compatible with the classical view of linguistic gist as faded verbatim information (e.g., Jarvella, 1971). At the other extreme, subjects could extract a range of *potentially* relevant gist from each verbatim fact as it is encoded. We have previously reviewed certain classes of experimental findings that provide tests for serial versus parallel gistification (Brainerd & Reyna, 1990b).

On the whole, both empirical and theoretical considerations favor the parallel scenario (Brainerd & Reyna, in press-a, in press-b; Reyna & Brainerd, 1991a). Empirically, evidence from a variety of sources shows that information in many tasks is sufficiently redundant and pattern-like that subjects begin to extract relevant patterns from the incoming verbatim flow before all of that information has been presented (Reyna & Brainerd, 1991a; Townsend, 1990). Indeed, the background phases of some tasks are so configured as to permit comprehensive gistification after presentation of only a fraction of the background facts. Transitivity tasks are illustrative (for a review, see Reyna & Brainerd, 1990). As premises are presented ($A > B$, $B > C, \ldots$), subjects catch on to patterns such as "things are getting bigger," especially after having been administered a few problems. We have conducted experiments in which probes for such overall, series-level gist were inserted at selected points during premise presentation (Brainerd, Fulginiti, & Reyna, 1992). We found that such gist was usually stored after only two or three premises had been encoded and that this process became more routine with age.

On the theoretical side, there are at least two arguments favoring parallel gist extraction. First, because extracting gist involves storing patterns, early gist extraction takes immediate advantage of regularities and redundancies in incoming information, something that the circuitry of the human brain seems particularly well equipped to do (cf. Estes, 1989). This, in turn, means that reasoners can "get to the point" sooner by extracting relevant gist from the start. Second, verbatim memory is notoriously unstable. Basing reasoning on unstable information sources is obviously a maladaptive procedure. Here, a ubiquitous finding about memory is that verbatim information is lost more rapidly than gist (Brainerd & Reyna, 1990b; Kintsch & Bates, 1977; Kintsch et al., 1990). To take a recent example, Zimny (1987) studied the comparative forgetting rates of the three types of traces posited by Kintsch et al. (1990) across a 4-day interval. She found that although Level 2 and Level 3 information was still available at the end of this interval, Level 1 information had been lost a short time after encoding. In addition, much experimentation suggests that verbatim traces are more sensitive than gist to interference from subsequently encoded traces and from processing (Brainerd & Reyna, 1989; Brainerd, Reyna, Howe, & Kingma, 1990).

In short, serial gistification operates under the severe memory constraint that encoded information must be preserved intact up to the point of reasoning, which is often impossible. If the objective is to deposit at least some stable representations that comport with all the background facts, a way around this obstacle must be found. The parallel method does the job by generating a spectrum of candidate gists from the start. Because gist is durable, patterns that are consistent with all the data and are therefore pertinent to the task at hand are unlikely to be forgotten before they can be used (Brainerd & Reyna, in press-a). Thus, parallel gistification is theoretically optimal because it processes labile verbatim traces immediately, before they are lost, to build up a usable stock of gist. Of course, building up a usable stock of gist requires that patterns that are consistent with initial inputs but are inconsistent with later inputs must be weeded out (cf. below).

The Verbatim → Gist Shift

How does the derivation of gist vary with age? FTT's answer takes the form of a developmental interaction. On the one hand, we have reviewed findings showing that the sheer ability to extract fairly abstract patterns emerges very early in life (Brainerd & Reyna, in press-b; Reyna & Brainerd, 1990). For instance, Wagner, Winner, Cicchetti, and Gardner

(1981) found that 11-month-olds stored nonverbal analogies, and Greco, Hayne, and Rovee-Collier (1990) reported that 3-month-olds stored cross-modal analogies. The conclusion that gist is primitive is also suggested by the animal work reviewed above.

On the other hand, there are any number of well replicated ontogenetic trends that appear to implicate age increases in reliance on gist. To illustrate, when subjects encode isolated relational statements (e.g., A is longer than B, X is longer than Y) and equivalent statements that form a pattern, such as a linear series (e.g., A is longer than B, B is longer than C), younger children remember the isolated statements better but older children and adults remember the patterned statements better (Perner & Mansbridge, 1983). Similarly, in face memory, there is an age trend away from remembering individual facial components toward remembering facial configurations (Carey & Diamond, 1977). As another illustration, on tests of frequency memory children rely on retrieval strategies that process verbatim event frequencies (e.g., counting), whereas adolescents and adults rely on retrieval strategies that process global strength impressions (Marx, 1986). Therefore, there is an *increasing* reliance on gist throughout childhood.

Within this framework of overall movement toward gist, FTT places special emphasis on a concentration of such movement during the late preschool and early elementary school years. This is the verbatim → gist shift (Brainerd & Reyna, in press-a; Reyna & Brainerd, 1991b). The verbatim → gist shift consists of three interconnected proposals. The first is that the memory systems that support retention of verbatim information develop rapidly and complete their emergence rather early in life, presumably by the midelementary school years. The second claim is that the memory systems that support retention of gist evolve slowly and complete their development later on. The third claim is that the discrepancy between verbatim and gist growth functions is most prominent during early childhood, when the former is approaching asymptote but the latter is still in its preliminary stages. We have assembled many results that bear on these proposals in earlier reviews (Reyna, 1992; Reyna & Brainerd, 1991b). Data from three literatures are especially probative: the development of recognition versus recall, the development of short-term memory span, and mnemonic development.

Recognition Versus Recall

Since Bartlett (1932), it has been common practice to regard long-term memory tests as varying in their degree of reliance on verbatim memory versus gist. In particular, recognition tests have been viewed as being weighted toward verbatim memory, whereas recall tests have been viewed as allowing considerable latitude for reconstruction from gist. The fact that reconstructive memory errors occur more often with recall than with recognition (e.g., Signorella & Liben, 1984) is often mentioned in support of this view. Developmentally, recognition memory for many materials is asymptotic as early as age 3 (Perlmutter & Myers, 1974), but recall of the same material improves gradually from early childhood through young adulthood (Bjorklund & Muir, 1988). The recognition-recall disparity is most marked during the preschool years, when it is possible to produce near-ceiling recognition coupled with near-floor recall for the same materials.

Convergent evidence on this point is available in the developmental literature on forgetting (for reviews, see Brainerd, Reyna, Howe, & Kingma, 1990; Howe & Brainerd, 1989). There are negligible age trends after age 5 in rate of forgetting from long-term memory when recognition tests supply the retention measures, but there are large age trends when recall tests are used. The obvious interpretation is that recognition tests are tapping verbatim memory systems whose development is largely complete, and recall tests are tapping gist systems that are still evolving.

Span of Recall

Span of recall is the maximum number of items that can be reproduced immediately after encoding. Intuitively, span, in sharp contrast to recall from long-term memory, seems to be a strongly verbatim measure, an idea that is supported by the fact that span is not much affected by mnemonic strategies (e.g., chunking) that help children organize incoming verbatim information (Dempster, 1981). Consistent with this interpretation and with the verbatim → gist shift, span exhibits only limited age variation after midelementary school. However, large age changes are observed when span tasks are modified so as to measure retention of the gist than can be extracted from sets of items (Schmidt, 1990).

Mnemonics

An important dimension on which mnemonic strategies vary is the extent to which they focus on preserving verbatim information or preserving the senses and patterns that are present in such information. Looking, pointing, and rehearsing are familiar examples of verbatim mnemonics, whereas category clustering, elaboration, and subjective organization are equally familiar examples of gist mnemonics. Spontaneous use of mnemonics of the first type has been noted in preschoolers and young elementary schoolers, but spontaneous use of mnemonics of the latter type is uncommon before late childhood or early adolescence (Schneider & Pressley, 1988).

Storage: On-Line Gist Editing and Fuzzy-to-Verbatim Continua

On-Line Gist Editing

We have seen that the instability of verbatim traces, as well as direct demonstrations of on-line gistification (Brainerd, Fulginiti, & Reyna, 1992), favors the hypothesis that gist is extracted in parallel with the encoding of background facts. However, deriving a spectrum of candidate gists from early information, rather than waiting and deriving only gist that agrees with all the data, creates the problem of possible *local-global gist mismatches* (Brainerd & Reyna, in press-a). Specifically, gists will often be extracted from early information that are inconsistent with subsequent information, which leads to the undesirable accumulation of representations that are *locally valid but globally wrong.*

With transitivity, for instance, suppose that the task is to make inferences about nonadjacent relationships in the series A > B > C > D > E after encoding the four nonadjacent relationships in left-to-right order as background facts. After A > B and B > C have been encoded, subjects might store relational gist such as "things get smaller to the right" and/or nominal gist such as "the left side is the big end," both of which are locally and globally correct. If, on the other hand, the relationships between the five objects happened to instantiate some other pattern than is rarely encountered, such as the V-shaped series A > B > C < D < E, both gists would be locally valid but globally wrong for the series as a whole, and they would produce errors if inferences about nonadjacent relationships were based upon them. Similarly, with probability judgment, suppose that the task is to make forecasts about the four-set sampling space described earlier, and that the cardinal numbers are presented in the order $A_1 = 5$, $A_2 = 4$, $B_1 = 7$, and $B_2 = 1$. After the second number is presented, subjects might extract the relational gist "more A_1s than A_2s" and/or the nominal gist "A_1 has most." Whereas both gists are locally valid, the second is globally wrong.

Since gist is durable, parallel extraction creates the obvious need for an on-line editor that updates the gist store by deactivating locally valid representations as they become globally wrong. Essentially, a range of gist would be derived from the start, and then the editor would home in on globally correct gists as the background phase unfolds. In view of the evidence of both infantile and infrahuman gist extraction, it would be theoretically desirable if the editor were a basic, structural property of memory, rather than a metacognitive device requiring levels of inferential understanding that could only plausibly be attributed to older children and adults (Brainerd & Reyna, in press-b). A promising candidate mechanism, the construction-integration model, has been proposed by Kintsch (1988) in connection with discourse analysis. In this model, "dumb" encoding rules operate on the incoming verbatim flow so as to extract a variety of representations, many of which are wrong, that conform to Levels 2 and 3 of Kintsch et al. (1990). This is the construction stage, which roughly corresponds to parallel gist extraction in FTT. The representations that are activated by these dumb rules are embedded in a semantic network. As more and more inputs are received, activation necessarily settles in areas of the network that contain correct representations, thereby deactivating wrong representations. This is the integration stage, which corresponds to on-line editing in FTT. Kintsch (1988) reported extensive simulations of the construction-integration model, and some related simulations that implement FTT's assumptions have been reported by Kreindler and Lumsden (1992).

Fuzzy-to-Verbatim Continua

Thanks to these gist extraction and editing tendencies, a variety of task-relevant traces will accumulate as a sequence of background facts is encoded, some of which are only vaguely reminiscent of the original verbatim information. These traces will vary in specificity, forming *fuzzy-to-verbatim continua* (Brainerd & Reyna, 1988). At one boundary, there are verbatim traces—richly detailed, well-articulated, crystallized representations that conserve recently encoded information with exactitude. At the other boundary, there are fuzzy traces—schematic, degenerate, fluid representations that conserve only the senses and patterns of recently encoded information. At intermediate positions, there are traces that vary in their proximity to the verbatim and fuzzy boundaries. For cognition in general, the significance of fuzzy-to-verbatim continua lies chiefly in the fact that they confer options, options that allow thinking and reasoning to avoid some persistent memorial and processing pitfalls (Reyna & Brainerd, 1991c).

Trace Independence

If gist is stored and edited in parallel with the encoding of verbatim information, it is natural to imagine that the memorial fates of the various levels in a fuzzy-to-verbatim continuum will be closely linked. Surprisingly, however, both behavioral data, which show functional independence of verbatim and gist traces, and neurophysiological data, which show structural independence, argue against this assumption (for reviews, see Brainerd & Reyna, in press-a; Reyna, 1992).

Behavioral Data

Illustrative findings include (a) evidence of early storage of gist relative to verbatim information and (b) independent decay functions for verbatim and gist traces. Concerning a, some experiments on sentence memory (e.g., Reder, 1982) have shown that subjects can often make plausibility judgments about sentences, which presumably involve gist processing, before they can perform accurately on verbatim memory tests. Likewise, studies of pattern perception (e.g., Lamb & Robertson, 1989) have suggested that global pattern detectors extract relationships as local operators process features. The well known Reicher–Wheeler effect, wherein words are recognized more rapidly than the letters that comprise them, is yet another illustration of patterns being deposited more quickly than the verbatim elements that specify them (Ankrum & Palmer, 1989).

Concerning b, forgetting functions for verbatim and gist traces seem to be different. Zimny (1987) studied this phenomenon in some detail using the three levels of representation in Kintsch et al.'s (1990) theory of text memory. She developed methods of measuring each level in the context of recognition memory for sentences. She then assessed the relative availability of information at these levels across a 4-day interval, and found a different decay function for each. Level 1 (verbatim) information became rapidly unavailable after encoding, and was completely absent after 40 min. Level 2 (semantic) information declined slowly after encoding, and was still partially available 4 days later. Level 3 (situational) information displayed no forgetting over the 4-day interval and, in fact, it tended to be more available 40 min after encoding than immediately after.

Neurophysiogical Data

Relevant evidence comes from both animal preparations and humans. With respect to the former, we have introduced latent learning and learning set as illustrations of infrahuman gist extraction. These paradigms have also been used to study the question of whether verbatim information and gist are housed in different neurological structures. Granger and McNulty (1986), for example, concluded that the case for independent structures is strong. Findings reported by Staubli, Ivy, and Lynch (1984) were particularly clear-cut. Staubli et al. reported that rats' memory for specific cues that they had been trained to discriminate and their memory for the learning sets that were formed during the course of such training were neurologically separable. When connections between the dorsomedial nucleus of the hypothalamus and the frontal cortex were dissevered, the first type of memory remained intact but the second type was destroyed. Conversely, when the hippocampus was surgically lesioned, the first type of memory was destroyed but the second type was conserved.

Although such procedures cannot be used with humans, the advent of noninvasive brain imaging technologies has made it possible to detect variations in brain activity that are characteristic of performance on different memory tasks. Results of such studies have recently been reviewed by Carr (1990). Of particular interest, in FTT, as subjects become increasingly familiar with a task and isolate patterns in verbatim information, new areas of the brain become active and previously active areas shut down.

Law of Overdetermination

As mentioned, the significance of fuzzy-to-verbatim continua for cognition as a whole is that they provide memorial options for thinking and reasoning. Memory is, after all, a fallible thing. Since, by definition, traces that are not in storage cannot be processed, it would be highly desirable, for the sake of accuracy, if there were multiple memorial substrata that thinking and reasoning could draw upon to achieve their objectives.

Fuzzy-to-verbatim continua provide such options by informationally overdetermining reasoning situations. It has been suggested that the enhanced genetic fitness that would accrue from such overdetermination has been an important factor in the evolution of the human nervous system (Brainerd & Reyna, 1990b; Kreindler & Lumsden, 1992), especially the high levels of redundancy that are hallmarks of brain anatomy (e.g., Estes, 1989) and are probably the neurological bases of gist extraction. Since the presence of such continua means that memory holds a good deal more information than the actual verbatim background facts, the loss of any specific item of information is rarely catastrophic; backup information will normally be available. Thus, reasoning can adapt on-line to fallible memory by calibrating itself to whatever information is still available.

Processing: The Fuzzy-Processing Preference, Task Constraints, Memory Independence, and the Development of Intuition

The Fuzzy-Processing Preference (Intuition)

FTT's concept of intuition, the fuzzy-processing preference, is taken to be a fundamental property of reasoning. Essentially, the fuzzy-processing preference is a principle of cognitive downsizing: Operating on traces that are as near as possible to the fuzzy extremities of fuzzy-to-verbatim continua is a natural habit of mind (Reyna & Brainerd, 1991c). In short, there is a predisposition for intuitive, flexible thinking that informational inputs constrain in only general ways. Since this predisposition is tantamount to a preference for imprecision in thinking, it is a major point of divergence between FTT and traditional cognitive science. But, oddly, it is a proposal that receives much support from the cognitive science

TABLE 3.1. Six reasons for the fuzzy-processing preference (intuition).

Reason	Synopsis
1. Trace availability	Traces that are not available in storage cannot be processed. Verbatim traces fade more rapidly than fuzzy traces (e.g., Kintsch et al., 1990) and, hence, are less likely to be available for processing.
2. Trace accessibility	Traces that are in storage cannot be processed unless they can be activated by appropriate retrieval cues. Fuzzy traces accept a broader range of inputs as retrieval cues (e.g., Alba & Hasher, 1983; Kintsch & Bates, 1977).
3. Trace malleability	Traces that are in storage and retrievable must be transformed via processing to solve problems. The flexible, fluid architectures of fuzzy traces make them easier to manipulate than verbatim traces (e.g., Reyna & Brainerd, 1989).
4. Processing complexity	Complex processing operations are more error-prone than less complex processing. Processing complexity decreases and one approaches the fuzzy boundaries of fuzzy-to-verbatim continua (e.g., Chapman & Lindenberger, 1988).
5. Parallel processing	Memory limitations make parallel processing in reasoning desirable (e.g., Estes, 1989). Reasoning operations can process fuzzy traces in parallel with the encoding of verbatim background information (e.g., Reyna & Brainerd, 1990).
6. Processing effort	The less processing that is required to achieve a cognitive objective the better (e.g., Zipf, 1949). Reasoning that is based on fuzzy traces involves less estensive processing than reasoning that is based on verbatim traces (e.g., Moore, Dixon, & Haines, 1991).

literature. We have previously reviewed six major lines of evidence, three concerned with memory and three concerned with reasoning, that confer support on the fuzzy-processing preference (Brainerd & Reyna, 1990b). They are summarized, along with references to primary literature, in Table 3.1.

An interesting payoff of the fuzzy-processing preference is that it delivers straightforward explanations of two common but baffling qualities of human thought: its ineffability and its insightfulness. Insofar as the former is concerned, when humans introspect on the mental operations that they use to solve problems, it is difficult for them to say exactly how they get from critical informational inputs to solutions, and their explanations are inclined to be poor predictors of their performance (e.g., Nisbett & Wilson, 1977). Such ineffability is a corollary of the fact that reasoning does not directly interrogate memories of those inputs in the first place and that it does not therefore employ the processing operations that would normally be associated with them. Instead, it interrogates distillates that bear limited resemblance to inputs, that function independently of inputs, and that subjects are even unaware that they have encoded (Brainerd & Kingma, 1984). Consequently, the true informational substratum of reasoning eludes attention and baffles description during the course of introspection. The reader will perhaps have noticed that this also suggests an explanation for the unreliability, especially in adults, of introspection.

Turning to insight, a familiar by-product of reasoning is the subjective impression of having locked onto a problem's solution suddenly, in a flash, without extensive processing of ostensibly critical information. Indeed, insights are often produced by expressly avoiding thinking about the details of a problem (e.g., Brainerd & Reyna, 1990c). The reason, obviously, is that if accurate performance can be achieved by processing simple gist that can be detected on the basis of early, fragmentary data, then, logically, a systematic exploration of all the background information will not usually improve performance and may do more harm than good (Reyna & Brainerd, 1991a).

It should be stressed that despite the fuzzy-processing preference, the products of reasoning are *not fuzzy* in the sense of being inaccurate, sloppy, irrational, or erratic. This is the most common misinterpretation of the predisposition for intuitive thought. We have noted elsewhere (Reyna & Brainerd, 1991a) that the question of precision in reasoning products can be decomposed into three smaller questions, the answers to which all argue against this misinterpretation. First, when memorial options like those in fuzzy-to-verbatim continua are available, so that solutions can be achieved either by processing verbatim information or by processing gist, do subjects prefer to operate on the most precise information available or do they gravitate toward gist? With both children and adults, many findings converge on the latter alternative (e.g., Brainerd & Reyna, in press-b; Chapman & Lindenberger, 1988; Reyna & Brainerd, 1989, 1990; Smedslund, 1963, 1969).

Second, can accurate responses only devolve from highly faithful memory representations and their associated processing operations? The answer is clearly no; accurate solutions can be achieved by processing crude sensory gist with symbolic analogues of simple perceptual discriminations—for example, solving transitive inference problems by processing the global direction of magnitude flow with left-right position discriminations (for a review, see Reyna & Brainerd, 1990). More generally, Estes (1980) observed that processing approximate, gist-like representations of information makes for more accurate "general purpose thinking machines" than the use of faithful verbatim representations.

Third, is it always or even usually possible to achieve precise reasoning products by processing detailed, verbatim representations of critical informational inputs? Again, the answer is no. The literature is replete with examples of reasoning problems that humans readily solve but for which the processing of detailed verbatim information is impossible because the amount of it is too vast (Brainerd & Reyna, in press-b). Consider, for instance, a 20-term transitive inference task in which the background phase involves encoding information about 19 different adjacent relationships, or consider a 20-set probability judgment task in which the background phase involves encoding 20 different cardinal numbers. In each case, the items of background information exceed short-term memory capacity by such a wide margin that the high levels of accuracy that subjects achieve cannot be explained without assuming that some sort of elementary gist is being processed (e.g., "things get bigger in that direction" for transitivity and "there are more Xs than anything else" in the case of probability judgment).

Task Constraints and Formatting

Fuzzy-to-verbatim continua contain levels of task-relevant information that vary in their degree of point-for-point fidelity to the verbatim background facts. That is, there is a hierarchy of gist that can be derived from the same baseline information. The place in such a hierarchy where reasoning is actually centered is determined by task considerations. Issues such as the form of the response that subjects must produce (e.g., point estimates vs. two-choice preference tasks), the amount of uncertainty that is inherent in the background information, and the degree to which accuracy suffers from processing levels of gist that amalgamate distinctions fix the level of specificity at which reasoning operates (Reyna & Brainerd, 1991a, 1991c).

We assume that the fuzzy-processing preference is expressed by calibrating reasoning to the lowest possible level in a fuzzy-to-verbatim continuum, given such task considerations. For example, suppose that the numbers 4, 7, 14, and 16 are presented as background facts. Then, suppose that the subject must solve one of four problems: (a) Was *any* number larger than 20? (b) Is the *sum* of the numbers larger than 20? (c) *What* is the sum of the numbers? Note there is a natural progression in just how precise one's representation of the these facts must be to solve each successive problem: Only primitive plausibility information (only a certain range of numbers was encoded) is required in the first case, relational gist will do in the second case (some numbers close to 20 were encoded), but the exact values of all four numbers must be retrieved and summed in the final case. More generally, research to date (e.g., Brainerd & Reyna, 1988; Reyna & Brainerd, 1991b) has suggested that distinctions without difference in background inputs are ignored, with reasoning flowing toward the level in a fuzzy-to-verbatim continuum where the number of distinctions that can be ignored is maximal (Reyna & Brainerd, 1991c).

Although reasoning favors the most impoverished level in a fuzzy-to-verbatim continuum that will support accurate performance, this tendency can be influenced by *formatting manipulations* that highlight or foreground certain types of gist at the expense of others. Class-inclusion and framing (e.g., Kahneman, Slovic, & Tversky, 1982; Tversky & Kahneman, 1986) problems are standard illustrations. From a logical standpoint, class-inclusion problems seem trivially easy. Children are presented with the cardinal numbers of two disjoint sets, A and A′, which belong to a common superordinate set, B, so that the relationship A + A′ = B holds. The task is to make judgments about the relative numerosity of the superordinate set and the larger subset ("Which has more, A or B?"). According to FTT, the best way to do this is to store a simple form of qualitative gist (namely, that the target sets form an inclusion sequence) and to process it with a cardinal ordering rule (namely, that any inclusion sequence is an ordering of relative numerosity). Processing either the verbatim numbers or their relational gist ("X has more things than Y") impairs accuracy because the part-part relationship between the subset numbers induces an illusion of judgment in which it is difficult to focus on the part-whole relationship between subset and superordinate numbers (Reyna, 1991). Further, part-whole relationships are intrinsically nonnumerical, which is another source of confusion in that processing numbers or their relational gist is apt to lead reasoning astray (Brainerd & Reyna, 1990c). Unfortunately, the presentation format of such problems causes numerical information to pop out and inclusional gist to sink into the background, which encourages both children and adults to succumb to such illusions.

Concerning the second example, framing (e.g., Tversky & Kahneman, 1986), these problems confront reasoners with a choice between two alternatives, an outcome that is certain (e.g., 400 of 600 people die) and an outcome that is probabilistic (e.g., a 2/3 chance that all 600 die). The expected values of the alternatives are always mathematically equivalent, so that neither is objectively preferable. However, a standard result in the literature is that subjects prefer certain alternatives when these problems are framed as gains ("people live") and uncertain alternatives when they are framed as losses ("people die"). Because subjects have strong preferences for maximizing gains and minimizing loses, this leads to marked preferences for the gamble in framing of losses (because everyone may live) and for the sure thing in framing of gains (because some people will definitely live). Note that these preferences are logically inconsistent with each other: Subjects are neither consistently risk-seeking nor risk-averse, but choice depends on how alternatives are framed. Subjects are not indifferent, either, even though the alternatives are mathematically equivalent.

Memory Independence

Yet another advantage of the fuzzy-processing preference is that when it is combined with fuzzy-to-verbatim continua, it accounts for one of the more puzzling outcomes of recent research on cognitive development: the reasoning-remembering independence effect (memory independence for short). Suppose that children are administered some standard problem such as transitive inference or probability judgment and that after answering reasoning questions, memory probes for the original background facts are administered. What should the data show about how reasoning is influenced by the ability to remember those inputs? Both commonsense and traditional theories of cognitive development say that the two should be connected via a necessity relationship: Better memory for critical information should translate into more accurate reasoning. Indeed, no less than three types of reasoning-remembering dependency are expected: *horizontal* (variations in memory should predict variations in reasoning within age levels), *vertical* (age increases in memory should produce age increases in reasoning), and *experimental* (manipulations that produce better memory should enhance reasoning).

However, horizontal, vertical, and experimental *in*dependence have lately been reported in several developmental studies (for reviews, see Brainerd & Reyna, in press-a, in press-b; Reyna, 1992; Reyna & Brainerd, 1990). In probability judgment, for instance, the accuracy of kindergartners' judgments does not depend on their ability to remember the numerical details of sampling spaces, age improvements in judgments are unrelated to age improvements in number memory, and manipulations that improve number memory do not enhance judgments (Brainerd & Kingma, 1985). In addition to developmental data, memory independence findings have been common in the recent adult literature. For example, judgments of relative frequency do not depend on memory for the actual frequencies of target events (e.g., Shelder & Manis, 1986), changes in attitudes do not depend on memory for attitude-relevant inputs (e.g., Hastie & Park, 1986), and text comprehension does not depend on memory for text inputs (e.g., Cooney & Swanson, 1990; Katz, Lautenschlager, Blackburn, & Harris, 1990; Swanson, 1990). Adult data are instructive because they suggest that memory independence is a fundamental property of reasoning, not a quirk of cognitive immaturity.

The memory independence effect falls naturally out of FTT because it is a by-product of the fact that memory probes and reasoning problems involve processing different (and independent) memory representations via distinct processing operations (Reyna, 1992). Thanks to the fuzzy-processing preference, reasoning flows toward the more impoverished levels of fuzzy-to-verbatim continua and involves the operations that are appropriate to processing such information. But, memory probes typically require that the verbatim traces of background inputs be read out, although gist-based reconstructive retrieval is possible in special circumstances (e.g., Brainerd & Reyna, 1988; Brainerd, Reyna, Howe, & Kingma, 1990). Since the operations that process verbatim and gist representations are different, memory dependency would not be expected on grounds of processing overlap. Dependency could result if the fates of corresponding verbatim and gist traces were linked in memory. As we have seen, however, there is evidence of both functional and structural independence. Thus, memory independence is the baseline situation in FTT, as it seems to be empirically, because there is neither representational nor processing overlap on memory probes versus reasoning problems. However, FTT can also explain memory dependency in situations where performance on memory probes is based on reconstructive processing of the same traces that are processed on reasoning problems (Brainerd & Reyna, 1988).

Development of Intuition: Representation and Processing

Does the inclination to think intuitively vary with age? As with the ontogeny of gist extraction, FTT's answer is somewhat complex, and it ultimately depends on segregating representational development from processing development. To begin with, the fuzzy-processing preference per se may be developmentally invariant as long as the relevant gists can be extracted (Brainerd & Reyna, 1990b, 1990c). On the other hand, we assume that from a purely normative standpoint, the strength and frequency of expression of the fuzzy-processing preference increase with age.

The basis for this claim lies primarily in the development of representation rather than processing. Regarding processing, we have seen (e.g., Table 3.1) that gist processing tends to be less complex than verbatim processing, which means that gist-processing operations have an accuracy advantage relative to verbatim-processing operations. Because they are simpler, gist-processing operations may also develop earlier in life. To illustrate, preschoolers are known to possess the ordering and classificatory operations that are necessary to process relational and nominal gist in probability judgment (Brainerd, 1981). The ratio operations that process verbatim numbers are typically not detected before late childhood (Callahan, 1989). Similarly, with transitive inference, the perceptual operations that process "flow" gist are present in preschoolers (Brainerd & Kingma, 1984). Most investigators (e.g., Moore, Dixon, & Haines, 1991; Surber & Haines, 1987) have interpreted the fact that verbatim-processing operations develop more slowly than gist-processing operations as demonstrating the opposite of FTT's proposal that thought becomes more intuitive with age. The modal position in the literature, enshrined in Piaget's (e.g., 1967) definition of the preoperational stage as "intuitive" and the concrete- and formal-operational stages as "logical," is that intuition is a primitive form of thought that children must suppress or otherwise overcome if their thinking is to become truly logical.

The weak link in this interpretation is that it overlooks the fact that verbatim-processing operations usually require a good deal more specific knowledge than gist-processing operations and that, naturally, it takes time to acquire such knowledge. That is, the interpretation fails to control for that fact that since intuitive reasoning operations make fewer specific knowledge demands than logical reasoning operations, it is unremarkable that the former tend to develop earlier. The critical question is whether or not, given the presence of both types of reasoning operations in some domain, intuitive reasoning tends to become more dominant with age.

Another property of memory development that seems to favor FTT's answer to this question is the phenomenon of verbatim decline, the fact that verbatim memory begins to deteriorate much earlier in life than gist memory and that, therefore, reasoning is driven in the direction of gist as a default option. For example, parents whose semantic and situational grasp of sentences and stories is vastly superior to their children's cannot remember verbatim sentences nearly as well as their children can. Our own preschooler constantly corrects small errors in recitations of stories that we have heard many times more than he has (e.g., because we have often read them to other children, or because they were read to us when we were children). It seems that the memories of preschoolers are highly specialized for storing and retrieving verbatim traces. Although verbatim memory continues to increase thereafter, it begins to decline before physical maturity, when gist memory still has far to go.

Since memory deterioration has traditionally been the province of aging researchers, there has been little work documenting verbatim decline by students of child development. However, there are two sources of apparent confirmation. First, there are experiments in which memory for both verbatim items and their gist have been studied from early childhood through young adulthood. These experiments have typically found that gist memory improves with age, and, in addition, it has sometimes been found that verbatim memory declines after childhood. In one such study, Perner and Mansbridge (1983) reported that retention of verbatim information about ordered series peaked by age 7 and gradually declined thereafter, whereas retention of the overall patterns in ordered series increased steadily between age 5 and adulthood. In another such study, Marx (1986) reported that retention of verbatim event frequencies declined after pubescence, but retention of global impressions of frequency differentials improved.

The second and more extensive source of evidence comes from language development, especially acquisition of first versus second languages. Acquiring a language demands remarkable feats of verbatim memory. The fact that young children are able to learn the thousands of words of their lexicons, as many as 5–10 new words per day between the ages of 15 months and 6 years (Gleitman & Gleitman, 1992), attests to their prodigious verbatim memory capabilities. These capabilities do not last long, however. It becomes progressively more difficult to acquire a lexicon after middle childhood, a phenomenon that has most often been studied with reference to second-language learning. In one recent study, Johnson and Newport (1989) found that the ability to learn English as a second language did not vary between the ages of 3 and 7, but that there was a linear decline between the ages of 7 and 19. This decline has typically been interpreted as favoring critical periods in language development (e.g., Lenneberg, 1967). In FTT, it is treated as a by-product of memory development, specifically as a by-product of verbatim decline.

Output: On-Line Interference, Concurrent-Processing Deficits, Cognitive Triage, and Reconstruction

On-Line Interference: Scheduling and Feedback

When a correct response is made on a reasoning or memory task, it can have many beneficial consequences. In free recall of categorized lists, recalling an exemplar of a category (e.g., robin) may encourage subjects to focus further retrieval effort on that category (e.g., birds). Similarly, solving a reasoning problem may improve the accuracy of subsequent solutions by supplying an external validity check. Such beneficial effects are widely acknowledged. What is not commonly recognized, however, is that responding can have adverse consequences for later performance. This notion of on-line, response-produced interference (and of age changes in sensitivity to such interference) is emphasized in FTT (see Dempster, 1992), both because it explains some classical results (children's concurrent-processing deficits) that are usually accounted for in other ways and because it predicts a new, counterintuitive pattern of findings about memory (cognitive triage in children's recall). In this subsection, we summarize FTT's analysis of on-line interference. In the next two subsections, we show how it explains concurrent-processing deficits and predicts cognitive triage effects.

Recent analyses of on-line interference (Brainerd & Reyna, 1989; Howe & Rabinowitz, 1989; Reyna & Brainerd, 1989) have suggested two general ways in which subsequent performance is degraded by current performance: response *scheduling* interference and response *feedback* interference. Scheduling interference is inherent in the fact that whereas response-output systems are serially organized, the memory and reasoning processes that lead to outputs can operate in parallel (cf. above and Estes, 1989). This induces a *parallel-to-serial bottleneck* at the point of output: Parallel processing delivers many potential outputs, but the serial response constraint necessitates selection and ordering of alternatives (Brainerd & Reyna, 1989, 1990b). Free recall is illustrative. If a list of words is reasonably well learned, several of them may be present in consciousness at any point during a free recall test. However, the fact that items can only be articulated one at a time means that subjects must queue them up for output, and then ensure that they do not reenter the queue after they are read out.

The second form of interference, response feedback, is released as responses are emitted. Response outputs inevitably produce a variety of irrelevant, off-task noise that propagates back through the system (Brainerd, Reyna, Howe, & Kevershan, 1991). Generally speaking, emission of a response carries in its wake the forced recoding of a variety of information that is irrelevant to processing and must, therefore, be suppressed, ignored, or otherwise gated out. Continuing with the free recall example, suppose that subjects learn to recall a list of unrelated words. Memory researchers view the articulation of a word on a free recall test as a "functional study trial" for its orthographic, phonological, and semantic features (e.g., Wilkinson & Koestler, 1983). But, such information is noise from the standpoint of the words that remain to be recalled. At a more global level, interference from feedback has long been a component of theories of perceptual discrimination (e.g., Helson, 1947). Sensitivity to such on-line interference from feedback increases in the aged (e.g., Hasher & Zacks, 1988).

Concurrent-Processing Deficits: Resource and Interference Explanations

One motivation for emphasizing on-line interference is that it allows FTT to avoid the notion of cognitive resources. According to this construct, there exists a generic limited capacity pool of mental energy (variously called *working-memory capacity* or *attentional capacity* or simply *the processing resource*), the amount and/or efficiency of which increases with development (Bjorklund, 1989). Short-term memory span is the standard index of resource capacity (Rabinowitz, Howe, & Lawrence, 1989). The processing resource is generic in the sense that its capacity units can be taxed to perform most of the usual functions of reasoning and remembering (Brainerd & Reyna, 1988).

Since Piagetian stages became unfashionable, the processing resource has become the nearest thing to a universally accepted principle of cognitive growth. It allows reasoning and remembering to be conceptualized as flexible activities in which performance is optimized through efficient allocation of resource capacity to component operations (Brainerd, 1981). Developmentally, the growth of resource efficiency/capacity can be used to explain age changes in performance on a panoply of reasoning and memory tasks (Bjorklund, 1987). Despite these up-front advantages, a strong case against some of the resource construct's most basic predictions has accumulated (for reviews, see Brainerd & Reyna, 1989, 1990b; Reyna, 1992; Hasher & Zacks, 1988). For example, Hasher and Zacks (1988) reported data showing that at least two independent resources had to be postulated to account for aging declines in text comprehension. Similarly, the fact that age changes in the accuracy of children's reasoning are often independent of age changes in their ability to remember critical background facts is inconsistent with the notion that both are controlled by the same generic resource (Brainerd & Kingma, 1985). These and other findings have fostered the conclusion, even among resource theorists, that the construct may be more trouble than its worth (cf. Bjorklund & Harnishfeger, 1990; Howe & Rabinowitz, 1990).

But, jettisoning the processing resource leaves one with the problem of accounting for the sorts of data that it is usually invoked to explain. As Hasher and Zacks (1988) and others have remarked, the job reduces to finding alternative explanations of concurrent-processing deficits, which have long been the major empirical basis for the processing resource (e.g., Kahneman, 1973). Such deficits are characteristic of the dual-task paradigm, wherein a simple motor activity (e.g., finger tapping) is paired with either a memory task (e.g., free recall) or a reasoning task (e.g., transitive inference). In developmental studies, this paradigm has produced two characteristic findings that have been thought (e.g., Bjorklund & Harnishfeger, 1987; Guttentag, 1989; Halford, Maybery, & Bain, 1986) to implicate the processing resource. First, children's baseline performance on simple motor tasks is better than it is in the presence of a concurrent memory or reasoning task. Second, the magnitude of children's concurrent-processing deficits decreases with age. The first datum is said to show that the same processing resource fuels performance on both motoric and memory/reasoning tasks. Resource capacity must be reallocated from motor performance to memory/reasoning performance when the two types of tasks are performed concurrently, thereby degrading the former. The second datum is said to show that as the amount and/or efficiency of the resource pool develops, the slack capacity that can be tapped by the secondary task also increases. So, secondary tasks impose progressively smaller resource drains on the primary motor task as development proceeds.

In FTT, these two findings are explained as on-line interference phenomena (Brainerd & Reyna, 1989; Reyna & Brainerd, 1989). Concerning the first result, it is self-evident that the total amount of on-line noise, in the sense of either scheduling interference or feedback interference, is greater when a primary task is performed in the presence of an irrelevant secondary task than when it is performed alone. Concerning the second result, age fluctuations in dual-task deficits are explained as functions of age fluctuations in sensitivity to such interference. There is independent evidence from a variety of paradigms that sensitivity to on-line interference decreases during birth-to-adult development and then increases during aging (for reviews, see Dempster, 1992; Hasher & Zacks, 1988).

FTT's interference explanation of dual-task deficits has the further advantage of accounting for certain results that pose difficulties for the resource construct (Brainerd & Reyna, 1989; Reyna & Brainerd, 1989).

The most obvious one is asymmetries in such deficits. As noted, the dual-task paradigm conjoins a rather decerebrate motor activity with a more cognitively engaging reasoning or remembering activity. According to resource theory, the latter consumes more resources than the former. Hence, adding a secondary memory/reasoning task to a primary motor task necessarily causes more "resource borrowing" from the primary task than adding a secondary motor task to a primary memory/reasoning task. Consequently, dual-task deficits should be larger in the former case. The interference explanation expects the opposite. Because memory/reasoning tasks are more complex than motor tasks, they will be more sensitive to noise of all sorts. Thus, adding a motor task will produce more degradation in interference-sensitive memory/reasoning tasks than will adding memory/reasoning tasks to interference-insensitive motor tasks. So far, experimentation has supported the interference prediction (cf. Bjorklund & Harnishfeger, 1989).

Cognitive Triage

It is one thing to postdict phenomena such as dual-task deficits. It is quite another to forecast unexpected phenomena. The interference principle does just this in a well mined area of memory development: free recall. The specific pattern of findings, the cognitive triage effect, is concerned with the relationship between the *order* in which children retrieve words on free recall tests and the *memory strengths* of those words. To see why the triage effect is interesting, we first consider what commonsense and traditional memory theories have to say about the strength-ordering relationship. We then summarize the effect itself and show how FTT predicts it.

The concept of memory strength, that words can be arrayed on a subjective magnitude dimension and that their positions on this dimension affect performance on memory tests, is as old as scientific psychology. These ideas were present in the work of Ebbinghaus and Marbe (see Osgood, 1953), and they are preserved in contemporary theories (e.g., Shiffrin & Murnane, 1989). Commonsense argues that during unconstrained recall, words with higher memory strengths necessarily come to mind before words with lower strengths, which implies that the strength-ordering relationship will be stronger → weaker. Beginning with Marbe's Law (Marbe, 1901; Thumb & Marbe, 1901), which says that the activation speed of a word's memory representation is a logarithmic function of the representation's strength, this prediction has been incorporated in many theories (e.g., Shiffrin, Ratcliff, & Clark, 1990). Since memory strength is a theoretical dimension, an empirical measure that is monotonically related to strength is required before the stronger → weaker prediction can be tested. The standard measure is recall *accuracy*. Thus, in free

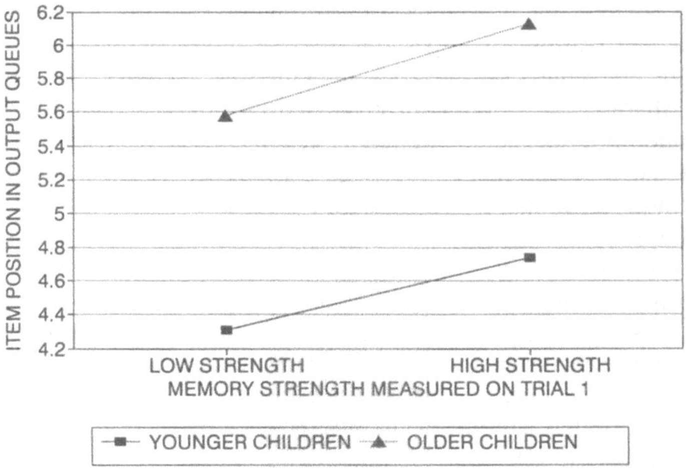

FIGURE 3.1. Cognitive triage effect on Trial 2 of free recall experiments. These plots are based on data from Brainerd, Reyna, Howe, & Kevershan (1991). The younger children were 7-year-olds, and the older children were 12-year-olds.

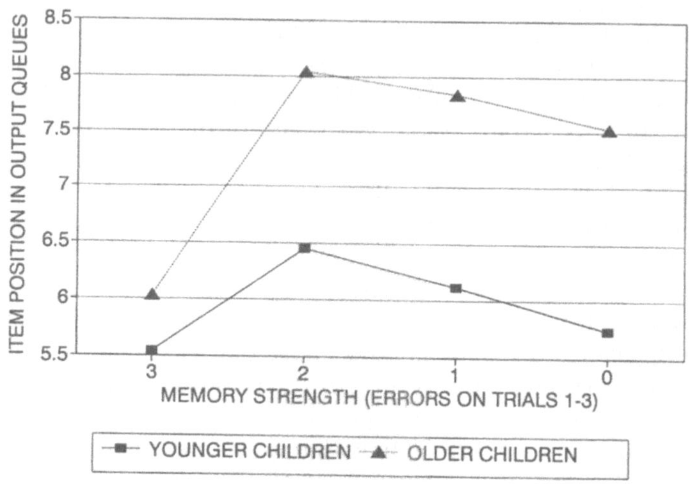

FIGURE 3.2. Cognitive triage effect on Trial 4 of free recall experiments. These plots are based on data from Brainerd, Reyna, Howe, & Kevershan (1991). The younger children were 7-year-olds, and the older children were 12-year-olds.

recall, the accuracy-ordering relationship is used to investigate the strength-ordering relationship.

When this is done, however, the observed relationship is not stronger → weaker. We have reported a series of studies that support a different

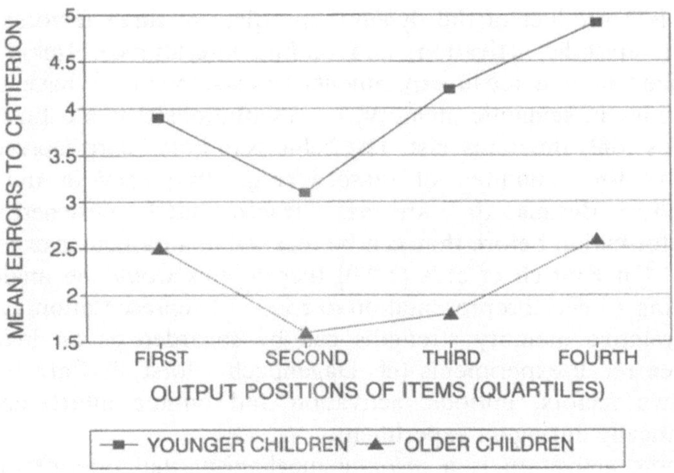

FIGURE 3.3. Cognitive triage effect on criterion trials (all items recallable) of free recall experiments. These plots are based on data from Brainerd, Reyna, Howe, & Kevershan (1990). The younger children were 7-year-olds, and the older children were 12-year-olds.

strength-ordering relationship, which we call the cognitive triage effect (Brainerd, Reyna, & Howe, 1990; Brainerd, Reyna, Howe, & Kevershan, 1990, 1991). The overall picture consists of four findings: (a) At the start of free recall learning, on Trial 2, if recalled words are classified as "strong" or "weak" on the basis of Trial 1 accuracy (i.e., strong = recalled on Trial 1, weak = not recalled on Trial 1), then weak words are recalled earlier on average than strong words (see Fig. 3.1); (b) If words recalled on later trials are classified in terms of their *degree* of memory strength on the basis of degree of accuracy on earlier trials (e.g., strongest = no prior errors, next-strongest = 1 prior error, etc.), a nonmonotonic strength-ordering relationship is obtained. Specifically, the very weakest words (all errors on previous tests) are recalled first, then the very strongest words (all successes on previous tests) are recalled, then the next-strongest words (1 error on previous tests) are recalled, and so on (see Fig. 3.2); (c) If words recalled at criterion (when performance is perfect) are classified in terms of memory strength using their complete accuracy history on precriterion trials, the overall strength-ordering relationship tends to be weaker → stronger → weaker (see Fig. 3.3); and (d) Findings a–c vary with age in the sense that each is more robust in older children and adults than in younger children. This can be see in Figs. 3.1 through 3.3, where each finding is plotted separately for younger and older children.

FTT predicts these results because it assumes that recall order is not under the exclusive control of a static memory-strength variable but, rather, is a product of the dynamic interplay of three factors: memory strength, episodic activation, and on-line interference. Items that are memorized in free recall experiments (nouns, pictures) have core representations in semantic memory, representations that are fuzzy in that they house only the items' gist. The richness of items' core representations may vary for a number of reasons (e.g., frequency in the lexicon, imagability). Because they are fuzzy, traces must be enriched with episodic information before they can be recalled in a particular experimental context. (In Kintsch et al.'s [1990] theory, this would be analogous to converting a Level 2 representation to a Level 1 representation.) Although items' relative memory strengths can be regarded as an invariant in most free recall experiments (cf. Dagenbach, Horst, & Carr, 1990), the other two factors, episodic activation and on-line interference, vary systematically during an experiment.

Episodic activation is a *priming* mechanism that operates on recall tests. Recalling a given word triggers information that promotes the recall of other words. Words with higher memory strengths apparently form more extensive episodic connections than words with lower memory strengths. Hence, recalling a strong word produces more priming than recalling a weak word and, thus, the overall rate of priming during a free recall test will depend on the strength-ordering relationship. Experiments on reminiscence effects in recall (e.g., Brainerd, Reyna, Howe, & Kingma, 1990) suggest that, other things being equal, such priming occurs in a negatively accelerated fashion and recedes if it is not refreshed by the recall of additional words.

As we have seen, on-line interference is an *inhibitory* mechanism. When words are read out, off-task noise (scheduling effects and feedback effects) is released as well as episodic activation. FTT makes two assumptions about such noise. First, on-line interference inhibits the recall of weaker words more than the recall of stronger words. Second, like priming, interference dissipates with time after it is released. Thus, neither priming levels nor noise levels simply rise inexorably as more and more words are recalled. Rather, they rise and fall as functions of the strength-ordering relationship.

FTT combines these ideas as follows to predict the triage effect. To begin with, the classical strength-ordering relationship has the previously unsuspected weakness that it is a *fixed relationship* that does not accommodate the influences of dynamic variables such as priming and on-line interference. A more optimal relationship would be one that calibrates recall to the current noise level, in particular, so that *weaker words are retrieved whenever the interference level is low and stronger words are retrieved whenever it is high.* There are two junctures in a free recall protocol when accumulated interference is low. First, it is low at the start of a protocol, which favors the recall of weaker words. (Note that Finding a above has now been explained, as well as the first part [initial recall of the weakest words] of Findings b and c.) Second, interference will be low after a run of strong words because such words produce large amounts of priming and small amounts of interference, which allows time for previously accumulated interference to recede.

Under FTT's analysis, therefore, recall could be maximized if subjects begin by recalling weaker words, then rotate in stronger words as interference builds, and then return to weaker words as interference recedes and priming builds. Thus, the *basal* strength-ordering relationship expected by FTT is weaker → stronger → weaker, which is also the observed relationship (Findings b and c). More complex concatenations of this relationship (e.g., weaker → stronger → weaker → stronger → weaker) could occur in situations (e.g., with very long or very difficult lists) where recall could be maximized only if there were multiple build-recede cycles for interference. Last, Finding d (developmental trends in triage) falls out of the previously discussed evidence that sensitivity to on-line interference fluctuates with age. As can be seen in Figs. 3.2 and 3.3, the key age difference is that the initial weaker → stronger segment of the strength-ordering relationship is smaller in younger children. The magnitude of this part of the relationship will depend on subjects' ability to resist the initially rapid accumulation of interference from recalling weaker words. Since younger children are more interference sensitive than older children, they will be less resistant, and it will be necessary for them to switch to stronger words sooner.

For FTT's optimization model of recall to function smoothly, reliable informational inputs must be available that allow children to make *in situ* diagnoses of words' relative memory strengths. We have proposed (Brainerd, Reyna, Howe, & Kevershan, 1991) that the usual error-success feedback supplied in free recall experiments is a trustworthy source of such information. Since weaker words are harder to recall, discriminating words in terms of their relative error-success histories is equivalent to discriminating them in terms of their relative memory strengths. Frequency memory, which has been found to be highly accurate even in preschoolers (Brainerd, 1981), can be exploited to effect such discriminations. As study and test trials accumulate, so do error-success frequency counts for individual items (Ekstrand, Wallace, & Underwood, 1966), which allows frequency discriminations (and, therefore, strength discriminations) to become more exact. The fact that frequency memory improves with age is relevant to Finding d above because it implies that the memorial basis for cognitive triage becomes more reliable with age.

Reconstruction in Short-Term Memory

The final two issues to be covered under the output heading are the nature and development of information retrieval in short-term memory. FTT takes nontraditional positions on these issues that, not surprisingly, emphasize the roles of fuzzy traces and reconstructive retrieval operations. Historically, the view that the memory systems that control reproduction of recently encoded information, normally called primary or short-term memory, are distinct from those that control reproduction of information after long delays has enjoyed great influence (e.g., James, 1890). Over the years, investigators have postulated certain criterial distinctions between short- and long-term memory in an attempt to dissever them (for a review, see Baddeley, 1986). Perhaps the most familiar one is the proposal that short-term memory is a limited-capacity system that involves simple readout of verbatim traces (also called surface traces), whereas long-term memory is an infinite-capacity system that involves reconstructive retrieval of schematic, gist-like traces.

FTT does not postulate separate short- and long-term stores. Such an assumption would overlook the fact that there is not a one-to-one relationship between the nature of retrieval (readout vs. reconstruction) and the nature of the traces being operated on (verbatim vs. fuzzy). On short-term memory tests, it is possible both (a) to respond by reconstructively processing recently encoded verbatim traces and (b) to respond by reading out the pattern information in recently encoded gist. Concerning a, we have investigated a family of mental arithmetic tasks that produce such performance (Brainerd, 1983). Children solve sequences of problems of the form $m + n = k$ and $m - n = k$. After certain problems, a recall probe is administered for the value of m. Theoretically, such probes could be answered either by reading out a verbatim trace of this value or by reconstructing it from a verbatim trace of the solution value; for example, if the probed problem was $5 + 2 = 7$, either the stored value "5" can be read out or the stored value "7" can be reconstructively processed ($7 - 2 = 5$). Children as young as age 5 are capable of the latter type of recall and, indeed, they prefer verbatim reconstruction over verbatim readout when both options are available (Brainerd & Reyna, 1988). Concerning b, although the memory probes in studies of reasoning-remembering relationships (cf. above) have focused on children's immediate memory for verbatim background facts, one could easily administer memory probes for gist that children extract from those facts. We have done this in the case of both transitivity (Brainerd, Fulginiti, & Reyna, 1992) and probability judgment (Brainerd, 1981), and have found that children as young as age 4 can read out the information in stored gist in these tasks.

At a more global level, FTT stresses that fuzzy traces and reconstructive retrieval play more pivotal roles in short-term memory performance and its development than has traditionally been thought. On tests of verbatim memory for recently encoded information, memory must confront the problem that readout becomes rapidly unavailable as a retrieval option because verbatim traces are sensitive to on-line interference (Brainerd & Reyna, in press-a, in press-b). There are two ways to compensate for poor verbatim memory: reconstruction and memory for gist. In FTT, reconstruction refers to using information-processing operations, including inference, to restore or redintegrate faded verbatim information (Reyna & Brainerd, 1991b). We assume that reconstruction contributes to span of immediate recall, the standard measure of short-term memory, and thanks to the verbatim → gist shift and the verbatim decline, these contributions increase with age. That is, although a certain proportion, perhaps most, of the items recalled on a span test involve verbatim memory, there is a residue of items that are recalled via reconstruction, and this residue tends to become greater as development proceeds.

To test such proposals, we have devised procedures for separating the verbatim and reconstructive portions of span performance (Olney & Brainerd, 1990). We have used these procedures to study the word and picture spans of preschool- to college-age subjects, finding that reconstructive recall makes at least some contribution to span at all age levels. However, the size of the contribution varies developmentally in ways that comport with earlier proposals. For example, the number of reconstructed items in output sets is smallest among preschoolers and kindergartners, which is consistent with the assumption that their memories are specialized for storing and retrieving verbatim traces. Further, although the number of reconstructed items in output sets increases with age throughout childhood and adolescence, by far the largest increase occurs between kindergarten and grade 2, which is consistent with the claim that the verbatim → gist shift is concentrated within these years. Finally, the number of verbatim items in output sets increases up to age 7 to 8, remains constant up to age 10 to 11, and declines thereafter, which is consistent with the claim that verbatim decline begins in adolescence.

Episodic Forgetting: Developmental Invariance, Storage/Retrieval Failure, Disintegration/Redintegration, and the Trace-Integrity Model

The study of forgetting occupies a unique niche in child psychology in that it is simultaneously relevant to some of our most basic theoretical questions and to some of our most important applied concerns (e.g., child psychotherapy, children's testimony, retention of classroom instruction). It is also one of those topics that has stimulated a mountain of speculation but only a modicum of data. There are two traditional theoretical stances (Campbell & Spear, 1972)—namely, that children forget less as they mature (e.g., because they acquire strategies that help them preserve stored information) or that they forget more (e.g., because their brains are less new). On the empirical side, there has been only a limited number of developmental studies of forgetting (for reviews, see Brainerd,

Kingma, & Howe, 1985; Howe & Brainerd, 1989). Although this seems perplexing given the theoretical centrality of forgetting, it can be traced to an elementary fact: Such studies failed to produce robust age trends.

In the present section, we begin by examining this surprising developmental invariance result. We then consider what has long been the fundamental theoretical distinction in forgetting research, forgetting *from memory* (or trace unavailability or storage failure) versus forgetting *in memory* (or trace inaccessibility or retrieval failure). Next, we sketch FTT's analysis of the development of forgetting. We conclude by summarizing the results of recent experiments that bear upon this analysis.

Developmental Invariance?

The Ebbinghaus long-term retention paradigm is the standard tool for studying the development of forgetting, owing perhaps to its resemblance to everyday forgetting. The procedure consists of a minimum of three phases. During the first phase, the acquisition session, children learn a set of target materials. This may consist of studying a list of words or pictures (e.g., Brainerd et al., 1985), of viewing a film about everyday events (e.g., Ceci, Ross, & Toglia, 1987), or of listening to a story (e.g., Howe, 1991). During the second phase, the forgetting interval, children resume their daily lives for a few days or weeks. It is especially important that the second phase last at least a few days because there is period called the *consolidation interval*, spanning a few hours to a couple of days, when memory may actually continue to improve before forgetting sets in (Howe, Brainerd, & Clark, 1992). Certain variables that are designed to accelerate forgetting, such as the familiar misinformation manipulation (cf. Ceci et al., 1987; Howe, 1991), may be introduced during this interval. During the third phase, the retention session, children receive a series of memory tests for the material that they learned during the first phase. A critical feature of these tests is that no opportunities to relearn the material are provided; the objective is purely to assess retention. The decline in performance between the end of the acquisition session and the retention session is the measure of forgetting.

The preponderance of developmental studies that have implemented this design have failed to detect age differences in forgetting. This has precipitated claims such as, "information is not lost more rapidly by children than by adults. Forgetting rates . . . were invariant from childhood to young adulthood" (Lehman, Mikesell, & Doherty, 1985, p. 27), "children organize and retrieve autobiographic memories in much the same manner as do adults" (Hudson & Nelson, 1986, p. 253), and "acquisition and/or retrieval differences are more likely sources of memory development in early childhood than are differences in rate of forgetting" (Merriman, Azmita, & Perlmutter, 1987, p. 273). Despite what seems to be monolithic support for such claims, analyses of the designs of these studies have isolated a number of variables that could have masked age differences in forgetting.

The three most common ones are floor effects, recognition insensitivity, and stages-of-learning confounds. Concerning floor effects, it is obvious that an experiment is incapable of detecting developmental trends in forgetting unless it produces some forgetting; that is, unless there are statistically reliable declines between the acquisition and retention sessions. Oddly, this criterion has often not been met. The literature contains several examples of studies in which acquisition-retention declines were either not significant or, although significant, were less than 10%. Concerning recognition insensitivity, a fundamental design axiom of developmental research is that one's measurement procedures must be maximally sensitive to age variation (Rushton, Brainerd, & Pressley, 1983). Thus, if the objective is to diagnose some aspect of memory development, memory tests that are insensitive to age variation are to be avoided. We know (cf. above) that recognition tests fall into this category because once children are old enough to understand the procedure, there is little age change in recognition memory for most materials. And yet, recognition tests were used almost exclusively in early developmental studies of forgetting.

Concerning stages-of-learning confounds, it is a truism that younger children will learn almost anything more slowly than older children, which means that older children will have reached more advanced stages of learning than younger children by the end of an acquisition session. Because learning curves are negatively accelerated, this age x learning confound will be maximal with one-trial acquisition sessions (Brainerd & Howe, 1982). Now, suppose that forgetting rates are correlated with learning stages. More explicitly, suppose, as many theorists would, that the initial, "primary" things that are learned about the target material are more resistant to forgetting than subsequent, "secondary" things. In short, earlier learning stages enjoy a retention advantage over later stages. Even if older children forget the information associated with specific learning stages at a slower rate than younger children, this age trend will be obscured by the fact that the information that younger children have learned is more memorable on average.

Since 1985, we have reported a series of experiments in which these three design problems have been corrected (Brainerd et al., 1985; Brainerd & Reyna, 1990a). Ceiling effects have been eliminated by devices such as longer retention intervals (e.g., 2 weeks rather than 1–2 days) and more difficult materials (e.g., words rather than pictures). Recognition insensitivity has been dealt with by switching to some form of recall (e.g., associative, cued, free). Stages-of-learning confounds have been controlled by switching to criterion learning coupled with the application of mathematical models that measure the proportions of subjects who attain different learning levels. When controls of this sort are in place, age declines in forgetting rates have been consistently observed between early childhood and young adulthood. It has also been found that normal children forget more slowly than children who have been classified as learning disabled (Brainerd & Reyna, 1991).

Storage Failure and Retrieval Failure

For many years, the fundamental question in the study of forgetting has been whether acquisition-retention declines are due to an inability to gain access to otherwise intact traces (the *retrieval-failure hypothesis*) or to the fact that traces do not remain intact (the *storage-failure hypothesis*). There have been many versions of both hypotheses. Hoffding (1891) and Freud (1914), for instance, were early proponents of the retrieval-failure hypothesis. Hoffding viewed retrieval as a perceptual process, and he proposed that interference from subsequent experiences made it progressively more difficult for perception to make contact with previously deposited traces. Freud, on the other hand, stressed the repression of past experiences that have emotionally unpleasant associations. Fugue states, Freudian slips, and guilt blocks are illustrative of this version of retrieval failure. Concerning storage failure, gestalt psychologists (Kohler, 1929; Wulf, 1922) thought that spontaneous reorganization produces trace mutations over time, gradually remolding traces in accordance with gestalt principles of perception. Historically, storage-failure models have been of two basic sorts: eradication metaphors and fading metaphors. Eradication metaphors assume that traces are physically destroyed through either complete or partial erasure by subsequently stored traces. Loftus' (e.g., 1979; Loftus & Hoffman, 1989) concepts of substitution and destructive updating are illustrative of complete and partial erasure, respectively. The ancient concept of trace decay, the gestalt concept of reorganization, and our own notion of episodic disintegration (cf. below) are exemplars of the class of fading metaphors.

The retrieval-failure hypothesis has been in ascendance throughout most of this century. Indeed, as Loftus and Loftus (1980) pointed out, this could be called the textbook view of forgetting. As Loftus and Loftus also remarked, there are two lines of evidence that comprise the major empirical support for this view. First, a series of brain stimulation experiments reported in the 1940s appeared to demonstrate that weak electrical stimulation of the cortex causes subjects to retrieve long-dormant and supposedly forgotten memories. Further, subjects' experiences of these memories are exceptionally vivid. Second, there is the familiar experience of reminiscence, which refers to the fact that it is often possible to remember something at Time 2 that could not be remembered at Time 1 although there has been no opportunity for relearning during the interim. The interpretation, of course, is that retrieval failed at Time 1 but succeeded at Time 2. In long-term retention experiments, the *reminiscence effect* is the finding that performance steadily improves across a retention session even though only memory tests (e.g., free recall) are being administered.

Despite the popularity of the retrieval-failure hypothesis, the issue of whether forgetting is exclusively or even chiefly due to a growing inability to access intact traces is far from settled. Neither brain stimulation data nor the reminiscence effect are necessarily probative. The problem with the former is that since the reexperienced events occurred in the distant past and cannot be verified for accuracy, stimulation-induced hallucinations may be causing these vivid "memories" (Loftus & Loftus, 1980). Likewise, the reminiscence effect only supports the retrieval-failure hypothesis if it can be safely assumed that memory traces are completely unaffected by memory tests. However, Howe and Brainerd (1989) reviewed evidence suggesting that memory tests produce trace redintegration and that this may be the source of the improvement between Time 1 and Time 2.

The Disintegration/Redintegration Hypothesis

Developmental studies of forgetting have been concerned with *episodic* forgetting. The materials that are studied during acquisition sessions are familiar items that have core (gist) representations in long-term memory. Hence, in FTT, learning consists of enriching these representations with sufficient episodic information that they can be retrieved in the experimental context. Conversely, since core representations are stable, forgetting consists of deactivating these episodic-semantic bonds. The *disintegration/redintegration hypothesis* is FTT's implementation of these general ideas.

During an acquisition session, FTT assumes that episodic traces are formed via a *featural integration* process, which consists of somehow bonding encoded episodic features to core gist. Although the mechanism is not well understood, there is some evidence that a spreading activation process operates when episodic and semantic features are jointly activated (Brainerd, Kingma, & Howe, 1986). The rate of featural integration depends on the strengths of items' core representations—stronger representations produce faster integration. Since strength varies with age, so does the rate of featural integration. Retrieval is conceptualized as a trace-discriminability process, a sort of memorial analogue of figure-ground discrimination. Retrieval operations are characterized as general-purpose rather than trace-specific procedures that perform these discriminations when they are "instructed" by episodic information on memory tests (Brainerd, Reyna, Howe, & Kingma, 1990).

During a forgetting interval, the opposite process, featural disintegration, ensues. This is the forgetting mechanism in FTT. The bonds between episodic features and core gist weaken, and the trace fades out against the background of memory noise. There are at least two reasons why featural integration levels drop (Brainerd, Reyna, Howe, & Kingma, 1990). First, continued joint activation of episodic features and core gist, which does not usually happen during a forgetting interval, may be necessary to maintain integration (Reyna & Brainerd, 1991b). Second, the episodic features that are stored in certain traces may be jointly activated with *other core gists* during the forgetting interval, and, conversely, the core gists of certain traces may be jointly activated with *other episodic features*. The decline in featural integration levels makes traces progressively less disinctive in the experimental context. This makes it progressively harder for retrieval operations to discriminate them on the basis of the episodic information that is available on memory tests. Note that this is a storage-failure explanation in the sense that it assumes that acquisition-retention declines are primarily due to changes in trace structure. The rate of featural disintegration is assumed to depend on the strength of the core gist to which episodic features are bonded; lower strength means faster distintegration. Developmentally, disintegration should exhibit developmental variations that parallel those for strength.

During a retention session, FTT assumes that a process that is analogous to acquisition-session integration, *featural redintegration*, operates on memory tests (Brainerd, Reyna, Howe, & Kingma, 1990). Under the standard definition of redintegration (e.g., Schweickert, Guentert, & Hersberger, 1990), some of a trace's features are activated when attempts are made to retrieve it on memory tests, even when retrieval is unsuccessful. This activation spreads out, both among activated features and among nonactivated features that are only weakly connected to the activated features. Like acquisition-session integration, the result is to increase the level of featural integration in the trace. Thus, attempting to retrieve traces on retention tests initiates a redintegration process that leads to net improvements in featural integration. This is how FTT explains the reminiscence effect. Even though the target material is not restudied on retention tests, redintegration makes traces more distinctive and, hence, more retrievable.

Recent Evidence: Findings from the Trace-Integrity Model

The disintegration/redintegration hypothesis generates several predictions about episodic forgetting and its development. In recent experiments, we have focused attention on four predictions that are of particular interest from the standpoint of previous research. First, contrary to the dominant retrieval-failure hypothesis, forgetting should be more a matter of storage failure than of retrieval failure. Second, contrary to the supposed developmental invariance pattern, forgetting rates should decline during age ranges where core gist is becoming stronger (i.e., birth to young adulthood) and should increase during age ranges where core gist is becoming weaker (i.e., young adulthood to late adulthood). Third, age changes in forgetting rates should be rooted in developmental variations in storage failure as well as retrieval failure. Fourth, because retention tests induce featural redintegration of traces, it should be possible during a retention session to *restore* some of the traces that have undergone storage failure, even though the target material is not restudied.

There is a preliminary obstacle that must be dealt with before such predictions can be tested. The predictions are concerned with the behavior of theoretical processes, such as storage and retrieval failure, rather than observable features of the data. To test them, therefore, it is necessary to formulate a mathematical model containing parameters that measure these processes and that can be estimated from the performance data of long-term retention sessions (cf. Brainerd, 1985). Such a model, the *trace-integrity* model, has been formulated and the statistical machinery that is required to apply it to long-term retention data has been developed (Howe & Brainerd, 1989; Howe, Kelland, Bryant-Brown, & Clark, 1992). The model, which is summarized in Table 3.2, measures four types of theoretical processes that figure in the disintegration/redintegration hypothesis: storage failure, retrieval failure, restorage, and retrieval relearning. As can be seen in Table 3.2, the model contains a single parameter for each of the first three processes that gives the probability of each of these events. Retrieval relearning, the ability to relearn how to retrieve an intact trace across a series of retention tests, is measured by combining three of the parameters in Table 3.2—namely, R, f_i, and r_i. It can be seen that 1-R is the probability of being able to retrieve an intact trace at the start of a retention session. It can also be seen that f_i and r_i are probabilities of being able to retrieve an intact trace after i previous retention tests. So, the difference between the values of

TABLE 3.2. Processes measured by the trace-integrity model.

Parameter	
Forgetting parameters:	
S	The probability that a trace disintegrates to the point that it can no longer be retrieved.
R	The probability that a trace that is still intact can be retrieved.
Relearning parameters:	
a	The probability that a trace that has undergone storage failure can be restored on a memory test administered during a retention session.
f_i	The probability that an intact trace that could not be retrieved on i previous retention tests can be retrieved on Test $i + 1$.
r_i	The probability that an intact trace that was retrieved on i previous retention tests is also retrieved on Test $i + 1$.

these latter parameters and 1-*R* is a measure of how much retrieval accuracy improves over a retention session.

We have applied the trace-integrity model to a series of forgetting studies in which the subjects ranged from 7-year-olds to 70-year-olds (Brainerd, Reyna, Howe, & Kingma, 1990; Howe & Brainerd, 1989; Howe et al., 1992). In these experiments, lists of words or pictures were first learned under associative, cued, or free recall conditions, and then retention tests for these materials were administered 1 to 2 weeks later. The values of the trace-integrity model's parameters were consistent with all of the aforementioned predictions. Concerning the first one, at all age levels storage-failure rates during forgetting intervals were much higher than retrieval-failure rates. The value of parameter *S* was 2 to 3 times the value of parameter *R* during childhood and 3 times the value of parameter *R* during adulthood. Concerning the second prediction, age variations in forgetting rates were noted throughout the life span. The overriding pattern was large age declines during childhood, followed by smaller age declines during adolescence, followed by age increases during adulthood. In Experiments 3 and 4 of Brainerd et al., for example, the total decline in forgetting rates between early childhood and young adulthood almost exactly equaled the total increase between young adulthood and age 70.

Concerning the third prediction, there were ontogenetic variations in both storage failure and retrieval failure, but storage failure was the more prominent source of age changes in forgetting rates. Between early childhood and adolescence, storage failure exhibited more variation than retrieval failure in some experiments, whereas the two were equal in other experiments. However, it was never the case that retrieval failure developed more than storage failure. During adulthood, however, age changes in storage failure consistently swamped age changes in retrieval failure. Across the eight list conditions of Experiment 4 of Brainerd, Reyna, Howe, and Kingma (1990), for example, there was a 0.18 increase in the value of parameter *S*, but only a 0.06 increase in the value of parameter *R*. Finally, concerning the fourth prediction, there was consistent evidence that disintegrated traces could sometimes be restored on retention tests, even though the target material was not restudied, and that this ability was present early in life. To illustrate, in Experiments 1 and 2 of Brainerd et al., the average values of parameter *a* were 0.15 for 7-year-olds and 0.24 for 11-year-olds, and, for some types of materials (categorized lists) the probability of restoring a disintegrated trace at some point during a retention session was nearly unity. Such results provide striking support for the proposal that traces themselves, not just retrieval operations, can be refurbished by simply attempting to recall them on retention tests.

Synopsis: Dimensions of Development

FTT is, in its most general sense, a theory of the interface between memory development and the ontogenesis of higher reasoning. It is quite true that some aspects of the theory (e.g., the fuzzy-processing preference) focus on reasoning, others (e.g., cognitive triage) on memory, and that still others (e.g., memory independence) fall somewhere in between. However, FTT's overriding thesis is that the analysis of basic memory processes informs our understanding of reasoning and the analysis of reasoning informs our understanding of memory. This point is perhaps most apparent in FTT's inclusion of reasoning processes (e.g., reconstruction) in its accounts of memory development and memory processes (e.g., memory independence) in its accounts of the development of reasoning.

The present chapter has been organized around the topics of encoding, storage, processing, output, and forgetting. In this summary, we return to these topics for purposes of drawing out 10 dimensions of developmental variation that are emphasized in FTT:

1. *Gist extraction*. The derivation of gist in parallel with the encoding of verbatim information occurs in infrahumans as well as human infants. However, the literature on memory development contains many well replicated age trends that converge on the conclusion that gist-extraction abilities, in the sense of the frequency and range of stored gist, develop.

2. *Verbatim → gist shift*. In most children, there is a landmark shift in the relative reliance of memory on verbatim and gist traces during the first few years of elementary school. The developmental literatures on recognition versus recall, forgetting, short-term memory span, and mnemonic strategies suggest that whereas preschoolers' memories are specialized for storing and retrieving verbatim traces, this specialization begins to wane shortly thereafter.

3. *Informational overdetermination*. As development proceeds, children's increasing ability to extract gist from verbatim inputs means that their reasoning is more flexible and more resistant to on-line interference.

4. *Memory independence*. Memory for critical background inputs on reasoning problems and the ability to solve those reasoning problems tend to develop independently of each other.

5. *Intuition*. The tendency to reason intuitively increases with development. This tendency is presumably rooted in age changes in the relative availability of different memorial bases for reasoning (e.g., the verbatim → gist shift and verbatim decline).

6. *Verbatim decline*. Relative to memory systems that support retention of gist, memory systems that support retention of verbatim information mature more rapidly, complete their development earlier, and begin to decline sooner.

7. *Interference sensitivity*. Developmental studies of a variety of interference-sensitive phenomena (e.g., dual-task deficits, cognitive triage) point to the conclusion that younger children are more adversely affected by on-line noise, in the sense of either scheduling interference or feedback interference, than older children and adults are.

8. *Memory strength*. The strengths of core gists (e.g., for word meanings) in long-term memory increase with development. Since episodic traces are formed by integrating core gists with episodic features, the ability to form such traces also improves.

9. *Reconstruction in short-term memory*. Memory for a recently encoded item (as in short-term memory span) can involve readout of a verbatim trace of that item, reconstruction of the item from other verbatim traces, or reconstruction of the item from gist. The short-term memories of older children and adults depend more on reconstruction from gist than do the short-term memories of younger children.

10. *Episodic forgetting*. The rate at which episodic information is forgotten decreases between early childhood and young adulthood and increases thereafter. This trend is related to underlying age variations in the rate at which disuse of episodic traces causes the bonds between episodic features and core gist to weaken.

References

Alba, J.W., & Hasher, L. (1983). Is memory schematic? *Psychological Bulletin*, *93*, 203–231.

Ankrum, C., & Palmer, J. (1989, November). *The perception and memory of objects and their parts*. Paper presented at Psychonomic Society, Atlanta, GA.

Baddeley, A.D. (1986). *Working memory*. New York: Oxford University Press.

Bartlett, F.C. (1932). *Remembering: A study in experimental and social psychology*. Cambridge, England: Cambridge University Press.

Berlyne, D.E. (1970). Children's reasoning and thinking. In P.H. Mussen (Ed.), *Carmichael's manual of child psychology*. New York: John Wiley.

Bjorklund, D.F. (1987). How age changes in knowledge base contribute to the development of children's memory: An interpretive review. *Developmental Review*, *7*, 93–130.

Bjorklund, D.F. (1989). *Children's thinking: Developmental and individual differences*. Pacific Grove, CA: Brooks/Cole.

Bjorklund, D.F., & Harnishfeger, K.K. (1987). Developmental differences in mental effort requirements for the use of an organizational strategy in free recall. *Journal of Experimental Child Psychology*, *44*, 109–125.

Bjorklund, D.F., & Harnishfeger, K.K. (1989). In defense of resources. *Journal of Experimental Child Psychology*, *47*, 19–25.

Bjorklund, D.F., & Harnishfeger, K.K. (1990). The resources construct in cognitive development: Diverse sources of evidence and a theory of inefficient inhibition. *Developmental Review*, *10*, 48–71.

Bjorklund, D.F., & Muir, J.E. (1988). Children's development of free recall memory: Remembering on their own. *Annals of Child Development*, *5*, 329–344.

Brainerd, C.J. (1981). Working memory and the developmental analysis of probability judgment. *Psychological Review*, *88*, 463–502.

Brainerd, C.J. (1983). Young children's mental arithmetic errors: A working-memory analysis. *Child Development*, *54*, 812–830.

Brainerd, C.J. (1985). Model-based approaches to storage and retrieval development. In C.J. Brainerd & M. Pressley (Eds.), *Basic processes in memory development: Progress in cognitive development research* (pp. 143–208). New York: Springer–Verlag.

Brainerd, C.J., Fulginiti, J., & Reyna, V.F. (1992). [Unpublished data.] University of Arizona, Tucson, AZ.

Brainerd, C.J., & Howe, M.L. (1982). Stages-of-learning analysis of picture-word effects in associative memory, with illustrations from developmental interactions in picture-word effects. *Developmental Review*, *2*, 251–273.

Brainerd, C.J., & Kingma, J. (1984). Do children have to remember to reason? A fuzzy-trace theory of transitivity development. *Developmental Review*, *4*, 311–377.

Brainerd, C.J., & Kingma, J. (1985). On the independence of short-term memory and working memory in cognitive development. *Cognitive Psychology*, *17*, 210–247.

Brainerd, C.J., Kingma, J., & Howe, M.L. (1985). On the development of forgetting. *Child Development*, *56*, 1103–1119.

Brainerd, C.J., Kingma, J., & Howe, M.L. (1986). Spread of encoding and the development of organization in memory. *Canadian Journal of Psychology*, *40*, 203–224.

Brainerd, C.J., & Reyna, V.F. (1988). Generic resources, reconstructive processing, and children's mental arithmetic. *Developmental Psychology*, *24*, 324–334.

Brainerd, C.J., & Reyna, V.F. (1989). Output-interference theory of dual-task deficits in memory development. *Journal of Experimental Child Psychology*, *47*, 1–18.

Brainerd, C.J., & Reyna, V.F. (1990a). Can age x learnability interactions explain the development of forgetting? *Developmental Psychology*, *26*, 194–204.

Brainerd, C.J., & Reyna, V.F. (1990b). Gist is the grist: Fuzzy-trace theory and the new intuitionism. *Developmental Review*, *10*, 3–47.

Brainerd, C.J., & Reyna, V.F. (1990c). Inclusion illusions: Fuzzy-trace theory and perceptual salience effects in cognitive development. *Developmental Review*, *10*, 365–403.

Brainerd, C.J., & Reyna, V.F. (1991). Acquisition and forgetting processes in normal and learning-disabled children: A disintegration/redintegration theory. In J.E. Obrzut & G.W. Hynd (Eds.), *Neuropsychological foundations of learning disabilities* (pp. 147–178). New York: Academic Press.

Brainerd, C.J., & Reyna, V.F. (in press-a). Memory independence and memory interference in cognitive development. *Psychological Review*.

Brainerd, C.J., & Reyna, V.F. (in press-b). Explaining "memory free" reasoning. *Psychological Science.*

Brainerd, C.J., & Reyna, V.F. (1992). The memory independence effect: What do the data show? What do the theories claim? *Developmental Review, 12,* 164–186.

Brainerd, C.J., Reyna, V.F., & Howe, M.L. (1990). Children's cognitive triage: Optimal retrieval or effortful processing? *Journal of Experimental Child Psychology, 49,* 428–447.

Brainerd, C.J., Reyna, V.F., Howe, M.L., & Kevershan, J. (1990). The last shall be first: How memory strength affects children's retrieval. *Psychological Science, 1,* 247–252.

Brainerd, C.J., Reyna, V.F., Howe, M.L., & Kevershan, J. (1991). Fuzzy-trace theory and cognitive triage in memory development. *Developmental Psychology, 27,* 351–369.

Brainerd, C.J., Reyna, V.F., Howe, M.L., & Kingma, J. (1990). The development of forgetting and reminiscence. *Monographs of the Society for Research in Child Development, 55,* 3–4 (Whole No. 222).

Broadbent, D.E. (1957). *Perception and communication.* London: Pergamon.

Callahan, P. (1989). *Learning and development of probability concepts: Effects of computer-assisted instruction and diagnosis.* Unpublished doctoral dissertation, University of Arizona, Tucson, AZ.

Campbell, B.A., & Spear, N.E. (1972). Ontogeny of memory. *Psychological Review, 79,* 215–236.

Carey, S., & Diamond, R. (1977). From piecemeal to configurational representations of faces. *Science, 195,* 312–341.

Carr, T.H. (1990, November). *Automaticity and cognitive anatomy.* Paper presented as part of the symposium "Varieties of automaticity," Psychonomic Society, New Orleans, LA.

Ceci, S.J., Ross, D.F., & Toglia, M.P. (1987). Suggestibility in children's memory: Psycholegal implications. *Journal of Experimental Psychology: General, 116,* 38–49.

Chapman, M., & Lindenberger, U. (1988). Functions, operations, and decalage in the development of transitivity. *Developmental Psychology, 24,* 542–551.

Chapman, M., & Lindenberger, U. (1992). Transitivity judgments, memory for premises, and models of children's reasoning. *Developmental Review, 12,* 124–163.

Cooney, J.B., & Swanson, H.L. (1990). Individual differences in memory for mathematical story problems: Memory span and problem perception. *Journal of Educational Psychology, 82,* 570–577.

Dagenbach, D., Horst, S., & Carr, T. (1990). Adding new information to semantic memory: How much learning is enough to produce semantic priming? *Journal of Experimental Psychology: Learning, Memory, and Cognition, 16,* 581–599.

Dempster, F.N. (1981). Memory span: Sources of individual and developmental differences. *Psychological Bulletin, 89,* 63–100.

Dempster, F.N. (1992). The rise and fall of the inhibitory mechanism: Toward a unified theory of cognitive development and aging. *Developmental Review, 12,* 45–75.

Ekstrand, B.R., Wallace, W.P., & Underwood, B.J. (1966). A frequency theory of verbal-discrimination learning. *Psychological Review*, *73*, 566–578.
Estes, W.K. (1980). Is human memory obsolete? *American Scientist*, *68*, 62–69.
Estes, W.K. (1989). Toward a framework for combining connectionist and symbol-processing models. *Journal of Memory and Language*, *27*, 196–212.
Estes, W.K. (1991). Cognitive architectures from the standpoint of an experimental psychologist. *Annual Review of Psychology*, *42*, 1–28.
Flavell, J.H. (1963). *The developmental psychology of Jean Piaget*. Princeton, NJ: Van Nostrand.
Freud, S. (1914). *The psychopathology of everyday life*. In A.A. Brill (Ed.), *The writings of Sigmund Freud*. New York: Modern Library, 1938.
Gleitman, L.R., & Gleitman, H. (1982). A picture is worth a thousand words, but that's the problem: The role of syntax in vocabulary acquisition. *Current Directions in Psychological Science*, *1*, 31–35.
Greco, C., Hayne, H., & Rovee-Collier, C. (1990). Roles of function, reminding, and variability in categorization by 3-month-old infants. *Journal of Experimental Psychology: Learning, Memory, and Cognition*, *16*, 617–633.
Granger, R.H., & McNulty, D.M. (1986). Learning and memory in machines and animals: An AI model that accounts for some neurobiological data. In J.L. Kolodner & C.R. Reisbeck (Eds.), *Experience, memory, and reasoning*. Hillsdale, NJ: Erlbaum.
Guttentag, R.E. (1989). Age differences in dual-task performance: Procedures, assumptions, and results. *Developmental Review*, *9*, 146–170.
Halford, G.S., Maybery, M.T., & Bain, J.D. (1986). Capacity limitations in children's reasoning: A dual-task approach. Child Development, 57, 616–627.
Harlow, H.F. (1949). The formation of learning sets. *Psychological Review*, *56*, 51–65.
Hasher, L., & Zacks, R. T. (1988). Working memory, comprehension, and aging: A review and a new view. In G.H. Bower (Ed.), *The psychology of learning and motivation* (Vol. 22). New York: Academic Press.
Hastie, R., & Park, B. (1986). The relationship between memory and judgment depends on whether the judgment task is memory-based or on-line. *Psychological Review*, *93*, 258–286.
Helson, H. (1947). Adaption-level theory as a basis for a quantitative theory of frames of reference. *Psychological Review*, *55*, 297–313.
Hoffding, H. (1891). *Outlines of psychology*. New York: Macmillan.
Howe, M.L. (1991). Misleading children's story recall: Forgetting and reminiscence of the facts. *Developmental Psychology*, *27*, 746–762.
Howe, M.L., & Brainerd, C.J. (1989). Development of long-term retention. *Developmental Review*, *9*, 301–340.
Howe, M.L., Brainerd, C.J., & Clark, S.L. (1992). *Forgotten but not gone: Evaluating the ups and downs of "normal" forgetting*. Manuscript submitted for publication.
Howe, M.L., Kelland, A., Bryant-Brown, L., & Clark, S.L. (1992). Measuring the development of children's amnesia and hypermnesia. In M.L. Howe, C.J. Brainerd, & V.F. Reyna (Eds.), *Development of long-term retention* (pp. 56–102). New York: Springer–Verlag.

Howe, M.L., & Rabinowitz, F.M. (1989). On the uninterpretability of dual-task performance. *Journal of Experimental Child Psychology*, *47*, 32–38.

Howe, M.L., & Rabinowitz, F.M. (1990). Resource panacea? Or just another day in the developmental forest. *Developmental Review*, *10*, 125–154.

Hudson, J., & Nelson, K. (1986). Repeated encounters of a similar kind: Effects of familiarity on children's autobiographic memory. *Cognitive Development*, *1*, 253–271.

James, W. (1890). *The principles of psychology*. New York: Holt.

Jarvella, R.J. (1971). Syntactic processing of connected speech. *Journal of Verbal Learning and Verbal Behavior*, *10*, 409–416.

Johnson, J.S., & Newport, E.L. (1989). Critical period effects in second language learning: The influence of maturational state on the acquisition of English as a second language. *Cognitive Psychology*, *21*, 60–99.

Kahneman, D. (1973). *Attention and effort*. Englewood Cliffs, NJ: Prentice-Hall.

Kahneman, D., Slovic, P., & Tversky, A. (Eds.), (1982). *Judgment under uncertainty: Heuristics and biases*. New York: Cambridge University Press.

Katz, S., Lautenschlager, G.J., Blackburn, A.B., & Harris, F.H. (1990). Answering reading comprehension items without passages on the SAT. *Psychological Science*, *1*, 122–127.

Kendler, H.H., & Kendler, T.S. (1962). Vertical and horizontal processes in problem solving. *Psychological Review*, *69*, 1–16.

Kintsch, W. (1988). The use of knowledge in discourse processing: A construction-integration model. *Psychological Review*, *95*, 163–182.

Kintsch, W., & Bates, E. (1977). Recognition memory for statements from a classroom lecture. *Journal of Experimental Psychology: Human Learning and Memory*, *3*, 150–159.

Kintsch, W., Welsch, D., Schmalhofer, F., & Zimny, S. (1990). Sentence memory: A theoretical analysis. *Journal of Memory and Language*, *29*, 133–159.

Kohler, W. (1929). *Gestalt psychology*. New York: Liveright.

Kreindler, D.M., & Lumsden, C.J. (1992). *A zeroth-order FTT narrative gistifier*. Manuscript submitted for publication.

Lamb, M.R., & Robertson, L.C. (1989, November). *An evaluation of the empirical bases underlying global precedence theory*. Paper presented at the Psychonomic Society, Atlanta, GA.

Lehman, E.B., Mikesell, J.W., & Doherty, S.C. (1985). Long-term retention of information about presentation modality by children and adults. *Memory & Cognition*, *13*, 21–28.

Lenneberg, E.H. (1967). *Biological bases of language*. New York: Academic Press.

Loftus, E.F. (1979). *Eyewitness testimony*. Cambridge, MA: Harvard University Press.

Loftus, E.F., & Hoffman, H.G. (1989). Misinformation in memory: The creation of new memories. *Journal of Experimental Psychology: General*, *118*, 100–104.

Loftus, E.F., & Loftus, G.R. (1980). On the permanence of stored information in the human brain. *American Psychologist*, *35*, 409–420.

Marbe, K. (1901). *Experimentell-psychologische untersuchungen uber das utriel*. Leipzig, Germany: Englemann.

Marx, M.H. (1986). More retrospective reports on event-frequency judgments: Shift from multiple traces to strength factor with age. *Bulletin of the Psychonomic Society*, *24*, 183–185.

Merriman, W.E., Azmita, M., & Perlmutter, M. (1987). Rate of forgetting in early childhood. *International Journal of Behavioral Development*, *10*, 467–474.

Moore, C.F., Dixon, J.A., & Haines, B.A. (1991). Components of understanding in proportional reasoning: A fuzzy set representation of developmental progressions. *Child Development*, *62*, 441–459.

Newell, A., & Simon, H.A. (1972). *Human problem solving*. Princeton, NJ: Prentice-Hall.

Nisbett, R.E., & Wilson, T.D. (1977). Telling more than we can know: Verbal reports on mental processes. *Psychological Review*, *84*, 231–259.

Olney, C., & Brainerd, C.J. (1990, April). *Fuzzy-trace theory and short-term memory development*. Paper presented at American Educational Research Association, Boston, MA.

Osgood, C.E. (1953). *Theory and method in experimental psychology*. New York: Oxford University Press.

Perlmutter, M., & Myers, N.A. (1974). Recognition memory development in two- to four-year-olds. *Developmental Psychology*, *10*, 447–450.

Perner, J., & Mansbridge, D.G. (1983). Developmental differences in encoding length series. *Child Development*, *54*, 710–719.

Piaget, J. (1953). *Logic and psychology*. Manchester, England: Manchester University Press.

Piaget, J. (1967). *The psychology of intelligence*. New York: Random House.

Rabinowitz, F.M., Howe, M.L., & Lawrence, J.A. (1989). Class inclusion and working memory. *Journal of Experimental Child Psychology*, *48*, 379–410.

Reder, L.M. (1982). Plausibility judgments versus fact retrieval: Alternative strategies for sentence verification. *Psychological Review*, *89*, 250–280.

Reyna, V.F. (1990, November). *Categorical versus compensatory reasoning and inconsistent choices*. Paper presented at the meeting of the Psychonomic Society, New Orleans, LA.

Reyna, V.F. (1991). Class inclusion, the conjunction fallacy, and other cognitive illusions. *Developmental Review*, *11*, 317–336.

Reyna, V.F. (1992). Reasoning, remembering, and their relationship: Social, cognitive, and developmental issues. In M.L. Howe, C.J. Brainerd, & V.F. Reyna (Eds.), *Development of long-term retention* (pp. 103–132). New York: Springer–Verlag.

Reyna, V.F., & Brainerd, C.J. (1989). Output interference, generic resources, and cognitive development. *Journal of Experimental Child Psychology*, *47*, 42–46.

Reyna, V.F., & Brainerd, C.J. (1990). Fuzzy processing in transitivity development. *Annals of Operations Research*, *23*, 37–63.

Reyna, V.F., & Brainerd, C.J. (1991a). A fuzzy-trace theory of reasoning and remembering: Patterns, paradoxes, and parallelism. In A.F. Healy, R.M. Shiffrin, & S.K. Kosslyn (Eds.), *Festschrift for W.K. Estes*. Hillsdale, NJ: Erlbaum.

Reyna, V.F., & Brainerd, C.J. (1991b). Fuzzy-trace theory and children's acquisition of mathematical and scientific concepts. *Learning and Individual Differences*, *3*, 27–60.

Reyna, V.F., & Brainerd, C.J. (1991c). Fuzzy-trace theory and framing effects in choice: Gist extraction, truncation, and conversion. *Journal of Behavioral Decision Making*, *4*, 249–262.

Rushton, J.P., Brainerd, C.J., & Pressley, M. (1983). Behavioral development and construct validity: The principle of aggregation. *Psychological Bulletin*, *94*, 18–98.

Schmidt, C.R. (1990). *Individual differences in the development of rote and gist memory tendencies in young children*. Manuscript submitted for publication.

Schneider, W., & Pressley, M. (1988). *Memory development between 2 and 20*. New York: Springer–Verlag.

Schweickert, R., Guentert, L., & Hersberger, L. (1990). Phonological similarity, pronunciation rate, and memory span. *Psychological Science*, *1*, 74–77.

Shedler, J., & Manis, M. (1986). Can the availability heuristic explain vividness effects? *Journal of Personality and Social Psychology*, *51*, 26–34.

Shiffrin, R.M., & Murnane, K. (1989, November). *The list-strength effect in recognition memory*. Paper presented at the meeting of the Psychonomic Society, Atlanta, GA.

Shiffrin, R.M., Ratcliff, R., & Clark, S.E. (1990). List-strength: II. Theoretical mechanisms. *Journal of Experimental Psychology: Learning, Memory, and Cognition*, *16*, 179–195.

Siegler, R.S. (1981). Developmental sequences within and between concepts. *Monographs of the Society for Research in Child Development*, *46* (Whole No. 189).

Signorella, M.L., & Liben, L.S. (1984). Recall and recognition of gender related pictures: Effects of attitude, task difficulty, and age. *Child Development*, *34*, 55, 393–405.

Smedslund, J. (1963). Development of concrete transitivity of length in children. *Child Development*, *34*, 389–405.

Smedslund, J. (1969). Psychological diagnostics. *Psychological Bulletin*, *71*, 237–248.

Staubli, U., Ivy, G., & Lynch, G. (1984). Hippocampal denervation causes rapid forgetting of olfactory information in rats. *Proceedings of the National Academy of Sciences (USA)*, *81*, 5885–5887.

Swanson, H.L. (1990). *Individual differences in working memory: A model testing and subgroup analysis of learning disabled and skilled readers*. Manuscript submitted for publication.

Thorndike, E.L. (1911). *Animal intelligence*. New York: Macmillan.

Thumb, A., & Marbe, K. (1901). *Experimentell untersuchungen uber die psychologischen grundlagen der sprachlichen analogiebildung*. Leipzig, Germany: Engelmann.

Tolman, E.C., & Honzik, C.H. (1930). Introduction and removal of reward, and maze performance in rats. *University of California Publications in Psychology*, *4*, 257–275.

Townsend, J. (1990). Serial versus parallel processing: Sometimes they look like tweedledum and tweedledee but they can (and should) be distinguished. *Psychological Science*, *1*, 46–54.

Tversky, A., & Kahneman, D. (1986). Rational choice and the framing of decisions. *Journal of Business*, *59*, 251–278.

Wagner, S., Winner, E., Cicchetti, D., & Gardner, H. (1981). "Metaphorical" mapping in human infants. *Child Development*, *52*, 728–731.

Wilkinson, A.C., & Koestler, R. (1983). Repeated recall: A new model and tests of its generality from childhood to old age. *Journal of Experimental Psychology: General*, *112*, 423–451.

Wulf, F. (1922). Uber die veranderung von vorstellungen. *Psychologisch Forschung*, *1*, 333–373.

Zimny, S.T. (1987). *Recognition memory for sentences from a discourse*. Unpublished doctoral dissertation, University of Colorado, Boulder, CO.

Zipf, G.K. (1949). *Human behavior and the principle of least effort*. Boston, MA: Houghton Mifflin.

Part II
New Formal Approaches

4
The Role of a Global Mechanism in Developmental Change in Speed of Processing

ROBERT KAIL

Improvements during childhood and adolescence in performance on speeded tasks are ubiquitous. For tasks such as scanning the contents of short-term memory, retrieving names from long-term memory, verifying the truth of arithmetic statements, and reasoning analogically, the results are the same: Adults respond substantially more rapidly than do children (e.g., Ashcraft & Fierman, 1982; Bisanz, Danner, & Resnick, 1979; Sternberg & Rifkin, 1979). It has been proposed that these results reflect some global mechanism (i.e., one not specific to a particular task) that limits the speed with which all processes can be executed (Hale, 1990; Kail, 1988). As this mechanism changes with age, all processes are executed more rapidly.

My aim in this chapter is to examine the role of this global mechanism in developmental change in speed of processing. The chapter consists of three sections. In the first, I describe existing evidence that is consistent with the hypothesized global mechanism. In the second section, I present new evidence that is also consistent with this hypothesis. In the final section, I discuss several candidates for the hypothesized global mechanism.

Global Change in Processing Speed

Children's responses on speeded tasks are typically much slower than those of young adults (Wickens, 1974). These age differences in processing speed during childhood, adolescence, and young adulthood could be due to some general developmental factor. That is, the factor would not be specific to particular tasks and would change systematically with age. For example, in information processing theories, resources or attention are often required for performance on speeded tasks (Shiffrin & Dumais, 1981), and increasing resources typically increases processing speed (Anderson, 1983). Hence, an age-related increase in the processing resources (e.g., Case, 1985) would manifest itself in faster performance on all speeded tasks.

The possibility that a general mechanism is responsible for age-related change in processing speed has been tested using procedures derived from the study of cognitive aging (Birren, 1965; Cerella, 1985; Salthouse & Somberg, 1982). Specifically, suppose that young adults' response on a particular task consists of several processes, such that their response time (RT) is defined as

$$RT = a + b + c + \ldots \qquad (1)$$

where a is the time to execute process A, b is the time for process B, etc. If children execute each process more slowly, by a constant multiple, then the corresponding equation for children would be

$$RT = ma + mb + mc \ldots = m(a + b + c) \qquad (2)$$

where m is simply the slowing coefficient.

The validity of Equations 1 and 2 can be evaluated in experimental conditions that vary the number of processes included in RT or that affect the duration of those processes. The result is a range of RTs, for both children and adults. According to the hypothesis that a global mechanism is responsible for age-related change in processing speed, the correlation across these conditions between children's and adults' RTs should be 1, because this is simply a correlation between a variable and that same variable multiplied by a constant, m. Furthermore, the slope of the function relating children's RTs to adults' RTs from the corresponding experimental conditions provides an estimate of m. Thus, this explanation can be expressed as

$$Y = mX \qquad (3)$$

where Y and X are children's and adults' RTs, respectively, and m is the slowing coefficient.

To determine if a general factor is responsible for age-related change in processing speed, RTs from children and adolescents (hereafter referred to collectively as "youth") as well as adults' RTs can be fitted to Equation 3. The extent of slowing may change with age, so Y_i and m_i will be used to denote RTs and slowing coefficients at a particular age i.

The first study in which Equation 3 was evaluated with a range of tasks was reported by Hale (1990). She tested 10-, 12-, and 15-year-olds and adults on four speeded tasks: choice RT, letter matching, mental rotation, and matching abstract patterns. At ages 10, 12, and 15 years, eight mean RT times were derived and correlated with adults' RTs for those conditions. The correlations were greater than 0.99 at all ages. Values of m_i were 1.82, 1.56, and 1.00 for 10-, 12-, and 15-year-olds, respectively, indicating a gradual approximation to adults' processing time.

This result is consistent with the claim that some global factor is responsible for age differences in processing time. To provide a further test of this claim, I (Kail, 1991b) completed an exhaustive search for studies of speeded performance published in three primary empirical journals of child developmental psychology: *Child Development, Developmental Psychology*, and *Journal of Experimental Child Psychology*. This search yielded 75 studies, each with RTs for a sample of young adults and a sample of youth. Studies were included without regard to the specific cognitive task that was used; however, studies were included only if RTs were collected under speeded conditions. The studies included 1,826 pairs of youth–adult mean RTs. That is, each of 1,826 data points consisted of a mean RT for young adults from an experimental condition along with the mean RT for youth for that same condition. These data were divided into 11 sets based on the age of the youth: 3- and 4-, 5-, 6-, 7-, 8-, 9-, 10-, 11-, 12-, 13-, and 14-year-olds.

Each of the 11 data sets was fitted to Equation 3. At each age, Equation 3 accounted for substantial variance in youths' RTs, with R^2s $\geqslant$ 0.90. Values for m_i tended to be smaller for adolescents than for children, confirming the pattern observed by Hale (1990). For 3- to 5-year-olds, m_i values approximated 3; for 12- to 14-year-olds the mean m_i was 1.25. Values for m_i did not change linearly with age. Instead, they changed substantially in early and middle childhood, and more slowly thereafter.

Nonlinear changes with age such as these are often well described by exponential functions of the general form

$$Y = a + be^{-ci} \tag{4}$$

where a represents asymptotic processing time, e is the base of natural logarithms, $a + b$ is the intercept (for $x = 0$, $e^{-ci} = 1$), c indicates how rapidly the function approaches a, and i is age. Because the asymptotic value (a) should be 1, Equation 4 simplifies to

$$m_i = 1 + be^{-ci} \tag{5}$$

where b, e, c, and i are defined as before. In fact, as shown in Figure 4.1, age-related change in m_i is well described by Equation 5, which, with b = 5.16 and c = 0.21, accounts for 76.92% of the variance.

The analyses of archival data presented in Kail (1991b) thus indicate that (a) across an assortment of tasks, youth's RT can be expressed as a multiple of adults' RT for that condition, which is consistent with the view that some global factor is involved in age-related change in speeded performance, and (b) the m_i parameter from Equation 3 changes exponentially with age.

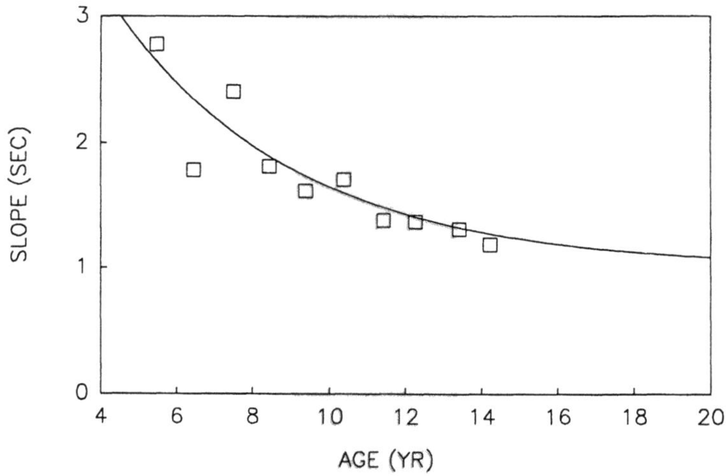

FIGURE 4.1. Change in m_i, the slowing coefficient, as a function of age. Also shown is the best-fitting exponential function, with $b = 5.16$ and $c = 0.21$. Adapted from "Developmental Change in Speed of Processing during Childhood and Adolescence" by R. Kail, 1991, *Psychological Bulletin*, *109*, p. 497. Copyright 1991 by the American Psychological Association. Adapted by permission.

New Evidence for Global Change

In this section, I present additional evidence that is consistent with the view that a global mechanism is implicated in developmental change in processing speed. In all cases, the evidence consists of evaluating predictions derived from the meta-analyses described in the previous section (Kail, 1991b). Specifically, if Equation 5 (with $b = 5.16$ and $c = 0.21$) is inserted into Equation 3, the result can be used to derive exact predictions regarding RTs at any age i:

$$Y_i = (1 + 5.16e^{-.21i})X \tag{6}$$

As before, Y is predicted RT for youth and X is an actual RT for adults. As age approaches maturity, $5.16e^{-.21i}$ approaches 0, so that predicted RTs approach X, adults' actual RTs. Thus, using Equations 5 and 6, predicted values of m_i and predicted RTs can be derived, using no free parameters.

In this section, predictions are evaluated in four cases. The first three cases involve additional analysis of archival data: (a) RTs from a supplementary meta-analysis of published studies, (b) reanalysis of RTs from individual studies involving multiple speeded tasks and multiple age groups, and (c) reanalysis of RTs from studies of the impact of practice on speed of processing. The fourth case involves data from an experiment that was designed explicitly to evaluate predictions from Equations 5 and 6.

Case 1: Supplementary Meta-analysis

To determine the robustness of the meta-analysis reported in Kail (1991b), a supplementary search of the literature was conducted. In this case,

TABLE 4.1. Studies included in the supplementary analysis.

Study (with ages of youth)	Number of conditions	Task
Brewer & Smith (1989, Expt. 2) 5.9, 7.6, 9.8, 11.7, 13.5, 15.5	21	Four-choice RT
Campbell et al. (1985) 7.8, 8.5, 9.5, 10.5	8	Multiplication
Carroll et al. (1985, Expts. 2 & 3) 5, 7, 10	4	Naming
Goodenough (1935) 3.5, 4.5, 5.5, 6.5, 7.5, 8.5, 9.5, 10.5, 11.5	1	Simple RT
Kerr (1979) 7	40	Two-choice RT
Kirshner (1972, Expt. 1) 9.1, 13.1	4	Naming and word recognition
(Expt. 2) 10.1, 14.2	4	Naming and word recognition
Klorman (1975) 10.4, 14.47	6	Simple RT
Krueger (1973) 9.92	8	Same–different decision
Lawler et al. (1976) 10.5	3	Two-choice RT
Leslie & Calfee (1971) 7.5, 9.5, 11.5	11	Visual search
Peretti (1969) 12, 15	1	Color–word interference
Salmoni & Bascoe (1979) 6.5, 10.5, 14.5	5	Tapping
Samuels et al. (1975–76) 9.5	1	Word recognition
Shea et al. (1982) 5, 9	36	Coincident timing
Surwillo & Titus (1976) 9.4	4	Simple RT
Svenson & Sjoberg (1983) 7.5, 8, 10, 12, 15	7	Dot counting
Williams (1985, Expt. 1) 5.8, 7.3, 9.7	6	Coincident timing
Young et al. (1980) 7.6	20	Identifying rotated letters; discriminating normal and backward letters

Child Development Abstracts and Bibliography was searched, from 1965 though 1989. This yielded the 18 studies listed in Table 4.1. (The number of studies is substantially less than the original search because the original search included the primary empirical journals for child developmental psychology.) The 18 studies included 448 pairs of means, where each pair consisted of a mean RT for adults and the mean for that same condition for a sample of youth. These data were divided into eight sets based on the age of the youth: 5 to 6, 7, 8, 9, 10, 11, 12 to 13, and 14 to 15 years.

At each age, Equation 3 accounted for substantial variance in youth's RTs (see Table 4.2). However, the R^2s tended to be smaller than those of the original meta-analysis (Kail, 1991b). Values for m_i generally decreased with age; Figure 4.2 shows observed values of m_i along with those derived from Equation 5 for $b = 5.16$ and $c = 0.21$. Equation 5 accounts for only 19.71% of the variance in m_i values. However, inspection of Figure 4.2 reveals that six of the eight obtained values correspond closely to those predicted from Equation 5. For these values, Equation 5 accounts for 96.63% of the variance in m_i.

There is a principled basis for questioning the two outlying values of m_i. One discrepant value—for 8-year-olds—is based on only 16 pairs and thus may simply represent an unstable estimate of m_i from a relatively small simple. The other discrepant value is for 5- and 6-year-olds. Here the fit to Equation 3 is satisfactory and the sample is reasonably large. Because most of the data came from two studies (Brewer & Smith, 1989, $N = 21$; Shea et al., 1982, $N = 36$), these data were analyzed separately in an effort to identify the reason for the unexpectedly small value of m_i. For the Brewer and Smith (1989) data, $R^2 = 0.59$ and $m_i = 3.65$; for Shea et al. (1982), $R^2 = 0.89$ and $m_i = 0.91$.

The small value of m_i in the Shea et al. data stems from qualitative age differences in performance. Specifically, the task was to adjust the rate

TABLE 4.2. Fit of youth–adult RTs from studies in Table 4.1 to Equation 3.

Age (yrs)	N	R^2	m_i
5–6	73	0.831	1.605
7	114	0.710	2.372
8	16	0.770	3.138
9	100	0.732	1.900
10	38	0.915	1.706
11	33	0.991	1.388
12–13	33	0.999	1.469
14–15	41	0.999	1.076

Note: N refers to the number of conditions (i.e., the number of pairs of youth–adult RTs). All R^2s are significant, $p < 0.01$. m_i denotes the slowing coefficient, estimated by the slope of the function relating youth's RTs to adults' RTs.

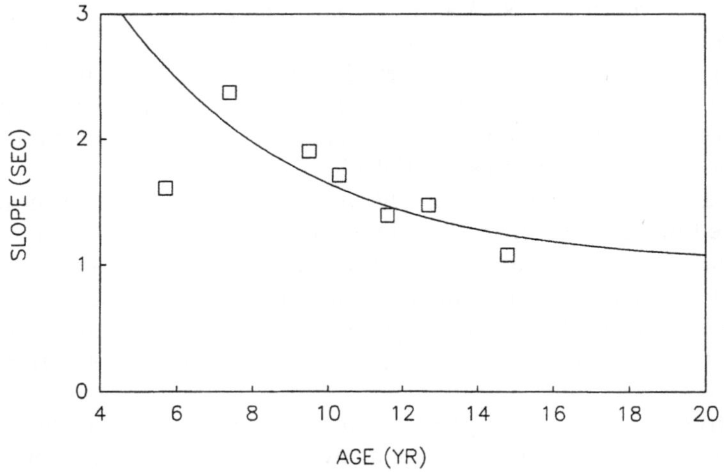

FIGURE 4.2. Change in m_i values obtained in the supplementary literature search as a function of age. Also shown are the expected values derived from Equation 5 with $b = 5.16$ and $c = 0.21$.

with which subjects moved their arms to coincide with a series of flashing lights. The 5-year-olds made these adjustments later in each trial than did adults. During those trial components when adults were adjusting (and thereby slowing) their response, 5-year-olds' responses were still unadjusted (and therefore, rapid). Qualitative differences of this sort violate the assumptions upon which these analyses are based. That is, Equations 1 and 2 do not hold, which means that there is no basis for predicting youth's RTs from adults' RTs.

Case 2: Studies of Developmental Functions

Evaluating predictions of Equations 3, 5, and 6 requires that a study include a sample of adults among multiple age groups and include numerous conditions (either multiple cognitive tasks with a few within-task conditions or a single task with many conditions). Relatively few individual studies in the literature meet these requirements. However, in the original meta-analysis (Kail, 1991b), three studies were described that met these criteria: Kail, 1986b; 1988, Experiments 1 and 2. In each case, Equation 3 was fitted to the data; estimated values of m_i were compared with those derived from Equation 5 with $b = 5.16$ and $c = 0.21$. For example, in Experiment 1 of the Kail (1986b) study, 8- to 21-year-olds were tested on two tasks: mental rotation and name retrieval. At each age, 12 mean RTs for youth and 12 for mean RTs for adults were fitted to Equation 3, which accounted for at least 99.65% of the variance in youth's RTs. Values of m_i declined exponentially in the predicted manner: Equation 5, with $b = 5.16$ and $c = 0.21$, accounted for 98% of the variance in the observed values of m_i. It is important to reiterate that there were no free parameters in this prediction. Predicted values of m_i were determined from Equation 5, which was derived from the original meta-analysis (Kail, 1991b).

This analysis was also performed on the data from two experiments described in Kail (1988). In Experiment 1, 8- to 21-year-olds were tested on visual search and memory search tasks that yielded 12 mean RTs at each age. Equation 3 accounted for at least 99.5% of the variance in youth's RTs. Here, too, change in m_i with age was exponential. Equation 5 with $b = 5.16$ and $c = 0.21$ accounted for 94% of the variance in observed values of m_i.

Experiment 2 in Kail (1988) included four tasks. For one task, analogical reasoning, the original analyses yielded several interactions with age that suggested qualitative change in performance with age. This means that Equations 1 and 2 are inappropriate because youth and adult RTs are comprised of different processes. Consequently, this task was deleted. The three remaining tasks consisted of mental rotation, memory search, and mental addition. At each age, 18 mean RTs were calculated, six for each task.

The 18 mean RTs at each of ages 8 to 17 years were fitted to Equation 3, along with the mean RTs for 18- to 21-year-olds. Equation 3 accounted for at least 97.68% of the variance in youth's RTs. Furthermore, Equation 5 accounted for 97.32% of the variance in age-related change in observed m_i values. Thus, analysis of these data, like the initial analyses of archival data, yielded two key results: (a) at each age, youth-adult RTs are highly related, and (b) m_i, the slope of the function that relates increases in youth RTs to increases in adult RTs, declines exponentially with age.

Here I report the results of these analyses applied to the findings reported in Kail (1991c). In this experiment, 7.5- to 21-year-olds and a separate comparison group of adults (17- to 43-year-olds) were tested on six speeded tasks: (a) a simple response time task in which they released a button upon presentation of a stimulus, (b) a tapping task in which they pushed a button as rapidly as possible for 5 sec, (c) a pegboard task in which they transferred 10 pegs from one row to another, (d) a modified form of the coding subtest from the WISC, (e) a matching task in which they judged if pairs of pictures were identical physically or in name, and (f) a mental addition task in which they judged the accuracy of addition statements such as $2 + 3 = 6$.

For the adult comparison group and for each of the 16 age groups, there were 25 mean RTs. These means were calculated as follows, with the number of means per task indicated in brackets:

1. for simple RT, the mean was based on raw RTs for 15 trials [1]
2. for tapping, on each of two trials, msec/tap was calculated by dividing, 5,000 msec (the length of the trial) by the number of taps [2]
3. for the pegboard task, the length of time needed to move 10 pegs was calculated for each of three trials [3]
4. for coding, the length of time needed to complete the entire page of 45 symbols was recorded [1]
5. for picture matching, a mean was calculated for each of the six conditions defined by two matching criteria (name match, physical match) and three types of pictures (identical physically and in name, physically different but with the same name; different physically and in name) [6]
6. for mental addition, a mean was calculated for each of the 12 conditions defined by six values of the sum of the problem (4–7, 8–9, 10, 11–12, 13–14, 15–17) × 2 responses (true, false) [12].

The 25 means for each age group were fitted to Equation 3, with the 25 means from the adult comparison group serving as X in that equation. As shown in Table 4.3, the fit to Equation 3 was excellent. Nonlinear change in m_i was well described by Equation 5, which, with $b = 5.16$ and $c = 0.21$, accounted for 94.1% of the variance (see Fig. 4.3).

TABLE 4.3. Fit of youth–adult RTs from Kail (1991c) to Equation 3.

Age (yrs)	R^2	m_i
7.5	0.95	2.48
8	0.97	2.11
8.5	0.96	2.20
9	0.99	2.24
10	0.99	1.71
11	0.99	1.43
12	0.99	1.21
13	0.98	1.37
14	0.99	1.17
15	0.99	1.16
16	0.99	0.99
17	0.99	1.15
18	0.99	1.01
19	0.99	0.97
20	0.99	1.08
21	0.99	1.04

Note: All R^2s are significant, $p < 0.01$. m_i denotes the slowing coefficient, estimated by the slope of the function relating youth's RTs to adults' RTs.

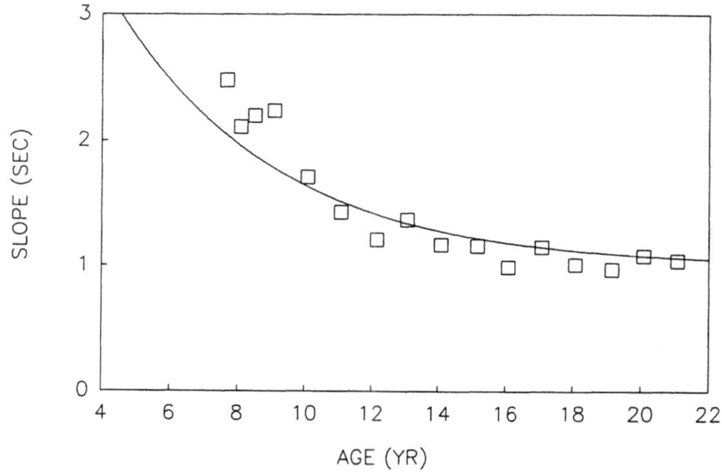

FIGURE 4.3. Change in m_i values obtained from Kail (1991c) as a function of age. Also shown are the expected values derived from Equation 5 with $b = 5.16$ and $c = 0.21$.

Case 3: Impact of Practice

With practice, adults and children execute cognitive processes more rapidly. For example, Elliott (1972) tested 7-year-olds on a simple auditory RT task. After approximately 1,000 trials, RTs had declined from 360 to 220 msec and had not yet reached asymptotic values. Similarly, adults perform many cognitive tasks substantially faster after practice (Newell & Rosenbloom, 1981).

Studies of practice provide another means by which to assess the accuracy of predictions from Equation 6. Improvements associated with practice often reflect more efficient performance, where efficiency often means that fewer steps are required for task performance (e.g., Anderson, 1983). To illustrate, whereas unpracticed performance might involve the component times a, b, and c of Equation 1, practiced performance might be represented by d, the time to execute process D, the single process that is responsible for task performance. Thus, assuming that the impact of practice does not differ qualitatively for youth and adults (i.e., Equations 1 and 2 apply), youth should still be slower than adults by the same value, m_i. That is, if adults' RTs after practice reflect a single time d, then youth's RTs should equal $m_i d$. Described in terms of change in youth's RT as a function of adults' RT, the expectation is that RTs before and after practice should both be well described by a straight line with a slope of m_i and intercept at the origin. The difference between unpracticed and practiced performance is that the latter points would be closer to the origin.

These predictions have been evaluated using data from a study of the impact of practice on mental rotation (Kail, 1986a). In this study, 9-year-olds, 13-year-olds, and adults were tested on a mental rotation task on 16 days, receiving 240 trials daily. To evaluate the predictions from Equation 6, RTs were used from the first and last days. Specifically, there were 24 mean RTs for each group: 6 (orientations) × 2 (responses) × 2 (days: first, last). For 9-year-olds, predicted RTs derived from Equation 6 accounted for 92.66% of the variance in actual RTs; for 13-year-olds, it accounted for 94.54% of the variance in actual RTs (Kail, 1991b). For the 9-year-olds, predicted RTs were quite accurate for practiced performance but slightly underestimated unpracticed performance; for 13-year-olds, there was no evidence of systematic mispredictions of RTs.

I have performed this same analysis on an additional set of practice data. In a study by Kail and Park (1990), 11-year-olds and adults were first tested on mental rotation and memory search tasks. In 11 subsequent sessions subjects received 3,168 mental rotation trials. In the final session, the mental rotation and memory search tasks were repeated. For the present analyses, 30 means were calculated for both 11-year-olds and adults. These values represented pre- and postpractice means for each of 15 variables. For memory search, a mean RT was calculated at each of three search set sizes (1, 3, 5). For mental rotation, a mean RT was calculated at each of six orientations, separately for letters and letter-like characters. As shown in Figure 4.4, Equation 6 accounted for 98.83% of the variance in actual RTs for 11-year-olds.

Case 4: Experimental Evidence

The results described thus far have been, with the exception of Hale's (1990) study, based on archival data. The aim of the study now described

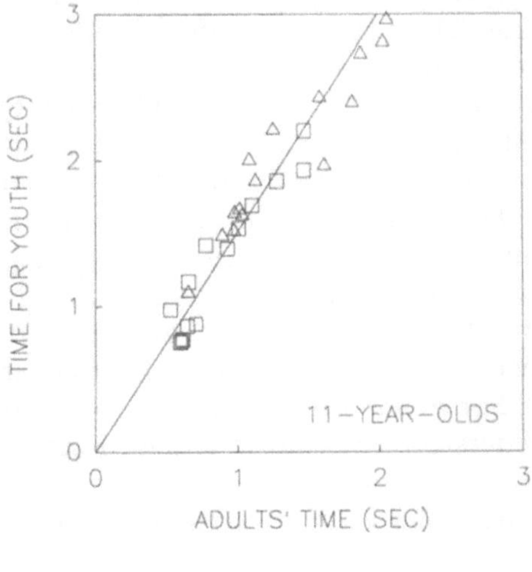

FIGURE 4.4. Change in youth's RT as a function of adults' RTs, from Kail and Park (1990). The triangles denote performance on the first day of practice; the squares, on the last day. Also shown is the function for $m = 1.51$ (derived from Equation 5 with $b = 5.16$ and $c = 0.21$) and the intercept = 0.

(Kail & Park, in press) was to provide additional evidence bearing on the hypothesis that a single, global factor may account for age differences in speeded performance. RTs for 8- through 20-year-olds were measured on four cognitive tasks that assessed reasoning, spatial, and arithmetic skill. The study was designed to extend Hale's (1990) work in two ways. First, the four tasks included 47 conditions. The large number of conditions allowed a more precise assessment of the fit of Equation 3 to youth's and adults' RTs. Second, many different age groups were used (14) in order to determine the precise manner in which m_i reaches asymptotic values.

The study included an adult comparison group and 14 different age groups. The adults in the comparison group had a mean age of 20.0 years. The remainder of the sample consisted of 16 subjects at each of the following ages: 8, 8.5, 9, 9.5, 10, 10.5, 11, 11.5, 12, 13, 14, 16, 18, and 20 years.

The four tasks were drawn from those used previously to study age-related change in cognitive processes and were selected to represent a spectrum of cognitive processes. *Figural matrices* included problems like those on Raven's Progressive Matrices. Each problem included three rows and each row consisted of three squares that contained different geometric objects. Moving from left to right in each row, the object changed systematically (e.g., increased in size or number). The subject's task was to identify the changes present in the first two rows, then determine whether these changes were present in the third row.

There were 72 problems, representing orthogonal combination of three factors: (a) the number of elements in each square in each row, (b) the number of transformations in each row, and (c) whether or not the squares in the last row adhered to the rule(s) illustrated in the first two rows.

For *geometric analogies*, taken from Bisanz (1979), there were two pairs of rectangles, with geometric figures inside each rectangle. The subject's task was to determine the relation between the objects in the first pair of rectangles, then decide whether the objects in the second pair of rectangles were related in like manner. The 80 problems included four types of true analogies and seven types of false analogies. Problems differed in the number and type of incorrect relations in the second pair of rectangles (see Bisanz, 1979, for details).

For *mental addition*, subjects determined the truth of addition statements of the form $m + n = y$. Subjects were presented addition facts involving seven values for m and n: 1, 3–4, and 6–9. For the 42 correct problems, $y = m + n$; for the 42 incorrect problems, the difference between y and $m + n$ was never larger than 2.

For *mental rotation*, subjects were asked to judge whether stimuli were letters or "backward" letters. Each of four letters was presented in six different orientations, once as a letter and once as a mirror image of a letter. The set of 48 problems was presented twice, for a total of 96 trials.

The four tasks yielded 47 means for each group: (a) for mental rotation, 12 means were derived from 6 orientations × 2 responses, (b) for geometric analogies, 4 means were derived from true problems and 7 from false, (c) for figural matrices, 12 means were derived from 2 numbers of elements × 3 numbers of transformations × 2 responses, and (d) for mental addition, 12 means were derived from 6 values for the sum (4–7, 8–9, 10, 11–12, 13–14, 15–17) × 2 responses. Group means were calculated for the 47 conditions, separately for the adult comparison and 14 age groups. These means were fitted to Equation 3, with X the means for the adult comparison group and Y the means for the age groups. At all ages RTs increased linearly as a function of adult control group RTs for the same condition. Equation 3 accounted for no less than 94.8% of the variance in age group RTs.

As before, change in m_i with age was nonlinear. Change was pronounced during childhood but smaller during adolescence (see Fig. 4.5). Also shown in Figure 4.5 are predicted values of m_i derived from Equation 5 with $b = 5.16$ and $c = 0.21$. The predicted values are quite similar to those actually obtained. In fact, Equation 5 accounted for 92.71% of the variance in observed m_is.

Thus, at each of 14 ages, RTs on four cognitive tasks were well described by Equation 3. In addition, change with age in m_i, the slowing coefficient, was exponential and well described by Equation 5.

These results are consistent with the hypothesis that a single, global factor is responsible for age differences in speeded performance. In the next section, I consider what this global factor might be.

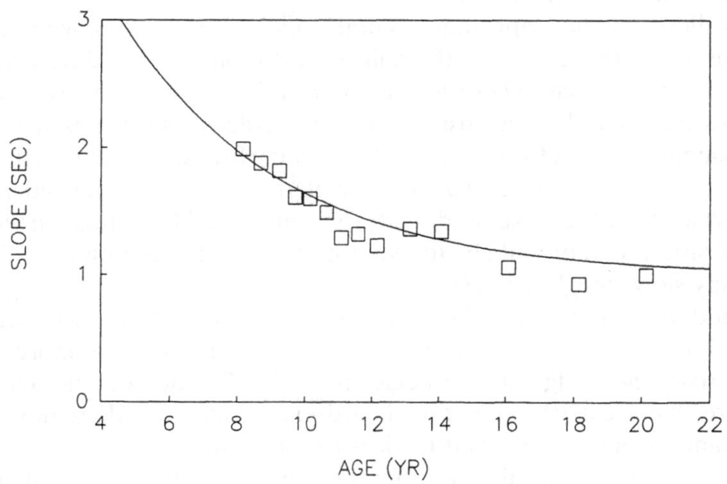

FIGURE 4.5. Change in m_i values shown as a function of age, from Kail and Park (in press). Also shown are the expected values derived from Equation 5 with $b = 5.16$ and $c = 0.21$.

Nature of the Global Mechanism

Each of the new analyses presented here provided additional evidence consistent with the view that a global mechanism is implicated in developmental change in processing speed. To summarize, predictions from Equations 3, 5, and 6 were confirmed with (a) a supplementary meta-analysis, (b) an additional study of developmental functions, (c) an additional study of practice, and (d) an experiment involving RTs for 7.5- to 21-year-olds on four cognitive tasks.

In this section, I first discuss an important limiting condition on the claim that a general factor is responsible for age differences in processing speed. Then I suggest several possible candidates for the proposed general factor. Finally, I consider the implications of global developmental change in processing speed for other aspects of cognitive development.

A Limiting Condition

Recall that the data from Shea et al. (1982) were problematic because 5-year-olds solved the timing task in a different way than did adults. Similarly, I mentioned previously that the data from the analogical reasoning task in Kail (1988, Expt. 2) were not pertinent because the strategies used to solve the reasoning task apparently varied with age. In cases like this, there is no basis for predicting youth RTs as a function of adult RTs because the processes that comprise RT are not the same for youth and adults. That is, youth RTs are expected to be a multiple of adult RTs only if the solution strategies represented in Equations 1 and 2 are the same for youth and adults.

This illustrates an important general point: The global slowing hypothesis is not intended to be the sole explanation for age differences in speeded performance. There are many instances in which these age differences clearly reflect acquisition of more efficient strategies with age. For example, age differences in the speed with which children solve addition problems can be explained, in part, by the fact that older children typically retrieve sums directly, which is rapid; younger children, in contrast, are more likely to determine sums by counting, which is relatively slow (Siegler, 1987).

In addition, sometimes the usual pattern of age differences will be reduced or eliminated because younger individuals have more task-appropriate knowledge and strategies (Chi, 1977). For example, children who are chess experts scan chessboards at a rate that does not differ significantly from that of adult novices (Roth, 1983).

Thus, it is clear that all age differences in processing speed cannot be explained solely in terms of age differences in some general factor. Instead, a complete account of age differences in processing speed will include both global and domain-specific components, and will specify how these components interact during performance of any particular cognitive task.

Possible Mechanisms

Given that the results implicate a single, global mechanism in age differences in speeded performance, what is that mechanism? As mentioned previously, one possibility concerns the quantity of processing resources available to execute speeded processes. The core ideas here are, first, that many cognitive processes require "resources" to be completed successfully, and second, that these resources are limited in supply. As Salthouse (1990) noted, the resource construct has been attractive because

> . . . it seems to be at a high enough level of abstraction to have relevance to many different types of cognitive activities, thereby offering the potential for a parsimonious and integrative interpretation, and yet, with certain conceptualizations of processing resources, explicit and testable hypotheses may be derived. (p. 102)

These conceptualizations have included *work space*, *capacity*, and *energy* models (Howe & Rabinowitz, 1990; Salthouse, 1988). However, when applied to the issue of developmental change, these conceptualizations lead to the common prediction that age-related change in processing resources (e.g., an increase in mental effort) should make possible improved performance on most cognitive tasks, including speeded ones.

The primary drawback to the process resources explanation is that a growing body of research casts doubt on the idea of a single, generic pool of resources. Particularly problematic is evidence from studies of dual-task performance, in which subjects perform a task alone as well as concurrently with another task. If both tasks require limited processing resources, then concurrent performance of the task should be inferior to performance without the concurrent task. In fact, the predicted pattern of interference is often not found. That is, concurrent performance is *not* inferior. For example, mental rotation by children and adults is just as fast when subjects perform a concurrent memory task as when mental rotation is performed alone (Kail, 1991a).

Because of results like these, some theorists have proposed multiple, domain-specific "pools" of resources, such as verbal and spatial resources (e.g., Wickens & Benel, 1982). To explain common patterns of developmental change across tasks with multiple resources, one would need to assume that either (a) all of the processes that show global slowing tap the same pool, or (b) these processes tap distinct pools, but these develop at the same rate. Alternative (a) is unlikely in light of the range of tasks investigated as well as some of the specific combinations of tasks that fail to produce interference (e.g., mental rotation speed is unaffected by both verbal and spatial memory tasks). Alternative (b) cannot, in my opinion, be dismissed on the basis of any extant findings. However, there is no principled basis for proposing strong dependencies in rate of development in resources that are otherwise thought to be independent.

Collectively, these shortcomings suggest the need to examine other potential global mechanisms. One possibility is based on an analogy to computer hardware (Salthouse & Kail, 1983). Many information-processing theories assume a cognitive architecture that includes a limited number of basic processes. For example, in theories based on production systems (e.g., Klahr, 1989), productions in working memory are scanned and those that match current goal conditions are implemented. A developmental decrease in the time to scan all productions in working memory would yield a similar pattern of development for all tasks that involved production scanning.

Another candidate for the global model is one developed by Myerson, Hale, Wagstaff, Poon, and Smith (1990) to explain slowing of cognitive processes in elderly subjects. In their model, processing occurs in many discrete steps. A small amount of information is lost at each step between input and response, which means that a processing unit must wait longer for sufficient information to accrue to begin processing a signal. Because information loss is greater for older than for younger adults, older adults must wait progressively longer at each processing step for information to accumulate.

This model leads to the prediction that a power function should relate older adults' RTs to those of younger adults. In fact, the deviation from linearity is usually slight (e.g., Myerson et al., 1990), which means that the information-loss model could be applied to results like those shown in Figure 4.4. Here, information loss would decrease gradually throughout childhood and adolescence, resulting in faster responding.

The information-loss model can also be linked to Bjorklund and Harnishfeger's (1990; Harnishfeger & Bjorklund, this volume) proposal that cognitive-developmental change reflects the ability to inhibit irrelevant processing. Bjorklund and Harnishfeger argue that, compared to older children, adolescents, and adults, younger children's processing is inefficient because they lack sufficient mechanisms to inhibit processing of irrelevant stimuli (also see Dempster, this volume). In the information-loss model, this could occur if information is not lost as it is transmitted from one processing step to the next but, instead, is transmitted to processing steps that are irrelevant to task performance. This functional loss of information would have the same result as the real loss proposed by Myerson et al.: At each subsequent step, processing would be slowed because units would need to wait for sufficient information to accrue to respond.

These various candidates for the global mechanism cannot be distinguished from the available evidence. Additional research will be needed to identify the global mechanism and to determine why its rate of development is exponential. However, common to all of the proposed global mechanisms are some general implications concerning cognitive change. These are considered in the next section.

Implications for Cognitive Development

One rule of thumb of cognitive-developmental research is that if children fail some cognitive task, try again but with a slower rate of presentation. In fact, there are numerous reports in the literature in which young children are found to be incapable of executing some cognitive process only to be able to do so when allowed more time.

One illustrative study was reported by Naus, Ornstein, and Aivano (1977), who investigated the impact of rate of presentation on children's memory. Specifically, children were asked to remember 18 words that were presented individually. In the condition of interest—spontaneous overt rehearsal—children ". . . were instructed to practice aloud the to-be-remembered words as they normally would do to themselves" (p. 240). For half of the children, a word was presented every 5 sec; for the remaining children, a word was presented every 10 sec.

The impact of presentation rate was complex because it interacted with the sex of the child. Consider, first, the impact of presentation rate on recall. For sixth-graders, recall was comparable for the fast and slow presentation rates. Recall by third-grade boys, too, was unaffected by presentation rate, and, predictably, was less than sixth-graders' recall. The key group was the third-grade girls: At the 5-sec rate, their recall approximated that of third-grade boys; at the 10-sec rate, it approximated that of sixth-graders. Thus, a slower rate of presentation eliminated age differences, at least for girls.

To determine the factors that mediate the impact of processing time, Naus et al. (1977) examined children's rehearsal. They examined the size of the rehearsal set, defined as the number of distinct words rehearsed together during the time between presentation of words. The pattern for this measure was similar to that for recall. Third-grade boys rehearsed approximately two different words regardless of presentation rate. Third-grade girls, too, rehearsed about two different words at the 5-sec rate but four words at the 10-sec rate. At grade 6, the rehearsal data do not correspond directly to the recall data, for sixth-graders rehearsed approximately four words at the faster rate but five at the slower rate.

Thus, for third-grade girls, increased processing time led to greater diversity in the words that subjects rehearsed together, which was associated with greater recall. For sixth-graders, increased processing again lead to greater diversity of rehearsal but not to greater recall. For third-grade boys, increased processing time affected neither rehearsal nor recall.

A second useful illustration comes from research on the characteristics of a word's meaning that are represented in long-term memory. These characteristics have been studied with the release from proactive interference (PI) paradigm developed by Wickens (1970). Each of several trials in this paradigm involves (a) presentation of two to three words to be remembered, (b) a distracting task (e.g., naming colors, counting) for a brief period, and (c) an interval to recall the words. Words that share a common feature are presented on successive trials. For example, all words might be drawn from the same taxonomic class or they might all have similar connotations. Typically, recall is nearly perfect on the first trial, but declines on successive trials. On the last trial (usually the fourth or fifth), words that are presented differ for subjects in control and experimental groups. For control groups, the words share the same feature as words on previous trials; recall is typically inaccurate. For experimental groups, the words presented on that trial share the same type of feature as on previous trials but a different value. For example, if words on trials 1 to 4 were from the category of animals, trial 5 would consist of a new category such as plants; if trials 1 to 4 consisted of words with positive connotations, trial 5 would consist of words with negative connotations. If the feature that is contrasted on trial 5 is encoded by children, then interference from preceding words that share a different feature should be reduced, with the result that (a) recall by children in the experimental group should improve from trial 4 to 5 and (b) recall on trial 5 should be greater for children in the experimental group than those in the control group.

To illustrate, Schroll and I (Kail & Schroll, 1974) tested 8- and 11-year-olds on the release from PI paradigm. On each of five trials, two words were presented that had similar evaluative connotations (Osgood, Suci, & Tannenbaum, 1957). Thus, children in control groups were asked to recall five pairs of negatively valued words (e.g., fear, cold) or five pairs of positively valued words (e.g., fresh, save). Children in experimental groups were asked to remember positively valued words on trials 1–4 but negatively valued words on trial 5 (or vice versa).

The results for 11-year-olds conformed to the pattern associated with encoding of a word's connotation: Recall by the experimental group increased from trial 4 to 5 and recall on trial 5 was greater for the experimental group than for the control group. In contrast, for the 8-year-olds, recall in trial 5 for the experimental group did not differ reliably from (a) their recall on trial 4, or (b) trial 5 recall for the control group. Thus, our results seemed to indicate that 11- but not 8-year-olds encode the evaluative connotation of a word, at least as encoding is assessed with this paradigm.

Subsequently, Douglas and Corsale (1977) showed that our conclusions concerning 8-year-olds were premature. They argued that our relatively rapid rate of presentation—1 sec/word—may have allowed insufficient time for younger children to encode evaluative connotations. Consequently, they examined second-graders' recall in the release from PI paradigm with presentation rates of 1 and 2 sec/word. At the faster presentation rate, the results replicated those of the 8-year-olds in Kail and Schroll's (1974) study. However, at the slower rate, recall conformed to the pattern associated with encoding of evaluative connotations. That is, trial 5 recall for the experimental group was significantly greater than (a) their trial 4 recall, and (b) trial 5 recall for the control group.

The work described here (as well as other studies not mentioned, e.g., Pezdek & Miceli, 1982) illustrate the usefulness of the cognitive developmental rule of thumb concerning additional processing time for younger children. What often appears to be a qualitative change in performance—before a certain age, children cannot perform *X*—is really an artifact of a rate of presentation that was too rapid to allow children to execute processes required for successful task performance.

Of course, increased processing time is not a developmental panacea. There are instances in which children's performance remains unchanged despite additional processing time. Illustrative is work by Siegler (1976, Expt. 3b) on rules that children use in solving balance-scale problems. Typically, when asked to predict which side of a balance scale will go down when supporting blocks are removed, 5-year-olds focus on the number of weights on the two sides but ignore the distance of the weights from the fulcrum. Siegler (1976) suggested that they

> . . . failed to encode the distance dimension simply because they were too slow in focusing their attention or in counting. In this view, the 5-year-olds might only have had time to encode one dimension, and therefore chose to encode the dimension they viewed as more important, weight. . . .

To test this view, 5-year-olds were allowed to evaluate the balance-scale problems for 15 sec instead of the original 10 sec. This additional time had no impact on their performance: Most of the children still considered weight only and ignored distance information.

Although it is possible that 5-year-olds would have encoded distance information with still more time, other experiments by Siegler (1976) make this unlikely. Instead, 5-year-olds need direct instruction in order to encode distance information.

Thus, increased processing time may often be a necessary component of improved performance for younger children but it may not always be sufficient for improved performance. The more general point, however, is that the impact of processing speed is not limited to performance on tasks with an obvious speeded component: Whenever there is external control on the rate of stimulation, on the pacing of responses, or, more generally, on the number of activities to be completed in a given period of time, performance may decline because children could not complete sufficient processing in the allotted time.

Acknowledgment. The research described here was supported by grant HD 19947 from the National Institute of Child Health and Human Development.

References

[* denotes a study listed in Table 4.1]

Anderson, J.R. (1983). *The architecture of cognition.* Cambridge, MA: Harvard University Press.

Ashcraft, M.A., & Fierman, B.A. (1982). Mental addition in third-, fourth, and sixth graders. *Journal of Experimental Child Psychology, 33*, 216–234.

Birren, J.E. (1965). Age changes in speed of behavior: Its central nature and physiological correlates. In A.T. Welford & J.E. Birren (Eds.), *Behavior, aging and the nervous system* (pp. 191–216). Springfield, IL: Thomas.

Bisanz, J. (1979). Processes and strategies in children's solutions of geometric analogies. Unpublished doctoral dissertation, University of Pittsburgh.

Bisanz, J., Danner, F., & Resnick, L.B. (1979). Changes with age in measures of processing efficiency. *Child Development, 50*, 132–141.

Bjorklund, D.F., & Harnishfeger, K.K. (1990). The resources construct in cognitive development: Diverse sources of evidence and a theory of inefficient inhibition. *Developmental Review, 10*, 48–71.

*Brewer, N., & Smith, G.A. (1989). Developmental changes in processing speed: Influence of speed-accuracy regulation. *Journal of Experimental Psychology: General, 118*, 298–310.

*Campbell, J.I.D., & Graham, D.J. (1985). Mental multiplication skill: Structure, process and acquisition. *Canadian Journal of Psychology, 39*, 338–366.

*Carroll, M., Burne, B., & Kirsner, K. (1985). Autobiographical memory and perceptual learning: A developmental study using picture recognition, naming latency, and perceptual identification. *Memory & Cognition, 13*, 273–279.

Case, R. (1985). *Intellectual development, birth to adulthood.* Orlando: Academic Press.

Cerella, J. (1985). Information processing rates in the elderly. *Psychological Bulletin, 98*, 67–83.

Chi, M.T.H. (1977). Age differences in the speed of processing: A critique. *Developmental Psychology, 13*, 543–544.

Douglas, J.D., & Corsale, K. (1977). The effects of mode and rate of presentation on evaluative encoding in children's memory. *Child Development, 48*, 46–50.

Elliott, R. (1972). Simple reaction time in children: Effects of incentive, incentive-shift and other training variables. *Journal of Experimental Child Psychology, 13*, 540–557.

*Goodenough, F.L. (1935). The development of the reactive process from early childhood to maturity. *Journal of Experimental Psychology, 18*, 431–450.

Hale, S. (1990). A global developmental trend in cognitive processing speed in children. *Child Development, 61*, 653–663.

Howe, M.L., & Rabinowitz, F.M. (1990). Resource panacea? Or just another day in the developmental forest. *Developmental Review*, *10*, 125–154.

Kail, R. (1986a). The impact of extended practice on rate of mental rotation. *Journal of Experimental Child Psychology*, *42*, 378–391.

Kail, R. (1986b). Sources of age differences in speed of processing. *Child Development*, *57*, 969–987.

Kail, R. (1988). Developmental functions for speeds of cognitive processes. *Journal of Experimental Child Psychology*, *45*, 339–364.

Kail, R. (1991a). Controlled and automatic processing during mental rotation. *Journal of Experimental Child Psychology*, *51*, 337–347.

Kail, R. (1991b). Developmental change in speed of processing during childhood and adolescence. *Psychological Bulletin*, *109*, 490–501.

Kail, R. (1991c). Processing time declines exponentially during childhood and adolescence. *Developmental Psychology*, *27*, 259–266.

Kail, R., & Park, Y. (1990). Impact of practice on speed of mental rotation. *Journal of Experimental Child Psychology*, *49*, 227–244.

Kail, R. & Park, Y. (in press). A global mechanism is implicated in developmental change in speed of processing. *Merrill-Palmer Quarterly*.

Kail, R., & Schroll, J.T. (1974). Evaluative and taxonomic encoding in children's memory. *Journal of Experimental Child Psychology*, *18*, 426–437.

*Kerr, B. (1979). Sequential predictablity effects on initiation time and movement time for adults and children. *Journal of Motor Behavior*, *11*, 71–79.

*Kirsner, K. (1972). Developmental changes in short-term recognition memory. *British Journal of Psychology*, *63*, 109–117.

Klahr, D. (1989). Information-processing approaches. In R. Vasta (Ed.), *Annals of child development* (Vol. 6, pp. 133–185). Greenwich, CT: JAI Press.

*Klorman, R. (1975). Contingent negative variation and cardiac deceleration in a long preparatory interval: a developmental study. *Psychophysiology*, *12*, 609–617.

*Krueger, L.E. (1973). Effect of letter-pair frequency and orientation of speed of "same"–"different" judgments by children and adults. *Bulletin of the Psychonomic Society*, *2*, 431–433.

*Lawler, K.A., Obrist, P.A., & Lawler, J.E. (1976). Cardiac and somatic response pattern during a reaction-time task in children and adults. *Psychophysiology*, *13*, 448–455.

*Leslie, R., & Calfee, R.C. (1971). Visual search through word lists as a function of grade level, reading ability and target repetition. *Perception & Psychophysics*, *10*, 169–171.

Myerson, J., Hale, S., Wagstaff, D., Poon, L.W., & Smith, G.A. (1990). The information-loss model: A mathematical theory of age-related cognitive slowing. *Psychological Review*, *97*, 475–487.

Naus, M.J., Ornstein, P.A., & Aivano, S. (1977). Developmental changes in memory: The effects of processing time and rehearsal instructions. *Journal of Experimental Child Psychology*, *23*, 237–251.

Newell, A., & Rosenbloom, P.S. (1981). Mechanisms of skill acquisition and the law of practice. In J.R. Anderson (Ed.), *Cognitive skills and their acquisition* (pp. 1–55). Hillsdale, NJ: Erlbaum.

Osgood, C.E., Suci, G.J., & Tannenbaum, P.H. (1957). *The measurement of meaning*. Urbana, IL: University of Illinois Press.

*Peretti, P.O. (1969). Cross-sex and cross-educational level performance in a color-word interference task. *Psychonomic Science*, *16*, 321–322.

Pezdek, K., & Miceli, L. (1982). Life-span differences in semantic integration of pictures and sentences in memory. *Child Development*, *51*, 720–729.

Roth, C. (1983). Factors affecting developmental changes in the speed of processing. *Journal of Experimental Child Psychology*, *35*, 509–528.

*Salmoni, A.W., & Bascoe, C. (1979). Fitt's reciprocal tapping task: a development study. In G.C. Roberts & K.M. Newell (Eds.), *The Psychology of Motor Behavior and Sport* (pp. 288–294). Champaign, IL: Human Kinetics.

Salthouse, T.A. (1988). The role of processing resources in cognitive aging. In M.L. Howe & C.J. Brainerd (Eds.), *Cognitive development in adulthood* (pp. 185–239). New York: Springer–Verlag.

Salthouse, T.A. (1990). Working memory as a processing resource in cognitive aging. *Developmental Review*, *10*, 101–124.

Salthouse, T.A., & Kail, R. (1983). Memory development throughout the life span: The role of processing rate. In P.B. Baltes & O.G. Brim (Eds.), *Life-span development and behavior* (Vol. 5, pp. 89–116). New York: Academic Press.

Salthouse, T.A., & Somberg, B.L. (1982). Isolating the age difference in speeded performance. *Journal of Gerontology*, *37*, 59–63.

*Samuels, S.J., Begy, G., & Chen, C.C. (1975–76). Comparison of word recognition speed and strategies of less skilled and more highly skilled readers. *Reading Research Quartery*, *11*, 72–86.

*Shea, C.H., Krampitz, J.B., Northam, C.C., & Ashby, A.A. (1982). Information processing in coincident timing taks: A developmental perspective. *Journal of Human Movement Studies*, *8*, 73–83.

Shiffrin, R.M., & Dumais, S.T. (1981). The development of automatism. In J.R. Anderson (Ed.), *Cognitive skills and their acquisition* (pp. 111–140). Hillsdale, NJ: Erlbaum.

Siegler, R.S. (1976). Three aspects of cognitive development. *Cognitive Psychology*, *8*, 481–520.

Siegler, R.S. (1987). The perils of averaging data over strategies: An example from children's addition. *Journal of Experimental Psychology: General*, *116*, 250–264.

Sternberg, R.J., & Rifkin, B. (1979). The development of analogical reasoning processes. *Journal of Experimental Child Psychology*, *27*, 195–232.

*Surwillo, W.W., & Titus, T.G. (1976). Reaction time and the psychological refractory period in children and adults. *Developmental Psychobiology*, *9*, 517–527.

*Svenson, O., & Sjoberg, K. (1983). Speeds of subitizing and counting processes in different age groups. *Journal of Genetic Psychology*, *142*, 203–211.

Wickens, C.D. (1974). Temporal limits of human information processing: A developmental study. *Psychological Bulletin*, *81*, 739–755.

Wickens, C.D., & Benel, D.C.R. (1982). The development of time-sharing skills. In J.A.S. Kelso & J.E. Clark (Eds.), *The development of movement control and coordination* (pp. 253–272). New York/London: John Wiley.

Wickens, D.D. (1970). Encoding categories of words: An empirical approach to meaning. *Psychological Review*, *77*, 1–15.

*Williams, K. (1985). Age differences on a coincident anticipation task: influence of stereotypic or "preferred" movement speed. *Journal of Motor Behavior*, *17*, 389–410.

*Young, J.M., Palef, S.R., & Logan, G.D. (1980). The role of mental rotation in letter processing by children and adults. *Canadial Journal of Psychology*, *34*, 265–269.

5 Individual Differences in Children, Studies, and Statistics: Applications of Empirical Bayes Methodology

Hoben Thomas

We Need a Richer Framework

The issue is individual differences and what might be done about them. There are, of course, a variety of meanings one might have in mind when individual differences are considered. However, a common occurrence is to find, even after careful stratification on variables thought to covary with the responses of concern, that the responses of some children appear quite different from the responses of others. Again, the nature of such differences will depend on the research setting, but one frequent observation is that some children have extreme scores relative to the rest of the group. Real data examples will appear below, but consider for illustration fictitious responses of five children on two measurement devices (2, 3), (3, 2), (3, 4), (4, 3), (15, 16) giving marginal values on one variable of 2, 3, 3, 4, 15 and 3, 2, 4, 3, 16 on the other. Attention naturally focuses on the individual with scores (15, 16).

Suppose our concern is with constructing confidence intervals or tests on mean values. The chances are good we might consider deleting the extreme individual, or adjusting the score in some way. Failing to do so results in a 30-fold increase in sample variance and correspondingly large confidence intervals relative to the result obtained should the extreme individual be deleted.

On the other hand, if our concern is with correlation, we might be delighted with the (15, 16) pair because $r = 0.98$, whereas $r = 0$ if the extreme pair is deleted. This suggests that our view of data and what we do with data is likely to be influenced by our goals and ambitions, and this is not a healthy condition. Still, it is not obvious that leaving the data points untouched is a better decision than altering the scores in some way, even if it is clear no blunder such as a scoring error has occurred. What is needed is an objective procedure for dealing with such situations. Although this example is extreme, it is only extreme in degree, and the fact is individual differences can be troublesome. I submit that one reason—perhaps the main reason—why such differences seem troublesome is because of our penchant for viewing different individuals as replicates of one another.

Take the simplest setting, a one-sample design. The conventional perspective is that each individual so sampled is an independent observation from a common distribution with the same mean and same variance. Within this framework, dominated by our thinking that the response distribution is normal or approximately so, any peculiarities in the distribution of responses, such as extreme responses and the like must be regarded as sampling error: a rare event has occurred. Thus, individual differences of any significant magnitude must be rare events! There simply is no other alternative to this interpretation under the conventional sampling perspective. Yet in the area of developmental psychology, and in particular where young children are concerned, each child has perhaps a unique rate of development and possesses his or her own idiosyncrasies.

If one agrees with this premise, does it make sense to view, for example, a group of 7-year-old boys even from the same school classroom as all being "observations" on identically distributed random variables with, of course, the same mean and variance, if concern focuses on aspects of cognitive development? At best, it seems, we might view the question as a hypothesis for test. As a general working assumption it seems far too unrealistic.

The only way to break out of this mode of thinking is to consider a broader class of models that explicitly allows for the consideration of individual differences. I'd argue that anyone having done even a modicum of research with children recognizes that there can be, and often are, very large individual differences. So it is not our own perceptions of children that are at fault. The fault lies with the models through which our data are viewed.

Consider each individual as having their own response distribution; it follows then that each individual may have a unique parameter value (possibly vector valued). Consequently, we can view a response of an individual as being a value generated from that individual's response distribution. With this change in thrust, we begin to think about estimating that individual's parameter value, and consequently shift our focus away from the conventional null hypothesis testing approach that is not congenial to ideas of individual differences. For instance, if our "conditions" happen to be samples of children in a one-way layout, the conventional null hypothesis specifies that the population means among the conditions are equal. This seems a very restrictive place to begin work, and it is of course by no means clear how best to interpret results if the null hypothesis is rejected, which is generally the research goal.

By regarding each individual as having their own response distribution, individual differences seem less problematic. The extreme individual (15, 16) may now be viewed as possibly having extreme parameter values. But there is another interpretation too, which resembles the dilemma of the conventional perspective: Our extreme observation may not be a good estimate of that individual's parameter value. And it typically will not be a good estimate if the response distribution of the subject has large variability. Consequently, with a broader model perspective we are faced with deciding between two possibilities: (a) Is the observed individual response representative of the individual, and thus a good basis on which to infer the value of the individual's parameter? Or could it be that (b) the response is a widely deviant atypical response of the individual, and thus perhaps a poor basis for estimating the individual's parameter value? In the real world, of course, it is probable that the truth lies somewhere in between. In any event, we must somehow decide which situation is closer to the truth. Fortunately, there appears to be a class of procedures that can help in the formulation of this decision: empirical Bayes (or EB) inference procedures.

What to Read Next

Some readers may wish to experience the message without the details. The next brief section tries to outline the basic ideas. The spirit of EB, not to be confused with Bayesian methods, is well captured by the baseball and car buying examples in the section titled "Examples of EB Approaches." The subsection "Form of the Data Required and Assumptions" specifies the data requirements for most applications of the simple approach considered here. The reader may then wish to skip to the section "Applications of EB Methodology" for several examples. In particular, the first example considers the artificial data presented above that hopefully will be intuitively helpful.

Empirical Bayes Philosophy

Because from an EB perspective individuals may be regarded as having different parameter values, the thrust of an analysis is different. The goal of EB is to obtain the best estimate of each individual's parameter value. This perspective differs considerably from the conventional perspective in which emphasis is placed on obtaining a group mean value, and where the individual plays, literally, a residual role. Consider for example, the ordinary sample mean. One justification for its use is that the sample mean is the value c, which minimizes

$$\sum_{i=1}^{n} (x_i - c)^2$$

This is not to say that constructing sample means is necessarily a bad thing to do. But in conventional estimation, it is the sample mean that is regarded as an estimate of a common population mean and the assumption there is one common mean often seems overly restrictive. Because EB focuses attention on estimating an individual's parameter value, it might be thought that the best way of doing so is by considering only the target individual's responses. Such intuition turns out to be wrong. EB procedures use information from other independent subjects, besides the information from the target subject, in order to arrive at a better estimate of the target subject's parameter value. Thus, EB literally says that we can know more about an individual by using not only information from that individual, but also information from other independent individuals. It is the contribution of information from other persons in providing an improved estimate of the target individual's parameter value that is a critical feature of the approach. This idea is illustrated below, and in particular, some intuition is provided as to why the idea actually works in practice.

EB methods are often termed *shrinkage* procedures, because they start with a parameter estimate of the individual, and together with information from other individuals revise this estimate. This new estimate is usually less extreme than the individual's original score. How much the new estimate differs from the estimate based only on the individual's response depends in part on the variance of the individual estimate. If the estimate has large variance it may be changed considerably; if not, it may be changed negligibly. This perspective provides the basis for a general strategy.

A Proposed General Strategy

Whether or not individual differences are worrisome is ultimately a judgement call. The artificial example above is illustrative. By ignoring the extreme individual's scores, and retaining the scores in the data set unaltered while forging ahead with conventional analyses, we are implicitly saying that the individual is simply typically expected random variation under the model of focus. Alternatively, by altering the data in some fashion, such as changing the individual's score or deleting the individual, there is implicit recognition that the score is not trustworthy.

There is, or should be, a natural reluctance to alter data without some justifiable reason for doing so, and the first thing to consider is whether a blunder, scoring error, or some other event occurred that could be the explanation for the deviant response. In this regard it is gratifying to note that some textbooks, even for the very first course in statistics, are now emphasizing computation *after* graphic examination of the data (Moore & McCabe, 1989). If nothing irregular can be turned up, then an objective procedure for considering data adjustment can implemented. EB is such a procedure.

Suppose after EB analysis the extreme scores of our hyopothetical individual were much more in line with the other scores. For example, the scores might now satisfy a normal model, whereas before they might have rejected such a model (in practice, more than five scores would be needed for such a test). If so, then it can be concluded that the extreme individual's scores were themselves untrustworthy, and consequently the individual differences are not of substantial concern.

Suppose, alternatively, that the individual's scores, after EB analysis, remain little changed from their original values. From a theoretical perspective this is critically important, and calls for more drastic action. At minimum, it suggests that any group-based statistic may be misleading.

Clearly what one should do next if EB procedures leave differences largely unaltered depends on substantive concerns such as the goals of the research, alternative possible explanations, and so forth. EB procedures do not by themselves provide a prescription for "what to do next." But EB procedures are capable of helping us decide when observed differences among individuals are worthy of concern and when they are not.

However, a useful follow-up when EB analysis reveals differences that cannot be (or should not be) ignored has been mixture decomposition analysis, which can be viewed as a form of cluster analysis. There appear to be many places in developmental psychology where mixtures can be usefully employed. Examples are given below.

In fact, there is a close connection between EB and mixture analysis. EB essentially says that different individuals have different parameter values, and usually we think of these differences among parameter values as representing differing values of a random variable with some smooth distribution. Finite mixture analysis allows for between-individual parameter value differences as well, but assumes that, for example, all individuals in a sample may have, say, two or three distinct common parameter values. Consequently, rather than thinking about a continuum of parameter values as in EB, from a mixture perspective we consider a specific small number of different discrete parameter values. Height may be regarded as an example. Although it is possible to consider different children as having different height parameters, it may be that within sex, at a fixed age, the parameter differences among children of the same sex are sufficiently negligible that a common parameter may be appropriate. But consider a sample of boys and girls at some fixed age. It is known that there are height differences among boys and girls at a common age. Consider all girls as having a common mean for height, and all boys as having a different common mean for height. Then a combined sample of boys and girls can be regarded as mixture distribution.

In particular, suppose boys' heights were modeled by a normal distribution with mean μ_b, variance σ^2, i.e., $n(\mu_b, \sigma^2)$, with density denoted by $f_b(x)$, and girls' height were modeled by $n(\mu_g, \sigma^2)$, with density $f_g(x)$. Then a mixture model for boys and girls combined would be

$$f(x) = \pi f_b(x) + (1 - \pi) f_g(x),$$

where π, $0 \leqslant \pi \leqslant 1$ is the mixing weight. π measures the proportion of boys, and $1 - \pi$ measures the proportion of girls in the population. In the most interesting examples, such as when a sample of heights for boys and girls are available but are not coded for sex, interest focuses on estimating π and the other parameters as well.

In summary, the present proposal is not intended to provide what might be called a "solution" for the "problem" of individual differences. Individual differences are not the problem: They are real features of people. The problem is to provide a framework within which such differences may be more constructively viewed. The fundamental idea, which is neither unique nor new, is to argue for a broader perspective, or to argue for a richer class of models through which to view children's behavior. One such class is to regard each child as having their own response distribution. This change in orientation alone has implications for how to do research and how to treat data.

Individual Differences Need Not Involve Persons

The previous development viewed individual differences as meaning differences between individual persons. But there is no need to restrict our focus in this way. We can just as naturally think of individual differences among groups, among studies (as in a meta-analysis), or among statistical quantities in general because the same general techniques apply. For instance, in the case of group means a group mean simply becomes the "individual" of focus.

There is a congenial connection between meta-analysis and EB (Maritz, Thomas, & Lombard, 1990). One way to view EB is to say EB addresses the question as to what past studies reveal about what might be expected from a current study. For example, suppose a study has just been completed in some content domain of interest. It is natural to consider how the results of the present or current study should be viewed against the background of past studies. EB provides a natural vehicle for accomplishing this goal. There is, however, no need to maintain a temporal perspective. The terms *past* and *present* are simply for convenience. One can just as well consider what an entire classroom of children (read "past studies") might say about a specific individual child (read "current study"). The approach is the same in either case.

Examples of EB Approaches

I know of no examples in developmental psychology where EB procedures have been employed. Thus, the approach must be regarded as perhaps holding promise. However, there are a number of examples in other areas where the power of the approach has clearly been demonstrated; consequently, there is good reason to think that its application within developmental contexts would also have beneficial effects as well. Consider two examples.

Baseball

Perhaps the most celebrated example concerns the prediction of batting averages of 18 baseball players during the 1970 baseball season (Efron & Morris, 1975). The problem is to use each player's batting average after the first 45 at bats to predict the player's batting average for the duration of the season. In most cases each player had several hundred additional at bats, and the batting average for these additional at bats was regarded as the parameter value of interest for each player.

A conventional estimate for predicting the subsequent batting performance would be to take the player's batting average for the first 45 at bats (number of hits divided by 45 at bats). One might think that Frank Robinson's batting average after 45 at bats would best predict Frank Robinson's subsequent performance for the rest of the season, and that knowing how well Roberto Clemente is doing is irrelevant for Frank Robinson. It is not so! Using the early season batting averages of Roberto Clemente and 17 other players, in addition to Frank Robinson's batting average, leads to a far better prediction of Frank Robinson's subsequent performance than simply using Robinson's own average after 45 at bats.

Robinson's early season average was 0.378, and normally that number would be used to predict his subsequent average. The EB estimate based on all the players predicted Robinson's average would be 0.286. His actual rest of season performance (parameter value) was 0.298. The EB method does far better in this example than the conventional estimate. When applied to all 18 players, the EB estimates were better for 15 players, and worst for only 3.

Referring to athletes as "hot" or "cold" when they seem to be performing especially well or especially poorly is common talk among sports fans. In a certain sense, EB methods may be viewed as a formal procedure that explicitly considers this fact in estimation. Referring to a player as "hot," for example, tends to reflect a belief that the player is currently performing above where the player would be expected to perform in the longer run, and correspondingly so for the "cold" player. From an EB perspective, these "hot" or "cold" players are those with rather extreme values; hot players are not expected to remain hot, and so the prediction of final performance should be somewhat less because the player is bound to "cool off." A similar situation holds for "cold" players. We would expect them to perform, in the longer term, much better than they are performing at the moment. Taking "hot" and "cold" into account, the revised estimates are shrunk toward the mean, and consequently, predictions are improved.

Car Buying

A second example (Morrison, 1979; Casella, 1985) concerns marketing behavior. Does an individual's stated intention to purchase a new car reflect the person's true car purchasing behavior? First, 447 people expressed their intentions to purchase automobiles; later, the sample was followed up to determine their actual purchasing behavior. EB estimates were far better for predicting actual purchasing behavior than was expressed intent.

The basic intuition in this example is similar to the baseball example. For instance, among individuals that claim they have no intention of purchasing a car, doubtlessly some individuals will do so. Similarly for those individuals expressing certainty about the prospects of buying a car, a few will have second thoughts. The EB methodology takes into account this information, and correspondingly adjusts the estimates.

Empirical Bayes from Bayes[1]

EB may be viewed as an application of the Bayesian calculations, but without the subjectivity of the Bayesian approach. Thus, EB may be regarded as an alternative to conventional procedures and in spirit is probably closer to conventional procedures than to Bayesian procedures. Indeed, it has been said that "noting is further from a Bayesian than an Empirical Bayesian" (Lindley, in Morris, 1983). Still, it is useful to approach EB through the Bayesian perspective. In what follows, the term *conventional approach* or the like will be used to denote the viewpoint exemplified in most traditional settings.

Consider a one-sample problem. From a conventional perspective, there is one stochastic process, and that concerns a model for the data. Suppose the data are sampled from a normal distribution with mean θ and variance 1; that is, the data are from a $n(\theta, 1)$ distribution. In the conventional perspective the parameter θ is fixed, and each individual is assumed to be an observation from a $n(\theta, 1)$ distribution.

---

[1] An effort has been made to maintain a consistent notation, although at times it is too cumbersome to do so. Capital X always denotes a random variable, typically a statistic, and often a mean; x denotes a value of X, and similarily in the Bayesian and empirical Bayesian settings for Greek letters. Θ is a random variable, θ is a value of Θ. $\hat{\theta}$ is an estimate of θ but sometimes $\hat{\theta}$ denotes a random variable, as in $\mathscr{E}(\hat{\theta} \mid \theta)$; other times it denotes a particular value of an estimate of θ as in Equations 6 to 9. f denotes a function, but $f(\theta)$ is not the same function as $f(\theta \mid x)$ or $f(x)$; different functions are distinguished by their arguments. There is an exception. The arguments of the function δ vary somewhat with the context but always refer to the same general quantity, expressed by Equation 6 or earlier, Equation 4. Also, no distinction is made between δ and an estimate of δ.

A Bayesian would want a richer model. A model for the data would also be specified, but in addition a model would be specified for the parameter θ which would now be regarded as the value of a random variable, Θ. Thus, there are two stochastic processes in the Bayesian approach: one for the data, another for the parameters. Furthermore, the Bayesian would typically assume that each data value, although still normal, could be sampled from a distribution with a different value of θ.

In the conventional perspective, interest would focus on the overall sample mean as an estimate of the unknown fixed mean θ, perhaps as the basis for constructing a confidence interval for θ. The Bayesian would proceed differently. The distribution for the random variable Θ would be termed the prior distribution, and each value of the data would be regarded as the data given a value of $\Theta = \theta$. That is, each observation can be from a distribution with a different $\Theta = \theta$. Once data are at hand, the Bayesian would be interested in estimating, for each observed data value, the mean for the distribution from which each data value has come. In Bayesian terminology, this is a posterior mean, or the expectation of the posterior distribution given a fixed data value.

The problem is to estimate this value of θ, which is the same as estimating $\mathscr{E}(\Theta|x)$; that is, the mean of the random variable Θ given X fixed at x. The Bayesian will typically specify the mean of Θ, $\mathscr{E}(\Theta)$, and the variance of Θ, $\mathscr{V}(\Theta)$ (typically after also specifying the distribution of Θ), based on knowledge of the content area, intuition, etc. EB is different from the Bayesian perspective. Although in EB the distribution of Θ is typically specified, the parameters of the distribution of Θ are not specified, but are estimated from data, thereby eliminating that subjective aspect of the approach. However, there is subjectivity involved in all approaches. Some judgement is generally made about the distribution for the data, and in the case of Bayesian and most EB approaches, the form of the prior distribution as well. The approach to be presented below is different in that it does not require that a specific form of the distribution for either the data or the prior distribution be specified. It is only assumed that the form of the distributions be continuous, and have moments, which are very weak conditions.

Bayes from a Regression Perspective

Figure 5.1 illustrates many of the basic ideas and communicates the idea that there are two random processes of focus: one for the data, and one for the prior parameter θ. The figure has no empirical reality and is only for didactic purposes.

We envision that the data have come from just three rectangular distributions pictured in Figure 5.1. These are the data distributions, and would be denoted generally as $f(x|\theta)$. Specifically, these distributions are

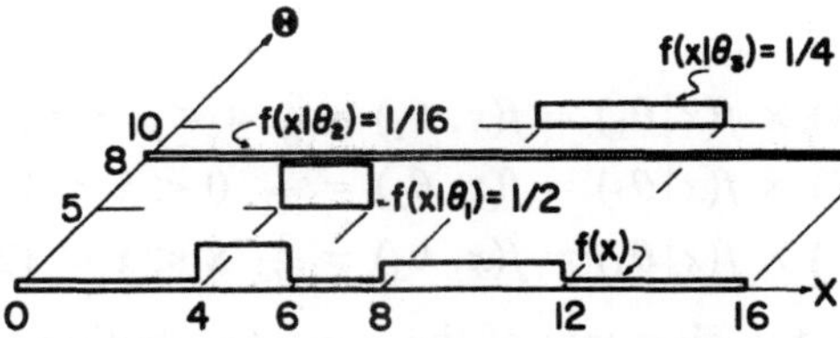

FIGURE 5.1. The joint space of Θ and X, the three conditional distributions of X given $\Theta = \theta$, and the marginal distribution of X.

$$
\begin{aligned}
f(x\,|\,\theta_1) &= \tfrac{1}{2},\ 4 < x < 6,\\
f(x\,|\,\theta_2) &= \tfrac{1}{16},\ 0 < x < 16,\\
f(x\,|\,\theta_3) &= \tfrac{1}{4},\ 8 < x < 12
\end{aligned} \tag{1}
$$

These data distributions have been placed in bivariate space, so that their means graph an identity function. That is, the mean of $f(x\,|\,\theta_i)$, $i = 1, 2, 3$, is θ_i, or $\mathscr{E}(X\,|\,\theta_i) = \theta_i$. Specifically, the means and variances of these distributions are

$$
\begin{aligned}
\theta_1 &= \mathscr{E}(X\,|\,\theta_1) = 5, & \mathscr{V}(X\,|\,\theta_1) &= 0.33\\
\theta_2 &= \mathscr{E}(X\,|\,\theta_2) = 8, & \mathscr{V}(X\,|\,\theta_2) &= 21.33\\
\theta_3 &= \mathscr{E}(X\,|\,\theta_3) = 10, & \mathscr{V}(X\,|\,\theta_3) &= 1.33
\end{aligned} \tag{2}
$$

To anticipate later developments, if X happened to be a statistic estimating θ, we would say that if $\mathscr{E}(X\,|\,\theta) = \theta$, then X is an unbiased estimator of θ; unbiased estimators, or at least approximately unbiased estimators, will be required for the procedure to be proposed.

Consider next the prior distribution of Θ; here that probability distribution is pictured as discrete, although in the real world it is typically continuous. The probability distribution for Θ is

$$
\begin{aligned}
f(\theta) &= \tfrac{1}{4},\ \text{if } \theta = \theta_1 \text{ or } \theta_3\\
&= \tfrac{1}{2},\ \text{if } \theta = \theta_2\\
&= 0 \text{ otherwise}
\end{aligned} \tag{3}
$$

$\mathscr{E}(\Theta) = 7.75$, and $\mathscr{V}(\Theta) = 3.1875$. The probabilities assigned for the prior Θ are again arbitrary. In this particular example, half the data (on average) have as their parameter value θ_2, and the remaining data have prior values θ_1 or θ_3.

Figure 5.1 does not portray the joint probability distribution $f(\theta, x)$ for the pair of random variables Θ and X. It shows the conditional distributions of $X\,|\,\theta$. But the picture is essentially the same for the joint distribution. From the definition of conditional probability distributions

$$f(x\,|\,\theta) = f(x, \theta)/f(\theta),\ f(\theta) > 0,$$

so

$$(1/4) \times f(x|\theta_1) = f(x, \theta_1) = \tfrac{1}{8},\ 4 < x < 6,$$
$$(1/2) \times f(x|\theta_2) = f(x, \theta_2) = \tfrac{1}{32},\ 0 < x < 16,$$
$$(1/4) \times f(x|\theta_3) = f(x, \theta_3) = \tfrac{1}{16},\ 8 < x < 12,$$

give the heights of the elements of the joint distribution. The conditional distributions are simply proportionally reduced, so the sum (integral) of all the elements of the joint distribution integrate to 1. Starting with a joint distribution and integrating out x would yield the marginal distribution of Θ, $f(\theta)$. Summing out θ provides the marginal distribution of the X, $f(x)$, which is also pictured in Figure 5.1.

Consider this X marginal distribution. Note that this distribution represents observations from three constituent components of the joint distribution. The proportions of these observations in the parent X marginal are as specified, in this example, by the marginal distribution of Θ. This marginal distribution is an example of a mixture distribution because it is a mixture of observations from different distributions. However, the notion of a mixture distribution does not need to be channeled through the Bayesian perspective. Mixture distributions are perfectly satisfactory non-Bayesian structures as noted above. Indeed, the marginal of X can be written as a three-component mixture:

$$f(x) = (\tfrac{1}{4})f(x|\theta_1) + (\tfrac{1}{2})f(x|\theta_2) + (\tfrac{1}{4})f(x|\theta_3).$$

This is the same as writing the marginal distribution of X as

$$\begin{aligned} f(x) &= \tfrac{1}{32},\ 0 < x < 4,\ 6 < x < 8,\ 12 < x < 16, \\ &= \tfrac{5}{32},\ 4 < x < 6, \\ &= \tfrac{3}{32},\ 8 < x < 12. \end{aligned}$$

Furthermore, the marginal mean and variance of X are

$$\mathscr{E}(X) = 7.75,$$
$$\mathscr{V}(X) = 685/48 = 14.27.$$

From a conventional data analytical perspective, one is generally content with simply calculating a sample mean and sample variance to construct confidence intervals or to perform certain tests. There usually is no recognition that the data distribution might have arisen from a more complicated process. Recognizing that the X marginal distribution "has a conceptual history in conditional distributions," so to speak, adds another dimension to the story.

From the Bayesian perspective, interest focuses on estimating the mean of Θ given a fixed $X = x$, that is, $\mathscr{E}(\Theta|x)$. From

$$f(\theta|x) = [f(\theta)f(x|\theta)]/f(x) = f(\theta, x)/f(x)$$

gives

$$f(\theta|x) = \tfrac{4}{5},\ \theta = \theta_1 = 5 \quad \left.\begin{matrix} \\ \end{matrix}\right] \quad 4 < x < 6.$$
$$= \tfrac{1}{5},\ \theta = \theta_2 = 8$$

$$f(\theta|x) = 1,\ \theta = \theta_2,\ 0 < x < 4,\ 6 < x < 8,\ 12 < x < 16.$$

$$f(\theta|x) = \tfrac{2}{3},\ \theta = \theta_3 = 10 \quad \left.\begin{matrix} \\ \end{matrix}\right] \quad 8 < x < 12.$$
$$= \tfrac{1}{5},\ \theta = \theta_2 = 8$$

Note these are discrete distributions with the specified probabilities for each value of X in the interval. Then the posterior means of θ for $X = x$ are easily given. For example, $\mathscr{E}(\Theta|x) = (\tfrac{4}{5}) \times 5 + (\tfrac{1}{5}) \times 8 = 5.6$ for $4 < x < 6$. Collectively, the means and the variance of these distributions are:

$$\mathscr{E}(\Theta|x) = 5.6,\ \mathscr{V}(\Theta|x) = 1.44,\ 4 < x < 6.$$

$$\mathscr{E}(\Theta|x) = 8,\ \mathscr{V}(\Theta|x) = 0,\ 0 < x < 4,\ 6 < x < 8,\ 12 < x < 16.$$

$$\mathscr{E}(\Theta|x) = 9.33,\ \mathscr{V}(\Theta|x) = 0.88,\ 8 < x < 12.$$

These mean values are graphed in Figure 5.2, as a function of X, and are the quantities that in practice are unknown, but which the Bayesian would be interested in estimating. The values are intuitively plausible. For example, for any value of x outside the intervals 4 to 6 and 8 to 12, the $\mathscr{E}(\Theta|x) = 8$, which is the mean of the distribution that must have contributed the observations.

Although different values of X can take on the same posterior expected value in this example, in realistic cases different X values have different expected values of Θ. Furthermore, $\mathscr{E}(\Theta|x)$ is often linear in x. For example, if $X|\theta$ is Poisson (i.e., if the data distribution is Poisson, which depends on a value θ) and Θ (with values θ) has a gamma distribution, or if $X|\theta$ is normal in distribution, and Θ is also normal, then for both of these examples the posterior mean $\mathscr{E}(\Theta|x)$ is linear in x (e.g., Maritz & Lwin, 1989, p. 6).

In fact, it is useful to consider predictions that are linear functions of x. If $\mathscr{E}(\Theta|x)$ is actually linear in x, then such functions may coincide with the

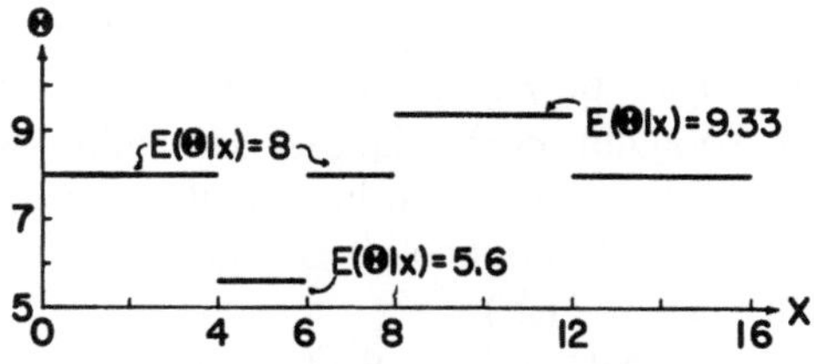

FIGURE 5.2. The joint space of Θ and X showing the conditional means of Θ given $X = x$, as a function of X.

true state of affairs. If the true posterior mean is not linear in x, as in the present example, then the linear function can be considered as an approximation to $\mathscr{E}(\Theta|x)$.

Because linear functions of x will be considered below, it is of some interest to consider linear functions of x here. Thus, consider

$$\delta(x) = Bx + (1 - B)\mathscr{E}(X) \tag{4}$$

where

$$B = \frac{\mathscr{V}(\Theta)}{\mathscr{V}(\Theta) + \mathscr{V}(X|\theta)} \text{ and } 1 - B = \frac{\mathscr{V}(X|\theta)}{\mathscr{V}(\Theta) + \mathscr{V}(X|\theta)} \tag{5}$$

and $\mathscr{E}(X)$ is the mean of the marginal distribution of X.

One might well wonder where these expressions came from. It turns out that in certain more realistic problems than the present one, $\delta(x)$ denotes the mean of the posterior distribution of Θ given $X = x$, that is $\mathscr{E}(\Theta|x) \equiv \delta(x)$. Actually, $\delta(x)$ is of the form of the mean of the posterior distribution for the normal case with normal prior distribution and it is the form of the expressions to be used for practical estimation discussed below. Therefore, it is useful to consider how B, $1 - B$, and $\delta(x)$ behave.

First, consider how $1 - B$ or B behaves when $\mathscr{V}(\Theta)$ is relatively fixed. Regard $\mathscr{V}(X|\theta)$ as the variance associated with an observation of interest on X. X might be a person's mean score on some measuring device. We would regard X then as estimating the parameter of interest, θ. The $\mathscr{V}(X|\theta)$ is the variance of that mean score [outside of the EB or Bayes content one would most likely write $\mathscr{V}(X)$, but within the EB context, $\mathscr{V}(X)$ is the variance of the *marginal* distribution of X]. If $\mathscr{V}(X|\theta)$ is small, we therefore have high confidence in the value of X, B, is large, $1 - B$ is small, and $\delta(x)$ is largely determined by x. So the "new" predicted value of Θ for the fixed $X = x$ is changed very little. In the above example, an observation from $4 < x < 6$ has a variance of 0.33, and because $\mathscr{V}(\Theta) = 5.6$, $B = 0.944$, so values of x in that interval are relatively unchanged. For example, $\delta(5) = 5.26$. On the other hand, the variance for observations from the second component have a very large variance, $\mathscr{V}(X|\theta_2) = 21.33$ (from Equation 2) and B for such observations is much smaller, $B = 0.13$; consequently, the observed value of x is strikingly changed. For instance, $\delta(0) = 6.74$, and $\delta(16) = 8.82$.

Consider now the role of $\mathscr{V}(\Theta)$. If $\mathscr{V}(\Theta)$ is very large, then B is relatively close to 1, so again, $\delta(x)$ is largely determine by the value of x. This says that the prior distribution, to be useful, must not have too large a variance. If it has a small variance, B is relatively smaller, and $\delta(x)$ is again determined largely by $\mathscr{E}(X)$.

It is instructive to compare values of $\delta(x)$ with the actual $\mathscr{E}(\Theta|x)$. (A casual attitude is taken with regard to the observations at the endpoints of the interval; in realistic models such problems do not arise.)

$$\left.\begin{aligned}\delta(4) &= 4.36\\ \delta(5) &= 5.26\\ \delta(6) &= 6.33\end{aligned}\right], \mathscr{E}(\Theta\,|\,x) = 5.35,\ 4 < x < 6$$

$$\left.\begin{aligned}\delta(0) &= 6.74\\ \delta(8) &= 7.78\\ \delta(16) &= 8.82\end{aligned}\right], \mathscr{E}(\Theta\,|\,x) = 8,\ x \text{ in other intervals}$$

$$\left.\begin{aligned}\delta(8) &= 7.92\\ \delta(10) &= 9.33\\ \delta(12) &= 19.45\end{aligned}\right], \mathscr{E}(\Theta\,|\,x) = 9.33,\ 8 < x < 12$$

The approximation of $\mathscr{E}(\Theta|x)$ by $\delta(x)$ even in this example where the posterior mean is not linear in x does not, in general, do too bad a job of approximating $\mathscr{E}(\Theta|x)$ for most values of x.

The goal here has not been to compare $\mathscr{E}(\Theta|X)$ with $\delta(x)$ for this particular example; rather, it has been to illustrate the general form of the estimator that will be used in practical situations.

The fundamental difference between EB and Bayes is that the former estimates the parameters from the data, whereas a Bayesian will specify them based on intuition, hunches, or prior knowledge. So next consider the estimation problem from an EB perspective.

Empirical Bayes Estimation

Most applications of EB are termed parametric EB because a specific model distribution is specified for both the distribution of the data and for the prior distribution. In the previous example the data model was Equation 1 (unrealistic) and the prior distribution was Equation 3. Perhaps the most common parametric EB model is the normal model. In this model the data are modeled by $f(x|\theta)$, which is assumed to be normal with mean θ. The prior distribution of Θ is also assumed to be normal as well. Such models are a fairly common basis for EB estimation (Morris, 1983).

Although in conventional data analysis it is common to model the data as normal, to model the distribution of Θ as normal may seem restrictive, and possibly unreasonable, particularily when there may be little information available that would suggest a suitable prior distribution for Θ. The concern is justified, but it turns out in practice that the specification of a parametric prior distribution (e.g., normal) may not be all that important anyway in determining results; the results of EB analyses tend to be "robust" with respect to the selection of different prior distributions (Maritz & Lwin, 1989, p. ix).

The emphasis here, however, will be on a nonparametric approach that does not assume any specific parametric distribution form for either the data distribution or the prior distribution. Rather, it is only assumed the data may be modeled by a smooth distribution that has moments, and similarly for the prior distribution. Besides providing a more general framework, the general form of the EB solution is easily implemented, so computation is simplified. In fact, the solutions can be obtained without need of a computer. However, except for small data sets, such an approach is not practical.

If it is possible to obtain EB solutions without assuming a parametric form for the data and prior, why would not such nonparametric approaches always be preferred? The main reason appears to be that results seem to be more satisfactory with small to medium data sets when a parameteric structure is assumed (Berger, in Morris, 1983). If so, given that much child data are based on small samples, wouldn't it be preferable to proceed with a parametric approach? Perhaps, but implementation of parametric approaches in a variety of situations is more difficult. Computer routines are not widely available, and almost always the approaches require iterative algorithms. A main attraction of the present approach is that it is widely applicable to a variety of real problems, and forming the estimates is generally straightforward. Thus, what will be presented is perhaps not the most efficient approach for the all EB problems, but the approach is nonetheless a generally accessible one that can be implemented easily.

Form of Data Required and Assumptions

1. Required are sample estimates $\hat{\theta}$s of an unknown parameter θs of interest. The estimates must be unbiased, or at least approximately so, which means that $\mathscr{E}(\hat{\theta} \mid \theta) = \theta$. For example, if there are n children, the data may be sample means based on the m responses of each child. The mean of a child's responses would typically estimate the child's θ.

Alternatively, suppose the focus happens to be on a meta-analysis. Then there might be, for example, several independent effect size estimates. Let d be an effect size estimate of the effect size δ. In general $\mathscr{E}(d \mid \delta) \neq \delta$, but under t-test-like assumptions, the bias in d can be eliminated (Hedges & Olkin, 1985, p. 81). Even without normality assumptions, the bias in d might not be troublesome. Distribution free estimators for effect size have been provided by Thomas (1986), which should be useful in more general settings.

2. For each parameter estimate of focus, there must be available an estimate of the variance of the estimate. For example, if $\hat{\theta} = \sum_x x/m$, where the x are the child's responses, and $\hat{\omega} = \sum_x (x - \hat{\theta})^2/(m - 1)$, then $\hat{\omega}/m$ can serve as an estimate of $\mathscr{V}(\hat{\theta} \mid \theta)$. Of course it may be that for

all $\hat{\theta}$ their variances are constant, but in the case of children, such an assumption seems difficult to justify a priori.

The procedure does not require that there be multiple measurements for each child, but in many applications this will be the case. A single response from each child could be used, but still an estimate of the variance of that response must be available.

There are many cases where the variances of summary statistics have a simple form and are often functions of a parameter divided by sample size. These are the kinds of situations of focus here. Some common examples of the kinds of estimates that may be used within the present framework are summarized in Table 5.1.

The lack of an easily obtained estimate of variance of an estimate does not prevent the methodology from being used. One can almost always obtain an estimate of variability of an estimator, provided one has the raw data available, by using bootstrap techniques (e.g., Efron & Tibshirani, 1986).

3. It is assumed that regression of posterior mean of Θ given X (the data) is linear in X or if it is not, that a linear approximation is a reasonable one. In the case of parametric EB where the data can be assumed to be normal or nearly so and the prior distribution is also normal, then linearity is known to hold. In many real applications, however, the assumption is difficult to evaluate. In most practical applications the assumption should not be troublesome.

TABLE 5.1. Some common parameters, and their conventional estimates, with variance estimates.

Parameter of interest		Estimate	Variance of estimate	Comment
Mean	θ	$\hat{\theta} = \Sigma x/m$	ω/m	$\hat{\omega} = \Sigma(x - \hat{\theta})^2/(m - 1)$ $\hat{\theta}$, $\hat{\omega}$ are distribution free estimators
Mean	θ	$\hat{\theta} = \Sigma x/m$	$\theta(1 - \theta)/(m - 1)$	For 0, 1 data
Variance	ω	$\hat{\omega} = \dfrac{\Sigma(x - \hat{\theta})^2}{m - 1}$	$\dfrac{2\omega^2}{(m - 1)}$	variance of estimate assumes normality of X
Correlation	ρ	$\hat{\rho} = r$	$(1 - \rho^2)^2/(m - 1)$	$\mathscr{E}(\hat{\rho} \mid \rho) \doteq \rho$, bias is typically small; variance is approximate; variance estimate based on bivariate normality. r is sample correlation coefficient
	$z(\rho)$	$z(\hat{\rho})$	$[m - 3]^{-1}$	$z(\rho) = 0.5 \log[(1 + \rho)/(1 - \rho)]$ $\mathscr{E}[z(\hat{\rho})] \doteq z(\rho)$
Slope	β	$\hat{\beta}$	$\omega/\Sigma(x - \bar{x})^2$	Standard normal errors regression model with $Y = \beta x + \alpha + E$, and fixed x; $\mathscr{V}(E) = \omega$,
Intercept	α	$\hat{\alpha}$	ω/m	$\mathscr{E}(E) = 0$

Specification of the Estimators

The development follows Maritz (Maritz, 1989; Maritz & Lwin, 1989), but is abbreviated here because the main concern is with providing practical estimators.

Suppose $\hat{\theta}$ is a conventional estimate of θ, $\mathscr{E}(\hat{\theta}|\theta) = \theta$, and $\hat{\theta}$ is based on m observations of X, and $\mathscr{V}(\hat{\theta}|\theta) = \upsilon(m)$. In many cases of application $\upsilon(m) = \omega/m$, as Table 5.1 indicates. For example, if $\hat{\theta}$ is a mean of m independent observations from a distribution with variance σ^2, then $\sigma^2/m = \omega/m = \upsilon(m)$.

The desired estimates are of the form $\delta(\hat{\theta}) = A + B\hat{\theta}$, and in a way similar to conventional regression, the criterion is to minimize $\mathscr{E}(A + B\hat{\theta} - \Theta)^2$. To do so the expectation first is taken, then taking derivatives of the resulting function with respect to both A and B yields two equations that, when solved, provide the following estimation equation:

$$\delta(\hat{\theta}, m) = B\hat{\theta} + (1 - B)\mathscr{E}(\Theta) \tag{6}$$

and where

$$B = \frac{\mathscr{V}(\Theta)}{\mathscr{V}(\Theta) + \mathscr{E}(\Omega)/m}. \tag{7}$$

To be useful, the unknown quantities must be estimated. The estimates are given by:

$$\hat{\mathscr{E}}(\Theta) = (1/n)\sum_{i=1}^{n}\hat{\theta}_i \tag{8}$$

$$\hat{\mathscr{E}}(\Theta^2) = (1/n)\sum_{i=1}^{n}(\hat{\theta}_i^2 - \hat{\omega}_i/m_i) \tag{9}$$

$$\hat{\mathscr{E}}(\Omega) = (1/n)\sum_{i=1}^{n}\hat{\omega}_i \tag{10}$$

Remembering that $\mathscr{V}(\Theta) = \mathscr{E}(\Theta^2) - [\mathscr{E}(\Theta)]^2$, then an estimate $\hat{B}$ of B can be obtained by replacing the parameters with their estimates. The method of estimation is the method of moments: replacing population moments with their sample values.

There are several important features of the above estimation equations that are critical to note. First, there are $n + 1$ individuals involved. Recall that a useful way to view EB, as noted earlier, is to consider how the n past observations (think n other children) can improve our estimate of our current observation (think target child). Consequently, the information from the n past observations form the Equations 8 to 10 and are recognizable as the i indexed quantities above. The unsubscripted quantities, $\hat{\theta}$ and m in Equations 6 and 7, refer to the current observation. Thus, B in Equation 7 changes as each child, in turn, becomes the target child. Second, it is always the case that $0 \leqslant B \leqslant 1$, but it can be that $\hat{\mathscr{V}}(\Theta)$ is negative. If so set $B = 0$, so that the estimate of $\delta(\hat{\theta}, m)$ will be $\hat{\mathscr{E}}(\Theta)$.

Note that the form of the estimators in Equations 6 and 7 is similar to Equations 4 and 5. The difference appears to be the difference between expectation term, $\mathscr{E}(\Omega)$ (divided by m) and a variance term, $\hat{\mathscr{V}}(X \mid \theta)$. Note how $\hat{\mathscr{E}}(\Omega)$ is constructed. It is the mean of the "parameter estimate part" of the variances $\hat{\mathscr{V}}(X = \hat{\theta} \mid \theta)$, averaged over the "past" observations; this average is then divided by the number of observations m in the "current" estimate, and the quantity is then used to construct B in Equation 7. In an EB model for normal data and normal prior, which Equations 4 and 5 represent, the conditional variance $\mathscr{V}(X \mid \theta)$ does not depend on the value of θ, so in this case, the structure of Equations 5 and 7 is the same.

Some Intuition

The form of the estimators does not necessarily reveal why the approach "works." Maritz and Lwin (1989) provide a full development but some intuition, based on their development, is provided.

In general, the only information available is information about the marginal distribution of X. The observed sample estimates, for example sample means, are regarded as samples from this marginal distribution, so information in the sample can provide information about the marginal distribution of X. The question is, therefore, what information about Θ, or more precisely the distribution of Θ, $f(\theta)$, can be retrieved from information in the marginal distribution of X?

One key idea is that if X estimates θ, that is, $X = \hat{\theta}$, and is unbiased, which means that $\mathscr{E}(X \mid \theta) = \theta$, then the marginal moments of X can be used to estimate the moments of the prior distribution Θ.

In the solution of the linear estimation equations for A and B, $\delta(\hat{\theta}) = A + B\hat{\theta}$, the following expression arises:

$$\int \mathscr{E}(X^r \mid \theta) f(\theta) d\theta, \; r = 1, 2,$$

where

$$\mathscr{E}(X^r \mid \theta) = \int x^r f(x \mid \theta) dx, \; r = 1, 2.$$

However,

$$\int \mathscr{E}(X^r \mid \theta) f(\theta) d\theta = \mathscr{E}(X^r), \tag{11}$$

where $\mathscr{E}(X^r)$ denotes the rth moment of the marginal distribution of X; values of X are the sample statistics of focus.

As before, suppose a sample mean X from a simple random sample of size m from a distribution with mean θ is an unbiased estimate of θ. Then $\mathscr{E}(X|\theta) = \theta$, and Equation 11 becomes $\int \theta f(\theta)d\theta = \mathscr{E}(\Theta) = \mathscr{E}(X)$, and similarily $\mathscr{E}(X^2|\theta) = \theta^2 + \mathscr{V}(X|\theta)$. Thus, estimates of the moments of X can be used to obtain estimates of the moments of Θ.

To see the equality of Equation 11 consider calculating the marginal moments of X, $\mathscr{E}(X^r)$, remembering that $f(\theta, x) = f(x|\theta)f(\theta)$; then:

$$\iint x^r f(\theta, x)d\theta dx = \int x^r f(x)dx = \iint x^r[f(x|\theta)f(\theta)d\theta]dx =$$
$$\iint [x^r f(x|\theta)dx]f(\theta)d\theta = \int \mathscr{E}(X^r|\theta)f(\theta)d\theta = \mathscr{E}(X^r).$$

Note that the form of the distributions above are not specified, and thus the approach is very general. In the example of the previous section the mean of the marginal distribution of X is the same as the mean of Θ, 7.75. The identity for $r = 2$ can be checked, if desired, by using Equations 2 and 3 and $\mathscr{E}(X^r) = \sum_{i=1}^{3} \mathscr{E}(X^r|\theta_i)f(\theta_i)$, where discrete summation replaces integration.

Applications of EB Estimation

In each of the examples below, the linear EB procedure is the analysis framework. Specifically, the estimator of focus is $\delta(\hat{\theta}, m) \equiv \delta$, Equation 6, with the estimation equations defined by Equations 7 to 10. The terms *EB estimator, shrunken estimator*, and similar expressions are used interchangeably and all refer to the estimator δ.

Example 1: Artificial Data

It is instructive to consider first how the estimator $\delta(x)$ behaves in artificial data. Focus on the values 2, 3, 3, 4, and 15, the first coordinate values of the artificial data presented in the introduction. Then $n = 4$ (not 5) and each observation becomes, in turn, the target observation for adjustment. Regard these data as values of $X = x$, and sample means based on a simple random sample of size m (which may vary with each x). Each observation may be from a different arbitrary continuous distribution with a different mean and different variance, σ^2. Because each x is regarded as a sample mean, it is unbiased.

Table 5.2 provides the EB estimators $\delta(x)$ for several values of σ^2 and sample size. For instance, suppose σ^2 is constant at 1, and each mean is based on $m = 10$ observations, in which case the variance of each sample mean is $\sigma^2/m = 0.1$. Table 5.2(A) shows that only the extreme observation 15 is altered significantly; the other values remain

TABLE 5.2. Behavior of $\delta(x)$ for $x = 2, 3, 3, 4, 15$ for various σ^2 and m.

			(A)						(B)		
x	2	3	3	4	15	x	2	3	3	4	15
σ^2	1	1	1	1	1	σ^2	10	10	10	10	10
m	10	10	10	10	10	m	1	1	1	1	1
$\delta(x)$	2.02	3.01	3.01	4.00	12.60	$\delta(x)$	4.48	4.64	4.64	4.9	3*
			(C)						(D)		
x	2	3	3	4	15	x	2	3	3	4	15
σ^2	2	3	3	4	15	σ^2	2	3	3	4	15
m	10	10	10	10	10	m	20	30	30	40	150
$\delta(x)$	2.10	3.06	3.06	4.04	7.80	$\delta(x)$	2.05	3.02	3.02	4.00	14.43

* $B \leqslant 0$, so $\delta(x)$ is the mean of the remaining observations.

essentially unchanged. On the other hand, if $\sigma^2 = 10$ and $m = 1$, in which case all means may be regarded as highly unreliable estimates, then all x are substantially altered; indeed, the value 15 is shrunk all the way to 3 as Table 5.2(B) illustrates. That result is a bit unusual. Because the estimate of B for this last observation was negative, the "new' estimate is shrunk to 3, the mean of the remaining observations.

In Table 5.2(C) the variances grow as the mean values grow, and the result is substantial shrinkage of the largest observation. Note in Table 5.2(D) that the sample size and variance both grow with the mean, but variance of the mean, σ^2/m, is constant, as in panel A. In this case each $\delta(x)$ remains largely unchanged, except for the largest: $x = 15$, whereas $\delta(15) = 14.43$.

Thus, how much an observation is altered depends importantly on how variable an estimate may be, and also on how deviant that observation is from the remaining observations.

Example 2: Psychophysics

Coello and Garriga (1990) were interested in individual differences in judgments of smell among 16 school children about 9 years old. Judgment differences were indexed by differences in the parameter estimates obtained from each child's data when estimated under Stevens' power law. Each child provided three kinds of judgments in response to seven stimuli, each of which differed in olfaction. The stimuli were vessels of water with varying concentrations of n-proponal measured in milligrams per liter. These concentration levels were taken as the stimulus measures.

The middle stimulus value was taken as the reference standard. Each child smelled the standard before providing a judgment for each comparison stimulus. The stimuli for comparison were hidden from view, and thus each child judged the standard as well.

For each stimulus, each child provided responses to three different judgment tasks. Only the data from their finger span task are used here; results for the other tasks were similar. In the finger span task the child's perceived strength of the smell was indicated by the size of the distance between the child's index finger and thumb. This distance was taken as the dependent variable of interest. Each child provided one finger span judgment for each of the seven stimuli.

Coello and Garriga's analysis assumes the following Stevens' power law model (Thomas, 1981):

$$P_i = \kappa c_i^{\beta} V_i, \quad i = 1, 2, 3, \ldots, m \tag{12}$$

where P_i is the judged sensory magnitude (the finger spans) associated with the fixed simulus magnitudes c_i (the smell stimuli) and β and κ are fixed unknown parameters. Here $m = 7$. V_i is a lognormal random variable with $Z_i = \log V_i$ so Z_i is $n(\mu, \sigma^2)$. The model is parameterized so $\mathscr{E}(V_i) = 1$, a natural requirement.

The standard data analytical procedure is to loglinearize the model of Equation 12 so $\alpha = \log \kappa$, $\log c_i = x_i$, and $Y_i = \log P_i$, then the model becomes almost a standard regression model in the form

$$Y_i = \beta x_i + \alpha + Z_i.$$

Estimation of the power (now slope) β and intercept α follows the standard least squares procedure, and the estimates of β and α for each child become the estimates of focus.

The slope and intercept estimates for each of the 16 children are listed in Table 5.3. The slope estimates correspond with those given by Coello and Garriga (1990), but the intercept estimates do not, and some estimates are substantially different from the ones they report. Under the log linearization of the power law, although $\mathscr{E}(\hat{\beta}) = \beta$, the intercepts can be quite biased because $\mathscr{E}(\hat{\alpha}) = \alpha - \sigma^2/2$ (Thomas, 1981), so it seems best to correct them by adding half the estimated residual variance to each $\hat{\alpha}$. The unbiased intercept, $\hat{\alpha}$, appears in Table 5.3. Of course another reason for correcting the estimates is because unbiased estimates are needed for the empirical Bayes analysis to be reported below.

The form of the analysis Coello and Garriga (1990) employed was a hypothesis testing approach typically testing both the slopes and the intercepts for equality. In the case of finger span judgments, such hypotheses were rejected, and for the other techniques the data generally rejected the same hypotheses. Based on these tests, Coello and Garriga concluded there were individual differences in the slope and intercepts among the children.

Certainly there is nothing wrong with their approach, but as noted earlier, trying to marry a hypothesis testing perspective with an individual difference perspective does not make for a happy union. A myriad of alternative hypotheses are possible once the null has been rejected, and it is not clear which one seems most appropriate. For example, a single child might have slope say, β_1, whereas the remaining children might have a common $\beta_2 \neq \beta_1$.

TABLE 5.3. Slopes and intercepts from a loglinearized power law, with their EB estimates for 16 children.

Subject	Slope	EB slope	Intercept	EB intercept
1	0.107	0.107	0.619	0.630
2	0.078	0.089	1.162	0.992
3	0.039	0.066	1.411	1.159
4	0.259	0.187	−0.820	−0.248
5	0.063	0.081	0.896	0.814
6	0.032	0.064	1.143	0.971
7	0.370	0.158	−1.648	−0.363
8	0.115	0.111	0.054	0.260
9	0.046	0.072	1.171	0.990
10	0.004	0.050	2.246	1.559
11	0.122	0.116	0.327	0.431
12	0.097	0.101	0.728	0.704
13	0.216	0.172	−0.039	0.176
14	0.054	0.073	0.832	0.779
15	0.054	0.074	1.208	1.029
16	0.047	0.071	1.128	0.967
Mean	0.106	0.099	0.651	0.678
S.D.	0.097	0.041	0.928	0.514

Data from Coello and Garriaga, 1990.

An examination of the slope and intercept data in Table 5.3 certainly suggests some rather different values for different children. However, there are associated with each estimate just seven observations, not a great many, and so it might be expected that at least some of these estimates would be rather untrustworthy, and good candidates for shrinkage.

Application of the linear EB procedure in this case requires some alteration of Equations 7 to 10 because the variance of the estimates is not of the form ω/m. Simply setting $m = m_i = 1$, then replacing $\hat{\omega}_i$ with the (estimated) variances of the estimates given in Thomas (1981, p. 31), produces the desired estimates for insertion into the equations. Separate analyses were performed for the slope and intercepts.

The EB estimates are also given in Table 5.3. Consider the slopes first. Many of these new estimates have undergone substantial change. The slope for the seventh child, for example, is less than half of what it was before, and some children with shallow slopes now have their slope estimates doubled, or almost so. The revised slope estimates do not display the magnitudes of individual differences that seem evident in the initial estimates. Note that the variance among the shrunken estimates is now less than 20% of what it was for the initial estimates.

The intercept data are similarily changed, and some intercept values have been altered by substantial amounts. For example, child 7's intercept was changed from −1.648 to −0.363, and child 13's initially negative value is now positive. There is also a large reduction in the variability among the estimates but not as much as in the case of the slopes.

This EB analysis provides a different picture of individual differences than is evident from the original estimates. The EB analysis would tend to suggest that the major source of individual differences among children would appear to reside primarily in the intercept, or multiplicative constant κ in Equation 12, and much less so in the slope or power function, β.

Example 3: Sex differences in Correlation Coefficients

Signorella and Jamison (1978) reported correlation coefficients among measures on three tasks: the water level task, a version of the embedded figures task, and a card rotation task. The later two tasks were regarded as measures of field dependence and spatial ability, respectively. The subjects were 48 boys and 45 girls from an eighth-trade elementary school. Correlation coefficients, computed from the original data, are shown in Table 5.4.

The most striking feature of the coefficients is the apparent sex differences in magnitudes of r. Assume approximate bivariate normality of the original data, an assumption needed to admit the usual hypothesis testing framework for population correlation coefficients (an assumption that will be questioned below). Then for the boys all the correlation coefficients reject the hypothesis that the population value is zero, while for the girls none of the observed r values do so. In addition, one might wonder if there is any psychological significance about the negative $r = -0.084$ between water level performance and card rotation for girls.

If there were more correlation coefficients within each sex, it would be more appropriate to consider shrinkage estimates within each sex separately. Here, we consider revised estimates for the six values. The EB procedure is straightforward. In Equations 9 and 10 $\hat{\omega}_i = (1 - r^2)^2$,

TABLE 5.4. Correlation coefficients among three tasks for boys (above) and girls (below) diagonal.

	Embedded figures	Card rotation	Water level
Embedded figures		0.498	0.590
	—	*0.401*	*0.400*
Card rotation	0.236		0.280
	0.251	—	*0.279*
Water level	0.152	−0.084	
	0.197	*0.172*	—

EB estimates are in italics.
Data from Signorella and Jamison, 1978.

and m and m_i are either 45 or 48. An alternative strategy would be to consider transformed values $z(r)$, noted in Table 5.1, reestimate the transformed values, then back-transform to an "updated" r at the end.

It should be noted that an assumption underlying the EB analysis is being violated here: namely, the within sex correlations are not independent of each other. It seems unlikely, however, that any fundamentally different pattern of shrinkage would appear under a model specifically parameterized to account for this dependency. The issue of violation of assumptions will be considered later.

The results of the EB analysis are given in Table 5.4. There is much less variability among the revised estimates within each sex than before, which suggests that the magnitudes of differences between certain task correlations may not be as important as might have been thought. However, the sex differences do not disappear; if anything, they seem more orderly, and the consistency of the sex differences seems more evident. The negative correlation is now positive, which seems more plausible.

This EB analysis does not reveal the source of the between-sex differences in correlation, but it does reaffirm that it is real and therefore worth worrying about. In fact, it is possible to provide an explanation for the between-sex differences based on the notion of population mixtures.

In the case of the water level task the between-sex differences observed in task performance are determined largely by distinct subgroups within each sex. Within age groups, for each sex there are two kinds of performers—those with highly accurate responses and those with inaccurate responses. It is the proportional composition of these subgroups that determines the between-sex differences (Thomas & Turner). The water level task is not the only task for which population subgroups provide plausible explanations of both within- and between-group membership differences. The rod-and-frame task and the embedded figures task are other examples (e.g., Thomas, 1987). The same kind of interpretation is possible in the bivariate case where the statistic of focus is the correlation coefficient. Thus, consider how correlation is influenced by distinct subgroup membership.

Bivariate Mixtures

In a manner analogous to the univariate case, consider a two-component bivariate mixture defined by

$$f(x, y) = \sum_i \pi_i f_i(x, y), \quad i = 1, 2.$$

The f_i can be any two bivariate distributions. In particular, they need not be normal. The π are the proportional weights, $0 \leqslant \pi_i \leqslant 1$, $\pi_1 + \pi_2 = 1$. Let μ_{xi}, σ_{xi}^2, ρ_i denote the within-component means, variances, and correlation for the X variable; and similarily for the Y. Then $\mathscr{E}(X) = \sum_i \pi_i \mu_{xi}$, $\mathscr{E}(X^2) = \sum_i \pi_i(\sigma_{xi}^2 + \mu_{xi}^2)$, and again, similarly for Y. $\mathscr{E}(XY) =$

$\sum_i \pi_i(\rho_i\sigma_{xi}\sigma_{yi} + \mu_{xi}\mu_{yi})$. The correlation between X and Y for the mixture density $f(x, y)$ is just

$$\rho = \frac{\mathscr{E}(XY) - \mathscr{E}(X)\mathscr{E}(Y)}{[\{\mathscr{E}(X^2) - [\mathscr{E}(X)]^2\}\{\mathscr{E}(Y^2) - [\mathscr{E}(Y)^2]\}]^{1/2}}.$$

When written out, ρ is a complicated function of 11 parameters, so it is useful to consider some special cases. Without loss of generality, we can set the first component means to zero, so $\mu_{x1} = \mu_{y1} = 0$. Now suppose all within-component standard deviations were standardized and set to one, and the second component means were equal; that is, $\mu_{x2} = \mu_{y2} = \mu_2$. Then ρ has a simple form:

$$\rho = \frac{\pi_1\rho_1 + \pi_2\rho_2 + \mu_2^2[\pi_2 - \pi_2^2]}{1 + \mu_2^2[\pi_2 - \pi_2^2]}$$

and if $\rho_1 = \rho_2$ then

$$\rho = \frac{\rho_2 + \mu_2^2[\pi_2 - \pi_2^2]}{1 + \mu_2^2[\pi_2 - \pi_2^2]}.$$

Let this last equation be the equation of focus. First, ρ is largest for $\pi_2 = \frac{1}{2}$, and ρ decreases symmetrically as π_2 differs from one half. That is, ρ is the same if π_2 is 0.2 or 0.8 for any values of the other two parameters; and of course even if $\rho_2 = 0$, $\rho > 0$. Suppose $\rho_2 = 0 = \rho_1$, so the within-component, between-task correlation is zero. And suppose that the second component means were separated by 2 standard deviations from the first component means with $\mu_{x2} = \mu_{y2} = \mu_2 = 2$. With $\pi_2 = 0.1$, $\rho = 0.26$. Suppose this example represents girls, and for boys the exact situation holds except that $\pi_2 = 0.2$ (or 0.8), then $\rho = 0.39$. Figure 5.3 illustrates this example. Alternatively, suppose $\rho_1 = \rho_2 = 0.1$, $\mu_2 = 1.5$, then with $\pi_1 = 0.1$, $\rho = 0.26$; with $\pi_1 = 0.2$, $\rho = 0.39$.

The parameter values selected for these examples were chosen to illustrate that the sex differences displayed in Table 5.4 are not difficult to reproduce approximately with parameter values that are not too implausible. The point is that if within each sex there are essentially two groups of individuals, then it does not require large differences in the between-sex proportional membership, particularly if the within-component correlations are low, for the between-sex correlational differences to be rather large.

The idea that between-task correlations may be largely a matter of subgroup membership differences, and not importantly determined by between-task intercorrelations, appears to be an interesting idea to explore further.

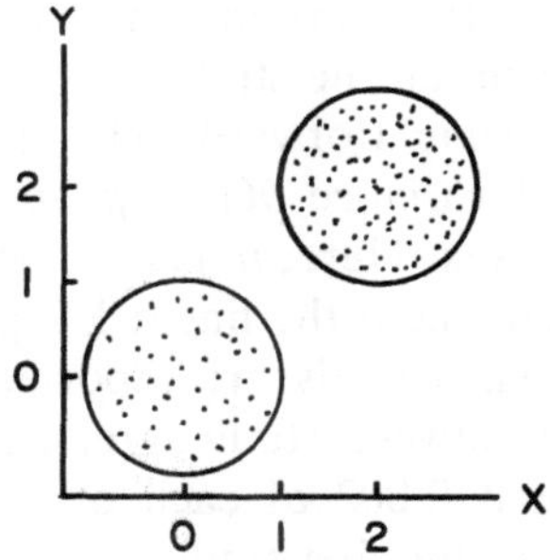

FIGURE 5.3. A representation of two-component bivariate normal mixture in the plane; one component centered at (0, 0), has weight of $\pi = 0.2$, the other centered at (2, 2) has a weight of $1 - \pi = 0.8$. In each case the within-component correlation is zero, and the within-component standard deviation is one on both marginals. The circles are 1 standard deviation in radius. Overall population correlation is 0.39.

Example 4: Water Level Performance: A Meta-Analysis

Data on the water level task can provide another illustration of EB procedures, namely, the variation in the performance across different studies. In today's jargon such an analysis would be called a meta-analysis.

A common scoring scheme of water level task performance is to classify subjects into two categories with respect to their water level task performance: accurate performers and inaccurate performers. The specific criterion for such classification tends to vary from study to study, as does the between study methodology, but typically subjects are classified as accurate if on several repeated trials their responses are within a few degrees of the horizontal. Usually the vessels are tilted to different angles on each of the trials.

Interest here focuses on the proportions of subjects in each of several different studies that have been classified as accurate or inaccurate. Because it is well known that the proportion of men who are accurate performers invariably exceeds the corresponding proportion of women, all studies report these proportions separately for each sex.

Thomas and Jamison (1981) reported data from seven independent studies conducted by different researchers. These data, taken from their Table 1, are in Table 5.5, and report the estimated proportion, $\hat{p}$, of accurate performers for each sex, which is simply the number of accurate performers over sample size. A clear sex difference is evident in each study, but among studies within each sex there is substantial variability among the p estimates. An EB analysis can provide improved estimates by using information from all the studies to improve the estimate of each study. Thus, it is of interest to determine how much each study's estimate is altered by using data from all the studies.

The EB procedure is straightforward. The unbiased estimate of the mean p, $\hat{p}$, has estimated variance $\hat{p}(1 - \hat{p})/m$, where m is the within study sample size for each sex. Here, $n + 1 = 7$ studies. This information is all that is needed to implement the linear EB procedure.

The EB estimates for each study are reported in Table 5.5. For the men, there is remarkable between-study agreement; all revised estimates of p $\delta(\hat{p})$ are within about 0.002 of each other, and hover very close to 0.7 with the exception of the first study.

For women the picture is similar, with the revised estimates just below 0.4. The first study appears to be an anomaly for both men and women. Note that the first study's estimate of p for women is the smallest of all those reported, and the revised estimate is now the largest women's estimate. This result occurred because the estimate of B in Equation 7 for the women in the first study was negative; consequently, the revised estimate is the average of the remaining six studies.

The results of this meta-analysis suggest that the between-study "individual differences" in proportions of accurate performers is negligible within each sex. However, the analysis reifies the hypothesis that there are striking between-sex differences in performance.

Example 5: Intelligence Test Scores

Skodak and Skeels (1949) report five IQ test scores for each child in their study of adopted children. Each child received an intelligence test on four occasions. The children were of different ages at the start of the study, so their ages at different test administrations were different as well. The first test administered was the Kuhlmann IQ test. This test was administered when children averaged about 2 years of age. The next three administra-

TABLE 5.5. Proportions of accurate performers on the water level task for 7 independent studies, and their revised EB estimates.

Study	Men			Women		
	m	$\hat{p}$	EB	m	$\hat{p}$	EB
1	30	0.60	0.669	30	0.266	0.417
2	123	0.724	0.712	191	0.492	0.393
3	33	0.818	0.695	33	0.515	0.380
4	59	0.525	0.718	69	0.319	0.385
5	24	0.708	0.695	22	0.409	0.397
6	62	0.758	0.719	72	0.403	0.398
7	43	0.698	0.693	58	0.362	0.387
Totals	374			475		

tions employed the 1916 Stanford-Binet. Children were about 4, 7, and 13.5 years old for these three tests. On the fourth test occasion, the children received the 1937 Stanford Binet as well. As expected, not all children received all tests on all occasions, but Skodak and Skeels (1949) published data for 100 children for whom all five test scores were obtained.

Because IQ is a relative measure, the different test scores may be regarded as replicated measurements, even though the children were not the same age at each administration. For this purpose, it seems safest to consider the replicated measurements with a common instrument, and so the focus is on the three administrations of the 1916 Stanford-Binet. The mean of these three scores was taken as the measure of focus, and the variability of this estimate, for each child, was simply the sample estimate of the variance of the mean; that is, the child's sample variance divided by 3. Thus, in this application, $m = 3$, and $n + 1 = 100$. Application of the EB procedure is once again straightforward.

Let $\hat{\theta}_i$ denote child i's estimated IQ based on three measurements, and let $\delta(\hat{\theta}_i)$ be the revised EB estimate for child i. From a practical perspective, the changes for most children were small. $\Sigma[\hat{\theta}_i - \delta(\hat{\theta}_i)]^2/100 = 5.25$; the largest change was from $\hat{\theta} = 77.6$ to $\delta(77.6) = 84.3$, a difference of 6.7 points. This is not much of a practical difference. However, for the group as a whole, there was a large reduction in total variance. The variance among the original estimates, with $\bar{\theta}$ and $\bar{\delta}(\theta)$ denoting means, was $\Sigma[\hat{\theta}_i - \bar{\theta}]^2/99 = 149.5$, while $\Sigma[\delta(\hat{\theta}_i) - \bar{\delta}(\hat{\theta})]^2/99 = 98.45$, a variance reduction of a third.

It might be expected that for tasks for which IQ was a good predictor, the improved individual estimates might be a somewhat better predictor than the original scores. Unfortunately, there appears to be no data to evaluate this prediction for these children.

Example 6: Classification Learning

Waxman, Chambers, Yntema, and Gelman (1989) report two largely identical experiments. In each experiment 3-year-old children were asked to sort pictures in one of two ways. Children in the Complementary condition were instructed to sort the pictures three times, first into classes A and not A (e.g., animals and nonanimals), then into B and not B, and finally into C and not C. Children in the Contrastive condition simultaneously sorted the pictures into categories A or B or C while passing through the pictures once. Four groups of 20 children, two in the Contrastive and two in the Complementary conditions, participated in the experiments.

Although the original motivation for the work concerned conceptual issues in cognition, a main focus of attention in the analysis concerned individual differences displayed in task performance, particularly per-

TABLE 5.6. Numbers of children with proportions of correct response and their EB estimates in experiments I and II.

Experiment I			Experiment II	
Number of subjects	EB	Proportion correct	EB	Number of subjects
10	0.977	12/12 = 1	0.974	6
0	—	11/12 = 0.917	0.899	4
1	0.823	10/12 = 0.833	0.823	2
0	—	9/12 = 0.750	0.746	1
0	—	8/12 = 0.667	—	0
1	0.589	7/12 = 0.583	—	0
0	—	6/12 = 0.500	0.516	2
1	0.433	5/12 = 0.417	—	0
2	0.355	4/12 = 0.333	—	0
3	0.279	3/12 = 0.250	0.289	3
2	0.203	2/12 = 0.167	0.167	1
0	—	1/12 = 0.083	0.146	1
0	—	0/12 = 0	—	0

Data from Waxman et al. 1989.

formance in the Contrastive groups. Table 5.6 gives numbers of children in each Contrastive group, Experiments I and II, for each of the possible proportions correct.

It is an interesting question as to how one might approach such data for analysis. (The Waxman et al. [1989] attempt to equate the two tasks through transformations makes their analysis highly problematic, and implies very strange conditions.) Upon examining the data in Table 5.6 in both studies there appear to be two relatively distinct groups: those children who perform extremely well (16 of 40 performed perfectly in both studies) and children who perform very poorly. In fact, because there was a one-third probability of being correct on each trial (under an equal probability guessing hypothesis in the Contrastive condition) four correct would be expected if the child guessed. With most poor performers having around four correct, they may have simply guessed.

It is of interest to consider how a linear EB procedure alters the picture in these data. There are several summary statistics that might be employed in such an analysis. The approach used here started with each subject's sample mean, which is simply the proportion of 12 trials that were correct, and used the ordinary sample variance of the mean as the estimate of each child's variability. Thus, the statistics for each child were simply $\hat{p}$, the proportion correct, and $\hat{p}(1 - \hat{p})/m$, an estimated variance of $\hat{p}$.

The EB analysis leads to an uninteresting result: There is essentially no shrinkage of any of the data for the two Contrastive groups, as the EB estimates in Table 5.6 make clear! There was some shrinkage for the subjects in the two Complementary conditions, but no major features of the data were altered by the linear EB procedure. This result is not necessarily bad, because it suggests something much more fundamental is occurring, and thus the search for other models is not misguided.

In fact, this example provides another instance of a case where a mixture model can be very useful. A model that mixes two binomial distributions results in a satisfactory model for the data, and that model accounts for 87% to 95% of the variance in four groups of data (Thomas, 1989).

Discussion

EB is statistical theory, not psychological theory. Thus, it should not be viewed as a replacement for substantive psychological theory. However, it would appear that EB can usefully refocus attention on which variables are important for consideration where individual differences are of concern, and which are not. For instance, in Example 2 (Coello & Garriga, 1990) where concern focused on individual differences in psychophysical responses, it would appear as if differences in intercepts are more susceptible to individual differences than are slopes. Alternatively, in Example 4 between-study differences in water level task methodology would seem to be unimportant as a contributor to the proportions of individuals categorized as accurate, relative to substantial between-sex differences. And although it is doubtful that EB is needed to reinforce the finding that there are substantial differences in children's classification responses in Example 6 (Waxman et al., 1989), that EB failed, in this case, to reduce substantially individual differences, is viewed as a strength, not a weakness of the approach. Note that in none of these examples is the EB focus explicitly on prediction of some future behavior, although that is one type of task for which EB would seem to be most suitable.

Some readers may be concerned that in certain applications of EB there appear to be violations of assumptions underlying the procedure. One issue that is likely to be raised in applications of EB to children's responses is that each child's response is assumed to be independent of the child's other responses, and on the surface at least, it appears that this assumption may be violated in some situations. Doubtlessly in some cases it is.

Such dependencies will not generally influence the main parameter estimate of interest (e.g., the child's mean) (e.g., in Example 5, the child's mean IQ scores), but such dependencies will influence the estimate of variance of the mean.

Precisely, suppose there are $Y_1, Y_2, \ldots, Y_m$ responses from an individual. Assume each Y_i has a common mean θ and variance ω^2 and $X = \sum_i^m Y_i/m$, then $\mathscr{E}(X|\theta) = \theta$, regardless of whether the responses are dependent or not. However, with $S^2 = \Sigma(Y_i - X)^2/(m - 1)$, in general $0 \leqslant \mathscr{E}(S^2|\omega^2) \leqslant m\omega^2/(m - 1)$ (David, 1985), whereas under independence $\mathscr{E}(S^2|\omega^2) = \omega^2$, and so consequently S^2/m, which estimates ω^2/m will likely be biased as well.

It is difficult to specify precisely the influence of such a lack of independence, but it appears as if it is not likely to be a serious problem in most settings. For example, multiple IQ tests obtained over intervals of several years are probably reasonably regarded as independent measurements. And simply because there are repeated measurements, even obtained at the same time points, does not mean there will always be assumption difficulties. For example, in the multiple psychophysical judgments, the only dependency of concern is the dependency of the response *errors*—that is, the random trial to trial variation—and there is little reason to think such errors are likely to be strongly dependent. In the final analysis, as Box (1976) has observed, all models are wrong models, so the issue becomes whether the model is importantly wrong. Given the useful application of EB procedures in other settings where similar assumption difficulties may have occurred, the guess is, in most applications, that the procedures are not likely to lead one far astray. More to the point, the very purpose of using EB, at least as proposed here, is to view it as a tool for distinguishing real and substantial individual differences from individual differences that are more apparent than real: those that reflect substantial within-subject performance variability.

The above presentation has not considered two important aspects of EB procedures. One concerns obtaining estimates of the variability of EB estimates; such procedures are discussed by Maritz and Lwin (1989), but for many EB applications, these estimates may be of secondary importance.

A second issue that is potentially an important extension of the EB procedure considered here is the issue of concomitant variables as they are known in the EB literature, or what are more commonly termed *covariates*. A common situation that occurs is that the concomitant variable may be a stratifying variable, such as age or sex. Thus, whereas for example sex does not itself provide an estimate of the unknown parameter of interest, it may be that estimates depend on sex. The correlational data of Example 3 is illustrative. Then in the case of sex, the variable would be a coded one (e.g., 1 male, 0 female) and this information would be used explicitly in the analysis. It is fairly straightforward to consider concomitant variables within the linear EB setting, but the estimation equations become more complex, as is to be expected. An example of such an application within the context of meta-analysis is in Maritz, Thomas, and Lombard (1990). Applications of this general framework within the context of child development will be considered elsewhere.

Summary

The problem of accounting for individual differences is the problem of providing a rich enough model for individual differences to be meaningfully interpreted. In conventional data analysis, different individuals within the same condition are regarded as being observations on a random variable with a common, typically normal, distribution. Thus, differences among individuals must be regarded as sampling differences. It appears more sensible in many situations to regard different persons as having their own response distribution and their own parameter values. EB methods allow for this perspective. By so doing, EB methods redirect our focus away from traditional issues of significance tests and toward the problem of obtaining the best possible parameter estimate for each individual. EB methods achieve this goal by using scores from *other independent* individuals to provide an improved estimate of the target individual. Knowing Jane's score does improve our understanding of Bill even though Bill and Jane do not know each other!

EB is not a Bayesian approach, because it avoids the subjectivity of Bayesian methods. Rather, it is an alternative to conventional methods. Like Bayesian methods, however, many EB methods present computation difficulties, and the procedures are generally not available in statistical computer packages. However, an easily implemented procedure, linear empirical Bayes, is described and applied to several real data examples. This procedure requires very weak assumptions; for example, normality of data is not required. In general, EB procedures are applicable to any situation where there are available replicated observations on individuals. Note that "individual" need not mean an individual person; it might be an individual group of different people or an individual statistic, such as an effect size in meta-analysis.

A main goal of EB methods in the present development is the identification of real differences among individuals; that is, the indentification of differences that are not simply attributable to random within-subject error variation. Several examples are provided illustrating the methodology and changes in perspective that result from using EB methods.

Acknowledgement. This research was supported in part by a grant from the Deutsche Forschungsgemeinshaft administered through the University of Muenster, Muenster, Germany. Appreciation is expressed to Teresa Coello and Peggy Signorella for providing data and to Arnold Lohaus for comments on an earlier draft.

References

Box, G.E.P. (1976). Science and statistics. *Journal of the American Statistical Association*, *71*, 791–799.

Coello, T., & Garriga, A. (1990). Assessing individual differences in psychophysical functions. Unpublished paper, Universidad Complutense, Madrid, Spain.

Casella, G. (1985). An introduction to empirical Bayes data analysis. *The American Statistician*, *39*, 83–87.

David, H.A. (1985). Bias of S^2 under dependence. *The American Statistician*, *39*, 201.

Efron, B., & Morris, C. (1975). Data analysis using Stein's estimator and its generalizations. *Journal of the American Statistical Association*, *70*, 311–319.

Efron, B., & Tibshirani, R. (1986). Bootstrap methods for standard errors, confidence intervals, and other measures of statistical accuracy. *Statistical Science*, *1*, 54–77.

Hedges, L.V., & Olkin, I. (1985). *Statistical methods for meta-analysis*. New York: Academic Press.

Maritz, J.S. (1989). Linear empirical Bayes estimation of quantiles. *Statistics & Probability Letters*, *8*, 59–65.

Maritz, J.S., & Lwin, T. (1989). *Empirical Bayes methods* (2nd ed.). New York: Chapman and Hall.

Maritz, J.S., Thomas, H., & Lombard, C.J. (1990). Empirical Bayes meta-analysis. Unpublished paper, Institute for Biostatistics, Medical Research Council, Tygerberg, South Africa.

Moore, D.S., & McCabe, G.P. (1989). *Introduction to the Practice of Statistics*. New York: W. H. Freeman.

Morris, C.N. (1983). Parametric empirical Bayes inference: Theory and Applications (with commentaries). *Journal of the American Statistical Association*, *78*, 47–65.

Morrison, D.G. (1979). Purchase intentions and purchase behavior. *Journal of Marketing*, *43*, 65–74.

Signorella, P., & Jamison, W. (1978). Sex differences in the correlations among field dependence, spatial ability, sex role orientation, and performance on Piaget's water-level task. *Developmental Psychology*, *14*, 689–690.

Skodak, M., & Skeels, H.M. (1949). A follow-up of one hundred adopted children. *Journal of Genetic Psychology*, *75*, 85–125.

Thomas, H. (1981). Estimation in the power law. *Psychometrika*, *46*, 29–34.

Thomas, H. (1986). Effect size standard errors for the non-normal non-identically distributed case. *Journal of Educational Statistics*, *11*, 293–303.

Thomas, H. (1987). Modeling X-linked mediated development: Development of sex differences in the service of a simple model. In J. Bisanz, C. Brainard, & R. Kail (Eds.), *Formal methods in developmental psychology*. New York: Springer–Verlag.

Thomas, H. (1989). A binomial mixture model for classification performance: A commentary on Waxman, Chambers, Yntema, and Gelman (1989). *Journal of Experimental Child Psychology*, *48*, 423–430.

Thomas, H., & Jamison, W. (1981). A test of the X-linked genetic hypothesis for sex differences in Piaget's water-level task. *Developmental Review*, *1*, 274–283.

Thomas, H., & Turner, G.F.W. (1991). Individual differences and development in water-level task performance. *Journal of Experimental Child Psychology*, *51*, 171–194.

Waxman, S.R., Chambers, D.W., Yntema, D.B., & Gelman, R. (1989). Complementary versus contrastive classification in preschool children. *Journal of Experimental Child Psychology*, *48*, 410–422.

6
On Determining the Dimension of Discontinuities in Human Learning and Development

John B. Cooney and Mark A. Constas

The Value of Psychological Science

The conduct of basic, as opposed to applied, research in any discipline is difficult to sell in a world with many pressing problems and limited resources. Justifiably then, those interested in the basic issues of a discipline are asked to speak to the potential contribution and benefits that would be derived from the funding of their endeavors. One theme of justification that is common, but not unique, to basic scientific psychological research is an assertion that the goal is to discover empirical laws for a particular phenomenon. Although the empirical laws may not be currently known, there is at least an implicit assumption that their eventual discovery will ultimately enable prescription—prescription for arranging circumstances that enhance physical, social, and intellectual development. Thus, the value of psychological research is proffered by attempting to equate the formulation of an empirical law with the ability to predict a phenomenon and perhaps even control it.

The passion or press for prescription has had the unfortunate and, we think, unintended effect of circumscribing our conception of determinism and hence the way in which we construct theories of learning and development. The problem, we think, is not with the idea of determinism or building deterministic models but with the idea that deterministic systems are, in the conventional sense, predictable. Models showing even a modest fit to data quickly gain the respect of researchers in the field although the percentage of unexplained variance exceeds, often by an order of magnitude, the variance that is explained by a model. We then bemoan the multitude of potentially important variables that could not be measured or controlled and claim that the best description that we can hope for is a probabilistic one. In a sense, we funnel all of our ignorance about the phenomena of interest into the error term of the model.

The pervasive belief in the idea that if we know enough about the organism and its surrounds that it is possible to predict and perhaps even control the course of learning and development is a vestige of the optimism expressed by Laplace for Newtonian mechanics. Laplace argued that Newton's laws of motion revealed a clock-like determinism in nature that afforded the investigator complete certainty. Once the initial conditions of the system are known, the laws of motion imply complete predictability about its behavior. Imprecise measurement of the initial conditions and ignorance of some causes prevented the investigator from achieving complete certainty. The uncertainty, however, could be captured by application of the calculus of probabilities.

The downfall of Laplacian determinism in this century, at least in the physical sciences, occurred for two reasons (Crutchfield, Farmer, Packard, & Shaw, 1986). First, Heisenberg's uncertainty principle, a central assumption of quantum mechanics, describes a fundamental limit on the accuracy with which the properties of a variable can be measured. Second, Poincare's (1913) principle of the sensitivity of phenomena on initial conditions meant that initial uncertainty about the properties of a phenomenon would quickly overwhelm the ability to make predictions about it. Numerous examples from mathematics and the physical sciences (Feigenbaum, 1980; Henon, 1976; Lorenz, 1963; Mandelbrot, 1982; May, 1976; Packard, Crutchfield, Farmer, & Shaw, 1980) provide illustrations that very simple deterministic models are capable of generating remarkably complex trajectories of behavior over time. Indeed, "all statistical tests will confer upon the numbers a pedigree of randomness" (Feigenbaum, 1980, p. 4). In other words, the trajectories from such systems are not predictable according to prevailing conceptions although we know *a priori* that the trajectory is governed by a simple rule. Moreover, we learn that even the slightest of differences in the initial values assigned to model parameters can give rise to very different trajectories.

Reevaluating the Value of Psychological Science

At first glance these findings may appear to signal the futility of our search for the variables and their rules of interaction that determine human behavior. On the contrary, we embrace the findings from the science and mathematics of nonlinear dynamical systems with the belief that they can in fact bring about the development of more powerful theories. There are two primary reasons why we believe that significant advances are in the offing.

First, recent (and some not so recent) advances in the field of nonlinear dynamical systems supply the analytical tools capable of revealing the orderliness of complex trajectories generated by deterministic systems. Furthermore, analytic tools exist that make it possible at least to identify the number of variables governing the trajectory of behavior in the absence of knowledge about the system that governs the trajectory. We view this low-level knowledge as exceedingly important. Given information about the number of variables that interact to govern the trajectory of behavior, we may divine the forms of human behavior for which there is hope of describing in determinsitic terms. An answer to the critical question of whether some aspect of human learning or development is governed by a few, several, or hopelessly many variables is within reach. For those aspects of behavior governed by a manageable number of variables we are confident that it will be possible to identify the nature of the variables and to begin the arduous task of describing the rules of interaction that govern the trajectory of learning and development. Accordingly, a primary goal of this chapter is to explicate the nature of these analytical tools and to illustrate their application with some concrete examples.

Second, the idea that simple deterministic models are capable of describing continuities, discontinuities, and the marked variability of data pertaining to human learning and development also holds considerable promise for fueling unification among the various subdisciplines of psychology. Reflecting on the relatively brief history of scientific psychology, Sameroff (1989) notes that periods of unity within the field of psychology are marked by periods when there was a shared metaphor, a role fulfilled by learning theory until the 1960s. Realizing that learning was only one of many possible metaphors, the trajectory of psychology underwent a series of bifurcations that represent the various subdisciplines of psychology as we know them today. The cost of the knowledge gained from the specialization of psychology, according to Sameroff (1989), was and is that it left the core of scientific psychology devoid of content. As a consequence of specialization, the responsibility for the explanation of "errors" was often delegated elsewhere. Everyone seemed to be passing their error terms off to another discipline. Aberrations in one psychological model of development are passed to one's colleagues in biology to explain. Likewise, cognitive psychology is quick to point to some recent developments in neuroscience as promising explanations for the aberrations in models of cognition.

The renewed focus on *General Systems Theory* (cf. von Bertalanffy, 1968) within developmental psychology (cf. Gunnar & Thelen, 1989) indicates a serious effort toward repatriating the various disciplines. Thelen (1989) cautions, however, that the success of a general systems approach will depend on the development of "principles that will guide empirical research, formulate testable hypotheses, and integrate data within and across species and domains" (p. 78). The concepts, principles, methods, and empirical examples that we offer in the present chapter represent a small step in that direction.

New Directions for the Science of Learning and Development

In the discussion that follows, we will speak about learning and development in general terms, often referring to psychological functioning or growth in the abstract. One may breathe psychological life into our abstract characterizations by thinking in terms of familiar constructs and dependent variables. For example, in language development one may think in terms of the growth of vocabulary or the nature and complexity of utterances. In the context of reasoning, one may think in terms of measures that are typically derived from such tasks as probability judgment, transitive inference, or memory span. In the context of learning, one may think in terms of the strength of a memory trace or of a production system (cf. Anderson, 1983) and the associated measures of probability of recall or speed of response. We will subordinate questions about what develops or what is learned to questions about how to model these processes in the domain of time (cf. Howe & Rabinowitz, 1991).

Simple Mathematical Models and Complex Behavior

A central problem for students of learning and development is to locate, describe, and explain the origin of psychological functioning. Equally important is the task of describing and explaining the changes in psychological functioning that occur with respect to the passage of time. Accordingly, it will be necessary for us to resort to some simple mathematical models. At the outset of our discussion, we apologize to the mathematically sophisticated reader for our lack of sophistication. Likewise, we hope our unabashed apology will encourage the readers who abhor mathematical models to persist with reading our chapter.

Linear Models

Consider a learning task that is repeated so often as to be taken for granted—learning the basic number facts. One may debate the value of teaching number facts, or how to teach them, and when to teach them. Nevertheless, learning the basic number facts is a task confronting every school-age child. Let us assume that a child has mastered the 100 basic multiplication facts over a period of 30 days. A central problem for students of learning and development is to describe and explain the growth in the child's knowledge of these facts.

The simplest model that could be proposed to describe the acquisition of the multiplication facts with respect to study time is the familiar linear model given by equation 1 below.

$$X_t = X_0 + (\beta * t) \tag{1}$$

In this model, X_t represents the proportion of problems known at time t and X_0 reflects the number of facts known before the investigation. The free parameter β in the model is the important psychological process that serves as the estimate of the rate at which the child learns for each unit of study time. Thus, the number of facts learned X after t units of study is determined by the sum of the initial level of learning (i.e., X_0) and the product of the learning rate parameter and the cumulative number of study units (i.e., $\beta * t$). This relationship is plotted in Figure 6.1. Note that this function implies unbounded growth and we would of course be taken to task to find an example of a child who exhibits this kind of learning.

Accordingly, we could revise our hypothesis to state that growth is linear but that the amount of growth decreases with the passage of time. Moreover, we might propose that there is some upper limit to the number of problems of this type that could be learned. The imposition of limitations in learning and development may take various forms. Hull (1952) proposed upper limits to the habit strength construct; more recently, Anderson's (1983) ACT* makes provisions for limiting the strength of declarative knowledge and production systems. In the context of cognitive development, van Geert (1991) implements the idea of a carrying capacity, which refers to the maximum allocation of limited resources to a task without having deleterious effects on other aspects of psychological

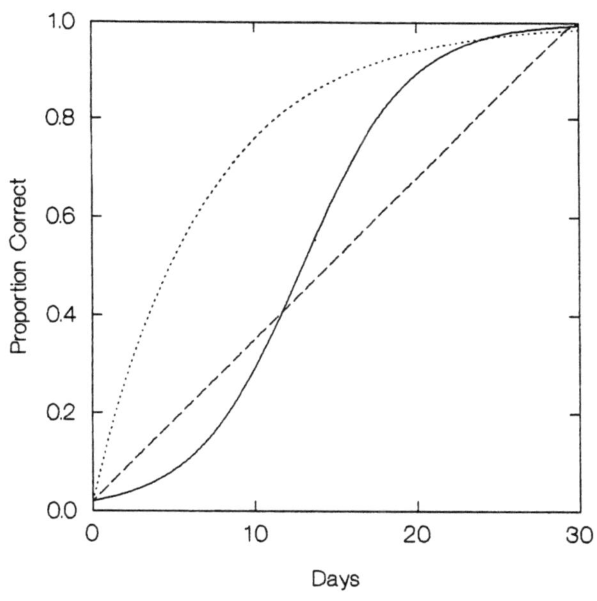

FIGURE 6.1. Theoretical growth curves for the acquisition of a cognitive skill given by ordinary differential linear (*dashed line*), exponential (*dotted line*), and logistic (*solid line*) equations.

functioning. Equation 2 reflects our revised hypothesis that the proportion of problems known after t intervals of time is a negatively accelerated function of an intrinsic learning rate parameter and the unused capacity for learning.

$$X_t = L - (L - X_0) * e^{-\beta * t} \tag{2}$$

In this model, L represents the maximal level of learnable items (or carrying capacity) and X_0 represents the number of facts that the child learned before the beginning of the investigation. The exponential negative rate of growth is determined by raising the base of the natural logarithm to the power of a negative product of an intrinsic learning rate parameter β and the amount of study time t. Multiplying the exponential function by the expression $(L - X_0)$ and subtracting the result from L makes explicit our belief that learning is a function of the unused capacity for growth or learning (van Geert, 1991). An example of this classical learning curve for our hypothetical subject is also plotted in Figure 6.1.

Alternatively, we might extend our hypothesis given by Equation 2 to assert that the proportion of problems that are known after t units of study is determined by the amount of prior learning in addition to the unused capacity. Specifically, we may hypothesize that the proportion of the problems known at time t is a function of an intrinsic learning rate parameter and the amount of prior learning relative to the unused capacity for learning: $X_t = \beta * X_0 * (L - X_0)$. Differentiating X with respect to t we may obtain the logistic growth function given by Equation 3:

$$X_t = \frac{L}{1 + \left(\frac{L}{X_0} - 1\right) * e^{(-L * \beta * t)}} \tag{3}$$

In this function, the proportion of problems known at time t is predicted by a fraction. The numerator L is the maximum learnable number of items and the denominator is a negative exponential function weighted by the maximum learnable number of items relative to the amount of prior learning. A plot of this function transformed to the unit interval is depicted in Figure 6.1. Note the sigmoidal shape of the curve. The early stage of learning is characterized by a period of positive acceleration followed by a period of negative acceleration.

There are many other mathematical models that can be constructed to describe more complex changes in psychological functioning. Regardless of the nature of change specified by models, the investigation proceeds by estimating the free parameters (e.g., β) using some minimization algorithm (e.g., ordinary least squares, quasi-Newton, simplex, etc. . . .) and evaluating the fit of the model to the data. What gets minimized in these procedures is the error or deviation of observations from the predictions made by the model. What we learn quickly is that our models only approximate these functions. That is, the data points exhibit deviation from the idealized functions and for each model we must add a term to describe these deviations. The nearly ubiquitous choice for the distribution of the deviations (i.e., error) is the normal (gaussian) law of errors. Being conscientous scientists we then plot the errors against the prediction of the model and calculate some statistic to verify that in fact the deviations conform to the normal or some other probability distribution that give unbiased tests of the model parameters.

Let us admit for the moment that the deviations of our measurements from our theoretical model conform to Gauss' law of errors; that is, we believe the errors are fortuitous. Some errors are positive and some negative but in the long run they are symmetrical with unit variance and a mean of zero. Tomorrow, an investigator refines the process by which a variable is measured that when included in the model reduces the magnitude of the errors. We must now admit that yesterday's errors were not fortuitous—that they did not obey the law of Gauss. How do we know beforehand which errors are systematic and which errors are unsystematic? It may very well be true that some errors are indeed unsystematic but we can never know a priori. Our ignorance on this point is absolute (Poincaré, 1913).

Nonlinear Models

Nonlinear finite difference equations offer an alternative way to view the sometimes simple and sometimes complex evolution of behavior of physical and living systems. In this scheme, the future behavior of the system at time $t + d$ is determined by some function of itself at time t, where d is a constant interval of time. We will start with a simple model to illustrate the variety of behavior that may be obtained under different parameter values. The assumptions are that the proportion correct at time $t + d$ is a function of the proportion correct at time $t + d$ is a function of the proportion correct at time t and the unused capacity for further learning at time t. The foregoing description suggests the following difference equation:

$$X_{t+d} = \beta^* X_t^* (1 - X_t) \tag{4}$$

Notice that at the core of this equation is a simple linear function, $\beta^* X_t$, which says that the proportion of problems known at time $t + d$ is in part a constant proportion of the problems known at time t. Again, we will think of β as some sort of intrinsic learning or growth rate parameter. Assuming that X_t is transformed to the unit interval, the expression $(1 - X_t)$ represents the amount of unused capacity for learning at time t. Unlike Equations 2 and 3, however, the unused capacity is not a constant. In Equation 4, the unused capacity is a dynamic property, a quantity that changes under iteration.

The range of behavior that Equation 4 is capable of generating is remarkable. We will focus on only a few properties of this equation that are relevant to our example (see Feigenbaum, 1981, for a thorough discussion of the properties of Equation 4). For $0 < \beta < 3$, the eventual behavior of X is known. For example, when $\beta = 2$, any $0 \leqslant X \leqslant 1$ will converge to a fixed point at $X = 0.5$. That is, no matter how close X_0 is to 0 (or 1), the iterates of X will eventually stabilize at 0.5. We will say that Equation 4 with $\beta = 2$ exhibits a stable attractor of period 1. The first 30 iterates of X for $X_1 = 0.02$ and $\beta = 2.00$ are shown in Figure 6.2. Higher values of $\beta < 3$ will increase the value of the fixed point attractor; however, an interesting feature is added to the behavior of the system. When $\beta = 2.90$, for example, X inceases rapidly over the first few iterations, overshoots its eventual level, and then vibrates toward the fixed point of 0.65. This pattern is also displayed in Figure 6.2. Now, when we investigate X_{t+d} for β in the range $0 < \beta < 1$, we find that all initial values of X are attracted (converge) to 0, another stable attractor of period 1.

In Equations 1 through 3, it should be obvious that increasing the value of β throughout its range would have the beneficial effect of increasing the rate or amount of learning. What we will see in what follows is that values of β in the range $3 \leqslant \beta < 4$ affect behavior in some peculiar and perhaps not so desirable ways. To illustrate, we will set $\beta = 3.25$, $X_1 =$

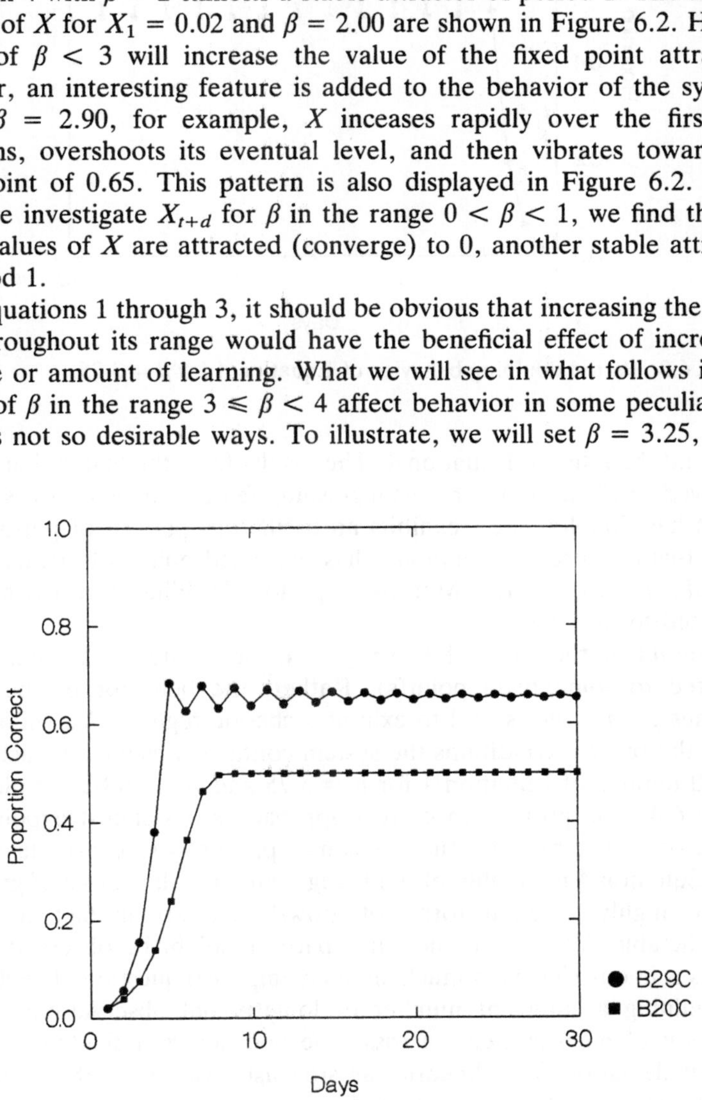

FIGURE 6.2. Theoretical growth curves for the acquisition of a cognitive skill given by the finite difference equation (Equation 4), $X_{t+1} = \beta * X_t * (1 - X_t)$, for $\beta = 2.0$ (*filled squares*) and $\beta = 2.9$ (*filled circles*).

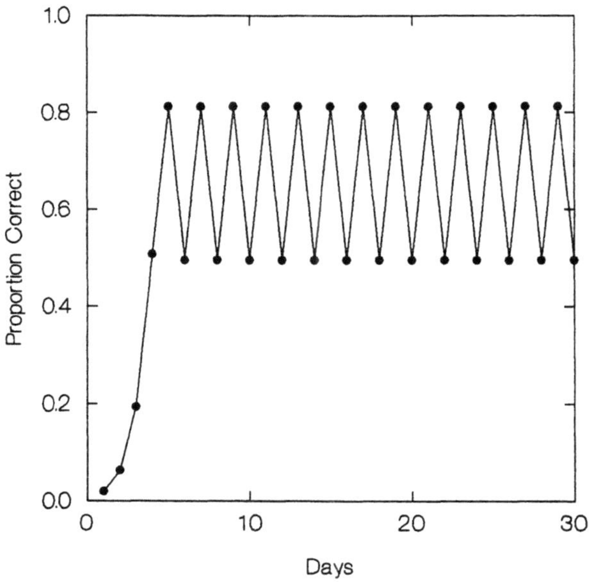

FIGURE 6.3. Period doubling behavior of Equation 4 for $\beta = 3.25$.

0.02, and then iterate Equation 4. The results from the first 30 iterates are displayed in Figure 6.3. The distinguishing feature of behavior is that its period has doubled (i.e., exhibits an oscillatory pattern of period two). Thus, this instance of Equation 4 has two fixed points of attraction (0.5 and 0.8, approximately). Moreover, period doubling progresses as β is increased toward 3.75.

When β is in the range of $3.75 \leqslant \beta < 4$, the iterates of X are no longer attracted to some fixed point(s). Rather, the behavior of the system becomes erratic and is said to exhibit a chaotic regime. We will say that under the present conditions the system contains a chaotic attractor. The first 30 iterates of Equation 4 for $\beta = 3.75$ and $X_1 = 0.02$ are plotted in Figure 6.4. The proportion correct approaches 0.8 almost exponentially fast before it begins to fluctuate in some apparently stochastic fashion. In sum, Equation 4 is capable of modeling highly regular forms of growth as well as highly irregular forms of growth that are in fact completely unpredictable. Whether or not such patterns might be observed in individuals is in our view very much an open empirical question. The difficulty of obtaining a sufficient number of longitudinal observations, the aggregation of measurements across time and across individuals, and the view of deviation from linearity as stochastic variation obfuscate information pertaining to the question. Our example raises the possibility that variation as marked as that seen in Figure 6.4 may be determined by only a few variables.

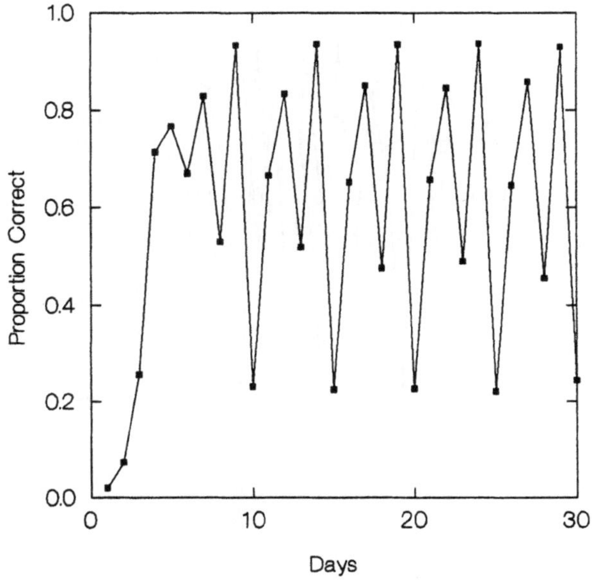

FIGURE 6.4. Chaotic behavior exhibited by Equation 4 for $\beta = 3.75$.

We may also demonstrate another interesting feature of the model for β in the range $3.75 \leqslant \beta < 4$—Poincaré's principle of sensitive dependence on initial conditions (SIC). We will illustrate this principle by example. Consider two individuals who differ negligibly at the outset of an investigation in terms of the value estimated for X_1. For one individual we measure $X_1 = 0.02$ and for another we find $X_1 = 0.021$. (These may also be two measurements of the same individual.) The first 30 iterates of X for each individual with $\beta = 3.75$ are plotted in Figure 6.5. Notice that the first few iterates yield nearly identical results; however, beyond that point it appears that all similarity ends. The student with the negligibly higher initial value appears to have achieved a steady state for another half a dozen iterates before making a transition to a chaotic regime.

Summary

Let us take stock of the differences in the two approaches to modeling the course of learning and development outlined thus far. When empirical observations are fitted with linear models such as those given by Equations 1 through 3, all of the nonlinearity is forced into an error term having many degrees of freedom. In the dynamical systems approach, the nonlinearity is not viewed as uncontrolled sources of variation to be described by a probability distribution. Rather, the nonlinearity becomes an integral part of the description and explanation of psychological func-

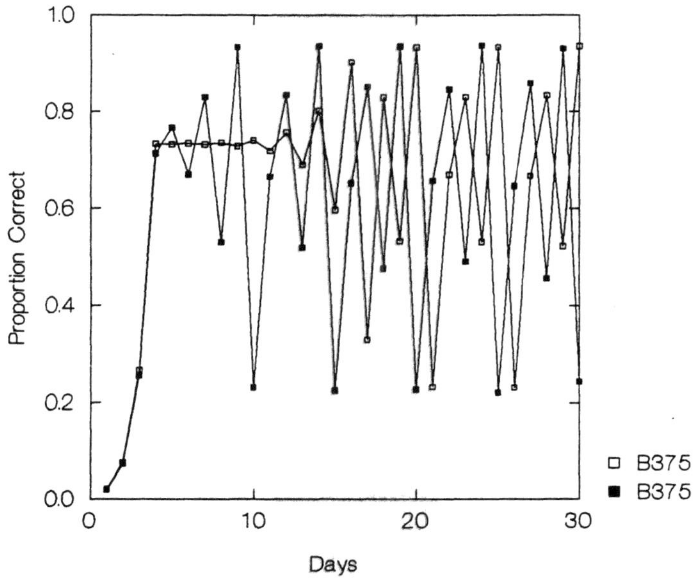

FIGURE 6.5. Sensitive dependence on initial conditions can be observed by seeding Equation 4 with negligibly different initial values of X_1, 0.02 (*open squares*) and 0.021 (*filled squares*). For both growth curves, $\beta = 3.75$.

tioning. It is clear in our example that the nonlinearity arises from a single degree of freedom (i.e., the value of β). From the standpoint of theory construction we will want to know (a) how many variables (i.e., degrees of freedom) underlie the apparent irregularity of a stream of data representing an individual's psychological functioning and (b) how those variables interact to determine the trajectory of psychological functioning. The question of prediction becomes an ancillary or practical issue rather than a theoretical issue. Indeed, there will be cases where psychological functioning governed by nonlinear dynamics may be predicted using a linear approximation (e.g., when $\beta = 2.5$ in Equation 4) althought there will be cases where linear approximations are of little practical import (e.g., when $\beta = 3.75$). In both cases, however, we would be prepared to accept the fact that X is determined and to focus efforts at theory construction on formulating the rules that govern the trajectory of psychological functioning no matter how irregular it may appear.

Analysis of Nonlinear Dynamical Systems

In this section we will begin to explicate more fully some procedures that are being used to analyze the nonlinear dynamical evolution of physical, chemical, electromechanical, and biological systems, and develop their extension to the analysis of psychological systems. The central problem is "How does one construct a representation of the deterministic aspects of a system given a stream of data from an experiment?" (Shaw, 1984). In Shaw's view, the representation is constructed from the recorded observations without preconceived notions of the underlying processes that relate the past behavior (X) of the system to the future behavior (X') of the system. Questions about the future behavior of the system (X') are posed abstractly in terms of the *state* and the *dynamic* of the past history (X) of the system. Knowledge about the *state* (or *dimension*) of the system provides essential information about the number of variables that determine the behavior of the system, whereas knowledge of the *dynamic* specifies the rule (i.e., a set of deterministic equations) that describes the way in which the essential variables interact to govern the evolution of the system. In general, we wish to specify what information is required to describe the instantaneous state of the system when (a) analytic integration of the differential equations for a system proves impossible or (b) we do not know the underlying system of equations (Bergé, Pomeau, & Vidal, 1984).

Geometrical Representation of Nonlinear Dynamical Systems

One tool that is useful toward the goal of obtaining information about the state and dynamic of a nonlinear system is to visualize the behavior of the system in two dimensions as a *first-return map* (i.e., a special case of a *Poincaré section*) or in three dimensions as *state space portrait*. We will illustrate this tool with a concrete example rather than a formal definition (see Bergé et al., 1984, and Shaw, 1984, for further discussion). Consider again the data plotted in Figure 6.4. Now, if we take as our coordinates the values of the variable X at fixed time delays (i.e., t and $t + 1$) and plot them in the Cartesian plane we have created a first-return map of the system. The result of this procedure is graphically depicted in Figure 6.6. The first return map clearly reveals that there is indeed order in our hypothetical variable of psychological functioning where before we thought none to exist. To some readers, the geometry revealed in the first return map may come as no surprise given that there exists a simple rule that determines the values of X. Undeniably, though, the trajectory of psychological functioning is confined or "attracted" to well defined regions of this space. More appropriately, we say that psychological functioning is governed by a *attractor*. We will say more about attractors later.

In this scheme, the measured values of a single variable at fixed time delays are treated as though they are a new dimension (i.e., variable). The important idea is that the evolution of any one component of a

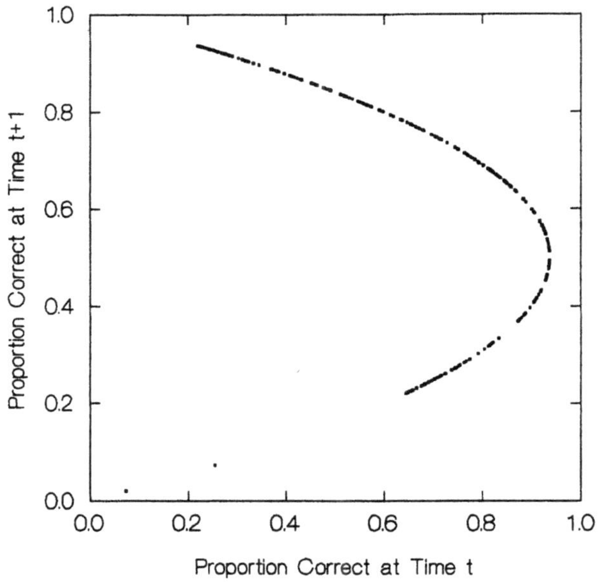

FIGURE 6.6. The data of Fig. 6.4 reconstructed as a first-return map. The x-axis represents the original series whereas the y-axis represents the lagged values of the original series.

system is determined by the other components with which it interacts (Crutchfield et al. 1986). Consider, for example, the Henon (1976) system consisting of the coupled difference equations given below:

$$X_{t+d} = Y_t + 1 - \beta^* X_t^2$$
$$Y_{t+d} = \alpha^* X_t \quad (5)$$

A state space portrait based on the fixed time delays of any one of the variables is geometrically equivalent to the representation of the original system based on both variables (Packard et al., 1980). We have plotted the first 200 iterates of X and Y for $\alpha = 1.4$, $\beta = 0.3$, $X_1 = 0.02$, and $Y_1 = 0$ in Figure 6.7A. In Figure 6.7B we have plotted X against itself with a fixed time delay, $d = 1$. Geometrically the two figures are identical. For the sceptics, Ruelle and Takens (1971) provide the formal proof of the conjecture that information about other relevant components of the system is implicitly contained in the temporal aspects of any single component.

Constructing first-return maps and state space portraits of experimental data is the first level of analysis from which the investigator may gain some insight about the complexity of the state and dynamic that underly the stream of data. The purpose of a visual analysis of first-return maps and state space portraits is to examine the geometry of the map for

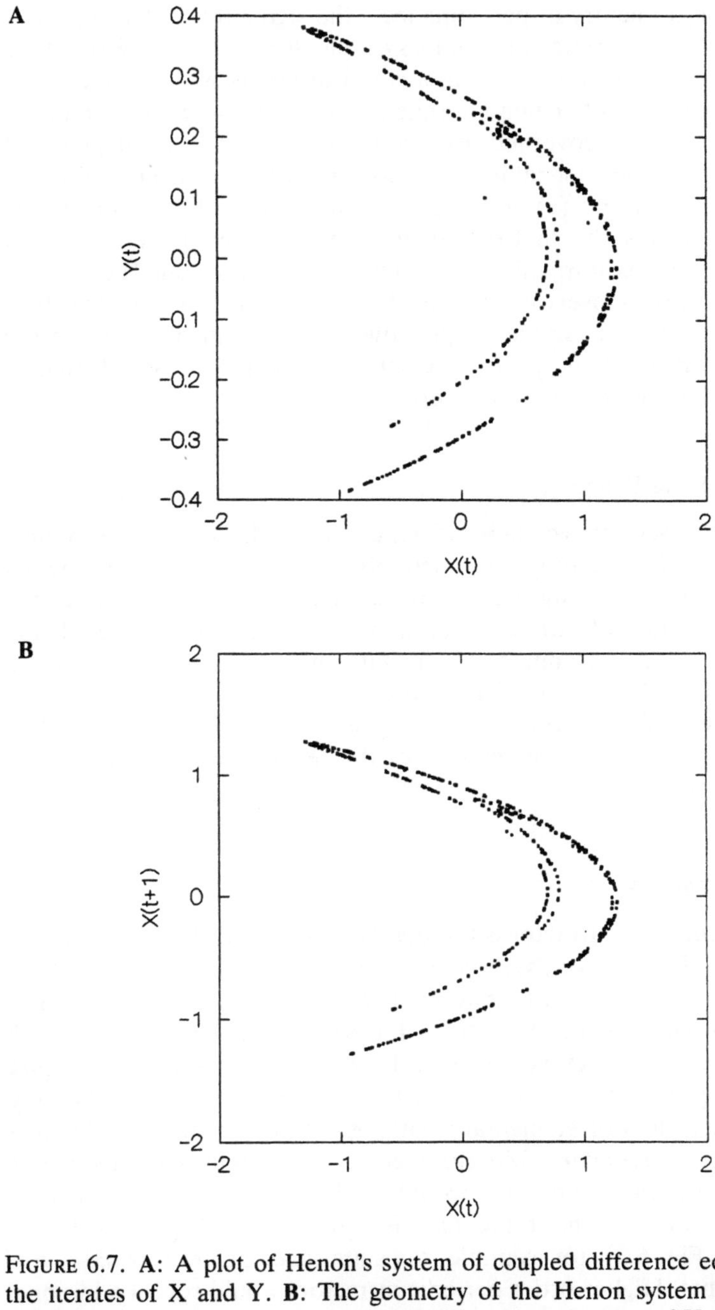

FIGURE 6.7. **A**: A plot of Henon's system of coupled difference equations using the iterates of X and Y. **B**: The geometry of the Henon system revealed by a first-return map constructed from knowledge of only iterates of X.

patterns in the trajectory of performance—the signature of determinisitic as opposed to nondeterministic chaotic systems. Bergé et al. (1984) argued that a state space portrait depicting a cloud of points without fine structure is characteristic of a nondeterministic chaotic (stochastic) number stream—one that is governed by an infinite number of degrees of freedom. Inspect the first-return map constructed from a normally distributed random variate (z) with a $\mu = 0$ and $\sigma = 0.10$ in Figure 6.8A. Figure 6.8B depicts the first-return map for the data generated from Equation 3 with this normally distributed error component (i.e., $X_t' = f(X_t) * (1 + z)$). Observing the evolution of this system reveals a trajectory, beginning near the origin, toward the cloud of points in the upper right portion of the portrait. Contrast these portraits with that of Figure 6.6 where there is fine structure.

Attractors in State Space

In the foregoing section we made reference to the idea that the seemingly erratic nature of psychological functioning could be governed by an attractor. In this section we will try to clarify the concept of an attractor and the classification of attractors. Farmer, Ott, and Yorke (1983) define an attractor as "... a compact set, A, with the property that there is a neighborhood of A such that for almost every initial condition the limit set of the orbit $[X_1, X_2, X_3, \ldots X_n, \ldots]$ as $n \ldots \rightarrow +\infty$ is A .... The basin of attraction of A is the closure of the set of initial conditions that approach A" (p. 154).

Elementry Attractors

The most elementary attractor is the *point attractor*, which characterizes a system at rest. In terms of psychological functioning a system in a state of equilibrium or one that has achieved asymptote would reveal a single fixed point in state space. Equations 1 through 3 and Equation 4 with $\beta < 3$ all reveal a trajectory toward a fixed point in state space. Figure 6.8B shows logistic growth, with normally distributed error, toward a fixed point. Another class of elementary but slightly more complex attractors are the *periodic attractors*. Measurements of psychological functioning governed by a periodic attractor would oscillate (cycle) between two or more fixed points. Without the first few iterates of Equation 4 with $\beta = 3.25$ (see Fig. 6.3), for example, the state space portrait would reveal two fixed points. Higher order periodic attractors would reveal additional fixed points in the state space portrait. In sum, both types of elementary attractors are predictable in the sense that if we know the state of the system at one instant in time we can predict its state at all future points in time.

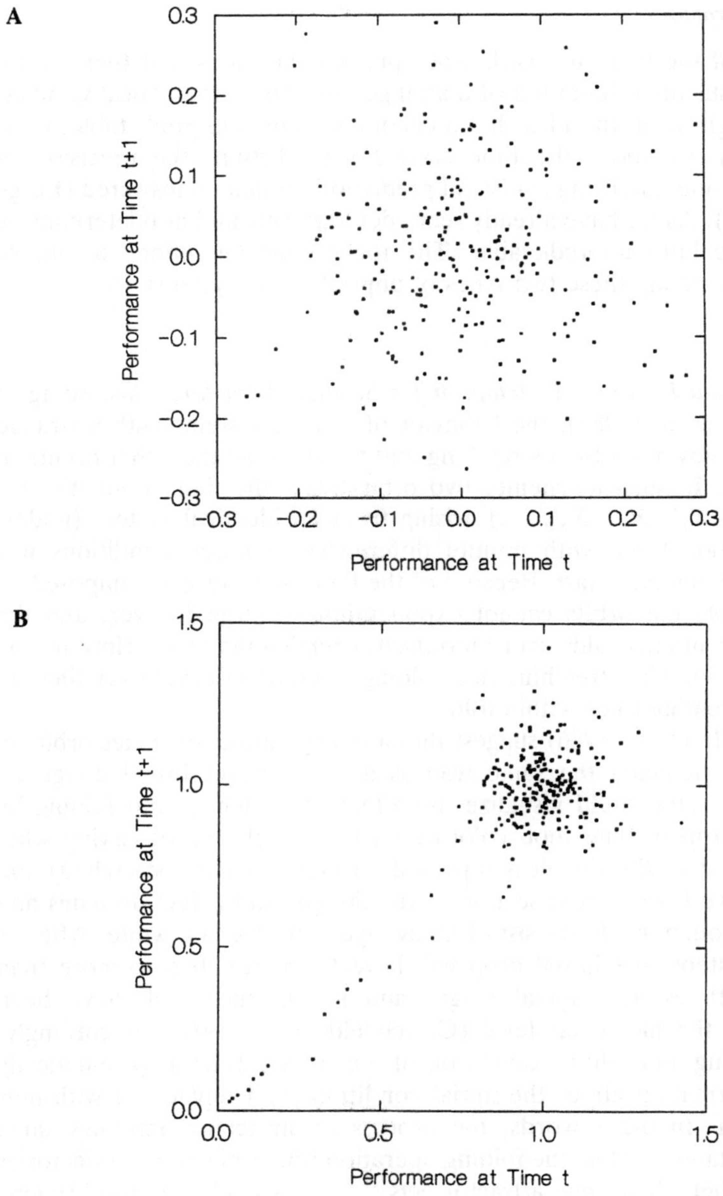

FIGURE 6.8. **A**: A first-return map constructed from a normal random variate with $\mu = 0$ and $\sigma = 0.10$. **B**: A first-return map constructed from the ordinary differential logistic growth equation with normally distributed error ($\mu = 0$, $\sigma = 0.10$).

Strange Attractors

A survey of the literature within our purview indicates that there is not yet consensus on a definition of a strange attractor. Pragmatically, investigators begin from the idea that a chaotic system is unpredictable; however, questions about the time scale for prediction, the precision of prediction, and admitting statistical prediction remain unanswered (Bergé et al., 1984). As we have already seen, deterministic and nondeterministic systems are both unpredictable. The focus must be refined to enable distinctions among these two types of unpredictable systems.

Stretching and Folding: A Metaphor for Strange Attractors. According to Crutchfield et al. (1986), the behavior of chaotic systems with a strange attractor is governed by a stretching and folding operation that occurs in state space. In such a scheme, two orbits (i.e., the time-series X_1, X_2, X_3, . . . and X_1', X_2', X_3', . . .) arising from an identical system (underlying equations) but with minute differences in initial conditions will diverge exponentially fast. Because of the limit on state space imposed by the attractor, the orbits cannot exponentially diverge forever, and the attractor eventually folds over onto itself, bringing the orbits close to one another again. The stretching and folding operation occurs over time *ad infinitum* creating folds within folds.

Crutchfield et al. (1986) suggest that a strange attractor mixes orbits in state space in much the same way as a baker mixes bread dough by kneading it. One could visualize the effect of stretching and folding by placing a drop of blue food coloring on the dough and observing what happens to it as the dough is repeatedly rolled out (i.e., stretched) and folded. If we take a cross section of the dough after a few stretches and folds, the dough would consist of many layers of blue and white. After as few as 20 steps, the initial drop will have been stretched to more than a million times its original length and its thickness will have been reduced to the molecular level (Crutchfield et al., 1986). Accordingly, the stretching and folding operation of a chaotic attractor systematically erases information about the initial conditions and replaces it with new information. In other words, the process of stretching amplifies small scale uncertainties while the folding operation brings divergent trajectories close together. A strange attractor acts ". . . as a kind of pump bringing microscopic fluctuations up to a macroscopic expression . . ." (p. 53). Thus, uncertainty in the measurement of initial conditions eventually covers the entire attractor, rendering prediction of the behavior of the system impossible. Nevertheless, we are dealing with a deterministic system.

Thus, a first-return map or state space portrait may provide our first clue to the existence of a strange attractor in a chaotic time-series; however, it is essential to obtain more precise information about the dimension of the attractor (i.e., the number of variables that determine the behavior of the system). In the examples given thus far, we know a priori the dimension and the dynamic of the system. This is not the case with a time series obtained from experiment. The dimension of the system must be evinced from more formal methods.

Numerical Representation of Nonlinear Dynamical Systems

A penultimate goal of dynamical systems analysis is to estimate the number of variables contained in the dynamic that governs the behavior of a system. Knowledge that measurements are governed by a few degrees of freedom would direct the investigator's attention to the construction of deterministic models. In contrast, finding that a system contains very many degrees of freedom (i.e., more than 10), then probabilistic models would be the best that could be achieved (Bergé et al., 1984). In the following sections, we describe two analytical tools used to achieve this level of knowledge.

Discrete Fourier Transform

A first step in the numerical analysis of a time series obtained by experiment is to search for the existence of a periodic dynamic. We may evaluate this hypothesis via the Fourier transform of the discrete time series and the construction of its spectrum. Should the time series be governed by a periodic dynamic, a plot of the Fourier components against frequency (i.e., inverse time, $1/t$, $2/t$, . . . , n/t) would reveal at least one nonzero component. For example, the oscillatory behavior of Equation 4 with $\beta = 3.25$ would exhibit a spectrum with one nonzero component with a frequency of $1/t$. The Fourier spectrum of Equation 4 in its higher order periodic regime would exhibit nonzero components of decreasing amplitude at specific frequencies. Should the Fourier spectrum reveal some periodic or harmonic structure, the task of modeling and predicting the behavior of the system is considerably simplified. If the Fourier spectrum reveals a continuous structure (i.e., no peaks at specific frequencies), one must proceed to thinking about the series of measurements as being nonperiodic (i.e., chaotic). The Fourier spectrum, however, does not allow us to distinguish between a quasiperiodic system with a high number of frequencies and an aperiodic (i.e., chaotic) system governed by a single parameter (e.g., β in Equation 4): Each will exhibit a continuous spectrum. At this point it is necessary to proceed with the arduous task of estimating the complexity of the underlying dynamic.

Measuring the Dimension of a Strange Attractor

According to Farmer et al. (1983), the dimension of an attractor is the first level of knowledge necessary to characterize its properties.

Specifically, the dimension of the attractor indicates (a) the amount of information needed to specify a point on the attractor and (b) the lower bound on the number of variables necessary to model the dynamics of the system.

The Correlation Integral

One technique for measuring the dimension of strange attractors from a single stream of data is the *correlation integral*, $C(r)$, developed by Grassberger and Procaccia (1983). Consider any series of measurements obtained by experiment plotted as a first-return map. Let $N(r)$ be the number of m points that are located inside a circle (sphere or hypersphere for higher dimensional state space) of radius r. The correlation dimension ν is calculated from the variation of $N(r)$ with r. Specifically, $N(r)$ behaves as a power of the radius r [i.e., $N(r) \sim r^{\nu}$].

One may better grasp this relation by thinking in terms of familiar objects in Euclidean space. Recall that a point has no length, width, or volume—its dimension is zero. Accordingly, the number of points in a state space captured by circles of increasing radius would not increase. Thus, $\nu = 0$. A time series governed by a fixed point attractor would therefore have a dimension of zero. Given a set of points uniformly distributed on a curve in state space, the object (i.e., a line) has the property of length but not width. Consistent with this expectation we find that $\nu = 1$. For a set of points uniformly distributed in state space on a plane, the object has the properties of length and width, and we find that $\nu = 2$.

We may also generalize this technique to maps whose dimension in noninteger, permitting the characterization of fractal sets. Maps whose dimension is noninteger (i.e., fractal) are often said to contain a strange attractor. One such fractal object that may be familiar to some readers is the Cantor set. To construct the Cantor set begin with a line of finite length and remove the middle third, then remove the middle third of the two remaining segments, and so on. The result of this repetitive operation is an object, a dust of points that are infinitely many with a total length of zero. Accordingly, we would expect the dimension of the Cantor set to lie somewhere between 0 and 1. By the method described above, $\nu = 0.63$. We will now show how this basic principle may be generalized to data where the underlying dynamic is not known.

The correlation integral $C(r)$ is obtained in a manner analogous to $N(r)$ by considering the correlations among the pairs of points on the attractor. Grassberger and Procaecia (1983) defined the correlation integral as:

$$C(r) = \lim_{N \to \infty} \frac{1}{N^2} \sum_{ij=1}^{N} \theta(r - |X_i - X_j|) \qquad (6)$$

where $\theta(r - |X_i - X_j|)$ is the Heaviside function, $\theta(H)$. If $(|X_i - X_j| \leqslant r)$, then $\theta(H) = 1$, otherwise, $\theta(H) = 0$. Bergé et al. (1984) show that the number of pairs of points satisfying the relation $(|X_i - X_j| \leqslant r)$ is also the sum of all $N(r)$, the number of points contained in circles (for the two-dimensional case) of radius r centered at every point of the time series. From the relation $C(r) \sim N(r)$, it follows that $C(r) \sim r^{\nu}$. Estimates of ν can be obtained in a straightforward manner by plotting $C(r)$ against r in standard log-log space and calculating the slope of their relationship. This method yields a very close approximation to the actual dimension of many known strange attractors (Bergé et al., 1984; Grassberger & Procaccia, 1983). The Henon map (see Fig. 6.7), for example, contains a strange attractor with a fractal dimension of 1.25. Additionally, it can be shown that ν bounds two other well known measures of dimension (i.e., the Hausdorff-Besicovitch dimension, D, and information-theoretic entropy, σ) from below, and in some special cases all three measures converge.

In practice, a more accurate estimate of ν is obtained when the experimental series is embedded in a dimension that is higher than the dimension of the attractor. For example, ν is a more accurate measure of the dimension of the Henon map when the trajectory of one of the variables is mapped in three-dimensional state space (i.e., $p = 3$). In exploratory work, where there are no a priori notions about the dimension of the system, it is necessary to calculate ν for increasing values of p. It is also important to note that $C(r)$ behaves as a power of r for a limited range of r. To avoid spurious estimates of ν, the calculation of ν is restricted to the range where the relation of *log* $[C(r)]$ with *log* (r) is linear. Using ordinary least squares, one may find the portion of the function that is linear. The best estimates of ν then are those obtained for the range of the *log* $[C(r)]$, *log* (r) relation that is most closely approximated by a linear function as indicated by R^2. When calculating the dimension from noisy data, Rapp, Bashore, Martinerie, Albano, Zimmerman, and Mees (1990) suggest that the degree of variation not exceed 10% (i.e., $1 - R^2 < 0.10$).

Summary

In a dynamical systems analysis, hypotheses about the dynamics underlying psychological functioning are delayed until information about the dimension can be evinced from the data. Information about the dimension of the data indicates the lower bound on the number of variables that are required to model the evolution of psychological functioning. Analysis begins with the construction and inspection of state space diagrams of the time series. The distribution of points in state space may give the investigator important clues about the dynamics that underly the data, particularly if the dynamics are of low dimension. Evidence for the existence of a chaotic dynamic underlying the data may be obtained from the Fourier transform. A Fourier spectrum that is continuous in nature indicates the potential presence of a chaotic regime. The dimension of the chaotic regime may be obtained by calculating the correlation integral. Once the lower bound of the dimension is obtained, the investigator is informed about the complexity of the dynamic that must be specified (i.e., how many variables must be considered to model some aspect of psychological functioning that is of interest).

Application of Dynamical Systems Analysis to the Study of Human Learning and Development

In this section of the chapter we will illustrate the application of the techniques discussed in the foregoing section to data that may be found in the literature of human learning and development. In the first example, we will consider a set of data collected from an adult subject practicing a simple cognitive skill. In our second example we will consider a data set reported by Dromi (1987) reflecting the growth in the one-word vocabulary of a child.

Analysis of Human Learning

We take as our starting point for illustrating dynamical systems analysis the literature concerned with the relationship between learning and practice. Although interest in this relationship appears to have waned over the past two decades, it continues to occupy an important niche in modern scientific psychology. Tradition in the psychology of learning is also one that has been strongly influenced by Newtonian and Laplacian conceptions of determinism. Nowhere is this influence more apparent than in the quantitative laws of practice advanced throughout the 20th century (Blackburn, 1936; Hull, 1952; Mazur & Hastie, 1978; Newell & Rosenbloom, 1981; Restle & Greeno, 1970; Thurstone, 1919). The work of Newell and Rosenbloom (1981) represents one of the most thorough and lucid treatments of this literature. After inspecting the data from a broad range of learning experiments these investigators accepted two propositions:

> Practice learning is described by performance-time as a power function of the number of trials since the start of learning (the hyperbolic is included as a special case). The same law is ubiquitous over all types of mental behavior (possibly even more widely). (p. 34)

The general form of the power law is given by Equation 7:

$$X_t = A + X_1 * (t + T)^{-\beta} \tag{7}$$

where X_t represents a measure of learning on trial t; A is the asymptote of learning, if any; X_1 = the amount of prior learning, measured on the first trial; T is the amount of prior practice (i.e., trials), if any; and β is a learning rate parameter.

The fit of this law to data stands in the history of psychology as one of the most accurate statistical descriptions of human behavior. Often the percentage of variance in performance accounted for by the power law exceeds 90%. In accepting the power law description of learning, one forces all of the nonlinearity into the error term of the model (Newell & Rosenbloom, 1981). The temporal irregularity in learning over time is treated as random jitter. Stated differently, learning may be predicted from the sum of a deterministic component, with one or two free parameters (i.e., A and β) and a stochastic component, with infinitely many free parameters.

The dynamical systems analysis outlined above provides an interesting way to evaluate the adequacy of the power law. Namely, the dimension of the raw time series would give us a clear indication of the number of variables (or degrees of freedom) that are involved in learning this task. For this purpose, we obtained data from an adult subject who practiced an elementary cognitive task for 250 trials a day for 8 days. The elementary cognitive task used in the experiment was a variant of the visual short-term memory scanning task (cf. Sternberg, 1966). The memory set, which remained constant across all trials of the experiment, consisted of four letters selected at random from the alphabet. The remaining letters of the alphabet served as distractor items. Target and distractor items occurred with equal probability in a random sequence. The presentation of specific target and distractor items were also randomized. Latency of response to the probe item, recorded to the nearest millisecond, served as the dependent variable. All latencies, independent of accuracy, were entered into the analysis.

Statistical Analysis

The results of this experiment are depicted in the traditional form in Figure 6.9. For visual clarity, we have averaged the data points into blocks of four trials. Parameter estimation, however, is based on the original 2,000 observations. The results of this analysis produced the model $X_t = 1.597 * t^{(-0.13)}$ with an $R^2 = 0.97$ (corrected $R^2 = 0.44$). Predicted values are plotted along the solid line in Figure 6.9. The fit of such a simple model is indeed impressive. The power function provides an exceptionally good statistical description of the data. In sum, we have replicated a basic finding of the learning literature. One could hardly hope to achieve a better fit of a model to data than a function that accounts for 97% of the variability in the stream of data. (We did not, as is common practice, omit data points from either the beginning or end of

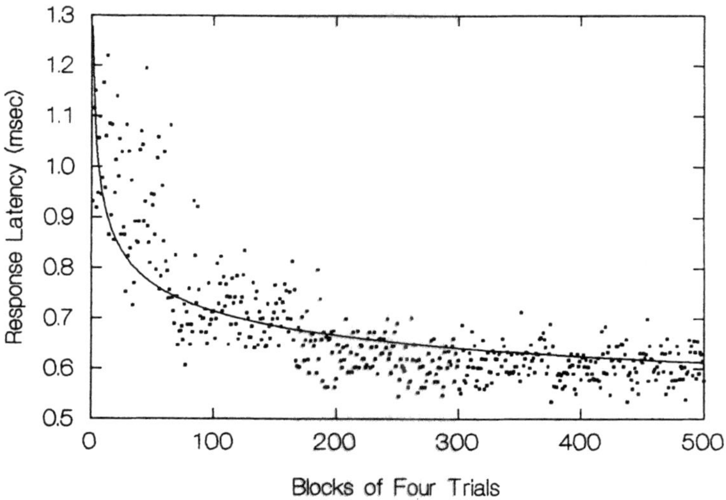

FIGURE 6.9. Response latency to targets and distractors in a visual short-term memory scanning task as a function of practice. Predicted values from the fit of a power function are plotted along the smooth line.

the time series.) As a statistical description, we find the model adequate and of practical utility, yet we are compelled by emergent views in the physical sciences to investigate the nature of the omnipresent temporal irregularity of the data. Can we assume that this temporal irregularity is governed by the laws of chance?

Dynamical Systems Analysis

Applying the tools supplied by the theory of dynamical systems, we will begin by constructing a first-return map of our time series, which is displayed in Figure 6.10. Notice that the trajectory of learning performance depicted in Figure 6.10 is confined to a region that shows systematic variation. Unlike the normally distributed random variates in Figure 6.8, some regions of state space in Figure 6.10 are visited quite frequently whereas other regions are never visited. The trajectory of performance forms sort of a grid. The empty space in the state space portrait represents some physical impossibility for combination variables. It is also interesting to note that the pattern observed in Figure 6.10 is invariant under various lags of the time series, X_t, X_{t+d}, X_{t+2d}, for values of d ranging from 1 to 50. In other words, the fluctuations are independent of the time scale. Thus, the system exhibits self-similarity in the temporal irregularities at different time scales. We believe that the irregularities are more than blemishes or chance fluctuations that distort the classical power function. No doubt, there is noise in

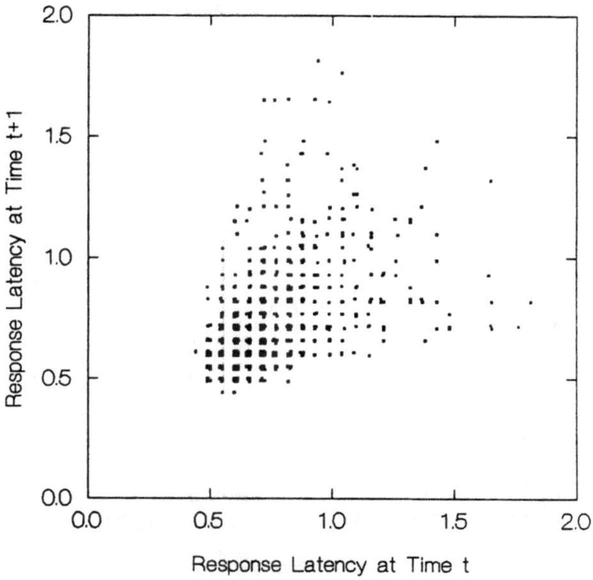

FIGURE 6.10. First-return map constructed from the response latency data.

our measurements (e.g., resolution of our clock); however, a working hypothesis is that the fine structure perceived in the maps indicates the existence of a chaotic attractor. What may not be apparent to the reader is the realtime trajectory of the dependent variable. Although the general pattern observed in Figure 6.10 emerges early, the trajectory appears to be attracted to a set of points nearer to the origin. In other words, it may be possible to describe the acquisition of this elementary skill as an increasingly stable attractor or some periodic regime.

The possibility that there exists some periodic regime in the time series was evaluated by a Fast Fourier Transform of the data. The Fourier spectrum can be seen in Figure 6.11. Note the continuous nature of the spectrum indicating that the time series is aperiodic or perhaps quasiperiodic with a high number of frequencies. Clearly, we can rule out the existence of periodic attractors underlying this system. Calculation of the dimension of the system will be necessary to resolve the question of how many variables would be required to model the experimental series.

As a first approximation toward estimating the dimension of the system we calculated the correlation integral (Equation 6) for the time series embedded in two-dimensional state space, three-dimensional state space, and so on up to a 10-dimensional state space. The correlation integral can be calculated for any number of dimensions; however, the tremendous number of machine cycles required by the correlation integral made 10-dimensional state space a good place to stop and take stock of what

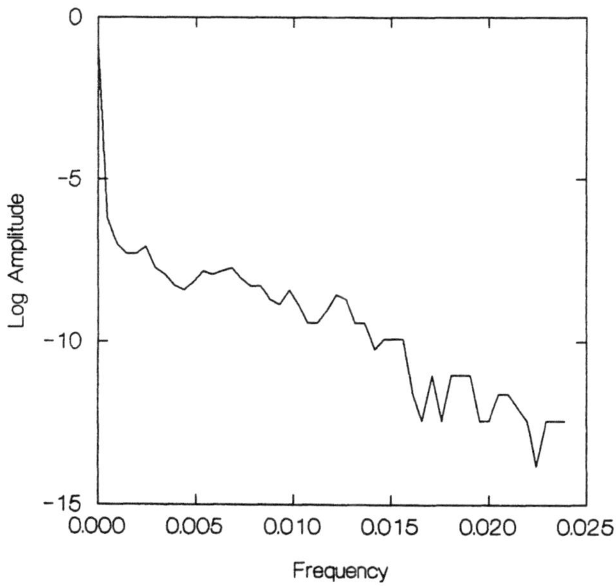

FIGURE 6.11. The Fourier spectra of response latency data.

was happening. Also, recall that $C(r)$ behaves as a power of r for a limited range of r and it was necessary to find that portion of the relationship between log $C(r)$ and log r that was linear. We relied on the method of least squares to indicate the range that was linear as indicated by an $R^2 \geqslant 0.95$. The smallest value of R^2 obtained by this method was 0.992. The slope of the line was taken as our estimate of ν. The slope (i.e., values of ν) and R^2 values are presented in Table 6.1.

One useful presentation of these results is to plot the variation of the exponent ν with the embedding dimension p. It is also useful to compare this relationship with that which would be obtained if the time series were a nondeterministic chaotic regime (e.g., white noise). This information is displayed in Figure 6.12. For a time series governed by an infinite number of independent variables we would expect to find that ν increase linearly with p. Put differently, the trajectories of such a system would densely cover any state space of dimension p (Bergé et al., 1984). In contrast, if ν at some point becomes independent of p, we would then conclude that the chaotic behavior of the system is in fact deterministic. The point at which ν exhibits stability in p is also our approximation of the dimension of the system. Note that in Figure 6.12 the estimate of ν is proportional to p up to $p = 6$, at which point it becomes independent of p. Specifically, our estimate of ν is 6.20. Contrast this relationship with that of the relationship that would be obtained from a nondeterminisitic chaotic regime.

TABLE 6.1. Variation of the exponent ν as a function of the dimension p for the learning of a cognitive skill.

	Dimension p								
	2	3	4	5	6	7	8	9	10
Exponent ν	1.84	2.66	3.69	4.91	5.53	5.98	6.18	6.20	6.20
R^2	0.994	0.999	0.998	0.997	0.992	0.999	0.996	0.999	0.999

R^2 values indicate the best linear approximation of the relationship between $log(r)$, the log of the radius, and $log\ [C(r)]$, the log of the correlation integral.

In sum, the results of our analysis indicate that the time series representing measurements indexing the effects of practicing an elementary cognitive skill contains an *attractor* and that the dimension of the attractor is *fractal* and therefore a *strange attractor*. We conclude from our numerical analysis that the measurements of our subject's performance of the elementary cognitive skill are embedded in a topological dimension on the order of seven. The estimate of the dimension gives us the number of variables that govern the irregular temporal pattern of behavior (i.e., the number of variables necessary to specify a point on the attractor).

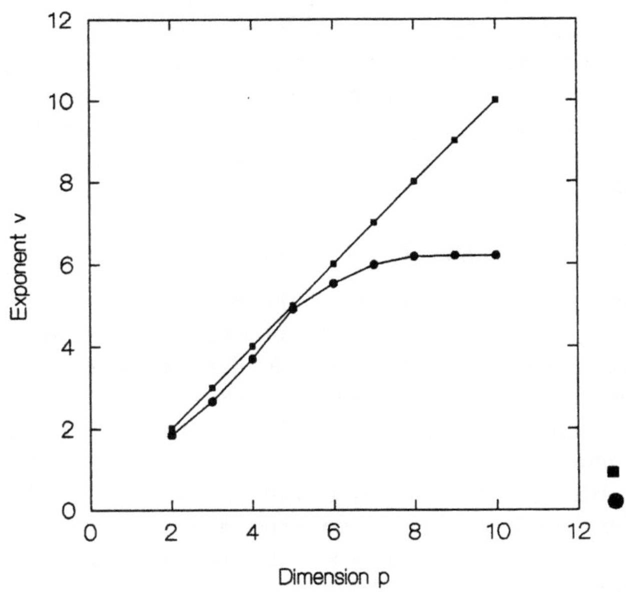

FIGURE 6.12. The exponent ν as a function of the embedding dimension p for white noise process (*filled squares*) and the response latency data (*filled circles*).

Discussion

Without question, the power law is an adequate probabilistic model of our subject's responses to this elementary cognitive task and the practical utility of such findings should not be underestimated. What we find remarkable about the results of the dynamical systems analysis is that there exists the possibility of specifying a completely determinisitic model to describe our subject's performance without appealing to the laws of chance. Of the great many variables that could potentially affect the behavior of our subject, the present analysis indicates that only a handful are required to describe the temporal irregularities evident in the raw data.

The variables pertaining to the dynamic underlying the acquisition of this elementary cognitive skill are part of the larger question about learning. At this point, we know only approximately the number, but not the nature, of the variables or their rules of interaction. Moreover, we do not know how the dimension would vary among individuals learning the same task or within an individual performing the task under varying conditions. The more difficult task of identifying the nature of the six or seven functionally independent variables indicated by our present analysis and specifying their rules of interaction (i.e., the dynamic) lies ahead of us.

For reasons that we will address in the general discussion below, our plan is to proceed with the study of interindividual and intraindividual differences in the dynamical properties of data obtained from larger scale experiments similar to that described in this section of our chapter. For example, we would like to know if estimates of dimension vary within an individual when the size of the memory set is varied. Such information would be useful for identifying scalar changes in one or more control parameters or whether control parameter(s) change over time (cf. Thelen, 1989).

Analysis of Language Development

Our second example is drawn from the work of Dromi (1986, 1987), which provides an extremely rich set of data describing her daughter's (Keren) acquisition of a one-word vocabulary. Beginning with the first word ("haw haw") symbolizing a dog's bark at an age of 10 months, 12 days and continuing until Keren uttered her first two-word sentence at an age of 17 months, 28 days, Keren's initial extension of new comprehensible words were meticulously recorded. Dromi (1987, Appendix A) provides the data necessary to reconstruct Keren's complete cumulative lexicon of 337 words at the one-word stage on a day-by-day basis. These data are plotted in Figure 6.13A.

Given our focus on determining the complexity of the underlying dynamic, we will sidestep much of the theoretical dabate surrounding this period of language development. It will be useful, however, to summarize

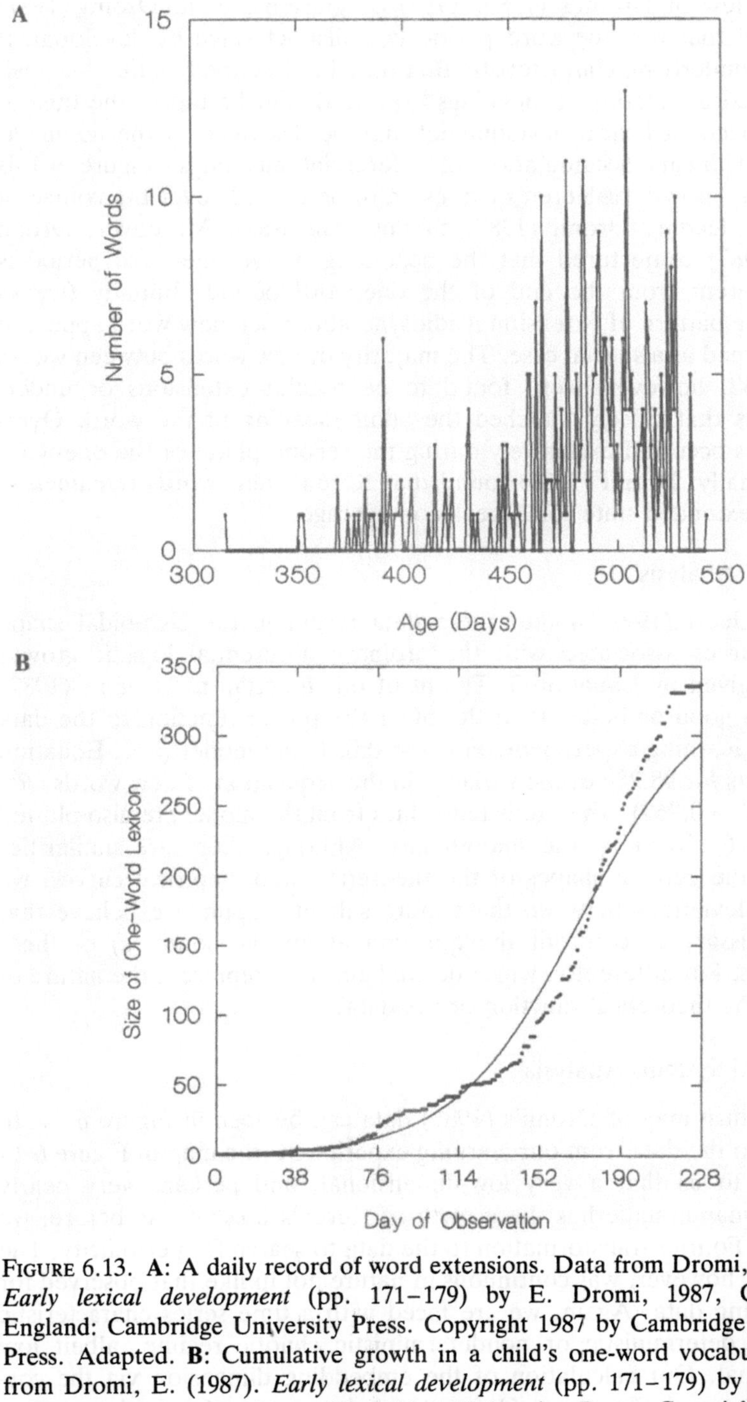

FIGURE 6.13. **A**: A daily record of word extensions. Data from Dromi, E. (1987). *Early lexical development* (pp. 171–179) by E. Dromi, 1987, Cambridge, England: Cambridge University Press. Copyright 1987 by Cambridge University Press. Adapted. **B**: Cumulative growth in a child's one-word vocabulary. Data from Dromi, E. (1987). *Early lexical development* (pp. 171–179) by E. Dromi, 1987, Cambridge, England: Cambridge University Press. Copyright 1987 by Cambridge University Press. Adapted.

briefly a few of Dromi's (1986, 1987) conclusions. First, Dromi (1987) concluded that the one-word period is a distinct stage of development with the underlying characteristic that may be described as the "acquisition of lexical referential meanings" (p. 154). Furthermore, the quantitative aspects of lexical development may be described as the nonlinear (i.e., curvilinear) accumulation of referential meanings. Figure 6.13B depicts the growth of Keren's extension of new words over the course of the study leading Dromi (1987) to this conclusion. Moreover, Dromi (1986, 1987) conjectured that the beginning of the one-word period is very different from the end of the one-word period. Initially (weeks 1–18), the pattern of extension is idiosyncratic. Each new word appeared to be learned as a special case. The majority of new words between weeks 19 and 32, however, were found to be regular extensions or underextensions that closely matched the adult meaning of the word. Overextensions occurred exclusively during the second phase of the one-word stage. Finally, Dromi (1986) found that Keren's new words remained in an underextended state for 2 weeks on average.

Statistical Analysis

As van Geert (1991) noted, these data resemble the sigmoidal shape of the curves associated with the ordinary differential logistic growth function given by Equation 3. The fit of this function to Dromi's (1987) data is as good or better than the fit of the power function to the data from our learning experiment. For $\beta = 0.034$, the model (i.e., Equation 3) accounts for 98.2% of the variance in the acquisition of new words (R^2-Corrected = 0.969). The predicted values from the model are also plotted in Figure 6.14B along the smooth line. Although there are similarities between the general shapes of the theoretical and empirical curves, we find the deviations between them more salient. Again, we believe that it is necessary to confront the question about the source(s) of these deviations. Put differently, which do we believe to represent the nature of things—the theoretical function or the data?

Dynamical Systems Analysis

A first-return map of Dromi's (1987) data can be seen in Figure 6.14. In contrast to the data from our learning experiment, the map in Figure 6.14 indicates to us that a very low-dimensional, and perhaps very nearly linear, dynamic underlies the growth of Keren's lexicon. As before, we applied a Fourier transformation to the data to search for periodicity. The spectrum, however, was continuous in nature not unlike that observed for the learning data. Again, we are faced with a time series characteristic of either deterministic or nondeterministic chaotic regime, albeit low dimensional. Our calculation of the embedding dimension via the correlation integral (Equation 6) for dimensions up to 6 corroborate our

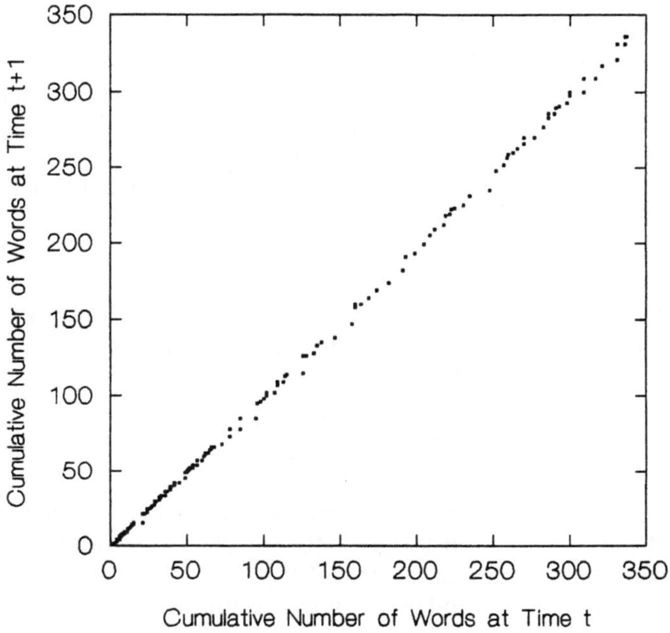

FIGURE 6.14. A first-return map of the growth in a child's one-word vocabulary. Data from Dromi, E. (1987). *Early lexical development* (pp. 171–179) by E. Dromi, 1987, Cambridge, England: Cambridge University Press. Copyright 1987 by Cambridge University Press. Adapted.

TABLE 6.2. Variation of the exponent ν as a function of the dimension p for the growth in a child's one-word vocabulary.

	Dimension p				
	2	3	4	5	6
Exponent ν	0.45	0.63	0.72	0.77	0.81
R^2	0.989	0.990	0.992	0.992	0.997

R^2 values indicate the best linear approximation of the relationship between *log*(r), the log of the radius, and *log* [$C(r)$], the log of the correlation integral.

hunch. Values of the exponent ν are presented in Table 6.2 where one can verify that $\nu < 1$. Our preliminary estimate of the dimension of the dynamic underlying Keren's accumulation of new word meanings is taken to be 0.81. The important finding is not so much the value of the estimate as the fact that the data exhibit a fractal property and that this aspect of a child's development may in fact be described by a very simple dynamic.

Discussion

Our finding of the existence of a low-dimensional dynamic underlying this subject's acquisition of a one-word vocabulary lends some support to van Geert's (1991) modeling of this process using a simple finite differences equation for logistic growth. van Geert (1991) proposed that Keren's acquisition of new word meanings could be described by an iterative equation for growth as follows:

$$X_{t+d} = (1 + \beta') * X_t \tag{8}$$

In this equation the parameter β' is taken to be a function of the unused opportunity for growth relative to the carrying capacity and a constant intrinsic growth rate parameter:

$$\beta' = \beta * \frac{(L - X_t)}{L} \tag{9}$$

The carrying capacity is viewed as the limit (L) or maximal number of words that the child could learn given the internal and external conditions of cognitive support (see van Geert, 1991, pp. 6–7 for further discussion). Combining Equations 8 and 9 gives the following equation for logistic growth after a specified feedback delay d:

$$X_{t+d} = X_t + \beta * X_t - \beta * \frac{X_t^2}{L} \tag{10}$$

Using Dromi's (1986) data aggregated by weeks, van Geert (1991) shows that Equation 10 with an estimated carrying capacity of $L = 350$ words, a growth rate parameter of $\beta = 0.71$, and a feedback delay interval of $d =$ 2 weeks provided a fit to the empirical data that was superior to the ordinary differential logistic equation (i.e., Equation 3 above). The choice of the feedback delay interval was based on Dromi's observation that new words existed in an underextended state for about 2 weeks. Moreover, proceeding from Dromi's (1986) argument that the one-word stage of language development really consisted of two distinct phases, van Geert (1991) reported an even better fit of the model to the data by assuming a two-step growth process (i.e., weeks 1–12 vs. weeks 13–32). Although the initial growth phase was not modeled, the second stage or substage was modeled quite accurately with $\beta = 0.35$ and $d = 1$ week.

Inspection of the data plotted daily indicate the possibility of a three-step process. The emergence of the first word referring to a dog's bark ("haw haw") at 10 months, 12 days of age was followed by a long period (35 days) in which no new words were recorded. The next longest delay (16 days) occurred after the acquisition of the fourth word ("ham" said while feeding) recorded at 11 months 18 days of age. This seems to be a period that is qualitatively and quantitatively distinct from the next stage where new extensions were idiosyncratic, and the following stage where new words were attached to categories similar to those of adult speakers of the language. We agree with Dromi (1986) and van Geert (1991) that it would not be prudent to generalize these conclusions to other children from an N of 1 study; however, it seems to be a reasonable hypothesis that bears scrutiny in future investigations. Regardless of the verity of the foregoing ad hoc conjectures, the important point is that complex and perhaps unpredictable changes in behavioral ontogeny can be modeled via scalar or gradual changes in the control parameters (i.e., β, L, or d) of a simple mathematical model.

General Discussion

Dynamical systems analysis has opened a veritable Pandora's box from which questions about how to conduct psychological research overwhelm us. One may retain the practical utility of stochastic modeling; however, one must not confuse such models with explanations of behavioral ontogeny when there is evidence that ontogeny is governed by the interaction of a finite number of variables. Moreover, it should be emphasized that adopting a dynamical systems approach does not necessarily advocate abandonment of the precepts of extant psychological theories of human development and learning. Rather, it suggests organization of those precepts around a shared metaphor—an ecosystem of cognitive and organismic "species" (van Geert, 1991). That is, one may continue to speak the language of Piagetian, neo-Piagetian (Pascual-Leone, 1970; Case, 1985), information processing (Newell & Simon, 1972), parallel distributed processing (Rummelhart & McClelland, 1986), or the new intuitionism (Brainerd & Reyna, 1990, this volume; Reyna & Brainerd, 1991) but not without addressing the question of how the "species" compete against or complement one another.

The metaphor of an ecosystem of cognitive and organismic species necessitates the specification of the nature and origin of the resources that contribute to cognitive and organismic growth and for which the species compete. van Geert (1991) specifies four general categories of resources: *spatiotemporal*, *informational*, *motivational*, and *material*. Each type of resource may further be defined to exist *internally* or *externally* with respect to the individual. Internal spatiotemporal resources, for example, refer to familiar constructs such as the span of apprehension, attentional capacity or working memory capacity (i.e., spatial resources), and the amount of time that may be allocated to some cognitive activity relative to other activities (i.e., temporal resources). External spatiotemporal resources, in contrast, refer to restrictions or structure in space and time imposed by caretakers, educators, and other persons with which the individual interacts. Internal informational resources are the knowledge and skills already acquired or developed, whereas external informational resources refer to the forms of knowledge and skills that are available to the individual such as language and other symbolic systems. Internal motivational resources consist of perhaps the level of arousal, activation, or cognitive effort that may be devoted to cognitive activity that are governed by external motivational resources in the form of task-specific payoffs. Finally, internal material resources consist of the physical, physiological, and neurological systems that have developed. External material resources, in contrast, refer to such things as nutrition, shelter, safety, and tools (see van Geert, 1991 for further discussion).

The calculated dimensionality of some measured aspect of learning or development gives us some clue about how many resources are "in play," so to speak. The best that we can do in our present state of knowledge to identify the relevant resources is to manipulate and control systematically (or observe the natural variation) those resources that we believe to be important and to observe their impact on the dimensionality of a measured variable. For example, in our learning experiment, manipulation of the size of the memory set or the introduction of a secondary task would constitute increased competition for internal spatial resources within the framework outlined above. Dimensionality that remains invariant to changes in resource systems hypothesized to be critical to the acquisition of a skill would serve as evidence to the contrary. Similarly, invariant dimensionality of lexical growth under variation of external informational resources such as the richness of the linguisitic context would send the investigator looking elsewhere for the critical resources. Sensitivity of the measured variable to resource manipulations, however, would serve as a strong signal that a critical resource system had been identified. The work of Thelen (1989) and her colleagues (Fogel & Thelen, 1987; Thelen, Kelso, & Fogel, 1987; Thelen, Ulrich, & Niles, 1987) on motor development provides many insights to the design of experiments from the perspective of the theory of dynamical systems.

Another approach that appears to have some immediate value is to proceed with analyzing and cataloging the dynamic properties of existing sets of data, with sufficient data points, published in the literature on human development and learning. Bergé et al. (1984) report that reasonably accurate estimates of the correlation integral are obtained with around 100 datum points. Although this number exceeds the number of datum points typically reported in the human development and learning literature, we hope that the present findings might spur investigators to reanalyze data sets originally analyzed in an aggregated form and in the future to design studies enabling more copious data collection.

Conclusions

Determinism is taking on new meaning in the light of advances in several branches of science and mathematics. Scientists working in many disciplines are finally coming to grips with the irregularities and unpredictability inherent in their data and increasingly are becoming unwilling to accept chance as a description of our ignorance about the causes of behavior—the laws of nature. We began this discussion by calling into question the practice equating the formulation of an empirical law with the ability to predict a phenomenon and perhaps even control it. The general tactic in psychology is to treat the deviations of empirical observations from the proposed lawful relationship as noise. Our motivation for writing this chapter was to explicate one framework for thinking about such problems without prematurely conceding that the ubiquitous irregularities in behavioral ontogeny are fortuitous.

The traditional mathematics of differential and partial differential equations and of statistics taught us to simplify rather than confront the complexity in our data. In many instances, this approach may supply information adequate for the purposes of prediction and prescription. There is, however, another kind of simplification that may be introduced into our models of nature. In an address to the Mathematics Panel of the American Association for the Advancement of Science, Fazarinc (1987) argued:

> We no longer need to ignore . . . complications that are all around us and that keep reminding us that our [closed-form] solutions are a mere shadow of the truth. Let us remove the crutch we use when the observations do not match our predictions. Let us use instead the mathematical tool [of finite differences] that has no excuses. This can only make our future generations more honest about their findings. (p. 39)

That is, by passing from the infinitesimal calculus to the finite difference calculus it is possible to arrive at a mathematical formalism, yielding statistical variation, that can be explored with modest mathematical knowledge (i.e., elementary algebra) and computational resources (i.e., desktop computers) (Bergé et al., 1984). For the serious student, software available from Yorke (1988) is a good place to start an exploration of dynamical systems.

As we toiled through the literature in the domains of physics, chemistry, biology, and the psychology of learning it became clear that nonlinearity is omnipresent. Moreover, there are phenomena in the physical sciences that, in our judgment, yield so-called error terms bounding those found in psychology. Despite the acknowledged ubiquity of nonlinearity in nature, we were not prepared for the indifference and resistance experienced in our attempts to discuss the ideas advanced in this chapter with members of the academy. The divorce of determinism from prediction is indeed a painful process. The ideas described above are not new and they are certainly not the product of our intellects. Rather, the foundation for the analysis undertaken herein was elucidated by Poincaré (1913) at the turn of this century and neither of us have a ready explanation for why psychology followed Laplace and Gauss rather than Poincaré. The substance of Poincaré's thinking, however, is conspicuously absent in our theorizing about human behavior. It would be reassuring to know that we were operating in the noise of our measuring instruments. The results of the present investigation serve as one contradiction to that claim.

A key concept that allows us to distinguish those forms of behavior governed by the interaction of a great multitude of variables from those that are governed by the interaction of only a few variables is that of dimension. We have argued that the dimension of a measured variable's trajectory reflects the complexity of the system in which behavior is embedded (Shaffer, 1984; Shaffer & Kot, 1985). Complexity, in this view, is equated with the number of resource systems interacting to govern the trajectory of behavior.

When one makes the shift to thinking about a system of resources in which behavior is embedded, it is possible to shed conventional dualisms (e.g., nature vs. nurture, basic vs. applied) and unidirectional causality (genotype → phenotype) (Oyama, 1989). Our search for the critical components that are assembled to meet the demands of a changing environment must span many levels of analysis, Moreover, no one level of analysis assumes importance over another. Thelen (1989) argues that the physical and social context in which development occurs is more than a supportive framework for the operation of phylogenetic mechanisms. They are integral components. For example, Bower (1989) reported that congenitally blind infants will exhibit patterns of intellectual development similar to those of sighted infants when the former are provided an opportunity to learn about the properties of objects in space via sonic representations. The point is that one cannot give priority to either the genetic component or the contextual component. Scalar changes to their critical parameters would greatly alter the course of intellectual development. Thus, our attention is focused on the important question of how relevant components interact rather than the question of which level of analysis is more important. It should now be clear that the theory of dynamical systems is one of radical interactionism. Additionally, it should be clear that there is much more to this view than token acknowledgment that behavioral ontogeny arises from the interaction of various factors. It necessitates answering the questions of which systems are involved and how those systems interact to govern behavioral ontogeny. It is the view of radical interactionism that we believe holds potential for bringing together the fractionated discipline of psychology.

Acknowledgments. The writing of this chapter was supported in part by funding from the Center for Research on Teaching and Learning at the University of Northern Colorado. We would like to thank Mark Howe, Bob Pasnak, and Teresa McDevitt for their encouragement and constructively critical comments on earlier drafts of this chapter.

References

Anderson, J.R. (1983). *The architecture of cognition*. Cambridgé, MA: Harvard University Press.

Bergé, P., Pomeau, Y., & Vidal, C. (1984). *Order within chaos: Towards a deterministic approach to turbulence*. New York: John Wiley & Sons.

Blackburn, J.M. (1936). *The acquisition of skill: An analysis of learning curves* (Report No. 73). London: His Majesty's Stationery Office.

Bower, T.G.R. (1989). *The rational infant: Learning in infancy*. New York: W.H. Freeman.

Brainerd, C.J., & Reyna, V.F. (1990). Gist is the grist: Fuzzy-trace theory and the new intuitionism. *Developmental Review*, *10*, 3–47.

Case, R. (1985). *Intellectual development: Birth to adulthood*. New York: Academic Press.

Crutchfield, J.P., Farmer, J.D., Packard, N.H., & Shaw, R.S. (1986). Chaos, *Scientific American*, *225*, 46–57

Dromi, E. (1986). The one-word period as a stage in language development: Quantitative and qualitative accounts. In I. Levin (Ed.), *Stage and structure: Reopening the debate* (pp. 220–245). Norwood, NJ: Ablex.

Dromi, E. (1987). *Early lexical development*. Cambridge, England: Cambridge University Press.

Farmer, J.D., Ott, E., & Yorke, J.A. (1983). The dimension of chaotic attractors. *Physica*, *7D*, 153–179.

Fazarinc, Z. (1987, March). A viewpoint on calculus. *Hewlett-Packard Journal*, pp. 38–40.

Feigenbaum, M.J. (1980). Universal behavior in nonlinear systems. *Los Alamos Science*, *1*, 4–27.

Fogel, A., & Thelen, E. (1987). The development of expressive communicative action in the forst year: Reinterpreting the evidence from a dynamic systems perspective. *Developmental Psychology*, *23*, 747–761.

Grassberger, P., & Procaccia, I. (1983). Characterization of strange attractors. *Physical Review Letters*, *50*(5), 346–349.

Gunnar, M.R., & Thelen, E. (Eds.) (1989). *The Minnesota symposia on child development: Vol. 22. Systems and development*. Hillsdale, NJ: Erlbaum.

Henon, M. (1976). A two-dimensional mapping with a strange attractor. *Communications in Mathematical Physics*, *50*, 69–77.

Howe, M.L., & Rabinowitz, F.M. (1991). Development: Sequences, structure, and chaos. *Annals of Theoretical Psychology*, *7*, 65–72.

Hull, C.L. (1952). *A behavior system: An introduction to behavior theory concerning the individual organism*. New Haven, CT: Yale University Press.

Lorenz, E.N. (1963). Deterministic nonperiodic flow. *Journal of the Atmospheric Sciences*, *20*, 130–141.

Mandelbrot, B.B. (1982). *The fractal geometry of nature*. San Francisco, CA: W.H. Freeman.

May, R.M. (1976). Simple mathematical models with very complicated dynamics. *Nature*, *261*, 459–467.

Mazur, J.E., & Hastie, R. (1978). Learning as accumulation: A reexamination of the learning curve. *Psychological Bulletin*, *85*, 1256–1274.

Newell, A., & Rosenbloom, P.S. (1981). Mechanisms of skill acquisition and the law of practice. In J.R. Anderson (Ed.), *Cognitive skills and their acquisition* (pp. 1–54). Hillsdale NJ: Erlbaum.

Newell, A., & Simon, H.A. (1972). *Human problem solving*. Englewood Cliffs, NJ: Prentice-Hall.

Oyama, S. (1989). Ontogeny and the central dogma: Do we need the concept of genetic programming in order to have an evolutionary perspective. In M.R. Gunnar & E. Thelen (Eds.), *The Minnesota symposia on child development: Vol. 22. Systems and development* (pp. 1–34). Hillsdale, NJ: Erlbaum.

Packard, N.H., Crutchfield, J.P., Farmer, J.D., & Shaw, R.S. (1980). Geometry from a time series. *Physical Review Letters*, *45*(9), 712–716.

Pascual-Leone, J. (1970). A mathematical model for the transition rule in Piaget's developmental stages. *Acta Psychologia*, *32*, 301–345.

Poincaré, J.H. (1913). *The foundations of science: Science and hypothesis; The value of science; Science and method.* (G.B. Halstead, Trans.). New York: The Science Press.

Rapp, P.E., Bashore, T.R., Martinerie, J.M., Albano, A.M., Zimmerman, I.D., & Mees, A.I. (1990). Dynamics of brain electrical activity. In S. Krasner (Ed.), *The ubiquity of chaos* (pp. 1–20) Washington, DC: AAS.

Restle, F., & Greeno, J.G. (1970). *An introduction to mathematical psychology*. Reading, MA: Addison Wesley.

Reyna, V.F., & Brainerd, C.J. (1991). Fuzzy-trace theory and children's acquisition of mathematical and scientific concepts. *Learning and Individual Differences*, *3*(1), 27–59.

Ruelle, D., & Takens, F. (1971). On the nature of turbulence. *Communications in Mathematical Physics*, *20*, 167–192.

Rummelhart, D.E., & McClelland, J.L. (Eds.) (1986). *Parallel distributed processing: Vol. 1: Foundations*. Cambridge, MA: MIT Press.

Sameroff, A.J. (1989). Commentary: General systems and the regulation of development. In M.R. Gunnar & E. Thelen (Eds.), *The Minnesota symposia on child development: Vol. 22. Systems and development* (pp. 219–235). Hillsdale, NJ: Erlbaum.

Schaffer, W.M. (1984). Stretching and folding in Lynx fur returns: Evidence for a strange attractor in nature. *American Naturalist*, *124*, 797–820.

Schaffer, W.M., & Kot, M. (1985). Nearly one dimensional dynamics in an epidemic. *Journal of Theoretical Biology*, *112*, 403–427.

Shaw, R. (1984). *The dripping faucet as a model chaotic system*. Santa Cruz, CA: The Aerial Press Inc.

Sternberg, S. (1966). High-speed scanning in human memory. *Science*, *153*, 652–654.

Thelen, E. (1989). Self-organization in developmental processes: Can systems approaches work? In M.R. Gunnar & E. Thelen (Eds.), *The Minnesota symposia on child development: Vol. 22. Systems and development* (pp. 77–117). Hillsdale, NJ: Erlbaum.

Thelen, E., Kelso, J.A.S., & Fogel, A. (1987). Self-oragnizing systems and infant motor development. *Developmental Review*, *7*, 39–65.

Thelen, E., Ulrich, B., & Niles, D. (1987). Bilateral coordination in human infants: Stepping on a split-belt treadmill. *Journal of Experimental Psychology: Human Perception and Motor Performance*, *13*, 405–410.

Thurstone, L.L. (1919). The learning curve equation. *Psychological Monographs*, *26*, (No. 114).
van Geert, P. (1991). A dynamic systems model of cognitive and language growth. *Psychological Review*, *98*, 3–53.
von Bertalanffy, L. (1968). *General system theory: Foundations, development, applications* (rev. ed.). New York, NY: George Braziller.
Yorke, J.A. (1988). *Dynamics, a program for IBM PC clones* [Computer Program]. College Park, MD: University of Maryland, College Park.

Part III
New Research Avenues

7
The Problem of Infantile Amnesia: Lessons from Fuzzy-Trace Theory

MICHELLE D. LEICHTMAN AND STEPHEN J. CECI

In recent years, developmental and cognitive psychology have provided a wealth of information about infancy that has forced us to reconsider James' celebrated observation that the baby's universe is "one big blooming buzzing confusion" (James, 1950). Studies of memory, coupled with those in other areas, have begun to confer a view of the organism as a powerfully prepared information processor, starting at birth and perhaps even earlier to shape and be shaped by its environment. Querleu and his colleagues, for example, have shown that a fetus' heart rate will accelerate in response to the sound of its mother's voice, as well as the voices of others by the third trimester (Querleu, Renard, & Crepin, 1981). Taking the notion of this early perceptual/mnemonic ability a step further, Spence and Decasper's (1982) results indicate that newborns can discriminate between stories that had been read to them while still in their mother's womb and those that had not been read. Such indications of an early ability to parse information from the world and store it for further use is supported by studies of short-term memory, which demonstrate, for example, that from as early as 2 months of age, infants distinguish between familiar and novel stimuli (e.g., Fantz, 1956, 1964; Fagan, 1985).

Short-term memory studies have dominated the infant arena over the past 30 years, with the development of visual attention paradigms opening the floodgate to studies of memory in infants as young as a few weeks of age (Bornstein & Sigman, 1986; McCall, 1979). Studies of long-term memory, in contrast, have been far less common. Part of the reason for this dearth of work on early long-term memory processes has been the domination of a focus on prediction of childhood intellectual functioning. Since short-term and long-term recognition memory indices appear to maintain similar developmental functions with later intelligence quotients (Fagan & Singer, 1983), researchers interested in intellectual development have focused on the former for practical reasons. That is, researchers primarily interested in early memory for the purpose of predicting subsequent intellectual development have found it equally useful and more expedient to focus on short-term memory paradigms. Putting aside the goal of predicting later intellectual status, however, other researchers have attempted to chart the developmental course and nature of long-term memory in infancy, with some promising results.

In this chapter, we incorporate recent insights from these studies of long-term memory into our discussion of one aspect of the long-term memory picture, *infantile amnesia*. We view infantile amnesia as only one dimension of a broader issue of the long-term memory capacity of infants. Specifically, we use the term *infantile amnesia* to refer to the inability of individuals to retrieve memories of events that occurred during the first few years of their lives. This definition is a critical beginning to our discussion, because the term *infantile amnesia* is sometimes used when discussing the more general issue of the inability of infants to remember from day to day. The inferior ability of infants and young children to demonstrate long-term recollection of events that have occurred within infancy and early childhood, relative to adult memory for events that have occurred within adulthood, for example, does not speak directly to the issue of infantile amnesia according to our conception. Such age-related differences in long-term retention are well known and have been accounted for by a variety of mechanisms that develop during the early and middle childhood years, such as rehearsal, organization, and metamnemonic insights (e.g., Kail, 1990). Although our understanding of this broader issue of age-related differences in long-term memory certainly has implications for conceptualizing infantile amnesia, it is not synonymous with it. For example, understanding the capacity of a 1-year-old to recall an event that she encoded a day earlier is not equivalent to explaining the inability she will experience later in life when she attempts to remember the same early event. This latter problem, infantile amnesia in the sense that we define it, is not directly treated within the framework of most models of developmental differences in long-term memory, and remains largely unresolved, despite some recent progress.

Our present purpose is to consider the problem of infantile amnesia in light of principles offered by one particular theoretical memory perspective, *fuzzy-trace* theory. This theory was developed as a general model of the memory system, and to date has not been explored in direct connection with infant memory. It is our contention, however, that fuzzy-trace theory offers a useful new framework within which to consider the infantile amnesia problem and it is from this perspective that we consider the problem in the present chapter. It is neither our intention to provide a comprehensive review of fuzzy-trace theory (see Brainerd & Reyna, 1990; Brainerd & Reyna, this volume), nor of the literature on infantile amnesia (see Howe & Courage, in press; Pillemer & White, 1989). Rather, we wish to illustrate how several select principles emerging from the fuzzy-trace perspective bring a new dimension to our thinking about how infantile amnesia occurs. To this end, we first provide an overview of these principles, highlighting essential aspects of the model from which they arise. We then consider some essential elements of the infantile amnesia problem, briefly treating pertinent infant memory data and historical perspectives. Following this brief overview, we apply the principles of fuzzy-trace theory specifically to the infantile amnesia problem. We conclude with a discussion of the implications of this view of infantile amnesia for future research.

Relevant Fuzzy-Trace Principles

Fuzzy-trace theory, developed by Brainerd and Reyna, is a gist-driven theory of cognitive development that has been presented as an alternative to Piagetian and information-processing perspectives (Brainerd & Reyna, 1990; Brainerd & Reyna, this volume). The theory takes into consideration a wide variety of experimental findings, in areas ranging from the traditionally social (attitudes, choice, and preference) to the cognitive and developmental (Piagetian tasks, memory, and inference). As explained by its authors, the dominant mental metaphor of fuzzy-trace theory is the concept of intuition, reminiscent of the approach suggested in the 1950s by Brouwer (1952) and by Heyting (1959). The overarching goal of the theory is to explain age differences that emerge in reasoning and memory on standard childhood cognitive tasks. In their synopsis of the theory, Brainerd and Reyna (1990) present seven guiding assumptions, that cross the spectre of memory processes from encoding and storage through retrieval. In this chapter, we concentrate on three principles of fuzzy-trace theory that we feel have direct implications for thinking about infantile amnesia. These three principles are *gist extraction*, the *fuzzy-to-verbatim continua*, and *fuzzy processing preference*. A fourth principle, the *fuzzy-trace concept of ontogenesis*, is a broader notion in that it applies to most other aspects of the theory. Given the fundamentally developmental nature of the infantile amnesia issue, this principle will also be treated in our discussion.

Gist extraction is a fundamental element of fuzzy-trace theory that is derived from the notion that as information is encoded, it is reduced to its essence. As Brainerd and Kingma (1984) have described, essential patterns and meanings are distilled from incoming information at this early point in the memory process. Evidence for gist extraction comes from several areas. The notion of learning sets, which allow individual discrimination-learning problems to be solved on the basis of generic representations, is one example. As Brainerd and Reyna (1990) note, the adult literature on discourse processes is replete with illustrations of gist-driven encoding, and childhood tasks have also been shown to reflect such processes (e.g., Reyna, Brainerd & Connolly, 1988).

Conceptually related to gist extraction is the notion of a fuzzy-to-verbatim continuum along which information being encoded may fall. Within Brainerd and his colleagues' conception of the memory system, information in working memory may be at any of several points along the line running between a detailed, verbatim (i.e., veridical) trace of incoming stimuli, and a pared down skeletal version of that information. Moreover, representations of information at a variety of stages along this continuum may coexist in working memory. Such a theoretical construction stands in contrast to the thrust of traditional information processing approaches, which consider the level of abstraction of traces at encoding to be limited. Although in their conception verbatim and fuzzy traces may be formed at the same time, Brainerd and Reyna favor the view that these traces are functionally independent, offering behavioral and neurophysiological evidence to support this. Clearly, this fact is important because it allows for the possibility that information at one level of abstractness may be retrieved while information at another level pertaining to the same episode, for instance, remains inaccessible. The bottom line is what Brainerd and Reyna term *the law of overdetermination*; that is, the availability of relevant information on the fuzzy-to-verbatim continua in working memory provides the individual with cognitive options. These options then allow for "finessing sources of memorial and processing failure" (Brainerd and Reyna, 1990, p. 17).

Following from the point that a continuum of representational levels exists within memory, is the assertion that fuzzy traces are actually advantaged with respect to their counterparts that are closer to verbatim, or more exact. According to this position, there is an inherent cognitive preference for employing those traces that are the most degraded. The general rule is that "when attempting to explain performance on some target task, the simplest gist that can support accurate responses is the probable basis for information processing" (Brainerd and Reyna, 1990, p. 19). There are a few convincing reasons for this fuzzy-processing preference offered by Brainerd and Reyna (Reyna et al., 1988; Brainerd and Reyna, 1990; Brainerd & Reyna, this volume). Pertaining to the traces themselves are the issues of trace availability, trace accessibility, and trace malleability. In short, traces that fall at the more skeletal, "fuzzier" end of the representational spectrum have advantages on all of these counts. Verbatim information in memory suffers from more rapid disintegration, a narrower range of effective retrieval cues, and less ease of cognitive manipulation than does information in fuzzy traces. It has also been noted that the operations required to process verbatim information are more complex, and thus more effortful and time consuming than those used to process more skeletal traces (Reyna et al., 1988). In many ways, then, gist-like traces are more effective and more expedient than the detailed, verbatim recollections that coexist with them.

Elements of the Infantile Amnesia Problem

A major difficulty in discussing the issue of infantile amnesia from any perspective is the dearth of important descriptive data relevant to the topic. To begin with, in contrast to the substantial work on early short-term memory using habituation and novelty preference designs, little is known about the fundamental properties of longer term memory in the prelinguistic years. Some research does exist that provides evidence for long-term recognition memory in infancy, although the retention periods explored have been limited. Fagan's research (1971, 1972, 1979), for example, has indicated that 5- to 7-month-olds can demonstrate memories lasting up to 2 days for abstract experimental stimuli, and for as long as 2 weeks for faces. Strauss and Cohen (1980) report 24-hour retention of abstract patterns by 5-month-olds. In addition, several studies that indicate longer term retention are reported by Fagan (1984). Fagan (1973), for example, reported delayed recognition for photographs of faces at intervals ranging up to 14 days in 5-month-olds. In addition, Topinka and Steinberg (1978) demonstrated a 2-week retention period for abstract patterns in 7-month-olds.

This evidence for delayed recognition abilities is clearly distinct from the possibility of recall or other types of reproductive memory abilities in infancy, as the cognitive operations involved in recognition are less effortful and conscious than those required for reproduction. Reproductive processes, which would provide more unequivocal evidence for conscious encoding, storage, and retrieval have rarely been rigorously studied before the onset of language. Some experiments of this nature have been carried out looking at infants' abilities to process and store event sequences or routines. Thus, it has been shown that infants between 5 and 18 months of age can become familiar with routines and use them to varying degrees for prediction (e.g., Kessen & Nelson, 1978; Smith, 1984). Methodologies using the infant's apparent surprise as an index, for example, upon encountering an object in a place other than where the infant saw it hidden, have also been a source of information about early event recollection (e.g., LeCompte & Gratch, 1972). These studies have focused on long-term memory; however, the retention intervals have been relatively short. Arguably, from the perspective of classical memory theory, the processes involved in memories lasting over long-term versus very long-term retention intervals (e.g., 2 days vs. 2 years) are the same. However, in light of the problem of infantile amnesia, the particular duration of the retention interval becomes quite important. Even if infants were to show a capacity for long-term storage that approximates the long-term memory of adults procedurally, there remains the important question of how closely this approximates the adult system of memory quantitatively at various points in the course of development. Both questions, that of the procedure and that of the quantity of infant memory, are central issues in the consideration of infantile amnesia.

Recent work by Meltzoff using the technique of deferred imitation contributes to our knowledge of both of these points. From a cognitive perspective, imitation requires reproduction of a behavior witnessed in the past, and thus illustrates recall, as opposed to pure recognition memory. In one set of studies, Meltzoff (1988a) first showed that 9-month-olds could imitate simple actions demonstrated by a researcher with novel objects. He then demonstrated that infants at this age could exhibit the same imitative behavior when a 24-hour retention interval was imposed between the researcher's modeling and the point at which the infant was permitted to interact with the object. Thus, significant recall for the researcher's behavior was evidenced by these infants over a day-long period. Even more strikingly, Meltzoff (1988b) studied imitation in 14-month-olds with a retention interval of 7 days. In this study, six actions, each perpetrated on a different object, were shown to each of the infants sequentially. The infants were not permitted to interact with any of the objects at the time of this demonstration or during the retention interval that followed. One of the six actions was an unusual behavior that had no probability of occurring spontaneously during play. After the week-long delay, infants were permitted to interact with the objects on their own. The findings show that infants who had witnessed the earlier modeling spontaneously produced significantly more of the modeled acts that infants in a control group that had not witnessed the modeling. In addition, the unusual, novel behavior was imitated by a large proportion (67%) of infants in the experimental condition, and, as expected, was not attempted by any of the control subjects. As Meltzoff notes (1988b, p. 474), "That the delay interval was 1 week effectively rules out any type of temporary 'motor set' or nonrepresentational explanation for what these children did."

Rovee-Collier and her colleagues have carried out a variety of studies exploring other dimensions of the memory of infants. In their mobile conjugate reinforcement paradigm, infants are trained to produce movement in a crib mobile overhead by footkicking, by way of a ribbon attached to their ankle and the mobile. Later, they are tested for their understanding of this response-reinforcement contingency. In such studies, long-term memory of up to 8 days has been demonstrated in 3-month-olds, and 6-month-olds have evidenced memory up to 21 days (Rovee-Collier & Hayne, 1987; Rovee-Collier, Patterson & Hayne, 1985). It appears from this work that situational specificity is decreasingly important in eliciting the behaviors indicative of memory as the retention interval is expanded. Interestingly, work by this group of researchers also indicates that under some conditions, the long-term memories of infants can be reactivated by the use of a reminder at some point during the retention interval (the *reactivation procedure*). From their work within this paradigm, Boller, Rovee-Collier, Borovsky, O'Connor, and Shyi (1990) have concluded that the functions describing memory processing at 3 and 6 months are essentially the same, but that the temporal parameters of memory at the two ages are different. The older subjects in their experiments appeared to demonstrate more rapid retrieval than the younger ones, but their reactivated memories also remained accessible for shorter periods. They summarize the implications of these findings as follows:

> The unexpected character of the temporal parameters of memory retrieval at 6 months suggests to us that memory processing is more dynamic at 6 months than at 3 months. If this supposition is correct, then infantile amnesia may be a consequence of the rapidity with which early memories are retrieved and modified rather than of the inability of young infants to store memories over the long term. (p. 778)

McDonough and Mandler (1990) have presented evidence for early recall with retention intervals spanning an even longer period than those observed using the Rovee-Collier reinforcement paradigm. Their study focused on the ability of 2-year-olds to remember actions that they observed or performed when they were only 11 months of age. Subjects from an experiment involving deferred imitation in infants around 1 year of age were brought back into the laboratory a year later. In the original experiment, subjects viewed the modeling of either familiar or novel actions, using props representing familiar objects. They were then given the opportunity to model immediately and/or after a 24-hour delay. In the session taking place the following year, the same infants were allowed to manipulate each object before any subsequent modeling. Comparison with a control group (subjects not present during the original experiment) indicated no overall differences in the number of target actions carried out by infants in these groups. However, for one particular familiar action (feeding a stuffed animal with an abstract bottle), there was a significant effect; subjects who had originally witnessed this action produced it more often than subjects who had not. The researchers concluded that this action, observed only twice and performed twice at most, could be recalled by 23-month-olds after a 1-year delay interval. Given the length of this interval, it is comprehensible that only one out of eight possible events was remembered. However, the reasons why this particular familiar action was recalled are unclear. The striking finding from our present perspective is that the action was recalled and reproduced by the infants after a full year away from the laboratory.

Consistent with this optimistic view of long-term memory capacities in infancy is a recent study by Perris and Myers (1990). In this work, 1.5- and 2.5-year-olds who had participated in a study of auditory localization at 6.5 months of age returned to the laboratory. In the original experiment, the infants had reached in the light or dark for a sounding object, on only one occasion. In the follow-up at the later ages, they were reintroduced to the procedure in the dark, and given uninstructed and then instructed trials, in which they were to find the sounding object. The results show that among 2.5-year-old subjects, those who had experienced the task in infancy reached out and grasped the object significantly more often than a control group without infancy experience. Among the 1.5-year-olds, however, this was not the case. The reason may be that subjects in the younger control group showed significantly higher reaching and grasping behaviors than their older counterparts, making the effects of infancy experience more difficult to assess in the 1.5-year-olds. The findings also indicate that a reminder of the past experience, the ringing of the same bell used in the original experiment just before the beginning of the trials, was an effective retrieval cue. Based on these data, the researchers conclude that the 2.5-year-olds remembered aspects of a single experience that they had around the age of 6 months.

In line with these findings, Cutts and Ceci (1988) reported that children as young as 8 months old were able to reproduce a learned behavior 4 months later. In their study, the children were originally exposed to a puppet that had a mitten that, if removed, would reveal a treat. Children were initially shown that the mitten could be pulled off the puppet to retrieve the treat; they grasped the contingency between pulling it off and eating the treat almost immediately. After 3 weeks of extensive practice removing the appropriate mitten, the puppet was taken away for 4 months. When it was re-presented, only 5% of the children seemed to remember that one of the mittens could be removed to recover a treat. They reacted indifferently to the puppet, preferring to play with other toys in the room. Yet, these same children engaged in reliably more touching of the appropriate mitten. In fact, they almost never touched the mitten that had not been associated with the treat 4 months earlier. They touched the appropriate mitten so much that it eventually fell off in 45% of cases within 5 min of playing. However, the children rarely looked for the treat when the mitten fell off, and did not express surprise when they were shown that there was no treat inside. Cutts and Ceci (1988) interpret this as evidence that early reproductive memory can be unconscious; infants and prelingual children may have encoded the early event in a way that does not survive the 4-month duration on a conscious level. However, from the automatic touching behavior they observed, it can be inferred that some memory exists on an unconscious level.

Notably, any serious inroads in resolving the question of the source and the development of infantile amnesia will rely on an understanding of the ontogeny of reproductive memory abilities, and not simply on an understanding of recognition memory abilities. This is the case because infantile amnesia implies the lack of an ability to retrieve early memories in a conscious, willful manner. This type of effortful retrieval is clearly a reproductive task closely resembling those laboratory experiments that require the subject to recollect (consciously) or reproduce an object or experience. In contrast, behaviors evidencing mere recognition of objects or stimuli dating from early exposure do not speak to the question of how distinctive events are processed in early infancy, despite their enormous importance for other purposes. Consequently, they do not offer substantial insight into the question of how such events are eventually forgotten.

Related to the distinction between effortful and unconscious processing is one that constrasts the fully developed self-concept of a toddler with the emerging self-concept of the infant. Children in the first 18 months of life are thought to be still developing a complete self-representational system, one that allows them to react appropriately to their own image in a mirror or to react with distress to an online film that shows their hands and feet moving out of sync. Recently, Howe and Courage (in press) have suggested that the developing self-concept provides a specific organizing system for establishing personal/autobiographical memories. According to this account, the earliest experiences may not be retrieved at a later time because they occurred when the self was too undeveloped to act as an anchor to yoke such events. An implication of this view is that early events that are not autobiographical (e.g., conditioning studies that depend only on the temporal contiguity between some stimulus and the organism's physical reaction) will be remembered better than events that are tied to personally meaningful experiences (e.g., spatial location of the perceiver) because the latter require an awareness of one's own self as the recipient of the experience, located in space and time. Thus, what characterizes early memory is apt to change with developments in the self system. Recently, Fivush and Hammond (1990) have reported on the results of their longitudinal study of children's recollections and have shown that most of what 30 month-olds recall from an experience that occurred 6 weeks earlier have to do with objects/persons ("I saw Santa Claus") and actions, not with locations ("I was at the beach") or other personally tied attributes.

Apart from issues centering around the question of what characterizes early memory, to discuss infantile amnesia as we have defined it requires substantiation of the claim that recollections of early experiences are indeed less easily retrieved than those of other periods in life. Further, our understanding of the problem would ideally be based on data documenting in detail the ontogeny of particular types of memories, experienced across the early life course and tested periodically at equivalent retention intervals. On this first point, some progress has been made. Data speaking to the second point, however, have never been presented in the literature, nor to our knowledge have investigators ever attempted to collect them (although Usher & Neisser, in press, present a first pass at this question). Although clearly critical to the infantile amnesia question, such data may be impossible to obtain in an unadulterated form because of developmental changes in responsiveness to various stimuli, and other task contraints.

As Pillemer and White (1989) have pointed out, most studies of the presumed lack of early memories in adults have been case studies, and only very recently have more rigorous investigations of the issue been undertaken. Freud, who first popularized the notion of a universal amnesia with respect to early memories, was clearly a champion of this case study method. In Freud's writing it also becomes clear that the personal phenomenology of the amnesia experience is a central part of his thinking about the problem. In his own words (Freud, 1920):

> You are all familiar from actual experience with the peculiar amnesia of childhood to which we are subject. I mean that the first years of life, up to the age of 5, 6, or 8, have not left the same traces in memory as our later experiences. True, we come across individuals who can boast of continuous recollection from early infancy to the present time, but it is incomparably more common for the opposite, a blank memory, to be found. In my opinion this has not aroused sufficient surprise. (p. 210)

Freud was not the only one to be surprised over the phenomenon of infantile amnesia. It is as though an organism becomes an adult after having erased the record of its own early development—a position troubling to those who maintain that development is an incremental, cumulative process in which the organism constantly builds on prior attainments. Sufficient surprise at this notion has prompted more recent investigators to explore empirically the retention of early memories in adolescence and adulthood. The conclusion from the majority of these studies has been that most adults' earliest memories date from the age of 3 to 4 years (Pillemer & White, 1989). Thus, for example, Wetzler and Sweeney's (1986) reanalysis of Rubin's (1982) data indicates that greater memory deficits exist for events occurring before the age of 3 years than for later memories of childhood and adulthood.

The critical problem, of course, is how to account for the apparent discontinuity between memories accumulated before and after the period at which the earliest memories begin. Investigators adhering to several theories of infantile amnesia have proposed that there is a "window" between the ages of 28 and 36 months. For example, Terr (1986) has argued that before and during this period children may behaviorally reproduce events they have experienced in the past. They may, for instance, reenact such events symbolically with the use of props or dolls, even though they cannot verbally recall them or otherwise describe them. According to Terr (1988), after the age of 3 years, however, children may be unable to verbally reproduce those events that they experienced before this age, although they can recreate them with actions. Below, she gives an example from a case study in which a child recreates with dolls a form of abuse that was known to have occurred to her, based on police photos that were confiscated at her grandparents' home:

> Gloria was 0 to 6 months old when she was enrolled in her grandparents' day care program. She did not see them again after age 6 months because of a family feud. At age 2 years, 11 months, she came into my office and shyly opened the toy cabinet, taking out a doll and looking under the doll's dress. Next, she piled dolls on top of other dolls, constructing a mess of twosomes á la mode de "Caligula." Her older brother had recalled group sex play in his separate session. Gloria then said, "I want to undress this baby." . . . She quickly, efficiently took all the clothes off Little Bo Peep . . . She then poked Bo Peep suddenly and violently in the vagina. (The photos confiscated at the grandparents' residence showed an erect penis poking Gloria's vagina.) (p. 256)

Recently, Usher and Neisser (in press) have pointed out that the "window" for infantile amnesia varies depending on the event being recalled. Adults can remember events associated with hospitalization and the birth of a sibling between the ages of 2 and 3 years, whereas events associated with moving to a new house or the death of a family member are not recollected if their onset predated their third birthday. Although the reason for this asymmetry is unclear, two possible explanations were ruled out by the authors. First, the two events that were remembered earliest (birth of a sibling and hospitalization) did not differ from the two that were not remembered early (death of a relative and house moving) in terms of their affective valence. Subjects were no more or less likely to rate early memories as positive, negative, or neutral than they were to rate later memories. Second, it is also the case that earlier memories were not obviously better rehearsed than later ones; subjects did not report having discussed them more or consulted photographs of them more, thus ruling out rehearsal and place-keepers as explanations for the earlier offset of infantile amnesia.

These studies provide an excellent starting point from which to approach the question of infantile amnesia. Still, despite their revelation that most childhood experiences before the age of 3 years are forgotten, we are left with an insufficiently detailed understanding of the trajectory of both memory processes and specific recollections throughout infancy and childhood to do more than speculate about the mechanism behind this phenomenon. Is the earliest offset of amnesia for moving or being hospitalized (between 24 and 35 months of age) coincident with the onset of complex grammar that enables such events to be coded more easily? Are the joint roles of language and rehearsal confounded with amnesia, insofar as caregivers of infants and very young children, sensing their charges' prelingual status, do not discuss prior events? If so, then the early amnesiac period may not represent a true critical period but rather a lack of reactivation of experience through language, the medium subsequently used to elicit memory. Early amnesia may reflect a condition wherein caregivers allow early experience to be coded nonlinguistically, and then use language at a later time to cue it, resulting in a mismatch of representations. Thus, the "critical period" for amnesia may be little more than the onset of the child's verbal skills, prompting discussion of events by caregivers.

As White and Pillemer (1979) have suggested, it may be the case that infantile amnesia is eventually attributable to multiple causes. Thus, this shift in language skills and the consequent changes in the child's personal environment may co-occur with other changes in the social, cognitive, and emotional spheres of an individual's development. Such changes may be either independent of or related to each other, and may work synergistically to create the phenomenon of infantile amnesia.

Lessons from Fuzzy-Trace Theory

As we have noted, then, in seeking to understand infantile amnesia we are faced with several unresolved issues. Among the most important of these are the descriptive questions of the procedural and quantitative characteristics of memory across infancy and childhood, and the apparent discontinuity of retrievability in memories accumulated before and after an apparently critical period around 3 years of age. We believe that fuzzy-trace theory offers an interesting theoretical grounding from which to approach all of these aspects of the problem.

The central message that we understand fuzzy-trace theory to offer the problem of infantile amnesia is contained in the notion that gist-like representations are in many ways superior to verbatim ones. Because the decay rate of fuzzy traces is understood to be slower than that of verbatim traces, it seems logical to look to these differential levels of trace detail for the locus of the infantile amnesia effect. Consider, for the sake of argument, the possibility that the fundamental properties of the memory system of the infant are very similar to those of the adult (we know, of course, that relevant biological changes such as myelinization constrict this statement, but in general the system architecture seems comparable well before the offset of the period of infantile amnesia). These younger and older memory systems might vary on just one dimension, and that is the ability to encode and to use fuzzy traces. Brainerd and others have postulated that gist-like representations are not used as much by younger subjects as by older ones, and the ability to encode in a "fuzzy" manner seems to improve with age. In their words,

> Distillation of gist per se is a primitive aspect of cognition that is present in infants and very young children, but the sheer frequency of gist extraction and the specific types of gist that are stored undergo protracted development. (Brainerd & Reyna, 1990, p. 34)

It may be the case that infants and young children use the same fundamental encoding processes as adults, and thus evidence procedurally similar long-term memory. However, working memory in these young subjects may still be replete with representations falling on the verbatim end of the verbatim-to-fuzzy continuum. This may be the case in part because their lack of language skills prevents them from transforming what are essentially perceptual-motor representations into more abstract (gist-like) propositional representations during encoding. In this case, no matter how efficient the operations used in the manipulation of the traces, infants' long-term memory performance would still be impoverished by comparison with that of older subjects. Quite simply, they would rely in their retrieval efforts on the verbatim products (traces) created by their immature language and representational systems. And such products fade faster, as argued by Brainerd and his colleagues (Brainerd, Reyna, Howe & Kingma, 1990; Brainerd and Reyna, 1990). Clearly, from Brainerd and Reyna's description one would predict that traces within the confines of the working memory of one individual could vary along the fuzzy-to-verbatim continuum at any given time. There is no a priori reason to expect that this would not be true of infants, as it is for adults. We can imagine, however, that a progressively larger proportion of traces become gist-like with development as a result, at least in part, of the greater efficiency of language to transform perception.

Although fuzzy and verbatim traces may be functionally independent (Brainerd & Reyna, 1988), there is nonetheless the possibility that they are related in their level of quality. If the way in which an infant is able to process information becomes better over time, then the gist-like representations in her working memory may also improve. This is closely related to the seemingly paradoxical idea that the greater the clarity with which the infant can perceive the details of the incoming information, the better her gist representations of this information will be.

So far, however, this interpretation of fuzzy-trace theory has not spoken directly to the more difficult and central question of infantile amnesia, that is, how the apparent discontinuity in retrievability between information obtained in early years and that obtained in later childhood and adulthood obtains. On this issue also, fuzzy-trace theory makes a unique theoretical contribution. If memories of events that occur before the critical "window" are confined to the verbatim end of the spectrum, then these would be expected to decay at a faster rate than the fuzzier traces accumulated later. Many skills follow a developmental course of gradual but nonlinear acquisition (e.g., language, causal reasoning, metamemory). The ability to extract gist at encoding may be among these. Suppose that this ability proceeded gradually, but accelerated at the point when a certain threshold of competency was met. If, in practical terms, this threshold were to fall just around the time of the critical period for infantile amnesia, then the development of the ability to encode in gist-like representations alone could be the factor determining the apparent discontinuity.

Notably, there is an interesting fit between this conception of infantile amnesia and the *dual memory system* hypothesis advocated by Pillemer and White to account for the phenomenon (Pillemer & White, 1989; White & Pillemer, 1979). According to this model, two functionally separate memory systems exist. The first, which is apparent from birth on, is concerned with social/emotional information, and operates through images, behaviors, or emotions. Thus, through this system experiences may be cued by people, locations, or feelings. According to Pillemer and White (1989), such memories are not linked to a specific past interaction, but afford general familiarity with an emotion, person, or context. Such memories are thus uninterpretable to others outside of the specific context indicating recognition. The second memory system, on the other hand, is a socially accessible one that kicks in during the preschool years. Within this system, specific past experiences and learned items can be retrieved, and intentional efforts can be made toward retrieving them. It is only when this second system is in operation that memories can be retrieved according to social demands. In this view, the two memory systems coexist throughout later life, but infantile amnesia is clearly evident because early memories are only encoded within a system of "global" memories that do not respond to intentional retrieval efforts.

Reframing this in terms of fuzzy-trace principles, however, we can imagine not two separate processes, but instead the tendency for particular types of memories to fall toward one end of the fuzzy-to-verbatim continuum or the other at encoding. It is indeed striking that the types of memories mentioned by Pillemer and White as constituting the more primitive memory system are all those that would appear to lend themselves to a gist-like interpretation. For example, the memory of a person who is habitually encountered, or the memory of a particular emotional experience, would appear to require processing as some manner of "gestalt" in order to be recognized on the next encounter. Such information may thus be encoded early on in a sort of primitive fuzzy-trace form. Since, other things being equal, the traces at the fuzzy end of the representational spectrum will maintain numerous advantages over those at the verbatim end, we would expect these to be retrieved more easily at a later time. However, because the content of this sort of early fuzzy trace does not lend itself to socially induced retrieval, such early memories will manifest themselves only in nonverbal forms. And, as infantile amnesia would suggest, those traces that are only encoded in an inadequate verbatim manner by the infant's memory system will be lost.

Conclusions

We have suggested that the offset of infantile amnesia is best viewed as an epiphenomenon of the developing child's mode of cognizing, rather than as a graduation from a critical period during which structural limitations on later recall were removed. Specifically, as the emergent information processing system unfolds, it is more likely that experiences get encoded at multiple levels of abstraction, including at the level of gist. Since gist is less vulnerable to being overwritten or erased by competing experiences, these types of encodings will be better preserved for later retrieval. Related to this shift toward greater gist-like representations in memory is the increased linguistic coding that comes with development. It is probably no coincidence that the offset for infantile amnesia is around the same time that the young child is gaining linguistic facility.

A prediction that flows from this view of infantile amnesia is that if we could design a situation in which the prelingual child were exposed to repetitive experiences that did not rely on the later cognitive apparatus to encode a durable trace, it would be possible to demonstrate memory from this early "preoffset" period of the infant's life. One possibility would be to expose infants to a fragrance that is associated with some positive or negative outcome, and then later in life present them with a preference test for various fragrances, including that one they were exposed to as infants. One should be able to show that this early time in the infant's life is not foreclosed to later probing, when the memory is not dependent on language coding. Affective, or gist-like, representations of fragrance experiences ought to be found for even the very youngest children, proving that the critical period analogy is ill-wrought.

Although Usher and Neisser (in press) have provided fascinating evidence that infantile amnesia is context-dependent (i.e., its offset differs for various experiences), the reasons for this are still poorly understood. Two possibilities suggest themselves, however. First, perhaps affect is an integral component of what gets permanently encoded and later retrieved, and the experiences that researchers have been studying have been of low to moderate intensity. Although Usher and Neisser did not find any affective correlate of early memories, it is important to note they did not ask subjects to rate the intensity of their early experiences, but merely to assign a positive, negative, or neutral valence to them. Perhaps extremely intense experiences of all types of affect are given privileged encodings. There is some evidence that intense stress, for example, might have facilitative effects on slightly older children's memory. Goodman and her colleagues have recently reported on four experiments that indicate that stress facilitates children's memory (Goodman, Rudy, Bottoms & Aman, 1990):

> Our general finding was that stress had a facilitative effect on the children's reports. Specifically, . . . children at the highest stress levels recalled more information than the other children and were less suggestible. Interestingly, the children had to reach a level of great distress before beneficial effects on memory were evidenced. . . . These children's reports were completely accurate. Not a single error in free recall was made by the highly stressed children. (p. 273–274)

On the other hand, Peters (1991) has criticized these studies on methodological grounds, reporting a series of his own studies that have not only failed to find facilitation for highly arousing experiences, but have usually found the opposite, namely impairment. The resolution of this issue obviously awaits further data, but the possibility exists that high levels of arousal at the time of encoding has some nontrivial effect on the later ability to recollect such experiences.

Another possible explanation for why certain memories survived the early infantile amnesia better than others, and one that borders on circularity, is that the events that get recalled from the earliest period of one's life are those that are perceived as most important to the organism. Naturally, the death of a relative and moving to a different house are important events to adults, but one wonders how they might be perceived by a 2-year-old. In contrast, being hospitalized for one or more nights or being separated for the first time in one's life from one's mother, while she enters the hospital to have another child, might be more salient. These are probably far more emotional times because they involve dramatic alterations to the young child's life. Thus, it is unsurprising that these are the first experiences to be recalled. One thought in this regard concerns the moving of one's house. Perhaps as adults we are unable to remember moving to a new house if this occurred before our third birthday, but that does not mean we do not recollect anything about our old house. In a small case study, we asked three students whose families moved to a new house between the ages of 20 and 33 months of age if they recalled anything about their old houses. To help them with this task, we provided the blueprints of their old homes—which they had not visited since their early move. Two of these students were able to place the kitchen, bathroom, family room, and some other rooms accurately in their old houses.

Finally, it is worth pointing out that our fuzzy-trace explanation of infantile amnesia complements other explanations that have been suggested, for example, schooling (Neisser, 1962), language ability, emotional control, and biology (Feger, 1985). That is, all of these factors that have been cited may actually be factors that contribute to the variance in the tendency to encode information in gist versus verbatim form.

Acknowledgment. Portions of this research were supported by a grant from the National Institutes of Health R01 HD24775-01A2.

References

Boller, K., Rovee-Collier, C., Borovsky, D., O'Connor, J., & Shyi, G. (1990). Developmental changes in the time-dependent nature of memory retrieval. *Developmental Psychology*, *26*, 770–779.

Bornstein, M.H., & Sigman, M.D. (1986). Continuity in mental development from infancy. *Child Development*, *57*, 251–274.

Brainerd, C.J., & Kingma, J. (1984). Do children have reason to remember? A fuzzy-trace theory of transitivity development. *Developmental Review*, *4*, 311–377.

Brainerd, C.J., & Reyna, V.F. (1988). Generic resources, reconstructive processing, and childrens' mental arithmatic. *Developmental Psychology*, *24*, 324–334.

Brainerd, C.J., & Reyna, V.F. (1990). Gist is the grist: Fuzzy-trace theory and the new intuitionism. *Developmental Review*, *10*, 3–47.

Brainerd, C.J., Reyna, V.F., Howe, M.L., & Kingma, J. (1990). The development of forgetting and reminiscence. *Monographs of the Society for Research in Child Development*, *55* (3–4, Serial No. 222).

Brouwer, L.E.J. (1952). Historical background, principles and methods of intuitionism. *South African Journal of Science*, *49*, 139–146.

Cutts, K., & Ceci, S.J. (1988). *Memory for cheerios of cheerio memory*? Paper presented at the annual meeting of the American Psychological Association, Atlanta, GA.

Fagan, J.F. (1971). Infants' recognition memory for a series of visual stimuli. *Journal of Experimental Child Psychology*, *41*, 453–476.

Fagan, J.F. (1972). Infants' recognition memory for faces. *Journal of Experimental Child Psychology*, *11*, 244–250.

Fagan, J.F. (1973). Infants' delayed recognition memory and forgetting. *Journal of Experimental Child Psychology*, *16*, 424–450.

Fagan, J.F. (1979). The origins of facial pattern recognition. In M. Bornstein & W. Kessen (Eds.), *Psychological development from infancy: Image to intention*. Hillsdale, NJ: Erlbaum.

Fagan, J.F. (1984). Infant memory: History, current trends, relations to cognitive psychology. In M. Moscovitch (Ed.), *Infant memory* (pp. 1–27). New York: Plenum Press.

Fagan, J.F. (1985). A new look at infant intelligence. In D.K. Detterman (Ed.), *Current topics in human intelligence* (pp. 223–246). Norwood, NJ: Ablex.

Fagan, J.F., & Singer, L.T. (1983). Infant recognition memory as a measure of intelligence. In L.P. Lipsitt & C.K. Rovee-Collier (Eds.), *Advances in infancy research* (pp. 31–78). Norwood, NJ: Ablex.

Fantz, R.L. (1956). A method for studying early visual development. *Perceptual and Motor Skills*, *6*, 13–15.

Fantz, R.L. (1964). Visual experience in infants: Decreased attention to familiar patterns relative to novel ones. *Science*, *146*, 668–670.

Feger, J. (1985). L'amnesie infantile: commentaire sur ses aspects neurobiologiques. *Psychologie Francaise*, *30*, 213–219.

Fivush, R., & Hammond, N. (1990). Autobiographical memory across the preschool years: Toward reconceptualizing childhood amnesia. In R. Fivush & J.A. Hudson (Eds.), *Knowing and remembering in young children* (pp. 223–248). New York: Cambridge University Press.

Freud, S. (1920, 1953). *A general introduction to psychoanalysis.* New York: Simon & Schuster.

Goodman, G.S., Rudy, L., Bottoms, B., & Aman, C. (1990). Children's concerns and memory: Issues of ecological validity in the study of children's eyewitness testimony. (pp. 249–284). In R. Fivush & J.A. Hudson (Eds.), *Knowing and remembering in young children.* New York: Cambridge University Press.

Heyting, H. (1959). *Constructivity in mathematics.* Amsterdam: North-Holland.

Howe, M.L., & Courage, M.L. (in press). On resolving the enigma of infantile amnesia. *Psychological Bulletin.*

James, W. (1950). *Principles in psychology.* New York: Dover.

Kail, R.V. (1990). *The development of memory in children.* San Francisco: W.H. Freeman.

Kessen, W., & Nelson, K. (1978). What the child brings to language. In B.Z. Presseisen, D. Goldstein, & M.H. Apperl (Eds.), *Topics in cognitive development* (Vol. 2). New York: Plenum.

LeCompte, G.K., & Gratch, G. (1972). Violation of a rule as a method of diagnosing infants' levels of object concept. *Child Development, 43,* 385–396.

McCall, R.B. (1979). The development of intellectual functioning in infancy and the prediction of later IQ. In J.D. Osofsky (Ed.), *Handbook of infant development* (pp. 707–741). New York: Wiley.

McDonough, L., & Mandler, J. (1990). *Very long term recall in two-year-olds.* Poster presented at the biennial meeting of the International Society of Infant Studies, Montreal, Canada.

Meltzoff, A.N. (1988a). Infant imitation and memory: Nine-month-olds in immediate and deferred tests. *Child Development, 59,* 217–225.

Meltzoff, A.N. (1988b). Infant imitation after a 1-week dalay: Long-term memory for novel acts and multiple stimuli. *Developmental Psychology, 24,* 470–476.

Neisser, U. (1962). Cultural and cognitive discontinuity. In W. Sturdevant (Ed.), *Anthropology and human behavior.* Washington, DC: Anthropological Society of Washington.

Perris, E.E., & Myers, N.A. (1990). *Expressing memory for an infant event.* Paper presented at the International Conference on Infant Studies, Montreal, Canada.

Perris, E.E., Myers, N.A., & Clifton, R.K. (1990). Long term memory for a single infancy experience. *Child Development, 61,* 1796–1807.

Peters, D.P. (1991). The influence of stress and arousal on the child witness. (pp. 60–76). In J.L. Doris (Ed.), *The suggestibility of children's recollections.* Washington, DC: American Psychological Association.

Pillemer, D.B., & White, S.H. (1989). Childhood events recalled by children and adults. In H.W. Reese (Ed.), *Advances in child development and behavior* (Vol. 21, pp. 297–340). Orlando, FL: Academic Press.

Querleu, D., Renard, X., & Crepin, G. (1981). Perception auditive et reactivite foetale aux stimulations sonores. *Journal de Gynecologie Obstetrique et Biologie de la Reproduction, 10,* 307–314.

Reyna, V.F. (1988). *Reiterative versus reconstructive memory in opinion change.* Paper presented at the First Annual Nagshead Conference on Judgement and Decision Making, Kill Devil Hill, NC.

Reyna, V.F., Brainerd, C.J., & Connolly, T. (1988). Just the bottom line please: A fuzzy-trace theory of framing effects in choice. Manuscript submitted for publication.

Rovee-Collier, C., & Hayne, H. (1987). Reactivation of infant memory: Implications for cognitive development. In H.W. Reese (Ed.), *Advances in child development and behavior, 20* (pp. 185–238). New York: Academic Press.

Rovee-Collier, C., Patterson, J., & Hayne, H. (1985). Specificity in the reactivation of infant memory. *Developmental Psychobiology*, *18*, 559–574.

Rubin, D.C. (1982). On the retention function for autobiographical memory. *Journal of Verbal Learning and Verbal Behavior*, *21*, 21–38.

Smith, P. Hull (1984). Five-month-old infant recall and utilization of temporal organization. *Journal of Experimental Child Psychology*, *38*, 400–414.

Spence, M.J., & Decasper, A.J. (1982). *Human fetuses perceive maternal speech.* Paper presented at International Conference on Infant Studies, Austin, Texas.

Strauss, M.S., & Cohen, L.B. (1980). *Infant immediate and delayed memory for perceptual dimensions.* Paper presented at the International Conference on Infant Studies, New Haven, Connecticut.

Terr, L. (1986). *Memory for traumatic episodes during childhood.* Paper presented at the Annual Meeting of the American Psychiatric Association. Washington, DC.

Terr, L. (1988). Anatomically correct dolls: Should they be used as a basis for expert testimony? *Journal of the American Academy of Child and Adolescent Psychiatry*, *27*, 254–257.

Topinka, C.V., & Steinberg, B. (1978). *Visual recognition memory in $3\frac{1}{2}$ and $7\frac{1}{2}$ month-old infants.* Paper presented at the International Conference on Infant Studies, Providence, Rhode Island.

Usher, J., & Neisser, U. (in press). Boundaries of childhood amnesia: Autobiographical memory for four early events. *Emory Cognition Project.*

Wetzler, S.E., & Sweeney, J.A. (1986). Childhood amnesia: An empirical demonstration. In D.C. Rubin (Ed.), *Autobiographical memory* (pp. 191–201). London: Cambridge University Press.

White, S.H., & Pillemer, D.B. (1979). Childhood amnesia and the development of a socially accessible memory system. In J.F. Kihlstrom & F.J. Evans (Eds.), *Functional disorders of memory* (pp. 29–73). Hillsdale, NJ: Erlbaum.

8
Development of Intentional Forgetting in Children

ELYSE BRAUCH LEHMAN AND MARGARET BOVASSO

The experience of deliberately trying to forget information, such as an old phone number when we move, is a common one in everyday life. Although the phenomenon has been extensively studied in adults, only a handful of studies have looked at intentional forgetting in children. This early work suggests that children begin to gain control over their forgetting in the elementary school years. However, partly because of the relatively complicated tasks used in these studies, many questions remain unanswered. How early in the school years, for example, can children make use of a forget instruction? By what mechanisms do children intentionally forget?

The present chapter has two main sections. In the first, the methodology and findings of published work on intentional (or selective/motivated/directed/instructed) forgetting will be reviewed. In the second, the results of a study on the development of intentional forgetting recently completed by the authors will be described. The goal of the chapter is to stimulate interest in forgetting, in general, and in intentional forgetting, in particular, among researchers of memory development by considering the developmental implications of work on directed forgetting.

General Background

Brief History

Experimental work on intentional forgetting began in the late 1960s with the development of the directed forgetting paradigm by Bjork (1972). In this paradigm, subjects are given cues that direct them to forget certain items that have been presented. Through the mid-1970s, an enormous number of studies using this paradigm were conducted with adults (see Bjork, 1972, and Epstein, 1972, for reviews). Of interest were questions about whether adults were able to delete information from storage voluntarily and about the mechanisms by which adults might make use of the forget cues.

More recent interest in the topic has emerged after a hiatus of almost a decade. There are several new papers on the mechanisms of intentional forgetting in adults, most notably by Geiselman and his colleagues (e.g., Geiselman & Bagheri, 1985; Geiselman, Bjork, & Fishman, 1983; Geiselman, Rabow, Wachtel, & MacKinnon, 1985). It is also more common now to see the directed forgetting paradigm used as a technique for investigating other aspects of memory in adults (e.g., retrieval processes) (Bjork & Geiselman, 1978; MacLeod, 1989).

Interest in the developmental aspects of intentional forgetting has been more limited. To date, 10 studies on intentional forgetting in children and adolescents have been published. Only four of these, however, are developmental (Bray, Justice, & Zahm, 1983; Bray, Hersh, & Turner, 1985; Foster & Gavelek, 1983; Posnansky, 1976). The rest include investigations of directed forgetting in 5- to 7-year-old normal children (Bray & Ferguson, 1976; Howard & Goldin, 1979), in mentally retarded children and adolescents (Bray, 1973, Bray & Ferguson, 1976; Bray, Goodman, & Justice, 1982; Bray, Justice, & Simon, 1978; Bray, Turner, & Hersh, 1985), and in reading-delayed boys (Foster & Gavelek, 1983). Much of this work with children has focused on finding the age at which children begin to use forget cues and on describing age changes in children's use of strategies to accomplish this feat.

Importance of the Problem

According to Geiselman, Bjork, and Fishman (1983), studies of intentional forgetting serve two broad functions. First, they expand our knowledge of how information is remembered by exploring how individuals keep their minds from being cluttered by outdated and useless information. James' (1890, p. 680) comment that "If we remembered everything we should on most occasions be as ill off as if we remembered nothing" underscores the point that in order to remember one thing effectively, individuals may need to forget something else. For example, learning a new phone number after a move often requires forgetting an old one. As proposed by Bjork (1972), this kind of memory updating is aided by the intentional forgetting of old information. For example, individuals may consciously use a strategy such as rehearsing only the new phone number when confusions between the new and the old arise. The idea is also illustrated by Luria's (1968) famous mnemonist who found that he could exert voluntary control over previously learned material so that it did not interfere with new learning.

The second function of the adult studies on intentional forgetting has been to provide a bridge between contemporary cognitive psychology and everyday forgetting experiences of interest to clinicians. The assumption here is that the mechanisms involved in intentional forgetting in the laboratory may be similar to those responsible for psychodynamic forgetting such as hysterical amnesia (see Gregg, 1986, for a review) and for posthypnotic amnesia (Geiselman, Bjork, & Fishman, 1983; Geiselman et al., 1983; Kihlstrom, 1983). Intentional forgetting studies could then be used to promote understanding of the clinical phenomena. How well this bridge is working, however, is still a matter of debate. Clearly, as Gregg points out, there are differences along the conscious awareness continuum between hysterical amnesia and the techniques most people use to avoid remembering painful and/or embarrassing events (e.g., deliberately thinking of something else). Likewise, not all researchers find support for the initial assumption that similar mechanisms mediate both intentional forgetting and posthypnotic amnesia (cf. Coe, Basden, Basden, Fikes, Gargano, & Webb, 1989).

From a developmental perspective, the first of these two broad functions is most likely the more important; that is, to expand our understanding of how children come to gain some measure of voluntary control over their memory functioning. Children, too, must encode and store in memory a substantial amount of information that may be outmoded or irrelevant for task solution. Thus, it is of interest to know whether children can prevent interference from the outmoded information through strategic behavior.

In a more general sense, information about the development of intentional forgetting adds to three bodies of literature: metamemory, selective attention, and forgetting. First, its proposed role in memory updating suggests that it will be of interest to researchers studying children's memory monitoring, an aspect of metamemory whose importance has been emphasized by Brown (1978). Available evidence suggests that skills for keeping track of and regulating performance are weak at all ages, although the studies in this area are relatively small in number and limited in scope (see Schneider & Pressley, 1989, for a review).

Second, the emphasis in intentional forgetting on selectivity in processing (i.e., focusing on the relevant and ignoring the irrelevant) specifies its relationship with studies of selective attention. A vast amount of research on the development of selectivity during the initial processing of a stimulus has demonstrated that with increasing age children acquire information more selectively and systematically (cf. Lehman, 1972; Miller & Weiss, 1981). How this regulation of early processing compares with the ability of children to engage in selective allocation of processing resources in memory is a question that has already received some attention (Howard & Goldin, 1979).

Finally, the focus on forgetting itself underscores the emphasis on an aspect of memory that has been relegated to secondary status by most researchers of memory development. A resurgence of interest, however, seems to be forthcoming. Recent work, for example, has challenged the notions that forgetting rates are invariant across age and that forgetting is primarily a retrieval problem (Brainerd, Reyna, Howe, & Kingma, 1990; Howe & Brainerd, 1989; Howe, Brainerd, & Reyna, 1992). What studies of intentional forgetting add to this literature is the reminder that (a) forgetting has positive aspects—memory updating can be constructive, and (b) forgetting can be an active process—individuals may use strategies to forget. The first point is illustrated by Ribot's (1882/1883) statement that "Were it not for our totally forgetting a vast number of states of consciousness and momentarily forgetting a great many, we could not recollect anything. Forgetfulness therefore is not, except in certain cases, a disease of memory, but rather one condition of its healthful action and of its life" (p. 14). The second point is discussed in the next section under mechanisms of intentional forgetting.

Published Research

The Directed Forgetting Paradigm

Procedural variations in the directed forgetting paradigm are legion. However, they can be categorized along two major dimensions (Bjork, 1972). First, subjects may be cued to forget either groups of items or individual items. In the cueing by item sets procedure, two sets of items are presented and a cue to forget (F) one and remember (R) the other is given. In the item-by-item cueing procedure, the two sets of items are mixed together and a forget or remember cue is given for each one.

Second, the temporal position of the cue may be varied. For example, in the cueing by item sets procedure, the cue to remember or forget may be given before, during, or after item presentation (i.e., preinput, intraserial, or postinput cueing). In the item-by-item cueing procedure, the cue may be presented at the same time as the stimulus (i.e., cueing at onset) or delayed until the offset of the item (i.e., cueing after offset). Both variations of item-by-item cueing have been labeled intraserial by Gregg (1986).

Directed Forgetting in Adults

The review presented in this section is not designed to be exhaustive. Its main purpose is to discuss the three questions that have been the focus of the adult research and to provide some general answers to these questions. More detailed reviews can be found in Bjork (1972) and Epstein (1972).

Is a Forget Cue Effective in Reducing Interference?

When the F cue is effective, there is minimal interference from the to-be-forgotten words on the recall of to-be-remembered words. When the F cue is ineffective, more interference occurs. The question may therefore be operationalized as: "What is the effect of the F instruction on memory for the R items?"

The evidence across many studies indicates that memory for the R items is considerably facilitated with intraserial cueing; that is, when the cue follows the set of items to be forgotten and precedes the set of items to be remembered as in the cueing by item sets procedure or when the R and F items are cued individually as in item-by-item cueing (see, e.g., Reitman, Malin, Bjork, & Higman, 1973; Geiselman & Bagheri, 1985). On the other hand, the facilitation is considerably reduced with postinput cues to forget in the cueing by item sets procedure (Bjork, 1970) and may even be completely absent when postcueing is employed in the item-by-item cueing procedure (Epstein, 1969). The conclusion then is that, under some conditions (e.g., intraserial cueing), adults can quite effectively make use of a forget cue to facilitate their processing of to-be-remembered items.

Are the F-Cued Items Erased from Memory?

Questions about the fate of F-cued items are important because they begin to ask about facilitation mechanisms. The studies indicate that, although recall of F items is low, recognition of F items is typically quite high (see, e.g., Reitman et al., 1973; Geiselman & Bagheri, 1985). Such findings suggest that the F-cued items are not erased from memory. Thus, a straightforward erasure or deletion mechanism will not account for the effectiveness of a forget cue in preventing proactive interference from outmoded information.

What Are the Underlying Mechanisms?

Four alternative mechanisms have been proposed. The first two are thought to operate primarily at encoding, the latter two at retrieval.

Selective Rehearsal

This mechanism was initially proposed by Bjork (1972) as one part of a two-process theory. The proposal was that after the F cue is presented, subjects devote all further rehearsal and other mnemonic activities to the R items. As noted by Bjork, this mechanism would apply only to conditions of intraserial cueing. With postinput cueing, all items would already have been rehearsed and encoded by the time the F cue is presented.

Selective Grouping

The second part of Bjork's (1972) proposal was that the forget cue reduces interference because it leads subjects to group to-be-remembered items in memory separately from to-be-forgotten items. Although there is controversy over exactly how this segregation might be accomplished (e.g., through tagging or through storage in separate areas), the notion of list segregation has received experimental support (Bjork & Geiselman, 1978).

Selective Search

Epstein (1972) proposed that when given a cue to forget, subjects limit their memory search to R items. Since there is no need to search items labeled to-be-forgotten, retrieval of R items in this situation should be better. Clearly, this mechanism assumes that some kind of selective grouping also takes place. Its strength lies in its ability to account for facilitation in postinput cueing conditions.

Retrieval Inhibition

Geiselman and his colleagues (Geiselman, Bjork, & Fishman, 1983; Geiselman & Bagheri, 1985) believe that an F cue does more than terminate rehearsal. Through a number of recent experiments, they have presented evidence for the idea that a forget cue can inhibit or block retrieval of items cued forget. Thus, in ordinary free recall the F items become inaccessible. However, when retrieval cues are present, as in a recognition test, it can be shown that F items are actually available.

All four mechanisms have received experimental support. Early work focused on the first three: selective rehearsal and selective grouping with intraserial cueing, and selective search with postinput cueing. Recent work is emphasizing retrieval inhibition.

Directed Forgetting in Children

With the exception of two studies that use item-by-item cueing (i.e., Foster & Gavelek, 1983; Posnanski, 1976, Exp. 1), all of the published work on directed forgetting in children has used the cueing by item sets procedure. This latter category can be subdivided into those that use postinput cueing (i.e., Howard & Goldin, 1979; Posnanski, 1976, Exp. 2), and those where the cueing is intraserial; that is, all of the research done by Bray and his colleagues (Bray, 1973; Bray & Ferguson, 1976; Bray, Goodman, & Justice, 1982; Bray, Hersh, & Turner, 1985; Bray, Justice, & Simon, 1978; Bray, Justice, & Zahm, 1983; Bray, Turner, & Hersh, 1985). The distinctions are important because of differences among the procedures in answers they give to the questions of interest; that is, age changes and individual differences in the ability to control forgetting and in the strategies children use to do so.

Can Children Use a Forget Cue to Reduce Interference from Irrelevant Information in Memory?

Age Changes

The cueing by item sets procedure has consistently failed to demonstrate that young children derive much benefit from the introduction of a forget cue. Howard and Goldin (1979), for example, found that kindergarten children had only limited ability to eliminate interference from irrelevant dimensions after initial encoding has taken place. Although the 6-year-olds in Bray and Ferguson's (1976) study did show higher recall of to-be-remembered words after an intraserial forget cue in comparison with trials involving the same number of items but no forget cues, Bray and Ferguson concluded from the pattern of results on control trials that the facilitation was not due to the elimination of interference from early items. In fact, there did not even seem to be any build-up of interference from the early items. What appeared more likely was that the forget cue served simply to engage the children more actively in the task, since there was more overt labeling and rehearsal of to-be-remembered items after a forget cue.

To date, the youngest age at which effective selective forgetting has been found with a cueing by item sets procedure is 11 years. Bray, Justice, and Zahm (1983) have even proposed that the developmental transition from ineffective to effective selective remembering occurs between 7 and 11 years of age. In their study, interference from the early items was not eliminated after an intraserial cue to forget those items for 7-year-olds (grade 1) and was just partially eliminated for 9-year-olds (grade 3). Only the 11-year-olds (grade 5) made good use of the forget cue. These findings are supported by Posnansky's (1976, Exp. 2) report that third-graders did not use a postinput cue to reduce interference at the time of recall whereas seventh graders did.

When item-by-item cueing is used, on the other hand, effective directed forgetting has been demonstrated at an earlier age. Posnansky (1976, Exp. 1), for example, found that more to-be-remembered items were recalled than forget items by both third- and seventh-graders. Also, more to-be-remembered items were recalled when they were the only ones asked for at recall than when all items were requested. There were no interactions with age. Additionally, Foster and Gavelek (1983) reported that even first-graders recalled more R- than F-cued items, although the differentiation between these two groups of items increased between first and fifth grade. Children's R-item recall varied as a function of grade, whereas F-item recall was similarly low at all grades.

Individual Differences

Directed forgetting has also been studied in both the learning disabled and the mentally retarded, and both groups have been shown to have some difficulties with the task. The learning disabled children in Foster and Gavelek's (1983) item-by-item cueing study were boys of average intelligence with a reading skill delay. Their difficulties were evident on two scores. First, they recalled fewer R-cued items than normal reading children. Second, they recalled more F-cued items than normal reading children. This latter score was especially interesting in light of the fact that none of the normal reading children, even first-graders, had any difficulty in refraining from recalling F-cued items when the instructions were to recall only those items cued R.

In their work with educable mentally retarded (EMR) children, Bray and his colleagues (Bray & Ferguson, 1976; Bray, Turner, & Hersh, 1985) have noted not only a delayed developmental progression, but also the possibility of a regression in adults. Nine- to 11-year-olds did not seem able to use the cue at all, even after extensive pretraining. For 15- and 18-year-olds, the forget cue facilitated performance but did not completely eliminate interference. Adults performed at the level of the youngest group. Bray, Turner, and Hersh (1985) therefore concluded that the developmental transition from ineffective to effective selective remembering found for nonretarded children by Bray, Justice, and Zahm (1983) is never completed by retarded individuals.

In summary, there is evidence that, under some conditions, elementary school-age children can use a forget cue to reduce interference from irrelevant information in memory. It is also known that some children (e.g., reading delayed boys and mentally retarded children) do not derive much benefit from forget cues. What is currently unknown is how early in the school years effective selective forgetting occurs.

Which Mechanisms do Children Use to Control Their Forgetting?

Three mechanisms have been studied in children's intentional forgetting: erasure, selective rehearsal, and selective search.

Erasure

It seems unlikely that items cued forget are simply erased from memory, although only one of the intentional forgetting studies to date has actually addressed this question in children. As with adults, that study found that recognition of F items by third- and seventh-graders was high (about 90%), even though recall of those items was low (Posnansky, 1976, Exp. 1). Thus, the items cued forget were still available in memory.

Selective Rehearsal

Possibly because of the emphasis on rehearsal strategies in the memory development literature itself (see Schneider & Pressley, 1989, for a review) and most certainly because of Bjork's (1972) proposal that selective rehearsal is the major mechanism involved in directed forgetting, most of the research on children's intentional forgetting has focused on the rehearsal strategies that children use in the directed forgetting paradigm. The results to date suggest that children's rehearsal does change after the introduction of an F cue, although again, procedural variations make it difficult to specify age changes with much degree of certainty.

Not surprisingly, with a cueing by item sets procedure, the use of a selective rehearsal strategy appears quite late. Bray, Justice, and Zahm (1983), in fact, propose that a second developmental transition occurs between 11 years of age and adulthood. The change is from no rehearsal to selective rehearsal. Evidence for this change comes from investigations of child-controlled study times across a trial. If subjects selectively rehearse, a decrease in study time on the first item after the introduction of an F cue would be expected (i.e., assuming that subjects cumulatively rehearse up to that point). In Bray's research, this result has appeared for 15- and 18-year-olds as well as adults, but not for 11-year-olds and younger children or for mentally retarded adolescents (CA = 11–18 years) and adults (Bray, Hersh, & Turner, 1985; Bray, Justice, & Zahm, 1983; Bray, Turner, & Hersh, 1985).

A study using an item-by-item cueing procedure with children, on the other hand, concluded that selective rehearsal occurs considerably earlier. Foster and Gavelek (1983) inferred from the pattern of study times that even first-graders were selectively rehearsing. Children from first to fifth grade spent more time after R- than after F-cued items as well as larger amounts of time as they progressed through a list. Interestingly, reading delayed boys, at least on trial 1, spent more time after F-cued items than did their normal-reading counterparts.

Selective Search

Both Bray (1979) and Posnansky (1976) have suggested that some selective retrieval mechanism must also be working. Bray cites his finding that 11-year-olds can make effective use of a forget cue, yet do not seem to be engaging in selective rehearsal, as the impetus for invoking another mechanism (see Bray, Justice, & Zahm, 1983). The selective retrieval strategy he describes (i.e., one using spatial-temporal cues to differentiate to-be-forgotten and to-be-remembered items) is similar to Epstein's (1972) selective search proposal.

Posnansky (1976) provides the only experimental evidence to date on children's use of a selective retrieval strategy. Seventh-graders, but not third-graders, recalled more of the to-be-remembered items when asked (postinput) to recall only this subset of items than when instructed to recall all items (the "Only" effect). Since there was no opportunity in this procedure to rehearse to-be-remembered and to-be-forgotten items differentially, any age effect must be occurring at retrieval. Based on Epstein's analysis of the task, Posnansky concluded that dividing items into remember and forget categories is more difficult for third- than for seventh-grade children. However, since the Only effect occurred at both ages when children were cued item by item, Posnansky also concluded that even third-graders were able to reduce interference through selective processing at recall if they could accomplish the differentiation between remember and forget items.

In summary, the research suggests that children's rehearsal does change after the introduction of an F cue, although exactly when the transition to selective rehearsal occurs is unclear. No conclusions can be drawn about retrieval mechanisms, however, because of the paucity of studies in this area.

An Unpublished Study

We have recently begun to study the development of directed forgetting in our laboratory at George Mason University with several goals in mind. The first has been to develop a modification of Bjork's directed forgetting paradigm that would be of interest to children. With the notable exception of Howard and Goldin's (1979) paper, the tasks used have been taken directly from the adult literature. At the very least, they are difficult for children to understand, and often require a pretraining session before the administration of the test (see, e.g., Bray & Ferguson, 1976).

The second goal has been to find some of the missing pieces in the developmental puzzle. Whereas the literature reviewed above suggests that children begin to gain control over their forgetting during the elementary school years, it is not clear how early in the school years children can make use of the forget instruction. With this question as our focus, we elected to use item-by-item cueing, since previous research with this procedure suggests the possibility of an early transition from ineffective to effective use of a forget cue (Foster & Gavelek, 1983; Posnansky, 1976, Exp. 1).

The third goal has been to study two proposed mechanisms: selective rehearsal and retrieval inhibition. As reviewed above, in previous studies an indirect method has been used to study use of a selective rehearsal strategy by children. The method requires the experimenter to infer when such a strategy is operating by examining subject-controlled interstimulus intervals. A decrease in this interval after the F cue has been given would suggest that a child is selectively rehearsing only the to-be-remembered items. The method also assumes, however, that children are engaging in cumulative rehearsal. The fact that children rarely use this strategy before the late elementary school years (Ornstein & Naus, 1978), however, suggests that some alternative method for discovering how children rehearse in the directed forgetting paradigm is in order. It also suggests that an investigation of retrieval mechanisms might be fruitful. No one has yet studied retrieval inhibition in children. Given the current interest in the development of inhibition processes (Bjorklund & Harnishfeger, 1990; Dempster, this volume; Harnishfeger & Bjorklund, this volume), it seems appropriate to do so now.

The Modified Directed Forgetting Paradigm

The modification consisted primarily of making the procedure more game-like for children by telling them a story about a bee who needed to find honey to save her hive and by giving children control over the appearance of pictures on a computer monitor. In the story the bee has decided to look everywhere for honey, since she wasn't sure where she would find it. She knows that she will need to remember those places where she finds honey so that she can tell the other bees. The places where she does not find honey, however, can be forgotten. Subjects were then invited to help the bee find the honey (e.g., "If you look for honey, too, it might help the bee.").

Each "place" was a black line drawing of an everyday object, for example, a lamp, train, drum, etc. Each one appeared in the middle of a computer screen for 5 sec, followed by either a honeypot (indicating she should remember this "place") or a red X (indicating she should forget this "place") for 5 sec. When subjects thought the bee was ready to fly to the next place, it was explained that they should press the button they were holding. Twenty-four pictures were presented in this manner. Since the objects represented in the pictures were not related to real "honey locations," it seems unlikely that children's prior knowledge of bees could have facilitated or interfered with their use of the cue presented with each picture.

Method

Seven-, 9-, and 11-year-old children attending parochial schools serving middle- and upper-middle-class families and a group of college students as a comparison (20 per age group) participated in a procedure similar in form to one used by Geiselman and Bagheri (1985). Trial 1 consisted of item-by-item cueing followed by recall of all the pictures. This procedure allowed us to compare recall of R-cued words with recall of F-cued words. Additionally, since subjects were told that if they said anything to themselves during the presentation of the pictures they should say it out loud, we had a very direct measure of rehearsal that could be compared with the subject-controlled interstimulus intervals that were also recorded.

On trial 2, subjects were instructed to remember all of the pictures (i.e., all were followed by an R cue). The trial 2 list included 18 of the drawings from trial 1 plus 6 new ones. Subjects' recognition of "old" pictures was tested in addition to their recall of the pictures on trial 2.

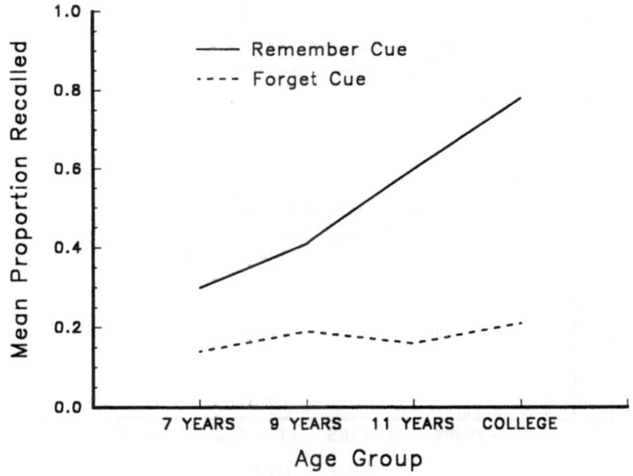

FIGURE 8.1. Mean proportion of pictures recalled on trial 1.

According to Geiselman and Bagheri (1985), evidence for retrieval inhibition would be indicated if trial 2 recall of F-cued pictures not recalled on trial 1 was higher than trial 2 recall of R-cued pictures not recalled on trial 1. The rationale here is that, with the repetition on trial 2, unrecalled F-items not only benefit from a second opportunity to rehearse, as do R-items, but also are enhanced by the release of retrieval inhibition from trial 1.

Results

Using the Forget Cue

Figure 8.1, which presents the mean proportions of R-cued and F-cued pictures recalled on trial 1, indicates that there was an interaction between age and cue. That is, the difference in recall between pictures cued remember and pictures cued forget increased with age.

Of special interest, however, was the finding that even 7-year-olds recalled more pictures cued remember. An increase with age in the number of pictures recalled occurred only for those followed by a remember cue. Recall of pictures cued forget was low at all ages. Thus, even 7-year-olds made use of a cue to forget information.

Fate of the Pictures Cued Forget

As has been found with adults, the forget cue did not erase the pictures from memory. Although recall of F-cued pictures was low, recognition of these items was high in all age groups (see Fig. 8.2). Nevertheless, more pictures were recognized after a remember cue (95.3%) than a forget cue (88.4%). This difference, although small, was statistically significant.

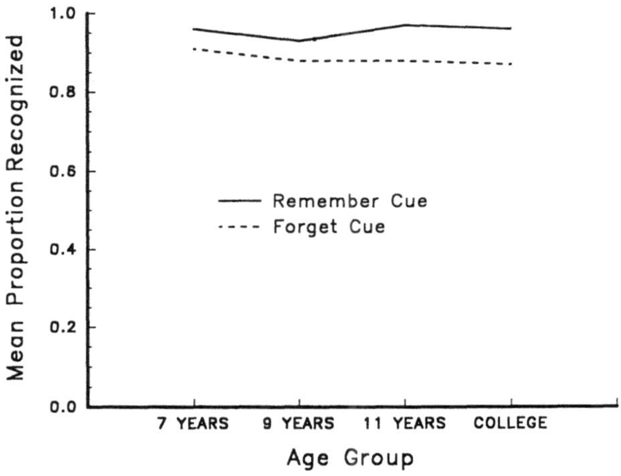

FIGURE 8.2. Mean proportion of pictures recognized on trial 2.

Selective Rehearsal Strategies

Direct Approaches

One strategy that is thought to be useful in the directed forgetting paradigm is to rehearse the R-cued pictures but not the F-cued pictures. Figure 8.3 shows the number of pictures rehearsed on trial 1 as a function of age and cue for subjects who rehearsed outloud. It includes the data

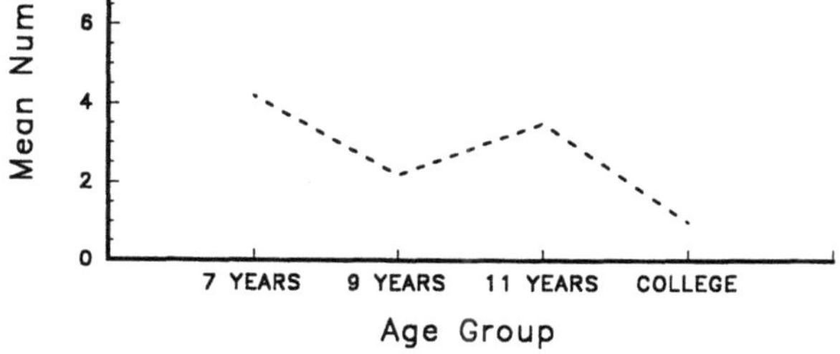

FIGURE 8.3. Mean number of pictures rehearsed on trial 1.

for eighteen 7-year-olds, sixteen 9-year-olds, eighteen 11-year-olds, and 20 college students. What is clear from the figure is that even the 7-year-olds rehearsed more R-cued pictures than F-cued pictures. Thus, it appears that 7-year-olds use the same selective rehearsal strategy that adults do.

Nevertheless, with increasing age this strategy seems to be applied more effectively. The figure indicates that the difference between the number of R- and number of F-cued pictures rehearsed increased with age. This effect can be accounted for by the fact that rehearsal of F-cued pictures dropped with age whereas rehearsal of R-cued pictures remained relatively constant. It can also be seen in the proportion of subjects who limited their rehearsals to only R-cued pictures. Those with a perfect use of this strategy included 27.8%, 62.5%, 50.0%, and 75.0% of the 7-, 9-, and 11-year-olds, and college students, respectively.

Developmental differences can also be seen in a more refined version of selective rehearsal; that is, waiting until the R cue is presented before rehearsing. For adults, 92.1% of the R-cued pictures rehearsed were not rehearsed until after the R cue appeared. The comparable proportions for 7-, 9-, and 11-year-olds were 51.6%, 75.1%, and 70.5%, respectively. Furthermore, the proportions of subjects with perfect use of this strategy also increased with age: 22.2%, 46.7%, 58.8%, and 70.0% for 7-, 9-, and 11-year-olds, and college students, respectively.

Interestingly, even though the proportion of rehearsers who rehearsed F-cued pictures decreased with age (72.2%, 37.5%, 50.0%, and 25.0%, respectively), many of the subjects who did rehearse F-cued pictures, regardless of age, seemed to have little idea of a good strategy for dealing with them. About half of the children who rehearsed F-cued pictures (53.8%, 50.0%, and 44.4% of 7-, 9-, and 11-year-olds) and 80.0% of the college students who rehearsed F-cued pictures waited until the cue was presented and then still rehearsed the picture.

Study Times

As has been reported before (see, e.g., Foster & Gavelek, 1983), study times were variable. Nevertheless, the analysis indicated that more study time followed an R-cued picture than an F-cued picture (means = 2.59 sec and 1.64 sec, respectively). Thus, both direct and indirect measures suggest greater rehearsal when pictures are followed by R cues.

Additionally, a trend appeared in the interaction between age and cue. Figure 8.4 shows that the differentiation between study times for R- and F-cued pictures tended to increase with age across the three child groups. Why this differentiation decreased for college students is not clear. It does not fit with evidence for increased differentiation in this age group when more direct measures of rehearsal are used. Since this interaction may be unreliable, however, caution is recommended in its interpretation.

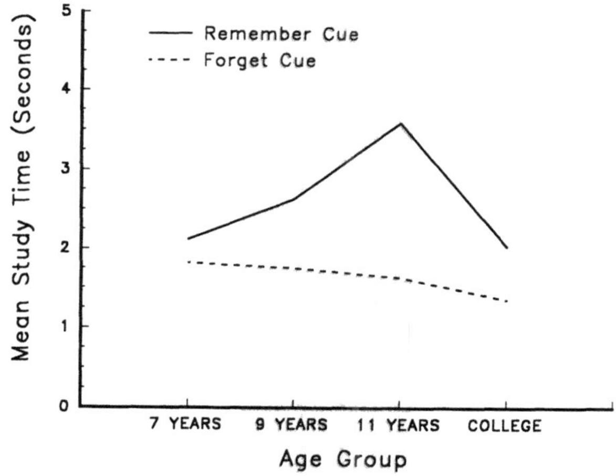

FIGURE 8.4. Mean study time on trial 1.

Retrieval Inhibition

No evidence was found for a retrieval inhibition mechanism, either in adults or in children. As Figure 8.5 indicates, there was no indication of better trial 2 recall of F-cued pictures not recalled on trial 1 than R-cued pictures not recalled on trial 1 at any age. It is possible that ceiling effects existing in the college students may have been responsible for the failure to replicate Geiselman and Bagheri's (1985) finding of a retrieval inhibition mechanism in this group. However, an analysis that was limited to those college students not showing ceiling effects still did not find any evidence for retrieval inhibition. Neither did an analysis that controlled for the amount of rehearsal time given to the F-cued items during the study of list 2.

Summary and Conclusions

From a developmental perspective there are two major issues on which to focus. First, how does intentional forgetting develop and how early can it be demonstrated in children? Second, how do the mechanisms by which intentional forgetting is accomplished change with age? A subissue here is whether the mechanisms occur primarily during storage, primarily during retrieval, or during both storage and retrieval.

The answer to the first question is still incomplete, although it is becoming clearer that the methodology used has a bearing on the answer. The directed forgetting studies completed to date demonstrate that, when each item is cued individually, even 6- and 7-year-olds can make use of a cue to forget. It does not seem to matter whether the cue appears at the

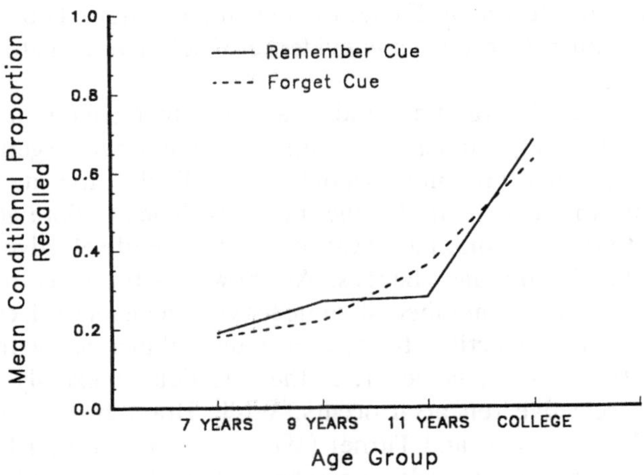

FIGURE 8.5. Mean proportion of pictures recalled on trial 2 conditionalized on trial 1 recall.

same time as the item to be remembered or forgotten (Posnansky, 1976, Exp. 1) or immediately after item offset (Foster & Gavelek, 1983; Lehman & Bovasso, this chapter). Effective directed forgetting appears later, however, when the cueing is done by item sets. With intraserial cueing in the cueing by item sets procedure, it has been proposed that the developmental transition from ineffective to effective selective remembering occurs between 7 and 11 years of age (Bray, Justice, & Zahm, 1983). With postinput cueing, the change may take place even later (Posnansky, 1976, Exp. 2).

It is not known whether these apparent differences in age of occurrence are simply an artifact of methodology; for example, stricter criteria for concluding that subjects are using forget cues in the cueing by item sets procedure or, more interestingly, whether they reflect real differences in the kinds of processing tapped by the two tasks. Updating memories during ongoing processing, for example, may require or allow different mechanisms than trying to forget information already stored in long-term memory.

Nevertheless, the studies reviewed make clear that, under some conditions, early elementary school age children can make use of a cue to forget. By this age, adult patterns of understanding the word "forget" are just beginning to emerge (Wellman & Johnson, 1979), so it would be expected that 7-year-old children would be able to comprehend the instructions in the directed forgetting paradigm. In the same vein, it is interesting to speculate that the failure to find instructed forgetting in even younger children is at least partially attributable to their often incomplete understanding of the numerous cognitive implications of the terms *remember/forget*. If such sophisticated knowledge of *forget* is necessary in order to use an F cue, then even more simplified versions of the task may still not produce any evidence of selective forgetting in very young children.

Both the directed forgetting studies and the metacognition literature thus suggest that developmental changes in intentional forgetting occur primarily after children enter school. Most likely, the development continues into the teen years. Furthermore, evidence to date gives clear-cut support to the idea that modifications in the use of selective rehearsal are responsible for the age changes. As shown by the work of Lehman and Bovasso, both the number of subjects who rehearse selectively and the extent to which selective strategies are applied increase with age.

What is still at issue, however, is the question of exactly when the transition to selective rehearsal occurs. While Bray, Justice, and Zahm (1983) and Bray, Hersh, and Turner (1985) propose a rather late transition from no rehearsal to selective rehearsal in the directed forgetting paradigm (i.e., between 11 and 15 years of age), other researchers find evidence for an earlier use of this strategy. Both Foster and Gavelek (1983) and Lehman and Bovasso (this chapter), for example, found that 6- and 7-year-olds rehearsed more after a remember cue than a forget cue, regardless of whether an indirect or direct measure of rehearsal was used.

Also at issue is the question of intentionality. Whereas Bjork (1972) seemed to focus on the conscious application of rehearsal strategies, recent discussions in the developmental literature challenge the notion that memory strategies must be conscious (e.g., Pressley & Levin, 1983a, 1983b). Likewise, in the directed forgetting literature there is current interest in retrieval processes that may or may not be under voluntary control (e.g., retrieval inhibition) (Geiselman et al., 1983; Kihlstrom, 1983).

Because the adult data suggested that intentional forgetting involves something more than simply terminating rehearsal, Geiselman et al. (1983) hypothesized that the F cue sets in motion some process that effectively blocks access of the forbidden material to working memory. They called this "missing mechanism" retrieval inhibition. The notion is of interest to developmentalists because of recent proposals that inhibitory processes become more efficient over childhood. One consequence of this increased efficiency is that, for older children, less irrelevant information would enter working memory, thus effectively increasing its functional capacity (Bjorklund & Harnishfeger, 1990; Dempster, this volume; Harnishfeger & Bjorklund, this volume). Developmental changes in the success of retrieval inhibition in a directed forgetting paradigm would provide support for Bjorklund and Harnishfeger's hypothesis.

Unfortunately, however, the evidence is equivocal. While Geiselman and his colleagues have found support for this mechanism in adults

(Geiselman et al., 1983; Geiselman & Bagheri, 1985), others working with this age group have not (Coe et al., 1989). Likewise, Lehman and Bovasso (this chapter) could not find evidence for retrieval inhibition in either children or adults.

Finally, there is the locus of forgetting issue. Is forgetting primarily storage-based, retrieval-based, or both? As discussed by Howe and Brainerd (1989), the common view in the memory literature is that forgetting is primarily a retrieval phenomenon. Since memory traces are presumed to remain intact (i.e., available), forgetting must be considered a failure to access the trace. The intentional forgetting studies, on the other hand, lend support to Howe and Brainerd's conclusions that storage failures also play a role in children's retention performance and that storage failures do not necessarily imply trace erasure.

Still an open question is the extent to which retrieval mechanisms apply in children's directed forgetting. Bray, Justice, and Zahm's (1983) suggestion that selective retrieval may be used by younger children who are not yet selectively rehearsing does not receive support from Posnansky's (1976) finding that it was precisely the younger children who had trouble partitioning items into remember and forget categories. Additionally, retrieval inhibition is not an established fact.

Nevertheless, Coe et al.'s (1989) conclusion that a storage deficit is the primary factor in the intentional forgetting of information seems premature. A better understanding of the role played by retrieval mechanisms would be useful for understanding the adult literature. It may be absolutely essential for putting together the pieces of the developmental puzzle.

Acknowledgments. This work was partially supported by a Student Research Grant to the second author from the George Mason University Sigma Xi Club. Portions were presented at the March 1990 Southeastern Conference on Human Development, Richmond, Virginia. We wish to thank Hanu Singh and Steven Kurtz for their help in designing the computer presentation.

References

Bjork, R.A. (1970). Positive forgetting: The noninterference of items intentionally forgotten. *Journal of Verbal Learning and Verbal Behavior*, *9*, 255–268.

Bjork, R.A. (1972). Theoretical implications of directed forgetting. In A.W. Melton & E. Martin (Eds.), *Coding processes in human memory* (pp. 217–235). Washington, DC: Winston.

Bjork, R.A., & Geiselman, R.E. (1978). Constituent processes in the differentiation of items in memory. *Journal of Experimental Psychology: Human Learning and Memory*, *4*, 347–361.

Bjorklund, D.F., & Harnishfeger, K.K. (1990). The resources construct in cognitive development: Diverse sources of evidence and a theory of inefficient inhibition. *Developmental Review, 10*, 48–71.

Brainerd, C.J., Reyna, V.F., Howe, M.L., & Kingma, J. (1990). The development of forgetting and reminiscence. *Monographs of the Society for Research in Child Development, 55* (3–4, Serial No. 222).

Bray, N.W. (1973). Controlled forgetting in the retarded. *Cognitive Psychology, 5*, 288–309.

Bray, N.W. (1979). Strategy production in the retarded. In N.R. Ellis (Ed.), *Handbook of mental deficiency: Psychological theory and research* (2nd ed., pp. 699–726). Hillsdale, NJ: Erlbaum.

Bray, N.W., & Ferguson, R.P. (1976). Memory strategies used by young normal and retarded children in a directed forgetting paradigm. *Journal of Experimental Child Psychology, 22*, 200–215.

Bray, N.W., Goodman, M.A., & Justice, E.M. (1982). Task instructions and strategy transfer in the directed forgetting performance of mentally retarded adolescents. *Intelligence, 6*, 187–200.

Bray, N.W., Hersh, R.E., & Turner, L.A. (1985). Selective remembering during adolescence. *Developmental Psychology, 21*, 290–294.

Bray, N.W., Justice, E.M., & Simon, D.L. (1978). The sufficient conditions for directed forgetting in normal and educable mentally retarded adolescents. *Intelligence, 2*, 153–167.

Bray, N.W., Justice, E.M., & Zahm, D.N. (1983). Two developmental transitions in selective remembering strategies. *Journal of Experimental Child Psychology, 36*, 43–55.

Bray, N.W., Turner, L.A., & Hersh, R.E. (1985). Developmental progressions and regressions in the selective remembering strategies of EMR individuals. *American Journal of Mental Deficiency, 90*, 198–205.

Brown, A.L. (1978). Knowing when, where, and how to remember: A problem of metacognition, In R. Glaser (Ed.), *Advances in instructional psychology* (pp. 77–165). Hillsdale, NJ: Erlbaum.

Coe, W.C., Basden, B.H., Basden, D., Fikes, T., Gargano, G.J., & Webb, M. (1989). Directed forgetting and posthypnotic amnesia: Information processing and social contexts. *Journal of Personality and Social Psychology, 56*, 189–198.

Epstein, W. (1969). Poststimulus output specification and differential retrieval from short-term memory. *Journal of Experimental Psychology, 82*, 168–174.

Epstein, W. (1972). Mechanisms of directed forgetting. In G.H. Bower (Ed.), *The psychology of learning and motivation* (Vol. 6, pp. 147–191). New York: Academic Press.

Foster, R.N., & Gavelek, J.R. (1983). Development of intentional forgetting in normal and reading-delayed children. *Journal of Educational Psychology, 75*, 431–440.

Geiselman, R.E., & Bagheri, B. (1985). Repetition effects in directed forgetting: Evidence for retrieval inhibition. *Memory and Cognition, 13*, 57–62.

Geiselman, R.E., Bjork, R.A., & Fishman, D.L. (1983). Disrupted retrieval in directed forgetting: A link with posthypnotic amnesia. *Journal of Experimental Psychology: General, 112*, 58–72.

Geiselman, R.E., MacKinnon, D.P., Fishman, D.L., et al. (1983). Mechanisms of hypnotic and non-hypnotic forgetting. *Journal of Experimental Psychology: Learning, Memory, and Cognition, 9*, 626–635.

Geiselman, R.E., Rabow, V.E., Wachtel, S.L., & MacKinnon, D.P. (1985). Strategy control in intentional forgetting. *Human Learning*, *4*, 169–178.

Gregg, V.H. (1986). *Introduction to human memory*. London: Routledge & Kegan Paul.

Howard, D.V., & Goldin, S.E. (1979). Selective processing in encoding and memory: An analysis of resource allocation by kindergarten children. *Journal of Experimental Child Psychology*, *27*, 87–95.

Howe, M.L., & Brainerd, C.J. (1989). Development of children's long-term retention. *Developmental Review*, *9*, 301–340.

Howe, M.L., Brainerd, C.J., & Reyna, V.F. (Eds.) (1992). *Development of long-term retention*. New York: Springer–Verlag.

James, W. (1890). *The principles of psychology* (Vol. 1). New York: Holt.

Kihlstrom, J.F. (1983). Instructed forgetting: Hypnotic and nonhypnotic. *Journal of Experimental Psychology: General*, *112*, 73–79.

Lehman, E.B. (1972). Selective strategies in children's attention to task-relevant information. *Child Development*, *43*, 197–209.

Luria, A.R. (1968). *The mind of a mnemonist*. New York: Basic Books.

MacLeod, C.M. (1989). Directed forgetting affects both direct and indirect tests of memory. *Journal of Experimental Psychology: Learning, Memory, and Cognition*, *15*, 13–21.

Miller, P.H., & Weiss, M.G. (1981). Children's attention allocation, understanding of attention, and performance on the incidental learning task. *Child Development*, *52*, 1183–1190.

Ornstein, P.A., & Naus, M.J. (1978). Rehearsal processes in children's memory. In P.A. Ornstein (Ed.), *Memory development in children* (pp. 69–99). Hillsdale, NJ: Erlbaum.

Posnansky, C.J. (1976). Directed forgetting among third and seventh graders. *Contemporary Educational Psychology*, *1*, 247–256.

Pressley, M., & Levin, J.R. (1983a). *Cognitive strategy research: Educational applications*. New York: Springer.

Pressley, M., & Levin, J.R. (1983b). *Cognitive strategy research: Psychological foundations*. New York: Springer.

Reitman, W., Malin, J.T., Bjork, R.A., & Higman, B. (1973). Strategy control and directed forgetting. *Journal of Verbal Learning and Verbal Behavior*, *12*, 140–149.

Ribot, T.A. (1883). *The diseases of memory* (J. Fitzgerald, Trans.). New York: Humboldt. (Original work published 1882).

Schneider, W., & Pressley, M. (1989). *Memory development between 2 and 20*. New York: Springer–Verlag.

Wellman, H.M., & Johnson, D.N. (1979). Understanding of mental processes: A developmental study of "Remember" and "Forget". *Child Development*, *50*, 79–88.

9
Direct and Indirect Assessments of Memory: Implications for the Study of Memory Development During Childhood

JAYNE ANN AUSLEY AND ROBERT E. GUTTENTAG

INTENTION, n. The mind's sense of the prevalence of one set of influences over another set; an effect whose cause is the imminence, immediate or remote, of the performance of an involuntary act.

The Devil's Dictionary
Ambrose Bierce

Most children become aware of the meaning of the term *remember* by the time they are 3 years of age (Wellman, 1985). Requests by adults for children to engage in deliberate recollection then become common (Perlmutter, 1980); young children often also set this task for themselves during the normal course of their daily activities. Although much that is remembered (by both children and adults) likely involves information committed to memory incidentally rather than having been intentionally memorized, the process of memorization as a deliberate act finds its origins during the preschool years (Wellman, 1988).

Research on the development of memory has been dominated by a focus on age differences in intentional aspects of remembering. Thus, for instance, most studies have examined children's performance on deliberate memorization tasks; that is, on tasks whose expressed goal is to commit information to mind for later recollection. This research has produced evidence for large age differences in mnemonic performance, attributable to a considerable degree to age differences in the types of procedures or strategies children deploy to help them commit the presented information to mind (see reviews by Kail, 1990, and Schneider & Pressley, 1989).

Even those developmental studies that have examined memory under incidental learning conditions (where the goal during information presentation is something other than memorization) have assessed remembering under deliberate recollection instructions; that is, under instructions that direct the subject to try to bring to mind aspects of a prior experience. Thus, for instance, most studies of both adults' and children's memory have used tests such as free recall, cued recall, and recognition. These tests have one thing in common: subjects are asked to try deliberately to remember the occurrence of a personally experienced prior event. For this reason, these tests have been referred to as intentional (Jacoby, 1984), episodic (Tulving, 1972, 1983), explicit (Graf & Schacter, 1985; Schacter, 1987), or direct (Johnson & Hasher, 1987) measures of memory.

Recently, the adult memory literature has witnessed a dramatic shift in attention toward examining memory with the use of tests that do not require deliberate recollection of prior information or of a prior event, but that nonetheless may reveal the influence of the prior experience on the performance of some task. Tulving, Schacter, and Stark (1982), for example, examined the effects of prior presentation of list items on the ability of subjects to perform a word fragment completion task (e.g., -ss-ss-, which can be completed as assassin). Unbeknownst to the subjects, some of the fragments could be completed by items from the previously presented list. The critically important feature of this task is that subjects were not instructed to refer to their memory for the list items to help them complete the fragments; nonetheless, subjects were able to complete successfully more list-item than non-list-item fragments.

Tasks such as this have been referred to as incidental (Jacoby, 1984), implicit (Graf & Schacter, 1985; Schacter, 1987), or indirect (Johnson & Hasher, 1987) measures of remembering. We prefer the terms *direct* and *indirect* because they avoid tacit acceptance of any of the prevailing theoretical views designed to account for the differences in performance that have been found with the two types of tasks.

In the present chapter, we will discuss the phenomenon of memory as indexed by indirect tests of retention; that is, memory in the absence of deliberate recollection instructions. In the first section of the chapter we describe recent theoretical and empirical work on this topic from the adult memory literature. In the sections that follow we will review findings from the few developmental studies that have been conducted using indirect tests of remembering, and then present the findings from two new studies of our own that tested for age differences in associative memory as assessed by an indirect test of memory. In the final section of the chapter we discuss some of the general implications of this new focus of memory research for the study of the development of memory.

Indirect Tests of Memory: Research with Adults

Most of the current research on adult cognition using indirect tests of remembering has been concerned with what is referred to as *repetition priming* (Cofer, 1967; see Richardson-Klavehn & Bjork, 1988, and Schacter, 1987 for reviews). Subjects typically study a list of items and at some later time are given a task to perform with old and new items, without reference being made to the items' old/new status. Priming is evidenced by facilitation in performance on items encountered a second time.

The most commonly used indirect memory tests are word stem and fragment completion, lexical decision, and word or perceptual identification. On word stem completion tests (e.g., Graf, G. Mandler, & Haden, 1982), old and new items are represented at test by their first three letters (e.g., cha__ for chair), and subjects are asked to complete each stem with the first word that comes to mind. Word fragment completion (discussed above) is a variant of this task. Priming on these two tests is revealed when subjects complete more old than new stems with target items or when more old than new fragments are correctly completed.

With lexical decision tasks (e.g., Scarborough, Gerard, & Cortese, 1979) subjects are presented with letter strings (only some of which spell real words) and are asked to indicate as rapidly as possible whether or not each string constitutes a word. Priming is revealed by shorter decision times on the second, compared to the first, presentations of letter strings. Word or perceptual identification tasks (e.g., Jacoby & Dallas, 1981) involve very brief presentations of old and new items, and subjects are simply asked to identify each word. Priming here is evidenced by greater identification accuracy for old as compared with new items or by shorter exposure times necessary to identify old as compared with new items.

Interest in memory as measured through indirect tests is not new (see review by Schacter, 1987); however, excitement recently has been generated by cognitive and neuropsychological research that demonstrates compelling functional dissociations in which a number of variables have been found to have different effects on direct and indirect tests. Such dissociations suggest inherent differences between the forms of memory assessed by the two types of tests and raise fundamental questions regarding the nature of memory generally. In the classic research by Warrington and Weiskrantz (1968, 1970, 1974, 1978), for example, patients with anterograde amnesia (characterized by normal intellectual functioning coupled with disastrous memory for recent events) performed poorly compared with normals on typical direct tests or memory (e.g., recall and recognition) yet demonstrated performance equal to that of normals when tested with word stem or fragment completion. Similar results have now been obtained with amnesics using a number of different tasks (see Shimamura, 1986, for a review).

Subsequent studies have demonstrated similar dissociations in performance on direct and indirect tests of memory in normal subjects after the manipulation of certain variables at encoding. For example, several papers have reported dissociations due to level of processing at encoding (e.g., Graf et al., 1982; Graf & G. Mandler, 1984; Graf, Squire, & G. Mandler, 1984; Jacoby & Dallas, 1981; Schacter & McGlynn, 1987; Winnick & Daniel, 1970). In these studies, subjects typically were presented list items under incidental learning conditions involving either a semantic orienting task (e.g., subjects rated how much they liked each word) or a nonsemantic orienting task (e.g., subjects decided whether each word shared vowels with the word preceding it). When memory for the presented information was tested, a large advantage for semantically encoded list items was found on direct measures of memory, replicating the well established levels of processing effect (e.g., Craik & Lockhart, 1972; Craik & Tulving, 1975). In contrast, indirect tests revealed significant priming of both semantically and nonsemantically encoded items, with either small or no effects of the nature of the orienting task on the magnitude of the priming produced.

Several papers have also reported dissociations due to changes between study and test in factors such as modality of presentation (e.g., Clarke & Morton, 1983; Graf, Shimamura, & Squire, 1985; Jacoby & Dallas, 1981; Kirsner, Milech, & Standen, 1983; Kirsner & Smith, 1974; Roediger & Blaxton, 1987a, 1987b) and other types of "surface information" (e.g., Kolers, 1975, 1976; Roediger & Blaxton, 1987a, 1987b; Roediger & Weldon, 1987; Scarborough et al., 1979). These studies have found that changes in modality (e.g., visual to auditory) or other surface information (e.g., type font) sharply reduced priming on various indirect tests but had small or no effects on memory measured by direct tests such as recognition and recall. Other studies have demonstrated differential effects of interference (e.g., Graf & Schacter, 1987) and retention interval (e.g., Jacoby & Dallas, 1981; Komatsu & Ohta, 1984; Tulving et al., 1982) on direct versus indirect measures of memory. Dissociations have also been demonstrated through findings of statistical independence between performance on the two types of tests (e.g., Eich, 1984; Graf & Schacter, 1985; Jacoby & Witherspoon, 1982; Kolers, 1976; Metcalfe & Fisher, 1986; Tulving et al., 1982).

Theoretical Accounts of Memory-Task Dissociations

As might be expected, a plethora of theoretical frameworks has been proposed to account for the dissociations obtained in performance on direct and indirect tests of memory. Each of these views has strengths and weaknesses with respect to accounting for existing data (Richardson-Klavehn & Bjork, 1988; Schacter, 1987). Multiple memory system views suggest that performance on direct and indirect tests of memory is mediated by different underlying memory systems with separate neuroanatomical substrates. A variety of frameworks for classifying memory systems have been proposed (e.g., Johnson, 1983; Oakley, 1983; O'Keefe & Nadel, 1978; Olton, Becker, & Handleman, 1979; Squire, 1986, 1987; Tulving, 1972, 1983; Warrington & Weiskrantz, 1982). The distinction that we will be concerned with is that made between semantic and episodic memory (Tulving, 1972, 1983). According to this view, episodic memory is a system that receives and stores information about temporally dated episodes or events, and that preserves information regarding the context in which a remembered event occurred. This system is considered to underlie performance on direct tests of remembering such as recognition and recall. Semantic memory, in contrast, is a system that contains general world knowledge and knowledge of language, and that consists of representations that are abstract and conceptual. This system is believed by some to underlie priming on indirect tests of memory; specifically, priming is viewed as being due to the temporarily heightened activation of preexisting representations in semantic memory (e.g., Cermak, Talbot, Chandler, & Wolbarst, 1985; Kinsbourne & Wood, 1975; Parkin, 1982; Schacter & Tulving, 1982; Tulving, 1983).

The memory systems view readily explains the differential effects of amnesic syndromes on direct and indirect measures of memory. Presumably, for amnesics, the semantic memory system is intact but the episodic system is impaired. This view also readily accommodates findings that variations in elaborative processing do not affect performance on indirect tests of item memory (e.g., Graf et al., 1982; Jacoby & Dallas, 1981), and Tulving's recent addition of a perceptual representation system enables this view to accommodate data demonstrating the effects of superficial study-test changes on repetition priming (Tulving & Schacter, 1990). Nonetheless, the systems view has been criticized for a number of reasons. For example, one problem with this perspective is the potential to hypothesize a new system to explain any newly discovered dissociation (McKoon, Ratcliff, & Dell, 1986; Roediger & Blaxton, 1987a, 1987b; Schacter & Tulving, 1982; Squire & Cohen, 1984; Tulving, 1983, 1986). Moreover, even the basic distinction between episodic and semantic memory has been called into question (Dagenbach, Horst, & Carr, 1990; McKoon et al., 1986), making reliance on the distinction to explain the findings from studies using indirect assessments of memory problematic.

Rather than postulating distinct memory systems to explain differences in performance on direct and indirect tests of memory, processing views focus on the nature of the encoding and retrieval operations (and the relations between them) required by the two types of tasks (e.g., Craik, 1983; Jacoby, 1983a, 1983b; Kolers & Roediger, 1984; Moscovitch, Winocur, & McLachlan, 1986; Roediger, 1990; Roediger & Blaxton, 1987a, 1987b; Roediger & Weldon, 1987; Roediger, Weldon, & Challis, 1989). According to this view the effects of a prior experience depend on the extent to which retrieval conditions reinstate encoding conditions, an assumption consistent with Tulving's principle of encoding specificity (Tulving & Thomson, 1973), Koler's theory of memory for operations (e.g., Kolers, 1973, 1979), and the principle of transfer-appropriate processing (Bransford, Franks, Morris, & Stein, 1979; Morris, Bransford, & Franks, 1977; Stein, 1978). Dissociations in performance on direct and indirect tests occur because encoding conditions interact with the different processing requirements of the two types of memory tasks.

For example, one prominent system for classifying types of processes distinguishes between data-driven and conceptually driven operations (Jacoby, 1983b; Blaxton, 1989; Roediger, 1990; Roediger & Blaxton, 1987a, 1987b; Roediger et al., 1989). Data-driven processes are guided by the stimulus information that is provided and tend to involve primarily the perceptual processing of surface structure, whereas conceptually driven processes (such as elaboration, organization, and imagery) are subject-guided and involve meaning. Most indirect tests, it is hypothesized, are sensitive to data-driven operations; that is, they rely primarily on a match of perceptual processing of surface features between study and test. Most direct tests, on the other hand, depend primarily on prior subject-guided, conceptually driven processing of an event.

This view accounts for the dissociations in performance on direct and indirect tests observed in amnesics by suggesting that it is a type of processing, and not a memory system, that is deficient. Presumably, with amnesia, conceptually driven processing is deficient but data-driven processing is preserved. Like the multiple systems view, this approach readily accounts for findings that item priming does not depend on prior elaborative processing (e.g., Graf et al., 1982; Jacoby & Dallas, 1981) and predicts demonstrations that study-test changes in modality and other aspects of surface structure affect performance on indirect but not direct tests of remembering (e.g., Jacoby & Dallas, 1981; Roediger & Blaxton, 1987b). This view, however, is not without problems (Richardson-Klavehn & Bjork, 1988; Schacter, 1987), including recent evidence that questions the correspondence between data-driven processing and indirect tests of remembering on the one hand, and conceptually driven processing and direct tests of remembering on the other (e.g., Hunt & Toth, 1990; Toth & Hunt, 1990).

More recently, Jacoby (e.g., 1991) has refined his ideas regarding the processing approach to understanding performance on direct and indirect tests of memory. In this work Jacoby has emphasized the fact that whereas performance on direct tests of memory depends on conscious recollection of a prior experience, savings in performance on indirect tests of memory does not require either an intention to remember or an awareness of past experience. Therefore, according to Jacoby, one way to describe differences between the two types of tests is in terms of the distinction between consciously controlled and automatic processing (Hasher & Zacks, 1979; Posner & Snyder, 1975; Shiffrin & Schneider, 1977). Specifically, effortful, controlled processing is presumed to contribute much more to performance on direct than indirect tests of remembering; performance on indirect tests, on the other hand, is presumed to be affected primarily by automatic, rather than controlled, operations. Supporting this view, Jacoby has recently demonstrated that whereas performance on direct tests of memory may show decreases when attention is divided, some indirect tests of memory are not affected by division of attention (e.g., Jacoby, Woloshyn, & Kelley, 1989b).

Developmental Studies Using Indirect Measures of Remembering

The extant literature on memory development has established that young children typically perform more poorly than adults on tasks that involve deliberate memorization and intentional recall (e.g., Bjorklund & Muir, 1988; Brown, Bransford, Ferrara, & Campione, 1983; Kail, 1990; Schneider & Pressley, 1989). Age differences in performance on such tasks have been traced to age differences in the processes or procedures that subjects deploy at the time of learning (e.g., rehearsal, organization, and elaboration). Traditionally, it has been presumed that these procedures are used deliberately as mechanisms to improve retention; hence the use of the term *strategies* to describe the procedures. More recently, it has begun to be recognized that strategies may often involve a mix of deliberate and automatic procedures (Ashcraft, 1990; Folds, Footo, Guttentag, & Ornstein, 1990; Howe & O'Sullivan, 1990), with the status of different components of a particular strategy potentially changing with age.

Although most of the research on children's memory has focused on age differences in the use of encoding procedures, a few studies have examined age differences in procedure use at the time of retrieval (e.g., Kobasigawa, 1977); here, as with the case of encoding, it has been found that, with increasing age, children come to use a broader variety of retrieval procedures, use those procedures more skillfully, and tailor their use of retrieval procedures more appropriately to the task at hand (Kail, 1990).

Even those studies that have focused on retrieval have typically examined performance only under deliberate recollection conditions; that is, using direct tests of remembering. It cannot be assumed, however, that patterns of age differences in performance found with direct measures of retention will be paralleled by similar patterns when retention is assessed using indirect indices. For example, in contrast to children's deficient memory under intentional conditions, it has been found that memory may occur involuntarily as part of ongoing activities in which the child is engaged, such as play (e.g., Greenbaum & Graf, 1989; Istomina, 1975; J.M. Mandler, 1984; Piaget & Inhelder, 1973). In addition, the finding of differential effects of a variety of variables (including subject variables, such as amnesia) on direct and indirect tests of retention with adults raises the clear possibility that the two types of measures may reveal different patterns of developmental change as well.

The different theoretical perspectives proposed to account for dissociations between direct and indirect indices of memory are each consistent with the possibility that the types of age differences in performance found with direct measures may not occur when indirect measures of memory are used. For example, Tulving (1985) has claimed that semantic memory is both phylogenetically and ontogenetically primary (see also Kinsbourne & Wood, 1975; Sherry & Schacter, 1987), and that young children may not possess episodic memory (see also Neisser, 1979; Nelson & Gruendel, 1981). From a processing perspective, one might hypothesize that whereas direct tests of remembering may be sensitive to processes that develop during childhood, the processes underlying performance on indirect tests may mature very early and may be developmentally invariant in their functioning beyond infancy or early childhood.

Of particular relevance here is Jacoby's (1991) observation that indirect tests of retention are affected primarily by automatic, rather than deliberate, procedures at the time of retrieval. Given the evidence that age differences in performance on direct tests of remembering are highly correlated with age differences in the use of deliberate encoding and retrieval strategies (Schneider & Pressley, 1989), it would be expected that age differences in performance would be diminished on tasks whose structure discourages the use of such procedures and that index instead the functioning of automatic retrieval procedures (Hasher & Zacks, 1979).

Experimental Evidence

Only a few studies comparing patterns of developmental change on direct and indirect measures of remembering have been conducted. Nonetheless, the findings from these studies have been fairly consistent in supporting the hypothesis that memory performance as assessed by indirect tests remains relatively invariant across ages between early childhood and adulthood. A review of this literature follows.

In what appears to have been the earliest developmental study comparing performance on direct and indirect tests of memory, Carroll, Byrne, and Kirsner (1985) presented subjects lists of pictured items; subjects were subsequently presented both old and new pictured items on either a picture recognition test or a picture naming task. It was found that although recognition memory performance improved significantly between 5 years of age and adulthood, picture naming priming (the difference in naming latencies between old and new items) remained invariant across age.

Parkin and Streete (1988; see also Parkin, 1989) used a picture completion paradigm to assess memory indirectly. Subjects, ages 3, 5, and 7 years and adults were shown pictures of objects degraded by deleting line segments. There were eight degraded picture versions of each of 15 objects, with each version less degraded than the one before. Subjects were shown the most degraded picture version of each object first and were asked to identify the object. If identification from the first picture did not occur, subjects were shown the next, less degraded version of the object, and so on until identification was successful. The same task was then repeated, either 1 hour or 2 weeks later, except that 15 new sequences of incomplete pictures were presented along with the 15 old series. Priming was assessed as a savings in the quality of the picture required to produce correct identification on the second, as compared with the first, presentation. Subjects also performed a recognition test in which they had to indicate which of the 30 pictures shown during the second session were repetitions of pictures presented earlier. The finding of interest from the study was that whereas performance on the recognition test improved with age and declined with retention interval, the indirect measure of memory (savings in picture identification) revealed no change as a function of age at either retention interval.

A very different type of indirect test of memory was used by Greenbaum and Graf (1989). The 3-, 4-, and 5-year-olds in their study were presented with six pictures related to one of four possible themes and asked to memorize them. After study, children were asked to generate as many items as possible relevant to two of the four possible themes (one new and one previously studied). The measure of priming here was the difference in the number of list items generated for previously studied themes as compared with the number of list items generated for new themes. After this category generation task, children were presented with a free recall test as a direct test of their memory for the list items. Greenbaum and Graf (1989) found that whereas free recall performance increased with age, priming of target items on the category production task was invariant across age.

The fragment completion test first used with adults by Tulving et al. (1982) was recently adapted for use with children in a series of experiments by Naito (1990). Children in grades 1, 3, and 6 and adults were presented with lists of printed words under either semantic or nonsemantic orienting task conditions. List presentation was followed by direct (free recall and recognition) and indirect (fragment completion) tests of memory. Retention interval was also manipulated, with testing done at 7 min or 6 days. Whereas performance on the direct tests of memory was affected by age, encoding task, and retention interval, priming of list items on word fragment completion was significant at all ages and was not affected by any of these three variables. Similar results were found in a study by Lorsbach and Worman (1989) comparing learning disabled and nondisabled children. Lorsbach and Worman (1989) found that older and nondisabled subjects performed reliably better on direct tests of memory, but that effects due to grade and subject group were not observed on priming of fragment completion.

In the one study reporting age differences during childhood on an indirect test of memory, Buller (unpublished Master's thesis, reported in Graf, 1989) used a levels of processing manipulation and found similar priming effects across age after semantic study but an age-related increase in priming after the nonsemantic study task.

To our knowledge, these studies exhaust the published literature comparing direct and indirect tests of memory with children, although a few additional studies have been presented at meetings (e.g., Anooshian, 1987, 1991; Anooshian & Pride, 1989; Harris & Durso, 1991). These studies as well are strikingly convergent in their findings of dissociations due to age between direct and indirect tests of memory. That is, whereas age-related improvements in performance have been found with direct tests such as recognition and recall, the amount of priming produced by prior item presentation on indirect tests of memory has been found to be invariant across age.

Indirect Tests of Memory for Associations: Research with Adults

The research discussed above with adults and children focused solely on memory for individual items. There is, however, a long history to the study of memory for associations between items, reflecting the important role that associative memory plays in many learning contexts (see review by Schneider & Pressley, 1989). Recently, Graf and Schacter (1985; 1987; Schacter & Graf, 1986) have extended the use of indirect measures of memory to the study of memory for associations.

Subjects in the experiments by Graf and Schacter were presented lists of unrelated word pairs under various encoding task conditions. After list presentation, memory was tested with a direct test of memory (cued recall) and an indirect test (cued word-stem completion). For the indirect test, only half the cues could be completed by items from the input list, and two different input lists were used (counterbalanced across subjects) so that baseline measures could be taken of the probability of completing a stem with a particular target item when that target was not on the input list.

One noteworthy feature of the procedure used in most experiments in this line of research is that the stimulus conditions present at retrieval were identical for the two types of memory tests; for both the direct and indirect tests, subjects were presented the first word from pairs as cues along with the first three letters of a word stem. The only difference between the direct and indirect tests involved the instructions given at retrieval; for the direct test, subjects were instructed to try to complete each stem with a word from the earlier presented list, whereas for the indirect test subjects were instructed to complete each stem with the first word that came to mind. Thus, differences in performance with the two types of test cannot be attributed simply to greater retrieval support provided by the indirect tests (Merikle & Reingold, 1991; Schacter, 1989).

Graf and Schacter found evidence for associative priming from the cue words on the indirect tests, but only after orienting tasks at the time of encoding that obliged subjects to encode an elaborative relationship between cue and response members of each word pair. Significantly, this effect was found even with amnesic patients, whose performance on direct tests of associative memory was extremely poor (Graf & Schacter, 1985). Furthermore, performance on the direct and indirect tests was differentially affected by a number of variables, including interference (both proactive and retroactive) (Graf & Schacter, 1987) and the degree of elaboration required by the orienting tasks. In the case of the latter variable, it was found that whereas variations in the degree and type of associative elaboration required by the orienting task had a large effect on performance on a direct test of associative memory, associative priming of word stem completion was affected only by the presence or absence of elaborative encoding and not by the degree or type of associative elaboration (Schacter & Graf, 1986).

Thus, as with research examining memory for individual items, studies of memory for associations have found evidence for dissociations in performance between direct and indirect tests. Some differences in the patterns of results, however, also have emerged. Most importantly, whereas indirect memory for individual items has been found to be unaffected by the strategies used by subjects to encode the stimulus, associative priming effects have been found only when subjects have encoded a meaningful relationship between items. There is also evidence that although associative priming is spared in many clinical populations, it has been found to be absent or diminished in magnitude in some forms of severe amnesia (Schacter, 1985; Shimamura & Squire, 1989), even though priming of individual items was demonstrated in the same populations.

The fact that performance on indirect tests of memory for associations exhibits a somewhat different pattern (in response to encoding and subject variables) than does either indirect memory for individual items or direct memory for associations raises the issue of developmental change in indirect associative memory. Although there are no studies in the literature examining this issue with children, a recent series of studies by Howard (1988) tested for age differences in indirect associative memory between younger and older adults.

In general, the pattern of memory deficits exhibited by older adults closely parallels the findings with children, with the largest age differences being found under task conditions that place a premium on the use of effortful, deliberate strategies at encoding and retrieval (Guttentag, 1985; Kausler, 1982). For example, paralleling the research with children, a fairly large number of studies have found that indirect memory for individual items does not vary with age during adulthood (Howard, 1988).

In the case of indirect memory for new associations, Howard (1988) found that the age-related decrement in performance that typically occurs when using direct measures of remembering was often reduced or eliminated when testing memory using indirect forms of assessment. However, after certain study conditions, age differences were found using both types of tests of retention. For example, in one experiment the word pairs were presented within meaningful sentences in preparation for a recognition test for the target nouns. Some subjects received just one presentation of each sentence before testing, whereas other subjects were presented each sentence twice. Age differences were found in recognition test performance regardless of the number of times each sentence was presented. In contrast, age differences in associative priming were found only for subjects receiving a single presentation of each sentence; when each sentence was presented more than once, the amount of associative priming that occurred was equivalent across age. Howard concluded that the age difference found in associative priming reflected a diminished ability on the part of the older adults to establish an enduring new association between the target nouns with just a single exposure to the material.

A Developmental Study of Associative Memory: Comparing Direct and Indirect Measures

Developmental studies using direct measures of memory for associations have found that there are large age differences in performance after deliberate paired-associate learning that extend well into the teen years (see reviews by Kail, 1990, and Schneider & Pressley, 1989). These age differences in recall performance have been traced to age differences in the frequency and degree to which subjects of different ages engage in meaningful or elaborative processing of the presented word pairs. For instance, assessments of deliberate use of elaborative procedures demonstrate a pattern of age changes that parallels the age differences found in associative recall performance (Beuhring & Kee, 1987; Pressley, 1982); moreover, age differences in performance are significantly diminished when younger subjects are instructed to generate meaningful elaborations (Pressley, 1982).

Recently, we conducted two experiments designed to study children's associative learning using indirect measures of memory (Ausley & Guttentag, 1991). The general procedure that we used was patterned after that used by Graf and Schacter (1985). Subjects were first presented a mixed list of 16 related and 16 unrelated word pairs. The related pairs consisted of moderately associated items, based on word association norms for fifth-graders (Palermo & Jenkins, 1964). Past research has demonstrated that when word pairs are presented whose members have a preexisting association with each other (even a moderate one), both children and adults are more likely to encode a meaningful relationship between pair members, resulting in improved paired-associate learning performance as assessed by direct, cued recall tests of memory (Guttentag, 1989; Pressley & Levin, 1977; Rohwer, Rabinowitz, & Dronkers, 1982). For the purposes of the present study, performance with associated pairs provided a baseline measure under indirect memory assessment conditions of the amount of priming produced in the absence of the requirement that subjects establish an entirely new association between items in semantic memory.

Two different lists were used, with half the subjects receiving A-list items and half receiving B-list items. After list presentation, half the subjects at each age were tested with a direct test of memory and half with an indirect test. The stimulus materials presented at the time of retrieval for the direct and indirect tests were identical; the two types of test differed solely with respect to the instructions provided at the time of retrieval. As was noted above, this feature of the procedure is necessary if meaningful comparisons are to be made between patterns of performance under direct and indirect testing conditions (Merikle & Reingold, 1991). Moreover, in the case of developmental research, it is necessary to control for the possibility that, in comparison with the direct test of remembering, the indirect measure of retention may simply involve the provision of greater retrieval support from the environment. Craik (1983), for example, has argued that age differences in remembering performance are likely to decrease as the amount of retrieval support increases. With the design used here, however, the amount of retrieval support provided by the direct and indirect tests was equivalent.

The tests consisted of 64 three-letter word stems presented in random order. Half the stems (*old item* stems) could be completed by a target item from the input list, whereas the remaining stems (*new item* stems) could not be completed by an item from the input list. Subjects in the direct test condition were told that many of the stems could be completed by items from the previously presented list, and they were instructed to try to complete each stem with a list item if possible. Subjects in the indirect test condition were told to complete each stem as quickly as possible with the first word that came to mind that began with that three-letter stem.

All subjects received the identical set of 64 stems on the retrieval tests. The set was constructed such that the 32 *old-item* stems for subjects receiving the A-list at input were *new-item* stems for subjects receiving the B-list, and vice versa. In addition, half the old and half the new stems

TABLE 9.1. Examples of study list items and retention test items for subjects receiving items.

Study items	A-list items	B-list items
Related pairs	Cry–Tears	Stem–Branch
Unrelated pairs	Girl–Plant	Bed–Peace
Retention test items		**Target response**
Old, related, context	Cry–Tea—	(Tears)
Old, related, no-context	–Tea—	(Tears)
Old, unrelated, context	Girl–Pla—	(Plant)
Old, unrelated, no-context	–Pla—	(Plant)
New, related, context	Stem–Bra—	(Branch)
New, related, no-context	–Bra—	(Branch)
New, unrelated, context	Bed–Pea—	(Peace)
New, unrelated, no-context	–Pea—	(Peace)

were presented with context (the corresponding cue or stimulus word from the A or B input list) and half were presented without context; that is, with no cue word at all. The assignment of stems to the context or no-context testing conditions was counterbalanced across subjects at each age. Thus, in combination with item relatedness (related vs. unrelated items on the input lists), the manipulation of context at test (context vs. no context) and item status (old vs. new stems) produced eight different types of items on each retention test (see Table 9.1).

This procedure permitted testing direct and indirect memory for both individual items (stem completion for stems presented with no context cues) and for associations between cue and target members of item pairs (stem completion for stems presented with context cues). For the indirect test of memory, responses to new-item stems provided a baseline measure of the frequency of stem completion with targets in the absence of prior presentation of those items on the input list. Accordingly, the measure of priming was the percentage of old-item stems completed with list items minus the corresponding baseline.

Two experiments were conducted using this general procedure; the experiments differed solely with respect to the study conditions that were required. In Experiment 1, each word pair was printed on a separate index card for serial presentation. As each pair was presented, a sentence was read to the subject containing both words from the pair; all sentences were constructed so that they presented the pair members in an interactive relationship. The orienting task required subjects to judge how well each sentence related the two words from the pair. Subjects were not told that their memory for the word pairs was to be tested. This task was designed to require subjects to encode a meaningful relationship between the members of each pair; in this way we were able to compare direct and indirect memory for items and associations after elaborative encoding.

Experiment 2 examined direct and indirect memory for items and associations after deliberate memorization of the presented pairs. Word pairs were presented serially printed on cards, but no sentences accompanied list presentation. Subjects were simply instructed to memorize each word pair in preparation for a cued recall test.

After study (in both Experiments 1 and 2), subjects in the direct memory assessment condition were presented the stem completion task and were asked to complete as many stems as possible with words from the previously presented list. Subjects in the indirect memory assessment condition also performed the stem completion task, but they were asked to complete each stem with the first word that came to mind; subjects in the indirect memory condition were told that the stem completion task was part of another experiment and their memory for the list items would be tested later.

Results

The results from the two experiments are presented in Tables 9.2 and 9.3. Turning first to the direct assessment of memory after incidental elaborative encoding in Experiment 1 (see Table 9.2), an analysis of variance revealed significant effects of Materials, $F(1, 30) = 26.85$, $p < 0.01$, and Context, $F(1, 30) = 98.45$, $p < 0.01$, and a Materials × Context interaction, $F(1, 30) = 49.13$, $p < 0.01$, but a nonsignificant effect of Age, $F < 1$. Simple effects tests revealed that the context effect was significant for both related, $F(1, 30) = 229.22$, $p < 0.01$, and unrelated, $F(1, 30) = 6.50$, $p < 0.02$ items, but was significantly larger for

TABLE 9.2. Direct memory scores (% stem completion with target items) and indirect memory scores (priming of word stem completion) at each age in each condition of Experiment 1 (incidental learning with a meaningful associative orienting task).

Direct memory (recall)			
Age	Materials	Context condition	
		Context	No-context
Children	Related	0.91	0.49
	Unrelated	0.64	0.56
Adults	Related	0.96	0.43
	Unrelated	0.65	0.50
Indirect memory (stem-completion priming)			
Age	Materials	Context condition	
		Context	No-context
Children	Related	0.28	0.19
	Unrelated	0.27	0.18
Adults	Related	0.20	0.03
	Unrelated	0.23	0.11

related than unrelated items. The effect of materials, on the other hand, was significant only when context was provided, $F(1, 30) = 83.14$.

This pattern of results is consistent with what was predicted. Context facilitated performance, reflecting the learning of associations between items, especially for pairs for which there was a preexisting association between the items. The preexisting relatedness of the materials also affected performance, as has been found in past research, but of course only when context was provided (there is no reason to expect an effect of relatedness when the related context cues were not presented at retrieval). The lack of any age differences in performance is also consistent with past studies that have found that age differences in paired-associate learning performance are diminished or eliminated when subjects at all ages are obliged to encode a meaningful relationship between pair members at input (Pressley, 1982). It should be noted that in the present case, not only was encoding constrained at input, but considerable support was provided at retrieval as well (in the form of the word stems). As Craik (1983) has noted, it is exactly under such conditions (constraint on encoding, support at retrieval) that age differences in remembering are apt to be least apparent.

A similar analysis of the priming scores in Experiment 1 revealed a somewhat different pattern of findings: significant main effects of Context, $F(1, 30) = 26.26$, $p < 0.01$, and Age, $F(1, 30) = 8.43$, $p < 0.01$, but no significant effect of Materials and no significant interactions. Inspection of Table 9.2 reveals that priming scores were significantly larger under context than under no-context conditions at retrieval; it is this difference that provides the measure of priming of associative memory. Importantly, the magnitude of the priming effect did not vary with relatedness. Consistent with the results from previous studies, this finding indicates that although the elaborative encoding of related items was more supportive of cued recall than was the encoding of unrelated pairs, performance on the indirect test of memory was not affected by this variable.

It may also be seen in Table 9.2 that priming scores were actually significantly larger for the children than for the adults, a difference that was present under both context and no-context conditions. Thus, the present findings suggest that the magnitude of priming of individual items (priming under no context conditions) may be even larger for children than for adults, and associative priming is at least as robust for children as for adults after elaborative encoding at input, even for unrelated items.

In Experiment 2, no attempt was made to constrain encoding at input; instead, the experiment was conducted under deliberate memorization conditions. An analysis of the scores on the direct test of memory (see Table 9.3) revealed significant main effects of Age, $F(1, 30) = 9.00$, $p < 0.01$, Materials, $F(1, 30) = 15.27$, $p < 0.01$, and Context, $F(1, 30) =$

TABLE 9.3 Direct memory scores (% stem completion with list items) and indirect memory scores (priming of word stem completion) at each age in each condition of Experiment 2 (intentional learning).

Direct memory (recall)			
Age	Materials	Context condition	
		Context	No-context
Children	Related	0.77	0.34
	Unrelated	0.46	0.42
Adults	Related	0.91	0.40
	Unrelated	0.63	0.43
Indirect memory (stem-completion priming)			
Age	Materials	Context condition	
		Context	No-context
Children	Related	0.32	0.13
	Unrelated	0.15	0.11
Adults	Related	0.25	0.13
	Unrelated	0.36	0.24

103.92, $p < 0.01$, and two significant interactions: Age × Context, $F(1, 30) = 5.44$, $p < 0.05$, and Relatedness × Context, $F(1, 30) = 29.46$, $p < 0.01$. The latter interaction parallels the findings from Experiment 1; relatedness affected recall performance when context was provided at retrieval, but did not affect performance when the stems were presented without context.

Further analysis of the Age × Context interaction using simple effects tests revealed that although there were no age differences in performance on the direct memory test in the absence of context, the adults completed more stems with list items than did the children when context was provided, $F(1, 30) = 12.83$, $p < 0.01$. Thus, whereas no age differences in performance were found in Experiment 1 when encoding was constrained, performance by the adults in Experiment 2 was superior to that of the children after deliberate memorization instructions, provided that context was provided at the time of retrieval. This result is consistent with the findings from previous studies suggesting that age differences in associative learning performance are primarily a reflection of age differences in the degree of encoding of meaningful associations between pair members.

The analysis of stem completion priming (the indirect measure of memory) in Experiment 2 revealed significant main effects of Age, $F(1, 30) = 6.01$, $p < 0.01$, and Context, $F(1, 30) = 16.32$, $p < 0.01$. There was also a significant Age × Materials interaction, $F(1, 30) = 18.27$, $p < 0.01$. Inspection of Table 9.3 reveals that, unlike the findings from Experiment 2, children in Experiment 3 experienced less associative priming for unrelated than for related pairs when context was provided at retrieval.

This pattern of findings is consistent with the assumption that the children did not deliberately encode a meaningful association between items in Experiment 2; consequently, they did not experience significant associative priming for unrelated pairs. In the case of related pairs, on the other hand, the preexisting association between items was sufficient to support priming on the stem completion task. The adults, in contrast, experienced significant associative priming even for unrelated pairs, reflecting their strategic use of elaborative encoding during list presentation. The findings from Experiment 2 suggest that the children experienced as much priming of individual items as did the adults, and experienced at least as much associative priming as did the adults for related items. It was only in the case of associative priming of unrelated pairs that an increase with age in the magnitude of priming was found, apparently reflecting the children's failure to encode intentionally a meaningful association between members of unrelated pairs.

Discussion

The purpose of these experiments was to compare associative memory in children and adults using both direct and indirect measures of memory. The findings using traditional, direct measures of memory (in this case cued recall) are consistent with previous evidence suggesting that age differences in associative learning performance result, at least in part, from age differences in the deliberate, spontaneous use of elaborative encoding procedures. It is noteworthy that age differences in performance emerged only when encoding was unconstrained at study and when context cues were provided at recall; this pattern of findings makes clear that the age differences in recall performance were a reflection of age differences in the encoding of associations between items, rather than resulting from age differences in the encoding of the individual words.

On the indirect memory task, there were no age differences found after elaborative encoding (Experiment 1) in the priming of either individual items or associations. Thus, whatever the nature of the mechanism underlying priming on indirect tests (in terms of either processes or memory systems), this mechanism of memory appears to function similarly across the age span tested here with respect to the priming of both individual items and associations between items. Our personal bias is toward use of Jacoby's (1991) automatic/controlled processing framework to discuss the findings from studies using indirect measures of remembering. Thus, one possible interpretation of these findings (and related findings from developmental studies using indirect measures) is that the functioning of the automatic components of memory retrieval is invariant across age during childhood.

Age differences in priming did emerge after intentional learning (Experiment 2), but were limited to priming of associations for unrelated items. The large priming effect found for the children with related items may reflect either an automatic increase in the activation of a preexisting association or may reflect a more deliberate and effortful encoding of an association between items with materials that are highly supportive of elaborative encoding. The relatively small amount of associative priming found for the children with unrelated items, on the other hand, suggests that in the absence of the support provided by either an elaborative encoding task or by materials with a preexisting relationship between the items, children at this age do not engage in even the minimal amount of elaborative encoding necessary to support associative priming.

In past studies of individual item priming, it has typically been found that priming effects remain invariant across age even under conditions that produce large age differences in performance using direct measures of retention. In the present study, this type of dissociation was found in only one condition: after deliberate memorization of related items (in which case adults recalled more list items than did the children whereas the children exhibited a larger associative priming effect than did the adults). Because the direct and indirect measures used here differed solely with respect to the instructions provided at retrieval, this pattern of results cannot be attributed simply to greater retrieval support with the indirect measure. Instead, the finding suggests that age differences in associative learning result in part from age differences in the use of deliberate retrieval procedures.

One final issue regarding the experiments that deserves mention concerns the extent to which the indirect test of memory used here really was an indirect test (Schacter, 1989). It is possible that subjects may have recognized the relationship between the indirect test and the earlier presented list, and accordingly may have deliberately referred back to their conscious memory of the list as a strategy to bring stem-completions to mind.

Certainly it was the case that virtually all subjects recognized that some of the cue words and some of their responses were items from the earlier presented list. We attempted to conceal the relationship between the indirect test and the earlier presented list by describing it as a filler task that was part of another experiment that used some of the same items, and we gave considerable emphasis to the instruction to subjects in the indirect test condition to report the first word that came to mind to complete each stem. We also inserted two filler tasks between list presentation and retrieval to dissociate the two procedures further in the subjects' minds.

Although it remains possible that some subjects may nonetheless have used a strategy of transforming the indirect test into a direct test, there are a number of reasons for believing that this was rarely the case. First, each stem could be completed by a number of different common words and only half the stems could be completed by a word from the list;

accordingly, referring deliberately back to memory for the list items was not likely to be an effective strategy for completing the stems quickly. Second, the different patterns of results using the two methods of assessment also argues against the view that subjects treated the indirect test as a direct one. Thus, for instance, relatedness affected performance on the direct test of memory in both experiments but did not affect word stem completion priming. This (and other) dissociations between the two types of tests provide perhaps the strongest evidence that subjects responded on the indirect test as they were instructed.

Further Implications of the Use of Indirect Tests for the Study of Memory Development

It is our view that the distinction between direct and indirect forms of remembering is relevant to a consideration of a number of important issues in the study of memory development. In this section we will discuss the use of indirect tests as they relate to the issues of continuities in memory between infancy and childhood, the development of recognition memory, and conscious and unconscious influences on memory.

Infant Memory

One goal of research on memory development is to trace the origins during infancy of the memory processes studied in children and adults. An obvious impediment to such efforts is the fact that so many of the methods that have been used to study memory in children depend on some minimal level of verbal skill. When testing memory in preverbal infants, alternative procedures must be used that do not require verbal responses and that do not depend on verbal knowledge.

Researchers have devised a variety of techniques to study infant memory by capitalizing on nonverbal behavioral responses. Visual habituation/preference paradigms, for instance, have been widely used to study memory during early infancy, as have variations on standard operant procedures. Research using such techniques has produced startling evidence regarding the early development of recognition memory. For example, Friedman (1972), using a visual habituation paradigm, demonstrated that even newborns are capable of visual recognition of a repeatedly presented visual pattern. Perhaps even more dramatically, DeCasper and Spence (1986) found that newborns whose mothers recited a particular story repeatedly during their last few weeks of pregnancy found it more rewarding to hear that "familiar" story than a different story; this finding has been taken as evidence of newborn recognition of a complex verbal stimulus that had previously been experienced only prenatally.

An important issue raised by these and other similar findings concerns the extent to which continuities exist between recognition memory as assessed with these paradigms and recognition memory as it has typically been assessed in research on memory development during childhood. The reason for questioning the existence of continuities is that the procedures used to study recognition memory during infancy are clearly indirect forms of assessment; unlike the direct memory tests typically used with children, the infancy procedures do not require any awareness on the subject's part that a stimulus has been presented before. Thus, there is little reason to expect continuity between the type of memory studied with indirect assessment procedures during infancy and the type of memory studied with direct assessment procedures during childhood. Indeed, it is unfortunate that the same memory terms have tended to be used in the two literatures; in particular, the use of the term *recognition* to describe the memory effects found with infants using indirect assessment procedures has connotations (such as awareness of a previous experience) that really may not apply. On the other hand, research using indirect methods of memory assessment with children probably does provide a real avenue of continuity with the infancy research, because these tests do not require an awareness of the previous occurrence of events for successful performance.

Components of Recognition: Developmental Implications

Past research has demonstrated that even preschool children possess an impressive capacity for stimulus recognition. Indeed, in some studies, little if any change in recognition memory performance has been found beyond early childhood (Brown, 1975; Olson, 1976). Other studies, however, have found evidence for substantial age-related improvement in the accuracy of recognition memory judgments (e.g., Dirks & Neisser, 1977; Mandler & Robinson, 1978). Recent research with adults using direct and indirect measures of memory may point the way toward a reconciliation of these conflicting sets of findings.

Current research with adults suggests that recognition memory is not a unitary phenomenon. Rather, dual process theories of recognition (e.g., Atkinson & Juola, 1974; Jacoby, 1991; Jacoby & Dallas, 1981; Mandler, 1980) hypothesize that recognition judgments may be based either on the conscious recollection of having experienced a stimulus on an earlier occasion or on a more general feeling of familiarity. Feelings of familiarity occur because previously presented stimuli tend to be processed more readily than novel stimuli, a phenomenon Jacoby and Dallas termed *perceptual fluency*.

Supporting this view, Jacoby and Dallas (1981) used a perceptual identification task to demonstrate that items seen for a second time could be identified at shorter exposure durations than could stimuli presented just once during the experiment. They concluded that perceptual fluency is often used as a basis for recognition. To test this proposition, Johnston, Dark, and Jacoby (1985) gave subjects a recognition test for previously studied words in which each word was gradually clarified until it could be identified, at which time subjects also made an old/new judgment. Johnston et al. found that the likelihood that a word would be judged "old" was affected not only by its actual old/new status (i.e., by conscious recollection), but also by its speed of identification; the more rapid the identification, the more likely subjects were to judge that the item had been presented before, demonstrating an effect of perceptual fluency on recognition judgments. Johnston et al. also found that the contribution of perceptual fluency to recognition judgments varied with the type of stimulus presented. When nonwords rather than words were presented, perceptual fluency (i.e., ease of stimulus identification) acquired a larger role in subjects' recognition memory judgments.

This work may have important implications for understanding the development of recognition memory. We hypothesize that conflicting findings in the developmental literature may reflect different patterns of developmental change for the two components of recognition. Whereas perceptual-fluency-based recognition may be developmentally invariant, conscious recollection as a basis for recognition judgments may improve throughout childhood. It would be productive in future research on the development of recognition memory to track patterns of developmental change in the two bases for recognition judgments.

Attributions of Unconscious Memory

When subjects respond on direct tests of recall or recognition memory, their responses imply a conscious awareness of the prior presentation of particular stimulus items. On indirect tests of memory, in contrast, *memory* effects are revealed without requiring any conscious awareness on the subject's part of the prior experience of the stimulus. Indirect measures of memory thus reveal unconscious influences of memory on current behavior.

In some cases, of course, subjects may be sensitive to the "indirect memory" effect being produced by the prior experience and may correctly attribute that effect to memory; indeed, this is assumed to be the process that occurs when the effects of perceptual fluency produce a feeling of familiarity and a judgment of recognition. Jacoby and colleagues (Jacoby & Kelly, 1987; Jacoby & Kelley, 1990; Jacoby, Kelley, & Dywan, 1989a; Jacoby et al. 1989b; Kelley & Jacoby, 1990) have also demonstrated, however, that unconscious influences of memory can be misattributed to sources other than the past. For example, it has been found that the increase in perceptual fluency produced by a single prior presentation of a name during the initial phase of an experiment is sufficient to increase the likelihood that people will later judge that name to be the name of a famous person (the "false fame" effect) (Jacoby et al., 1989b). In this case, the feeling of familiarity experienced by subjects when the name is presented a second time fails to be attributed correctly to its earlier presentation during the experiment; instead, the feeling of familiarity is misattributed to the stimulus being the name of someone famous. Similarly, the increase in perceptual fluency produced by prior presentation of a stimulus during an experimental session has been found, under certain conditions, to affect subjects' judgments of the level of background noise accompanying stimulus presentation (Jacoby, Allan, Collins, & Larwill, 1988) and judgments of the duration of presentation of a briefly flashed item (Witherspoon & Allan, 1985).

The point established by this evidence is that prior experiences can influence the interpretation of later events by increasing their ease of processing. How these events are interpreted, however, depends on an inference or attribution regarding the source of the increased efficiency of processing. Sometimes fluent processing is correctly attributed to an influence of the past, whereas under other conditions fluent processing may be misattributed to other sources.

Misattributions will occur, of course, only if subjects fail to recollect consciously the earlier occurrence of the event. Conscious recollection, however, is known to be affected by the kinds of effortful processes that vary with age, raising the possibility of systematic age differences in the likelihood of misattributions. Dywan and Jacoby (1990), for example, found that older adults showed a larger "false fame" effect than did younger adult subjects, suggesting that older adults may be more likely than young adults to make misattributions of perceptual fluency. An important question for future research is whether children also exhibit an increased likelihood of misattribution of indirect memory effects; at present there is almost nothing known about developmental change or invariance during childhood in these important attributional processes.

Summary

Most research on the development of memory has focused on the singular case of intentional memorization followed by deliberate recall or recognition. Much of what we remember, however, is information learned incidentally rather than deliberately. Moreover, the effects of past experience are not limited to situations in which we deliberately try to recall a prior experience. Studies using indirect indices of "memory" (which do not require that subjects be aware of the influence of the prior experience on their responding) thus complement studies using more traditional measures of retention by broadening the focus of research on the development of memory to encompass what is undoubtedly one of the most important contexts in which memory (broadly defined) operates—contexts in which past experiences affect behavior in the absence of deliberate attempts at recollection. Moreover, as findings from our own experiments demonstrate, the use of indirect measures of memory, in combination with more traditional direct indices, may help highlight sources of age differences in performance that occur under traditional deliberate recollection conditions.

At present, most of the developmental research using indirect tests of memory has been designed simply to demonstrate dissociations due to age on direct and indirect tests of memory. Given the consistency of the data so far, we would argue that the field is ready, even at this early stage, to shift attention away from indirect memory as an object of study toward the use of indirect memory paradigms as tools—tools whose use may help provide new insights into such issues as the nature of developmental change in the conceptual knowledge base (e.g., Harris & Durso, 1991), sources of developmental change in recognition memory, and the development of memory attribution processes.

References

Anooshian, L.J. (1987). *Implicit and explicit remembering by children and adults*. Paper presented at the biennial meetings of the Society for Research in Child Development, Baltimore, MD.

Anooshian, L.J. (1991). *Identifying and remembering pictures: Contrasting developmental trends for direct and indirect memory measures*. Poster presented at the biennial meetings of the Society for Research in Child Development, Seattle, WA.

Anooshian, L.J., & Pride, L. (1989). *Identifying and remembering pictures: Developmental trends for implicit and explicit memory*. Paper presented at the biennial meetings of the Society for Research in Child Development, Kansas City, MO.

Ashcraft, M.H. (1990). Strategic processing in children's mental arithmetic: A review and proposal. In D.F. Bjorklund (Ed.), *Children's strategies: Contemporary views of cognitive development*. Hillsdale, NJ: Erlbaum.

Atkinson, R.C., & Juola, J.F. (1974). Search and decision processes in recognition memory. In D.H. Krantz, R.C. Atkinson, R.D. Luce, & P. Suppes (Eds.), *Contemporary developments in mathematical psychology* (Vol. 1, pp. 243–293). San Francisco, CA: Freeman.

Ausley, J.A., & Guttentag, R.E. (1991). *Implicit memory for new associations: A developmental study*. Presented at the biennial meetings of the Society for Research in Child Development, Seattle, WA.

Beuhring, T., & Kee, D.W. (1987). Developmental relationships among metamemory, elaborative strategy use, and associative memory. *Journal of Experimental Child Psychology*, *44*, 377–400.

Bjorklund, D.F., & Muir, J.E. (1988). Children's development of free recall memory: Remembering on their own. *Annals of Child Development*, *5*, 79–123.

Blaxton, T.A. (1989). Investigating dissociations among memory measures: Support for a transfer-appropriate processing framework. *Journal of Experimental Psychology: Learning, Memory, and Cognition*, *15*, 657–668.

Bransford, J.D., Franks, J.J., Morris, C.D., & Stein, B.S. (1979). Some general constraints on learning and memory research. In L.S. Cermak & F.I.M. Craik (Eds.), *Levels of processing in human memory*. Hillsdale, NJ: Erlbaum.

Brown, A.L. (1975). The development of memory: Knowing, knowing about knowing, and knowing how to know. In H.W. Reese (Ed.), *Advances in child development and behavior* (Vol. 10). New York: Academic Press.

Brown, A.L., Bransford, J.D., Ferrara, R.A., & Campione, J.C. (1983). Learning, remembering, and understanding. In P.H. Mussen (Ed.), *Handbook of Child Psychology* (4th ed., Vol. III). J.H. Flavell & E.M. Markman (Vol. Eds.). New York: John Wiley & Sons.

Carroll, M., Byrne, B., & Kirsner, K. (1985). Autobiographical memory and perceptual learning: A developmental study using picture recognition, naming latency, and perceptual identification. *Memory and Cognition*, *13*(3), 273–279.

Cermak, L.S., Talbot, N., Chandler, K., & Wolbarst, L.R. (1985). The perceptual priming phenomenon in amnesia. *Neuropsychologia*, *23*, 615–622.

Clarke, R.G.B., & Morton, J. (1983). Cross modality facilitation in tachistoscopic word recognition. *Quarterly Journal of Experimental Psychology*, *35A*, 79–96.

Cofer, C.C. (1967). Conditions for the use of verbal associations. *Psychological Bulletin*, *68*, 1–12.

Craik, F.I.M. (1983). On the transfer of information from temporary to permanent memory. *Philosophical Transactions of the Royal Society of London*, *302*, 341–359.

Craik, F.I.M., & Lockhart, R.S. (1972). Levels of processing: A framework for memory research. *Journal of Verbal Learning and Verbal Behavior*, *11*, 671–684.

Craik, F.I.M., & Tulving, E. (1975). Depth of processing and the retention of words in episodic memory. *Journal of Experimental Psychology*, *104*, 268–294.

Dagenbach, D., Horst, S., & Carr, T.H. (1990). Adding new information to semantic memory: How much learning is enough to produce automatic priming? *Journal of Experimental Psychology: Learning, Memory, and Cognition*, *16*, 581–591.

DeCasper, A.J., & Spence, M.J. (1986). Prenatal maternal speech influences newborns' perception of speech sounds. *Infant Behavior and Development*, *9*, 133–150.

Dirks, J., & Neisser, U. (1977). Memory for objects in real scenes: The development of recognition and recall. *Journal of Experimental Child Psychology*, *23*, 315–328.

Dywan, J., & Jacoby, L.L. (1990). Effects of aging on source monitoring: Differences in susceptibility to false fame. *Psychology and Aging*, *5*, 379–387.

Eich, E. (1984). Memory for unattended events: Remembering with and without awareness. *Memory and Cognition*, *12*, 105–111.

Folds, T.H., Footo, M.M., Guttentag, R.E., & Ornstein, P.A. (1990). When children mean to remember: Issues of context specificity, strategy effectiveness, and intentionality in the development of memory. In D.F. Bjorklund (Ed.), *Children's strategies: Contemporary views of cognitive development*. Hillsdale, NJ: Erlbaum.

Friedman, S. (1972). Habituation and recovery of response in the alert human newborn. *Journal of Experimental Child Psychology*, *13*, 339–349.

Graf, P. (1989). *Life-span changes in implicit and explicit memory*. Paper presented at the meetings of the Psychonomic Society, Atlanta, GA.

Graf, P., & Mandler, G. (1984). Activation makes words more accessible, but not necessarily more retrievable. *Journal of Verbal Learning and Verbal Behavior*, *23*, 553–568.

Graf, P., Mandler, G., & Haden, P. (1982). Simulating amnesic symptoms in normal subjects. *Science*, *218*, 1243–1244.

Graf, P., & Schacter, D.L. (1985). Implicit and explicit memory for new associations in normal and amnesic subjects. *Journal of Experimental Psychology: Learning, Memory, and Cognition*, *11*, 501–518.

Graf, P., & Schacter, D.L. (1987). Selective effects of interference on implicit and explicit memory for new associations. *Journal of Experimental Psychology: Learning, Memory, and Cognition*, *13*, 45–53.

Graf, P., Shimamura, A.P., & Squire, L.R. (1985). Priming across modalities and priming across category levels: Extending the domain of preserved function in amnesia. *Journal of Experimental Psychology: Learning, Memory, and Cognition*, *11*, 385–395.

Graf, P., Squire, L.R., & Mandler, G. (1984). The information that amnesic patients do not forget. *Journal of Experimental Psychology: Learning, Memory, and Cognition*, *10*, 164–178.

Greenbaum, J.L., & Graf, P. (1989). Preschool period development of implicit and explicit remembering. *Bulletin of the Psychonomic Society*, *27*(5), 417–420.

Guttentag, R.E. (1985). Memory and aging: Implications for theories of memory development during childhood. *Developmental Review*, *5*, 56–82.

Guttentag, R.E. (1989). *Age differences in associative learning: Strategic propensity and knowledge access effects*. Presentation at the meetings of the Society for Research in Child Development, Kansas City, MO.

Harris, J.F., & Durso, F.T. (1991). *The impact of knowledge and frequency on implicit and explicit memory tasks*. Presented at the biennial meeting of the Society for Research in Child Development, Seattle, WA.

Hasher, L., & Zacks, R.T. (1979). Automatic and effortful processes in memory. *Journal of Experimental Psychology: General*, *108*, 356–388.

Howard, D.V. (1988). Implicit and explicit assessment of cognitive aging. In M.L. Howe & C.J. Brainerd (Eds.), *Cognitive development in adulthood: Progress in cognitive development research*. New York: Springer–Verlag.

Howe, M.L., & O'Sullivan, J.T. (1990). The development of strategic memory: Coordinating knowledge, metamemory, and resources. In D.F. Bjorklund (Ed.), *Children's strategies: Contemporary views of cognitive development*. Hillsdale, NJ: Erlbaum.

Hunt, R.R., & Toth, J.P. (1990). Perceptual identification, fragment completion, and free recall: Concepts and data. *Journal of Experimental Psychology: Learning, Memory, and Cognition*, *16*, 282–290.

Istomina, Z.M. (1975). The development of voluntary memory in preschool-age children. *Soviet Psychology*, *13*, 5–64.

Jacoby, L.L. (1983a). Perceptual enhancement: Persistent effects of an experience. *Journal of Experimental Psychology: Learning, Memory, and Cognition*, *9*, 21–38.

Jacoby, L.L. (1983b). Remembering the data: Analyzing interactive processes in reading. *Journal of Verbal Learning and Verbal Behavior*, *22*, 485–508.
Jacoby, L.L. (1984). Incidental versus intentional retrieval: Remembering and awareness as separate issues. In L.R. Squire & N. Butters (Eds.), *Neuropsychology of memory* (pp. 145–156). New York: Guilford Press.
Jacoby, L.L. (1991). A process dissociation framework: Separating automatic from intentional uses of memory. *Journal of Memory and Language*, *30*, 513–541.
Jacoby, L.L., Allan, L.G., Collins, J.C., & Larwill, L.K. (1988). Memory influences subjective experience: Noise judgments. *Journal of Experimental Psychology: Learning, Memory, and Cognition*, *14*, 240–247.
Jacoby, L.L., & Dallas, M. (1981). On the relationship between autobiographical memory and perceptual learning. *Journal of Experimental Psychology: General*, *110*, 306–340.
Jacoby, L.L., & Kelley, C.M. (1987). Unconscious influences of memory for a prior event. *Personality and Social Psychology Bulletin*, *13*, 314–336.
Jacoby, L.L., & Kelley, C.M. (1990). An episodic view of motivation: Unconscious influences of memory. In E.T. Higgins & R.M. Sorrentino (Eds.), *Handbook of motivation and cognition: Foundations of social behavior* (Vol. 2, pp. 451–481). New York: Guilford Press.
Jacoby, L.L., Kelley, C.M., & Dywan, J. (1989a). Memory attributions. In H.L. Roediger & F.I.M. Craik (Eds.), *Varieties of memory and consciousness: Essays in honor of Endel Tulving* (pp. 391–422). Hillsdale, NJ: Erlbaum.
Jacoby, L.L., & Witherspoon, D. (1982). Remembering without awareness. *Canadian Journal of Psychology*, *36*, 300–324.
Jacoby, L.L., Woloshyn, V., & Kelley, C.M. (1989b). Becoming famous without being recognized: Unconscious influences of memory produced by dividing attention. *Journal of Experimental Psychology: General*, *118*, 115–125.
Johnson, M. (1983). A multiple-entry, modular memory system. In G.H. Bower (Ed.), *The psychology of learning and motivation* (Vol. 17, pp. 81–123). New York: Academic Press.
Johnson, M.K., & Hasher, L. (1987). Human learning and memory. *Annual Review of Psychology*, *38*, 631–638.
Johnston, W.A., Dark, V.J., & Jacoby, L.L. (1985). Perceptual fluency and recognition judgements. *Journal of Experimental Psychology: Learning, Memory, and Cognition*, *11*(1), 3–11.
Kail, R. (1990). *The development of memory in children*. New York: Freeman.
Kausler, D.H. (1982). *Experimental psychology and human aging*. New York: Wiley.
Kelley, C.M., & Jacoby, L.L. (1990). The construction of subjective experience: Memory attributions. *Mind and Language*, *5*(1), 49–68.
Kinsbourne, M., & Wood, F. (1975). Short term memory and the amnesic syndrome. In D.D. Deutsch & J.A. Deutsch (Eds.), *Short term memory* (pp. 258–291). New York: Academic Press.
Kirsner, K., Milech, D., & Standen, P. (1983). Common and modality-specific processes in the mental lexicon. *Memory and Cognition*, *11*, 621–630.
Kirsner, K., & Smith, M.C. (1974). Modality effects in word identification. *Memory and Cognition*, *2*, 637–640.

Kobasigawa, A. (1977). Retrieval strategies in the development of memory. In R.V. Kail & J.W. Hagen (Eds.), *Perspectives on the development of memory and cognition*. Hillsdale, NJ: Erlbaum.

Kolers, P.A. (1973). Remembering operations. *Memory and Cognition*, *1*, 347–355.

Kolers, P.A. (1975). Memorial consequences of automatized encoding. *Journal of Experimental Psychology: Human Learning and Memory*, *1*, 689–701.

Kolers, P.A. (1976). Reading a year later. *Journal of Experimental Psychology: Human Learning and Memory*, *2*, 554–565.

Kolers, P.A. (1979). A pattern-analyzing basis of recognition. In L.S. Cermak & F.I.M. Craik (Eds.), *Levels of processing in human memory*. Hillsdale, NJ: Erlbaum.

Kolers, P.A., & Roediger, H.L. (1984). Procedures of mind. *Journal of Verbal Learning and Verbal Behavior*, *23*, 425–449.

Komatsu, S.I., & Ohta, N. (1984). Priming effects in word- fragment completion for short- and long-term retention intervals. *Japanese Psychological Research*, *26*, 194–200.

Lorsbach, T.C., & Worman, L.J. (1989). The development of explicit and implicit forms of memory in learning disabled children. *Contemporary Educational Psychology*, *14*(1), 67–76.

Mandler, G. (1980). Recognizing: The judgment of previous occurrence. *Psychological Review*, *87*, 252–271.

Mandler, J.M. (1984). Representation and recall in infancy. In M. Moscovitch (Ed.), *The transition from infant to child memory* (pp. 75–101). New York: Plenum.

Mandler, J.M., & Robinson, C.A. (1978). Developmental changes in picture recognition. *Journal of Experimental Child Psychology*, *26*, 122–136.

McKoon, G., Ratcliff, R., & Dell, G.S. (1986). A critical evaluation of the semantic/episodic distinction. *Journal of Experimental Psychology: Learning, Memory, and Cognition*, *12*(2), 295–306.

Merikle, P.M., & Reingold, E.M. (1991). Comparing direct (explicit) and indirect (implicit) measures to study unconscious memory. *Journal of Experimental Psychology: Learning, Memory, and Cognition*, *17*, 224–233.

Metcalfe, J., & Fisher, R.P. (1986). The relation between recognition memory and classification learning. *Memory and Cognition*, *14*, 164–173.

Morris, C.D., Bransford, J.D., & Franks, J.J. (1977). Levels of processing versus transfer appropriate processing. *Journal of Verbal Learning and Verbal Behavior*, *16*, 519–533.

Moscovitch, M., Winocur, G., & McLachlan, D. (1986). Memory as assessed by recognition and reading time in normal and memory-impaired people with Alzheimer's disease and other neurological disorders. *Journal of Experimental Psychology: General*, *115*, 331–347.

Naito, M. (1990). Repetition priming in children and adults: Age-related dissociation between implicit and explicit memory. *Journal of Experimental Child Psychology*, *50*, 462–484.

Neisser, U. (1979). Review of *Divided Consciousness* by E.R. Hilgard. *Contemporary Psychology*, *24*, 99–100.

Nelson, K., & Gruendel, J. (1981). Generalized event representations: Basic building blocks of cognitive development. In M.E. Lamb & A.L. Brown (Eds.), *Advances in developmental psychology*. Hillsdale, NJ: Erlbaum.

Oakley, D.A. (1983). The varieties of memory: A phylogenetic approach. In A.R. Mayes (Ed.), *Memory in humans and animals* (pp. 20–82). Wokingham, UK: Van Nostrand Reinhold.

O'Keefe, J., & Nadel, L. (1978). *The hippocampus as a cognitive map*. London: Oxford University.

Olson, G.M. (1976). An information-processing analysis of visual memory and habituation in infants. In T.J. Tighe & R.N. Leaton (Eds.), *Habituation*. Hillsdale, NJ: Erlbaum.

Olton, D.S., Becker, J.T., & Handleman, G. (1979). Hippocampus, space, and memory. *Behavioral and Brain Sciences, 2*, 313–365.

Palermo, D.S., & Jenkins, J.J. (1964). *Word association norms: Grade school through college*. Minneapolis, MN: Minnesota Press.

Parkin, A.J. (1982). Residual learning capability in organic amnesia. *Cortex, 18*, 417–440.

Parkin, A.J. (1989). The development and nature of implicit memory. In S. Lewandowsky, J.C. Dunn, & K. Kirsner (Eds.), *Implicit memory: Theoretical issues*. Hillsdale, NJ: Erlbaum.

Parkin, A.J., & Streete, S. (1988). Implicit and explicit memory in young children and adults. *British Journal of Psychology, 79*, 361–369.

Perlmutter, M. (1980). *Children's memory: New directions for child development (No. 10)*. San Francisco: Jossey Bass.

Piaget, J., & Inhelder, B. (1973). *Memory and intelligence*. New York: Basic Books.

Posner, M.I., & Snyder, C.R.R. (1975). Attention and cognitive control. In R.L. Solso (Ed.), *Information processing in cognition: The Loyola Symposium* (pp. 55–85). Hillsdale, NJ: Erlbaum.

Pressley, M. (1982). Elaboration and memory development. *Child Development, 53*, 269–309.

Pressley, M., & Levin, J.R. (1977). Task parameters affecting the efficacy of a visual imagery learning strategy in younger and older children. *Journal of Experimental Child Psychology, 24*, 53–59.

Richardson-Klavehn, A., & Bjork, R.A. (1988). Measures of memory. *Annual Review of Psychology, 39*, 475–543.

Roediger, H.L. (1990). Implicit memory: Retention without remembering. *American Psychologist, 45*, 1043–1056.

Roediger, H.L., & Blaxton, T.A. (1987a). Effects of varying modality, surface features, and retention interval on priming in word fragment completion. *Memory and Cognition, 15*, 379–388.

Roediger, H.L., & Blaxton, T.A. (1987b). Retrieval modes produce dissociations in memory for surface information. In D. Gorfein & R.R. Hoffman (Eds.), *Memory and cognitive processes: The Ebbinghaus centennial conference*. Hillsdale, NJ: Erlbaum.

Roediger, H.L., & Weldon, M.S. (1987). Reversing the picture superiority effect. In M.A. McDaniel & M. Pressley (Eds.), *Imagery and related mnemonic processes: Theories, individual differences, and applications* (pp. 151–174). New York: Springer–Verlag.

Roediger, H.L., Weldon, M.S., & Challis, B.H. (1989). Explaining dissociations between implicit and explicit measures of retention: A processing account. In H.L. Roediger & F.I.M. Craik (Eds.), *Varieties of memory and consciousness: Essays in honor of Endel Tulving*. Hillsdale, NJ: Erlbaum.

Rohwer, W.D. Jr., Rabinowitz, M., & Dronkers, N.F. (1982). Event knowledge, elaborative propensity, and the development of learning proficiency. *Journal of Experimental Child Psychology*, *33*, 492–503.

Scarborough, D.L., Gerard, L., & Cortese, C. (1979). Accessing lexical memory: The transfer of word repetition effects across task and modality. *Memory and Cognition*, *7*, 3–12.

Schacter, D.L. (1985). Priming of old and new information in amnesic patients and normal subjects. *Annals of the New York Academy of Sciences*, *444*, 41–53.

Schacter, D.L. (1987). Implicit memory: History and current status. *Journal of Experimental Psychology: Learning, Memory, and Cognition*, *13*(3), 501–518.

Schacter, D.L. (1989). On the relation between memory and consciousness: Dissociable interactions and conscious experience. In H.L. Roediger III & F.I.M. Craik (Eds.), *Varieties of memory and conscious experience: Essays in honor of Endel Tulving*. Hillsdale, NJ: Erlbaum.

Schacter, D.L., & Graf, P. (1986). Effects of elaborative processing on implicit and explicit memory for new associations. *Journal of Experimental Psychology: Learning, Memory, and Cognition*, *12*, 432–444.

Schacter, D.L., & McGlynn, S.M. (1987). Implicit memory: Effects of elaboration depend on unitization. *American Journal of Psychology*, *102*, 151.

Schacter, D.L., & Tulving, E. (1982). Memory, amnesia, and the episodic/semantic distinction. In R.L. Isaacson & N.E. Spear (Eds.), *The expression of knowledge* (pp. 33–65). New York: Plenum Press.

Schneider, W.E., & Pressley, M.J. (1989). *Memory development between 2 and 20*. New York: Springer-Verlag.

Sherry, D.F., & Schacter, D.L. (1987). The evolution of multiple memory systems. *Psychological Review*, *94*(4), 439–454.

Shiffrin, R.M., & Schneider, W. (1977). Controlled and automatic human information processing: II. Perceptual learning, automatic attending, and a general theory. *Psychological Review*, *84*, 127–190.

Shimamura, A.P. (1986). Priming effects in amnesia: Evidence for a dissociable memory function. *Quarterly Journal of Experimental Psychology*, *38A*, 619–644.

Shimamura, A.P., & Squire, L.R. (1989). Impaired priming of new associations in amnesia. *Journal of Experimental Psychology: Learning, Memory, and Cognition*, *15*(4), 721–728.

Squire, L.R. (1986). Mechanisms of memory. *Science*, *232*, 1612–1619.

Squire, L.R. (1987). *Memory and brain*. New York: Oxford University Press.

Squire, L.R., & Cohen, N.J. (1984). Human memory and amnesia. In J. McGaugh, G. Lynch, & N. Weinberger (Eds.), *Proceedings of the conference on the neurobiology of learning and memory* (pp. 3–64). New York: Guilford Press.

Stein, B.S. (1978). Depth of processing reexamined: The effects of precision of encoding and test appropriateness. *Journal of Verbal Learning and Verbal Behavior*, *17*, 165–174.

Toth, J.P., & Hunt, R.R. (1990). Effect of generation on a word-identification task. *Journal of Experimental Psychology: Learning, Memory, and Cognition*, *16*, 993–1003.

Tulving, E. (1972). Episodic and semantic memory. In E. Tulving & W. Donaldson (Eds.), *Organization of memory* (pp. 381–403). New York: Academic Press.

Tulving, E. (1983). *Elements of episodic memory*. Oxford: The Clarendon Press.

Tulving, E. (1985). Memory and consciousness. *Canadian Psychology*, *26*, 1–12.

Tulving, E. (1986). What kind of a hypothesis is the distinction between episodic and semantic memory? *Journal of Experimental Psychology: Learning, Memory, and Cognition*, *12*, 307–311.

Tulving, E., & Schacter, D.L. (1990). Priming and human memory systems. *Science*, *247*, 301–306.

Tulving, E., Schacter, D.L., & Stark, H.A. (1982). Priming effects in word-fragment completion are independent of recognition memory. *Journal of Experimental Psychology: Learning, Memory, and Cognition*, *8*, 336–342.

Tulving, E., & Thompson, D.M. (1973). Encoding specificity and retrieval processes in episodic memory. *Psychological Review*, *80*, 352–373.

Warrington, E.K., & Weiskrantz, L. (1968). New method of testing long-term retention with special reference to amnesic patients. *Nature*, *217*, 972–974.

Warrington, E.K., & Weiskrantz, L. (1970). Amnesia: Consolidation or retrieval. *Nature*, *228*, 628–630.

Warrington, E.K., & Weiskrantz, L. (1974). The effect of prior learning on subsequent retention in amnesic patients. *Neuropsychologia*, *12*, 419–428.

Warrington, E.K., & Weiskrantz, L. (1978). Further analysis of the prior learning effect in amnesic patients. *Neuropsychologia*, *16*, 169–176.

Warrington, E.K., & Weiskrantz, L. (1982). Amnesia: A disconnection syndrome. *Neuropsychologia*, *20*, 233–248.

Wellman, H.M. (1985). The child's theory of mind: The development of conceptions of cognition. In S.R. Yussen (Ed.), *The growth of reflection in children*. New York: Academic Press.

Wellman, H.M. (1988). The early development of memory strategies. In F.E. Weinert & M. Perlmutter (Eds.), *Memory development: Universal changes and individual differences*. Hillsdale, NJ: Erlbaum.

Winnick, W.A., & Daniel, S.A. (1970). Two kinds of response priming in tachistoscopic recognition. *Journal of Experimental Psychology*, *84*, 74–81.

Witherspoon, D., & Allan, L.G. (1985). The effects of a prior presentation on temporal judgments in a perceptual identification task. *Memory and Cognition*, *13*, 101–111.

Part IV
Afterword

10
Shifting Conceptions of Cognitive Development

MARK L. HOWE AND ROBERT PASNAK

Early in this century, interest in children's cognitive development was motivated by the need to cultivate standardized, psychometric tests of intelligence. The dominant force driving many of these early investigations of the ontogeny of children's cognition was that of associationism (e.g., Kendler & Kendler, 1962; Suppes & Ginsberg, 1963). As enthusiasm for this metaphor of cognition waned, Piaget's (e.g., Inhelder & Piaget, 1958) logicism grew in popularity. This new image of the child-as-logician was fueled in large part, at least in North America, by Flavell's (1963) masterful exposition of the tenets of Piaget's theory of cognitive development. As research began to expose a variety of shortcomings in Piaget's formalism, information-processing models (e.g., Siegler, 1981) and skills approaches (e.g., Fischer, 1980) began to appear. These newer models supplanted traditional Piagetian principles and enjoy a growing prominence in the cognitive development arena. As this century draws to a close, two major formalisms continue to dominate the cognitive development horizon: information-processing models in which the child is viewed as an abstract symbol manipulation device (e.g., Klahr, 1989; Klahr & Wallace, 1976) and Piagetian revivalism (for a review of neo-Piagetian theories, see Howe & Rabinowitz, 1990).

In addition to these shifts in theoretical dispositions, a number of different mechanisms have been proposed as being pivotal constructs necessary to explain cognitive ontogeny. For the past decade or so, theorists have stressed the importance of changes in metacognition and strategy use (see chapters in Volume II of this series; Bjorklund, 1990), resource allocation (see review in Howe & Rabinowitz, 1990), and the content and structure of the knowledge base (e.g., Bjorklund, 1987; Chi & Ceci, 1987) as key factors in the emergence of mature cognition (for a review of all of these mechanisms, see Howe & O'Sullivan, 1990). In this context, it is not unusual to liken cognitive development to some kind of emergent property that results from increases in one or all of these factors. For example, changes in the relative automaticity of some process (e.g., memory activation) or set of processes (e.g., memory activation, retrieval, and response production) involved in some cognitive skill (e.g., using a memorized prototype to match and classify objects) may result in the freeing of scarce resources. Consequently, freed resources may be reallocated to other more difficult aspects of the task, speeding their execution and lowering overall response time, or can be reallocated to an auxiliary task permitting unimpeded dual task performance (but see Howe & O'Sullivan, 1990; Howe & Rabinowitz, 1990). Indeed, a number of theorists have embedded these sorts of changes directly into their models of cognitive development (e.g., as in Case's [1985] framework where developmental changes in cognition are mediated by increases in working memory capacity).

The chapters in this volume, while borrowing from these earlier theories (particularly the notion of cognitive resources), represent a new generation of theories and models of children's cognitive development. Many of the writers have not only provided theoretical advances but have also contributed carefully crafted formal models and experiments that serve to evaluate aspects of their assumptions. The scope of these contributions is impressive. They range from innovative new ideas concerning the nature of the mechanism(s) that drives cognitive development (Dempster's and Harnishfeger & Bjorklund's changes in inhibition, and Brainerd & Reyna's fuzzy-trace theory) to new ways of modeling these developments (Kail's exponential model of changes in speed of processing, Thomas' empirical Bayesian analysis of individual differences, and Cooney & Constas' nonlinear dynamic modeling of learning and language), to the investigation of important research problems from a fresh perspective (Leichtman & Ceci's reanalysis of infantile amnesia) or the definition of new research agendas (Lehman & Bovasso's study of directed forgetting and Ausley & Guttentag's inquiry into children's nondeliberate memory). It is clear that these innovative proposals have culled the best from the past and will serve to direct much of future research in the decades to come.

The topics covered in this book are clearly eclectic and may be resistant to synthesis. However, in what follows we outline what we believe to be the major issues raised in this volume, ones that are critical to elucidating a complete theory of cognitive development. In particular, we focus our discussion on what is new in cognitive development (as reflected in the contributions to this volume) in an attempt to provide some answers to old questions about what develops. We round out this chapter by raising a number of questions that remain unresolved, ones that we hope will also serve to stimulate research into the next century.

What's New in Children's Cognitive Development?

One of the most interesting shifts that has occurred in thinking about what develops is a movement away from the idea that cognitive development is driven solely by an *increase* in some capacity or the acquisition of more powerful algorithms and toward the notion that this development may be spurred by some *decrease* in interference from extraneous information. That is, some aspects of cognitive development may be propelled by changes in the child's ability to resist interference from competing, task-irrelevant information. The chapters by Dempster (this volume) and by Harnishfeger and Bjorklund (this volume) both proclaim the importance of developments in such inhibitory processes and attempt to link these changes to the maturation of neurophysiological systems (i.e., the development of the frontal cortex).

Dempster provides a cogent review of tasks where interference is most likely to be observed (search, Wisconsin Card Sorting Test, measures of field dependence, conservation, selective attention, and the Brown-Peterson task) and argues that changes in levels of interference are related to changes in the efficiency of the functioning of the frontal lobes. Harnishfeger and Bjorklund review a number of sources of inhibition including inhibition of motor behavior, inhibition of external distracters (e.g., information from the environment), and inhibition of internal distracters (e.g., extraneous activation of nodes in a knowledge network). As Harnishfeger and Bjorklund argue, evidence from lexical decision, discourse processing, and memory tasks make a compelling case for the idea that advances in cognitive development may be related to children's growing ability to suppress extraneous information in working memory.

Both Dempster and Harnishfeger and Bjorklund agree that with decreases in interference from task-irrelevant internal and external stimuli, processing of the relevant information becomes easier and more efficient, speeding up processing and increasing accuracy. Although Dempster prefers to remain neutral concerning the locus of these improvements, Harnishfeger and Bjorklund argue that these changes are compatible with resource-based theories of cognitive development. Specifically, they propose a developmental theory of inefficient inhibition in which working memory figures prominently. Here, younger children's poor inhibitory mechanisms result in less efficient cognitive processing because working memory is consumed with irrelevant information, leaving less mental space available for relevant cognitive processing. This is basically a resource theory of cognitive development where efficiency of resource allocation varies with changes in the ability to inhibit irrelevant information in working memory.

Interestingly, in addition to the evidence concerning inhibition of irrelevant information provided by Harnishfeger and Bjorklund's (this volume) intrusion analysis, Lehman and Bovasso (this volume) provide direct evidence that children can intentionally and selectively inhibit what they retrieve from long-term memory. These authors examined children's ability to exhibit conscious control over their forgetting and found that children can monitor and inhibit recall of specific items. Whether this inhibitory ability is the result of processes involving storage mechanisms, retrieval mechanisms, or both is not immediately known (for a recent review of issues surrounding storage and retrieval in children's memory and retention, see chapters in Howe, Brainerd, & Reyna, 1992). However, it is clear that these findings are consistent with both Dempster's and Harnishfeger and Bjorklund's claims about the importance of effective inhibition in children's cognitive development.

Directly related to these issues involved in deliberate versus nondeliberate aspects of (and control over) children's cognition is Ausley and Guttentag's (this volume) examination of children's memory with and without awareness. Although much of the research on children's memory and cognition has centered on the deliberate aspects of these functions, the focus of Ausley and Guttentag's work was on indirect assessments of long-term memory. These authors posed the question of what the nature of the development of memory without awareness (e.g., potentially automatic aspects of memory) might be like. The results of experiments reviewed in their chapter lead to the conclusion that unlike the picture of memory development painted using deliberate tasks, age differences are not as easy to manufacture with indirect memory assessment techniques. Perhaps development takes a different route for automatic aspects of memory than it does for the more deliberate components.

In addition to these emerging theories concerning the contributions of effective inhibition and the nature of indirect (or nondeliberate) aspects of memory to children's cognitive development, this volume contains perhaps the most complete exegesis of Brainerd and Reyna's innovative fuzzy-trace theory of cognitive development. Although in its first generation stage (see Howe & Rabinowitz, 1991b), fuzzy-trace theory provides an important overarching framework for conceptualizing the development of children's reasoning and remembering. Perhaps the single most important of its basic assumptions about cognitive development concerns the shift from reliance on verbatim representations in memory early in development to the extraction of gist. According to their theory, memory representations range from verbatim to highly schematic or fuzzy, where the latter preserve only the critical or relevant features (the gist) of the display. Although verbatim traces are more faithful representations of the stimulus display, they have the disadvantage of being rapidly forgotten. On the other hand, fuzzy traces are less isomorphic with the stimulus display, but they carry the advantage of being more resistant to forgetting. One key to cognitive development, then, is that children learn to extract gist more reliably, producing longer lasting representations.

Although a number of other factors play an important role in Brainerd and Reyna's fuzzy-trace theory of cognitive development, the development of gist extraction is clearly preeminent. In fact, it is this verbatim to gist shift in development that Leichtman and Ceci exploit in their chapter to explain infantile amnesia. That is, early memories for personal experiences are quickly forgotten (relative to later experiences) because they were encoded and stored using highly volatile verbatim traces. Leichtman and Ceci argue that it is only when more stable, fuzzy representations are encoded and stored that autobiographical memories from childhood will be retrievable in later life.

As promising a framework as it may be, considerable research will be needed to test the implications of fuzzy-trace theory for cognitive development as well as its application to infantile amnesia. Indeed, some have suggested that the next step is to create a second generation version, one that affords greater formalization of the tenets of fuzzy-trace theory (Howe & Rabinowitz, 1991b). Kreindler and Lumsden (1992) have already taken a step in this direction, one that concerns what we have identified here as being of central concern; namely, the development of gist extraction. They have implemented a nonlinear dynamic model of gist extraction, one that is based on fuzzy-trace theory's assumptions. This mathematization of fuzzy-trace principles was remarkably successful and informative. Perhaps this represents the beginning of the next (or formalization) phase in the development of a viable alternative to the Piagetian (and neo-Piagetian) tradition.

Throughout science, formal models have played a critical role in the development, testing, and shaping of theories. Models make explicit a theory's assumptions by casting them in testable, falsifiable terms (e.g., equations). These formalizations can then be used to evaluate a theory's tenets rigorously, leading to subsequent acceptance, modification, or rejection of all or part of the theory. Modeling efforts in developmental psychology have played an equally important role in discriminating theories of cognitive ontogeny by providing a number of critical litmus tests. In the current volume, three such formalizations appear in the chapters by Kail, Thomas, and Cooney and Constas.

Kail provides us with an exponential model of changes in speed of processing that limits, rather than specifies, which theoretical alternative may be appropriate for understanding developments in children's cognition. Kail provides an excellent review of numerous tasks where developmental improvements in speed of processing are witnessed. Based in part on the ubiquitousness of these changes in processing speed across different tasks, Kail makes a cogent argument that a global mechanism must be responsible for driving such developments. He provides additional empirical evidence that the mechanism is global, and examines several hypotheses concerning the nature of this mechanism, including changes in inhibitory processing like those discussed by Dempster and by Harnishfeger and Bjorklund. Although the available evidence does not permit the excision of a single hypothesis concerning the nature of this mechanism, the form of the function relating age and changes in processing speed identified by Kail restricts the field of alternatives. As Kail sugggests, more research is required before we will be able to pinpoint the nature of this global mechanism and to understand why its developmental rate is exponential.

Perhaps one of the most important, yet often neglected, goals of studying patterns of development across individuals is to understand the nature of individual variations in ontogeny. Thomas provides us with an elegant way to model these individual variations. Rather than simply viewing individuals as being relatively homogeneous observations on some random variable, with variations being relegated the role of sampling variations or unwanted noise, Thomas argues that it is more sensible to treat different individuals as having their own response distribution with their own parameter values. He provides an outline of an empirical Bayesian (EB) approach, one that facilitates the examination of individual differences and illustrates its application in a variety of situations. By using EB, our focus is redirected away from traditional issues of significance tests and toward the problem of obtaining the best possible parameter estimate for each person. In this manner, EB permits identification of meaningful individual differences, ones not simply attributable to random within-subject error variation. As Thomas reminds us, an understanding of patterns of human development is gained by also understanding how the individuals comprising the trend develop.

Cooney and Constas show how a simple dynamic, deterministic model can also capture the vicissitudes of human development—continuity, discontinuities, and marked variability are all accounted for in their proposed nonlinear system. Recent applications of nonlinear dynamic modeling to problems in cognitive development have proved enormously useful and productive, and carry the advantage that they serve to integrate disparate aspects of development thought previously to be unmanageable within the confines of a single model (see Howe & Rabinowitz, 1991a; van Geert, 1991). Such models also map well onto models in other sciences, providing for an apparent "unification" of diverse areas through mathematics.

The authors contrast linear and nonlinear modeling approaches and develop and discuss nonlinear dynamic models in the context of language, learning, and cognitive development. Like Thomas' EB modeling, Cooney and Constas' nonlinear dynamic modeling changes the focus from treating deviations in empirical observations as noise to one that provides a rich source of information about a developmental process. Clearly one of their take-home messages is that because data are often related to our theoretical constructs in a nonlinear manner, we need to examine our data carefully and not simply use off-the-shelf analysis packages. It is also clear from their chapter that although dynamical systems analyses may appear somewhat complex at first blush, they provide a powerful tool in understanding (cognitive) development, one that is certain to become more visible and prominent in the field in the near future (also see Howe, Montevecchi, Rabinowitz, & Stones, 1991; Howe & Rabinowitz, 1991a, 1992; Rabinowitz, Grant, Howe, & Mason, 1992; Townsend, in press; van Geert, 1991).

Where Do We Go from Here?

We find the trends in cognitive development identified in this volume extremely promising. The changes that have transpired in thinking about cognitive development across the decades, ranging from the associative learning tradition that marked the early part of this century to the more recent models of the child as information processor, may now be supplanted at the end of this century by the innovative ideas of efficient inhibition (Dempster, this volume; Harnishfeger & Bjorklund, this volume) and fuzzy-trace processing (Brainerd & Reyna, this volume; Leichtman & Ceci, this volume). However, for these newer theoretical ideas to survive and flourish to the point of replacing extant models, it is important that they develop second generation formalisms. It will be in this context that the value of these theories can be explicitly evaluated and their explanatory power measured.

A number of researchers in this volume did use formal models to investigate the utility of their ideas about cognitive development. These included exponential models of age changes in speed of processing (Kail), modeling of individual differences (Thomas), and nonlinear dynamic modeling (Cooney & Constas). Each of these models is important because they bring with them not only a particular view of how some aspect of development proceeds but also a formal evaluative mechanism for testing its own validity. Although modeling efforts have always played an important role in developmental theories, it is perhaps only recently with the advent of high-speed desktop computers that more and more researchers are availing themselves of these powerful formal approaches. It is now clear that for a complete theory of cognitive ontogeny to emerge, a minimal criterion must be the formal testing of theoretical assumptions.

The focus of research has also shifted to new domains of development. Included in this volume are studies examining very early memory development (Leichtman & Ceci, this volume), the development of children's intentional control of their memory (Lehman & Bovasso, this volume), and memory without awareness (Ausley & Guttentag, this volume). All of these research programs show promise in helping elucidate basic mechanisms in cognitive development. As such, they should contribute substantially to our growing knowledge base in cognitive development and shape the course of future research as other, new phenomena suggest themselves.

Although it is always difficult to chart the course of future research, it is clear from this volume what such an agenda might look like as this century draws to a close. In addition to each of the specific research programs outlined in these chapters, it is imperative that we also extend our models and theories to incorporate the multitude of variables that influence cognitive development. Forwarding our understanding of the mechanisms driving cognitive development requires a more global perspective, one that is less specialized than has been the tendency in the past. Such a global approach demands the inclusion of social and motivational (among other) variables when answering questions about cognition and its development. We can no longer ignore the complexities of this interplay of factors in cognitive development. Moreover, because we now have the modeling techniques necessary to measure and analyze these complexities (e.g., Cooney & Constas), it is imperative that we take into account the many influences that shape cognitive development.

At the same time, our theories and models must be powerful enough to account for both the principal patterns common to cognitive development as a whole and individual variations in those patterns (e.g., Thomas). Indeed, it is paramount that our theories capture both the generalities of cognitive development as well as the irregularities in that development that occur within individuals. Such theories, although considerably more difficult to construct, convey the complexity that is ontogeny.

In this context, it is of more than passing interest to note that most of the authors in this volume, unlike those in previous books of this nature, have omitted consideration of whether cognitive development is continuous or discontinuous (also see Howe & Rabinowitz, 1991a). Indeed, lengthy discussions of whether development proceeds in a stage-like manner are conspicuously absent from this book. Although the theoretical orientations presented in this volume may be amenable to either stage or nonstage conceptions of development, perhaps the absence of more direct consideration of this issue in each of the chapters is a sign of the times. On the other hand, the question of developmental continuity may reemerge as these new theories evolve and are put to the empirical test (e.g., see Flavell, 1982).

Overall, we believe that the chapters in this volume represent a unique blend of both the global and specific, the collective as well as the individual aspects that comprise cognitive development. These chapters herald the future of what can be expected of research leading into the next century. The promise is that with the availability of more powerful models, a more comprehensive understanding of the foundations of the ontogeny of children's cognition will soon emerge.

Acknowledgments. Preparation of this chapter was supported by Grant OGP0003334 to Mark L. Howe from the Natural Sciences and Engineering Research Council of Canada.

References

Bjorklund, D.F. (1987). How age changes in knowledge base contribute to the development of children's memory: An interpretive review. *Developmental Review*, *7*, 93–130.

Bjorklund, D.F. (Ed.) (1990). *Children's strategies: Contemporary views of cognitive development*. Hillsdale, NJ: Erlbaum.

Case, R. (1985). *Intellectual development: Birth to adulthood*. New York: Academic Press.

Chi, M.T.H., & Ceci, S.J. (1987). Content knowledge: Its role, representation, and restructuring in memory development. In H.W. Reese (Ed.), *Advances in child development and behavior* (Vol. 20, pp. 91–142). New York: Academic Press.

Fischer, K.W. (1980). A theory of cognitive development: The control and construction of hierarchies of skills. *Psychological Review*, *87*, 477–531.

Flavell, J.H. (1963). *The developmental psychology of Jean Piaget*. Princeton, NJ: Van Nostrand.

Flavell, J.H. (1982). On cognitive development. *Child Development*, *53*, 1–10.

Howe, M.L., Brainerd, C.J., & Reyna, V.F. (Eds.) (1992). *Development of long-term retention*. New York: Springer–Verlag.

Howe, M.L., Montevecchi, W.A., Rabinowitz, F.M., & Stones, M.J. (1991). Modeling adaptation in the next generation: A developmental perspective. *Behavioral and Brain Sciences*, *14*, 100–101.

Howe, M.L., & O'Sullivan, J.T. (1990). The development of strategic memory: Coordinating knowledge, metamemory, and resources. In D.F. Bjorklund (Ed.), *Children's strategies: Contemporary views of cognitive development* (pp. 129–155). Hillsdale, NJ: Erlbaum.

Howe, M.L., & Rabinowitz, F.M. (1990). Resource panacea? Or just another day in the developmental forest. *Developmental Review*, *10*, 125–154.

Howe, M.L., & Rabinowitz, F.M. (1991a). Development: Sequences, structure, and chaos. *Annals of Theoretical Psychology*, *7*, 65–72.

Howe, M.L., & Rabinowitz, F.M. (1991b). Gist another panacea? Or just the illusion of inclusion. *Developmental Review*, *11*, 305–316.

Howe, M.L., & Rabinowitz, F.M. (1992). *Dynamic modeling, chaos, and cognitive development*. Manuscript submitted for publication.

Inhelder, B., & Piaget, J. (1958). *The growth of logical thinking from childhood to adolescence*. New York: Basic Books.

Kendler, H.H., & Kendler, T.S. (1962). Vertical and horizontal processes in problem solving. *Psychological Review*, *69*, 1–16.

Klahr, D. (1989). Information-processing approaches. *Annals of Child Development*, *6*, 133–185.

Klahr, D., & Wallace, J.G. (1976). *Cognitive development: An information processing view*. Hillsdale, NJ: Erlbaum.

Kreindler, D.M., & Lumsden, C.J. (1992). *A zeroth-order FTT narrative gistifier.* Manuscript submitted for publication.

Rabinowitz, F.M., Grant, M.J., Howe, M.L., & Mason, C. (1992). *Reasoning in middle childhood: A linear dynamic model of transitive inference.* Manuscript submitted for publication.

Siegler, R.S. (1981). Developmental sequences within and between concepts. *Monographs of the Society for Research in Child Development, 46* (Whole No. 189).

Suppes, P., & Ginsberg, R. (1963). A fundamental property of all-or-none models, binomial distribution of responses prior to conditioning, with application to concept formation in children. *Psychological Review, 70*, 139–161.

Townsend, J.T. (in press). Chaos theory: A brief tutorial and discussion. In A.F. Healy, R.M. Shiffrin, & S.K. Kosslyn (Eds.), *From learning to cognition: Essays in honor of William K. Estes.* Hillsdale, NJ: Erlbaum.

van Geert, P. (1991). A dynamic systems model of cognitive and language growth. *Psychological Review, 98*, 3–53.

Author Index

Note. Italicized entries refer to reference list citations.

Subject Index

MIX
Papier aus verantwortungsvollen Quellen
Paper from responsible sources
FSC® C105338

If you have any concerns about our products,
you can contact us on
ProductSafety@springernature.com

In case Publisher is established outside the EU,
the EU authorized representative is:
Springer Nature Customer Service Center GmbH
Europaplatz 3, 69115 Heidelberg, Germany

Printed by Libri Plureos GmbH
in Hamburg, Germany